LITURGY IN THE TWENTY-FIRST CENTURY

LITURGY IN THE TWENTY-FIRST CENTURY

Contemporary Issues and Perspectives

Edited by
Alcuin Reid

Bloomsbury T&T Clark
An imprint of Bloomsbury Publishing Plc

B L O O M S B U R Y
LONDON · OXFORD · NEW YORK · NEW DELHI · SYDNEY

Bloomsbury T&T Clark

An imprint of Bloomsbury Publishing Plc

Imprint previously known as T&T Clark

50 Bedford Square	1385 Broadway
London	New York
WC1B 3DP	NY 10018
UK	USA

www.bloomsbury.com

BLOOMSBURY, T&T CLARK and the Diana logo are trademarks of Bloomsbury Publishing Plc

First published 2016

© Alcuin Reid and Contributors, 2016

Alcuin Reid has asserted his rights under the Copyright, Designs and Patents Act, 1988, to be identified as Editor of this work.

British Library Cataloguing-in-Publication Data
A catalogue record for this book is available from the British Library.

ISBN:	HB:	978-0-56766-808-0
	PB:	978-0-56766-809-7
	ePDF:	978-0-56766-807-3
	ePub:	978-0-56766-810-3

Library of Congress Cataloging-in-Publication Data
A catalog record for this book is available from the Library of Congress.

Typeset by Forthcoming Publications (www.forthpub.com)

CONTENTS

INTRODUCTION

The cover of this book shows the liturgical procession of the feast of *Corpus Christi* crossing First Avenue in Manhattan, New York City, on the 4th of June last year *en route* to the beautiful church of St Vincent Ferrer, where *Sacra Liturgia USA 2015* came to an apposite conclusion with pontifical Benediction of the Most Blessed Sacrament. No one of the hundreds who participated in that procession, which followed the pontifical Mass of *Corpus Christi* celebrated in the *usus antiquior*—the more ancient form of the Roman rite, failed to be moved. The "spirit and power of the liturgy" (see: *Sacrosanctum Concilium* 14) hung in the air as tangibly as the incense and song rose in the evening light before Him with whom we processed and prayed. A little of New York paused that evening as He passed. Amidst the respectful curiosity, astonishment and stares that such unexpected order and beauty brought forth, hearts and minds were uplifted by a glimpse of He who is alive and at work in our world today in a singular and privileged manner in and through the Church's Sacred Liturgy.

Sacra Liturgia USA 2015 was the second *Sacra Liturgia* international liturgical conference, the first being in Rome in June 2013.[1] At the time of writing a third, in London, England, from 5–8 July 2016, is approaching. These conferences, publications and other initiatives seek to underline the centrality of liturgical formation and celebration in the life and mission of the Church, as well as the urgent need for genuine liturgical renewal in our time. *Sacra Liturgia* seeks to promote an authentic interpretation of the Second Vatican Council's mandate for liturgical reform, an assessment of the implementation of *Sacrosanctum Concilium* that is faithful to the Council, an ongoing consideration of the value of a possible reform of the reform, the integral celebration of the *usus recentior* with an optimal *ars celebrandi* (see: *Sacramentum Caritatis*, 38–42), and an openness to the value and riches of the *usus antiquior* in the Church today.

---

1. The proceedings are published: Alcuin Reid (ed.), *Sacred Liturgy: The Source and Summit of the Life and Mission of the Church* (San Francisco: Ignatius, 2014).

The New York speakers from 1–4 June 2015, whose papers are presented in this volume, have differing perspectives. Nevertheless each one shares the conviction that the Sacred Liturgy is the source and summit of the life and mission of the Church and that more needs to be done so that the Church of the twenty-first century may draw more deeply and efficaciously from the fount of her life. We may not agree with every opinion expressed by the authors herein—their opinions are their own. But their arguments are reasoned and critical discussion of the issues raised is to be welcomed.[2] If, in addition to moving hearts and minds—as was, thanks be to God, the case at all of the liturgical celebrations—the New York conference serves to advance liturgical scholarship, it will have made an important contribution. We are in the debt of all who gave of their time and expertise in speaking and who have so willingly prepared their texts for publication here.

That *Sacra Liturgia* came to the USA is thanks to the initiative of Dr Jennifer Donelson who, as her reward, carried the burden of its organization from the outset. In this she was supported by Fr Richard Cipolla as Co-organiser. All who benefitted from the June conference and who will draw treasures both old and new (see: Matt 13:52) from this book owe a profound debt to Dr Donelson and to her team, which comprised many generous volunteers, including a significant number from the student body of St Joseph's Seminary, Dunwoodie, New York.

That *Sacra Liturgia* came to the Archdiocese of New York is thanks to the warm welcome given to us by its Archbishop, His Eminence, Timothy Cardinal Dolan. Whilst it was a disappointment that he was prevented at the last minute from being present personally, the trouble he took in

---

2. In this respect it is unfortunate that some reports of *Sacra Liturgia USA 2015* displayed an unhealthy obsession with appearances and externals, seeming to wish to perpetuate "old" vs. "new" battle-lines, whilst failing to engage in the fundamental issues which are of vital importance to all liturgical formation and celebration, whether "old," "new" or both; see: Michael O'Loughlin, "In their quest to reform the liturgy, some Catholics hope to remake the culture" (Crux, 5 June 2015). So too, in more academic forums it is disappointing that some fail to engage the arguments advanced or to discuss their implications, preferring to fill their allotted space with tired generalisations and tangential observations; see: Kevin W. Irwin, review of *Sacred Liturgy: The Source and Summit of the Life and Mission of the Church*, *Worship* 89 (2015), pp. 275–77. These stances do not advance scholarship or legitimate debate. Nor do they contribute to genuine liturgical renewal in the contemporary Church. For a critical review which is worthy of an academic journal and begins to engage the issues raised, see: Michael Wahl, review of *Sacred Liturgy: The Source and Summit of the Life and Mission of the Church*, *Antiphon* 19 (2015), pp. 226–28.

sending a message of welcome, published herein, is very much appreciated. So too is the gracious message of His Eminence, Robert Cardinal Sarah, Prefect of the Congregation for Divine Worship and the Discipline of the Sacraments.

As ever, His Eminence, Raymond Leo Cardinal Burke was more than generous with his time and support. So too His Excellency, Archbishop Salvatore Cordileone kindly travelled from San Francisco to speak and to celebrate Holy Mass for us. We were blessed by the presence and inspiring preaching of Bishop Frank Caggiano of Bridgeport and Bishop John O'Hara, Auxiliary Bishop of New York, and by the beautiful celebration of the Mass of *Corpus Christi* by Bishop Joseph Perry, Auxiliary Bishop of Chicago.

Many other sacred ministers, masters of ceremonies, servers, musicians and others gave selflessly of their time, energy and resources in ways both great and small to ensure the optimal and integral celebration of the liturgical rites during the conference, and to them we owe profound gratitude. "Quantum potes, tantum aude: quia maior omni laude, non laudare sufficis" (As much as you can, dare that much: for even with praise greater than any, you cannot praise enough), we sang with the Church—using the words of St Thomas Aquinas—in the sequence of the Mass of *Corpus Christi*. The hundreds present at the conference and those who joined us for the liturgical rites can be in no doubt that we strove to be faithful to that injunction—something possible only given the sacrifices, large and small, made by many.

To the Prior and Dominican community of St Catherine of Siena, whose generosity, hospitality, support and patience in welcoming a liturgical conference to their inspiring church, we owe a profound debt, most particularly to Fr Jordan Kelly OP, St Catherine's then pastor. It is a privilege to be able to include his beautiful homily at the Solemn Votive Mass of the Holy Angels celebrated on the 2nd of June by a newly ordained priest of the Archdiocese of New York.[3] Fr Kelly also offered us the support of his parish team, and we are especially grateful to the indefatigable Steven Picciano, whose administrative and practical assistance at every turn enabled the smooth preparation and running of a major conference. To the Pastor of St John Nepomucene Church who welcomed the *Corpus Christi* procession for its station, and to the Prior and Dominican community of St Vincent Ferrer who so kindly welcomed us for the final Benediction, we express our heartfelt thanks.

---

3. It is regrettable that it has not been possible to publish the texts of the homily preached by Bishop Caggiano on the feast of Sts Charles Lwanga and his companions, or that of Bishop O'Hara on the feast of *Corpus Christi*.

Such a conference, and indeed this book, would not be possible but for the financial support of many sponsors, in particular the Knights of Columbus, the Knights of Malta, the Cardinal Newman Society, Granda Liturgical Arts, Extraordinary Faith, De Montfort Music, Cantica Nova Publications, the Monks of Norcia, the Society of St Hugh of Cluny, the Latin Mass Magazine, Roman Catholic Books, Bloomsbury Publishing, Ignatius Press and many generous individuals. For the prompt publication of this volume we owe a particular debt to Dominic Mattos, T&T Clark publisher at Bloomsbury, and the Bloomsbury team.

That almost 350 people registered to participate in the academic presentations at the Kaye Playhouse at Hunter College, and many more still joined us for the liturgical celebrations at St Catherine's, is a sign of the times: authentic liturgical renewal is of vital importance in our day, and many are committed to studying and promoting it. The predominance of young men and women, including a large number of seminarians, religious and clergy, amongst participants was noticeable. These are great signs of hope for the Church.

At the turn of this century Joseph Cardinal Ratzinger prefaced his book, *The Spirit of the Liturgy*, with an aspiration:

> If this book were to encourage in a new way, something like a "liturgical movement," a movement toward the liturgy and toward the right way of celebrating the liturgy, inwardly and outwardly, then the intention that inspired its writing would be richly fulfilled.[4]

The differing perspectives on contemporary issues facing the Sacred Liturgy in the Western Church at the beginning of the twenty-first century published herein cannot claim but to be a modest contribution to that movement. Hopefully they make a contribution to it nevertheless—the ideals of which are at the heart of all the *Sacra Liturgia* initiatives.

Dom Alcuin Reid
Sexagesima 2016

---

4. Joseph Cardinal Ratzinger, *The Spirit of the Liturgy* (San Francisco: Ignatius Press, 2000), pp. 8–9.

MESSAGE OF TIMOTHY CARDINAL DOLAN

Your Eminence Cardinal Burke, brother bishops, priests, deacons, consecrated women and men religious, and dearest faithful:

It is my privilege to welcome you, the distinguished participants of the *Sacra Liturgia* 2015 conference, to the Archdiocese of New York. It was my original intent to welcome you in person for the beginning of the conference, but necessary business at the state capitol in Albany fighting for parents who send their children to Catholic schools, has made it impossible. I hope I can count on your understanding and pardon.

In the life of the Church, there is no better subject to meet about than the Sacred Liturgy, our connection to the saving life, death, and resurrection of our Lord, the most profound act we can do.

It is in this light that I am happy to welcome you here, and let you know that you do the Church in New York, and indeed the whole Church, a service in continuing the conversation of authentic liturgical renewal and reform.

I am grateful to Bishop Dominique Rey, who sponsors the conference, to my brother, Cardinal Raymond Burke, to my brothers, Archbishop Salvatore Cordileone, Bishop Frank Caggiano, Bishop Joseph Perry, and my own auxiliary bishop, John O'Hara, for their participation in the conference. I thank the organizers, and all of you. I am honored that you have come to New York, and always know that you are welcome here.

Count on a *memento* as I stand at the altar these days!

Timothy Michael Cardinal Dolan
Archbishop of New York
1 June 2015

MESSAGE OF BISHOP DOMINIQUE REY

Your Eminences, Your Excellencies, dear priests, deacons and religious, dear lay brothers and sisters:

I wish to apologise for my absence from this important and historic conference. When the dates were finally determined it was impossible for me to travel to New York at this time due to a pre-arranged meeting of the French bishops. Please believe me when I say that I want to be with you and that if it were at all possible I would be with you. Please be assured of our union in prayer during these days. I have asked Dom Alcuin Reid, the coordinator of the *Sacra Liturgia* initiatives, to represent me in New York and to bring these greetings in my name.

In the first place I must thank His Eminence Cardinal Dolan, Archbishop of New York, for his generous and kind welcome of *Sacra Liturgia* to New York City. Communion with the bishop of the diocese is essential if we are to be truly followers of Jesus Christ, if we are to be truly Catholic. I thank His Eminence for strengthening those bonds of communion through his welcome and by making available one of his Auxiliary Bishops to be present at the concluding Mass of the Conference.

I must also thank His Eminence, Cardinal Burke, who, from the inception of *Sacra Liturgia* has done all that he can to support its different initiatives. Without your friendship and your support, Your Eminence, we would not be in the happy position of commencing a second major international conference today. We are profoundly in your debt.

From its outset, in planning our conference for 2013 in Rome, I have been clear that *Sacra Liturgia* is not about breeding liturgical narcissists or "sacristy rats" as I think the saying goes in English. No, *Sacra Liturgia* is about facilitating people's optimal connection with Christ who acts uniquely in the world today in the Church's liturgy. It is about coming to a working realisation of the implications of the teaching of the Second Vatican Council that "the liturgy is the summit toward which the activity of the Church is directed; at the same time it is the font from which all her power flows" (*Sacrosanctum Concilium* 10).

To be sure, that involves sacristies and sanctuaries and churches where everything is as it should be, indeed where everything is the best it possibly can be—for we rightly offer our first fruits to Almighty God in worship—and let us never forget that the right worship of God is our *first* duty. To be a Christian is first to "love the Lord your God with all your heart and with all your soul and with all your mind" (Matt 22:38). And this we do through the optimal celebration of the Sacred Liturgy. If our liturgical rites and celebrations are impoverished or are in any way not as they should be, we are not giving to Almighty God what is rightly his due: all our hearts, all our souls, all our minds.

The effect of 'getting the liturgy right' is the ability to fulfil Our Lord's second great commandment: "You shall love your neighbour as yourself" (Matt 22:39). Celebrating the Sacred Liturgy as the Church wishes us to celebrate it, as best as we are able, beautifully, with that *ars celebrandi* of which Pope Benedict XVI spoke (see: *Sacramentum Caritatis*, 38–42), forms Christians, it produces apostles, it empowers evangelisation. When our encounter with Christ acting in the liturgy of His Church is optimal our hearts and minds are filled with grace and light. In that encounter we can both discern and receive the grace to live our specific mission in this world, in the world which so desperately needs to meet Christ alive in each one of us.

That is why the Sacred Liturgy is central to Christian life. That is why its correct celebration matters, why it comes first. That is why liturgical formation for all, but above all for those with pastoral responsibility in the Church, is essential. That is why I was pleased to initiate *Sacra Liturgia* in Rome in 2013, and why I am delighted that it has now come to the United States of America!

I am sad not to be able to share these days with you and to greet each of you in person. I wish to thank the organisers for their vision and for all their efforts in preparing this conference. To the benefactors who have so generously enabled this initiative to become a reality, we are all profoundly grateful, most particularly to the Knights of Columbus who have shown *Sacra Liturgia*'s events constant support. Thank you, speakers, for giving of your time and insights in furthering the vital work of liturgical formation and scholarship. And thank you, dear participants: your presence in such numbers is an encouragement and a great sign of hope for the Church in our day.

Please know that I am united with you in prayer during these days. May God bless abundantly all who participate in *Sacra Liturgia USA* 2015!

Dominique Rey
Bishop of Fréjus–Toulon

MESSAGE OF ROBERT CARDINAL SARAH

1. It is my pleasure to greet all of you, gathered in New York City, for the inaugural conference of *Sacra Liturgia* in the United States of America. In particular, I greet His Eminence, Timothy Cardinal Dolan, the Archbishop of New York, and thank him for his interest in and support of this event underlining the essential role of liturgical formation and celebration in the life and mission of the Church.

I was very pleased to be present at the launch of the Italian and English editions of the proceedings of *Sacra Liturgia 2013* in Rome last November, and congratulate Bishop Dominique Rey and all who work with him on making this happy initiative a reality, now also in the United States of America.

I greet His Eminence, Raymond Leo Cardinal Burke, who will present the keynote address. And I greet all the bishops, priests and religious and learned lay men and women who will make presentations as well as those who will celebrate the Sacred Liturgy and preach in the coming days. Your apostolate in promoting the Sacred Liturgy is a most important one in our time: I thank you for all that you do.

2. Because the Sacred Liturgy is truly the font from which all the Church's power flows, as the Second Vatican Council insists (see: *Sacrosanctum Concilium* 10), we must do everything we can to put the Sacred Liturgy back at the very heart of the relationship between God and man, recognising the primacy of Almighty God in this privileged and unique forum in which we, individually and ecclesially, encounter God at work in our world. One cannot encounter God, my brothers and sisters, without trembling, without awe, without profound respect and holy fear. This is why we must rank what Cardinal Ratzinger called "the right way of celebrating the Liturgy, inwardly and outwardly" first amongst our concerns.[1]

---

1. Joseph Cardinal Ratzinger, *The Spirit of the Liturgy* (San Francisco: Ignatius, 2000), p. 9.

3. When the Holy Father, Pope Francis, asked me to accept the ministry of Prefect of the Congregation for Divine Worship and Discipline of the Sacraments, I asked: "Your Holiness, how do you want me to exercise this ministry? What do you want me to do as Prefect of this Congregation?" The Holy Father's reply was clear. "I want you to continue to implement the liturgical reform of the Second Vatican Council," he said, "and I want you to continue the good work in the liturgy begun by Pope Benedict XVI."

My friends, I want you to help me in this task. I ask you to continue to work towards achieving the liturgical aims of the Second Vatican Council (see: *Sacrosanctum Concilium* 1) and to work to continue the liturgical renewal promoted by Pope Benedict XVI, especially through the Post-Synodal Apostolic Exhortation *Sacramentum Caritatis* of 22 February 2007 and the Motu Proprio *Summorum Pontificum* of 7 July 2007. I ask you to be wise, like the householder in St Matthew's Gospel, who knows when to bring out of his treasure things both new and old (see: Matt 13:52), so that the Sacred Liturgy as it is celebrated and lived today may lose nothing of the estimable riches of the Church's liturgical tradition, whilst always being open to legitimate development (see: *Sacrosanctum Concilium* 23).

4. You have many days in which to consider these questions in depth. I would like to suggest two critical areas in which authentic liturgical renewal in the twenty-first century can be furthered. The first is by being utterly clear what Catholic liturgy is: it is the worship of Almighty God, the place where mankind encounters God alive and at work in His Church today. Please—never underestimate the importance of this. The liturgy is not some social occasion or meeting where we come first, where what is important is that we express our identity. No: God comes first. As Cardinal Ratzinger wrote in 2004:

> If the Liturgy appears first of all as the workshop for our activity, then what is essential is being forgotten: God. For the Liturgy is not about us, but about God. Forgetting about God is the most imminent danger of our age. As against this, the Liturgy should be setting up a sign of God's presence.[2]

The Church's liturgy is given to us in tradition—it is not for us to make up the rites we celebrate or to change them to suit ourselves or our own ideas beyond the legitimate options permitted by the liturgical books. That is why we must celebrate the Sacred Liturgy faithfully, with that reverence and awe of which I spoke earlier.

---

2. Joseph Ratzinger, *The Theology of the Liturgy*, Collected Works, vol. 11 (San Francisco: Ignatius, 2014), p. 593.

5. The second area in which I ask you to give of your time and expertise is in the promotion of sound liturgical formation. The Council's Constitution on the Sacred Liturgy went so far as to say that "it would be futile to entertain any hopes of realizing" the liturgical renewal it desired "unless the pastors themselves, in the first place, become thoroughly imbued with the spirit and power of the liturgy, and undertake to give instruction about it" (n. 14). We cannot truly participate in the Sacred Liturgy, we cannot drink deeply from the source of Christian life, if we have not been formed in the spirit and power of the liturgy. As our Holy Father, Pope Francis, said last year:

> Much remains to be done for a correct and complete assimilation of the Constitution on the Sacred Liturgy on the part of the baptized and by ecclesial communities. I refer in particular to the commitment to a strong and organic initiation and liturgical formation of the lay faithful as well as the clergy and consecrated persons. (Message to the participants of the Roman symposium on *Sacrosanctum Concilium*, 18 February 2014)

I hope and I pray that the different initiatives of *Sacra Liturgia* can do much to meet this urgent and crucial need.

6. Dear brothers in the episcopate, dear priests, deacons and religious, dear lay men and women, your participation in this conference is a sign that you are already aware of the importance of the Sacred Liturgy in the life of the Church. I thank you for your willingness to give of your time to study and consider this reality further. I pray that these days may increase your wisdom and knowledge, that they will help you to grow in holiness and that they will make you ever more zealous in promoting authentic liturgical renewal in the Church.

I hope I will be able to join you for the next *Sacra Liturgia* Meeting of July 2016 in London.

Please pray for me that I may faithfully exercise the service to which I have been called. May God bless you always!

Robert Cardinal Sarah
Prefect
Congregation for Divine Worship and the Discipline of the Sacraments

CONTRIBUTORS

Philip Anderson is the abbot of Our Lady of Clear Creek, a Benedictine abbey of the Congregation of Solesmes. After studying at the University of Kansas, he entered the French Benedictine abbey of Notre-Dame de Fontgombault, where he made profession and was ordained to the priesthood. In 1999, along with seven other Americans, three Frenchmen and two Canadians—all formed at Fontgombault abbey or its daughter houses—he helped found a monastery near Tulsa, Oklahoma that was raised to the status of abbey in 2010. Our Lady of Clear Creek Abbey currently has 46 members.

Kurt Belsole is a monk of St Vincent Archabbey in Latrobe, Pennsylvania. He is the Director of Liturgical Formation at the Pontifical North American College, Vatican City State. Professed in 1972, he was ordained to the priesthood in 1978. After ordination, he earned a license from the Patristic Institute "Augustinianum" in Rome. At the same time, he pursued studies at the Pontifical Liturgical Institute. From 1983 until 2006, he taught at St Vincent Seminary, Latrobe, Pennsylvania, where at various times he also served as Academic Dean and Rector. He earned a doctorate in theology from the Pontifical Athenaeum of St Anselm in Rome in 1993. Since August 2007 he has served as the Director of Liturgical Formation at the Pontifical North American College.

Fr Belsole's liturgical interests lie principally in the teachings of the liturgical movement of the nineteenth and twentieth centuries which were later enshrined in the Constitution on the Sacred Liturgy *Sacrosanctum Concilium*. The teaching of the Council in this document calls for a sound liturgical theology to animate those who preside over the Sacred Liturgy. In this manner, liturgical theology and liturgical celebration accompany one another and liturgy does not devolve into simply ceremonies and ritualism. He maintains that particularly important for a proper reading of *Sacrosanctum Concilium* is the liturgical life and theology that preceded it and which it presupposes. Important authors in this area are Lambert Beauduin, Romano Guardini, Odo Casel, Viktor Warnach, Jean Daniélou, Louis Bouyer, and Joseph Ratzinger (Pope Benedict XVI).

His publications include articles on Prosper Guéranger, Lambert Beauduin, Beuron, and Maria Laach, in the *Encyclopedia of Monasticism* and "The Christian as Pilgrim, the Church as Home" in *Sacred Architecture*.

Raymond Leo Cardinal Burke was born in Richland Center, Wisconsin, on 30 June 1948. He attended high school at Holy Cross Seminary in La Crosse, Wisconsin, before attending The Catholic University of America in Washington, DC, as a Basselin Scholar. He undertook his studies in preparation for ordination to the Holy Priesthood at the Pontifical Gregorian University in Rome, and was ordained to the priesthood by Pope Paul VI on 29 June 1975.

Ordained a bishop in 1995 by Pope John Paul II, he served for almost nine years as Bishop of La Crosse, where he founded the Shrine of Our Lady of Guadalupe. On 2 December 2003, Bishop Burke was named Archbishop of Saint Louis. From 2008–14, he served as Prefect of the Supreme Tribunal of the Apostolic Signatura in Rome. He was elevated to the College of Cardinals in 2010 by Pope Benedict XVI. In November 2014, he was named Patron of the Sovereign Military Hospitaller Order of Saint John of Jerusalem of Rhodes and of Malta.

Cardinal Burke has also served on the Congregation for Causes of Saints, the Congregation for Bishops, the Pontifical Council for Legislative Texts, the Congregation for Divine Worship and the Discipline of the Sacraments, and the Council of Cardinals and Bishops of the Section for Relations with States of the Secretariat of State.

Richard Gennaro Cipolla is a priest of the Diocese of Bridgeport and a Pastor of St Mary's Church in Norwalk, Connecticut. His academic degrees include a PhD in chemistry and a DPhil in theology from Oxford University. He is Chair Emeritus of the Classics Department of Brunswick School in Greenwich, Connecticut, where he teaches an advanced course in Vergil, Dante, and St Augustine. His main interests are liturgy, the thought of Blessed John Henry Newman, and all things Italian.

Salvatore Cordileone was born in San Diego on 5 June 1956. He attended public school through 12th grade and earned his BA in philosophy from the University of San Diego in 1978. He earned a second bachelor's degree in sacred theology from the Pontifical Gregorian University in 1981. Archbishop Cordileone was ordained to the priesthood on 9 July 1982. He continued his studies at Gregorian University from 1985–89, earning a doctorate in canon law.

He was appointed Judicial Vicar for the Diocese of San Diego in 1990 and served as an assistant to the Supreme Tribunal of the Apostolic Signatura from 1995–2002. On 5 July 2002, Pope John Paul II appointed him the Auxiliary Bishop of the Diocese of San Diego, where he served until his appointment as Bishop of Oakland on 23 March 2009. On 27 July 2012, Pope Benedict XVI appointed him as the ninth Archbishop of San Francisco, where he was installed on 4 October 2012.

Archbishop Cordileone chairs the Subcommittee for the Promotion and Defense of Marriage and sits on the Committee for Canonical Affairs. He is a member of the Board of Trustees, Catholic University of America; the Governing Board of the International Theological Institute; and the Subcommission on the Liturgy for the Anglican Ordinariates.

Jennifer Donelson is an associate professor and the director of sacred music at St Joseph's Seminary (Dunwoodie) in New York, where she also teaches sacred music courses in the St Cecilia Academy for Pastoral Musicians. She has co-edited *Mystic Modern: The Music, Thought, and Legacy of Charles Tournemire*, published by the Church Music Association of America (CMAA). Her publications also include articles in the *New Catholic Encyclopedia*, *Sacred Music*, *Antiphon: A Journal for Liturgical Renewal* and the proceedings of the Gregorian Institute of Canada. She serves on the board of the Society for Catholic Liturgy as well as the CMAA, and is the managing editor of the CMAA's journal *Sacred Music*. As academic liaison of the CMAA, she has organized and presented papers at several academic conferences on Charles Tournemire and the work of Msgr Richard Schuler; she was also co-organizer of the *Sacra Liturgia* USA 2015 conference in New York. Having studied Gregorian chant at the Catholic University of America and the Abbey of St Peter in Solesmes, for six years Donelson served as a co-organizer of the Musica Sacra Florida Gregorian Chant Conference, and has given chant workshops in dioceses and parishes across the USA. Before coming to Dunwoodie, Dr Donelson served on the faculty at St Gregory the Great Seminary in Lincoln, Nebraska, and at Nova Southeastern University in Fort Lauderdale, where she taught music theory, music history, piano, and directed the university chorale. As a church musician, Donelson has directed semi-professional, amateur, and children's choirs, including two choirs which she founded. Under her direction, the Schola Cantorum of St Joseph's Seminary sang for the 2015 papal Mass in New York, as well as Masses at St Patrick's Cathedral and academic symposia in New York.

Michael P. Foley is an associate professor of Patristics in the Great Texts Program at Baylor University. He holds a doctorate in systematic theology and works chiefly on the theology of St Augustine, political philosophy, and liturgical studies. A former president and current member of the Society for Catholic Liturgy, Foley's work on Sacred Liturgy has appeared in *Antiphon: A Journal for Liturgical Renewal*, *Studia Liturgica*, *Usus Antiquior*, *Journal of Early Christian Studies*, *Worship*, *Homiletic and Pastoral Review*, *Lay Witness*, *Crisis*, *Messenger of St Anthony*, and *The Latin Mass*. His most recent book is *Drinking With the Saints: The Sinner's Guide to a Holy Happy Hour* (Regnery, 2015).

Gregory A. Glenn is the Founder and Pastoral Administrator of the Madeleine Choir School, and the Director of Liturgy and Music at the Cathedral of the Madeleine in Salt Lake City, Utah. Glenn completed graduate work in liturgical studies at the Catholic University of America in Washington DC, and undergraduate studies in organ performance at Seattle Pacific University. While at Catholic University, he served on the music staff at the Basilica of the National Shrine of the Immaculate Conception. The Madeleine Choir School, a pre-kindergarten through eighth grade Catholic School serving over 400 students at the Cathedral, began as an after-school program for children in 1990, and opened as a full-time academic institution in 1996. At the Cathedral of the Madeleine Glenn oversees a liturgy and music program with over 150 regular volunteers and staff that serve daily and Sunday choral services, an annual Concert Series, and the Eccles Organ Festival. The choristers from the Madeleine Choir School have sung with professional arts organizations such as Utah Opera, the Utah Symphony, the San Francisco Opera and the Mormon Tabernacle Choir, and have also conducted biennial European performance tours throughout Italy, France, Belgium, Germany, Spain and Austria. The Choristers were featured in the music for the Opening Ceremonies of 2002 Winter Olympics in Salt Lake City. Glenn has served on the Steering Committee for the Conference of Roman Catholic Cathedral Musicians, and worked with M. Francis Mannion in facilitating the creation of the Snowbird Statement on Catholic Liturgical Music. In 2008 Glenn received the *Madeleine Award for Distinguished Service to the Arts and Humanities in Utah*, and in 2013, the *Yves Congar Award* for twenty-five years of service presented by the Congar Institute for Ministry Development. A native of Olympia, Washington, Glenn has served the Diocese of Salt Lake City since 1988.

Margaret I. Hughes is an Assistant Professor of Philosophy at the College of Mount Saint Vincent in Riverdale, NY. She received her PhD in philosophy from Fordham University, where she wrote her dissertation on the philosophy of Josef Pieper and the role of the perception of beautiful art in moral formation. Prior to entering graduate school, she taught for two years in Catholic elementary and middle schools while earning an MA in education from Seton Hall University. Her BA is in Philosophy and Medieval Studies from the University of Chicago.

Thomas M. Kocik (b. 1965) is a Catholic priest of the Diocese of Fall River, Massachusetts, where he has worked primarily in parish ministry. He is the author of *Apostolic Succession in an Ecumenical Context* (Alba House, 1996), *The Reform of the Reform? A Liturgical Debate* (Ignatius Press, 2003), *Loving and Living the Mass* (Zaccheus Press, 2007; 2nd edn 2011), *The Fullness of Truth: Catholicism and the World's Major Religions* (Newman House Press, 2013), and many published articles, book reviews and homilies. In addition, he has contributed several series of articles to his diocesan newspaper, *The Anchor*, including one on the liturgical movement and another on the Second Vatican Council. He is a member of the Society for Catholic Liturgy and former editor of its peer-reviewed journal *Antiphon*.

Peter A. Kwasniewski, born in Chicago, holds a bachelor's degree in liberal arts from Thomas Aquinas College in California and an MA and PhD in philosophy from The Catholic University of America in Washington, DC. After eight years as an assistant professor at the International Theological Institute in Gaming, Austria and a lecturer for the Austrian Program of the Franciscan University of Steubenville, he joined the founding team of Wyoming Catholic College in Lander, Wyoming, where he currently serves as professor of theology and choirmaster. In addition, he is a board member and scholar of The Aquinas Institute for the Study of Sacred Doctrine, which is publishing the *Opera Omnia* of the Angelic Doctor. As part of this project, Kwasniewski is editing and annotating the first complete translation of Book IV of Aquinas's *Commentary on the Sentences of Peter Lombard*.

Kwasniewski has taught and written extensively on a wide variety of subjects, especially the thought of St Thomas Aquinas, sacramental and liturgical theology, the history and aesthetics of music, and the social doctrine of the Church. He has published over 500 articles in popular and scholarly journals, and contributes regularly to weblogs such as New Liturgical Movement. He has published two books with The Catholic

University of America Press, *Wisdom's Apprentice* and *On Love and Charity*, as well as a volume of music for liturgical use, *Sacred Choral Works* (Corpus Christi Watershed, 2014). His latest book, *Resurgent in the Midst of Crisis: Sacred Liturgy, the Traditional Latin Mass, and Renewal in the Church* (Angelico Press, 2014), is being translated into eight languages.

He lives in Lander, Wyoming, with his wife, their son and daughter, a Russian Blue cat, and a host of early music instruments.

Matthew Menendez, born in Saint Louis, Missouri, is the founder of Juventutem Boston, a group dedicated to the joyful propagation of the Church's ancient liturgy. He was educated by the English Benedictine Monks at the Priory school of Saint Louis Abbey, where at the age of 18 he wrote a 90-page thesis on the proper orientation of the altar. In 2007, through the efforts of Raymond Leo Cardinal Burke, he was introduced to the extraordinary form of the Roman rite, for which he has ever since been a steady crusader.

In 2014, Mr Menendez graduated Phi Beta Kappa from Harvard University with an AB in Romance Languages and Literatures. In 2012, he founded Juventutem Boston to address a lack of transcendent liturgy for the many college students in the area. Juventutem Boston has introduced several hundred young people to the ancient rites, trained multiple priests to celebrate them, and brought countless lecturers to enrich the life of faith in the Archdiocese. At Harvard, he wrote his thesis on the mystical love poetry of St John of the Cross, led Harvard Right-to-Life, and coordinated the resistance movement that cancelled a planned Satanic Black Mass on campus. He is one of the founding organizers of the annual *Pro Civitate Dei* summer school (begun in 2015), which brings young Catholics together from around the world for solemn liturgies, convivial meals, and zealous discussions with top-notch professors about the implications of the Faith on politics, economics, and culture. He now works in the Leadership Development Program at TASER, International, based in Scottsdale, Arizona, where he runs their civilian weapons business.

Lauren Pristas, professor of Theology at Caldwell University, is the author of *The Collects of the Roman Missals* published by Bloomsbury and of articles published in the *Thomist, Communio, Nova et Vetera, New Blackfriars*, and *Antiphon.*

Alcuin Reid, International Coordinator of the *Sacra Liturgia* initiatives, is a monk of of the Monastère Saint-Benoît in the Diocese of Fréjus–Toulon, France. After studies in Theology and in Education in Melbourne, Australia, he was awarded a PhD from King's College, University of London, for a thesis on twentieth-century liturgical reform (2002), which was subsequently published as *The Organic Development of the Liturgy* with a preface by Joseph Cardinal Ratzinger (Ignatius, 2005). He has lectured internationally and has published extensively on the Sacred Liturgy, including *Looking Again at the Question of the Liturgy with Cardinal Ratzinger* (2003), *The Monastic Diurnal* (2004), *The Ceremonies of the Roman Rite Described* (2009). His new edition of *A Bitter Trial: Evelyn Waugh and John Carmel Cardinal Heenan on the Liturgical Changes*, was published by Ignatius Press in 2011. Dom Alcuin was the principal organiser of *Sacra Liturgia 2013* and edited its proceedings *Sacred Liturgy: The Source and Summit of the Life and Mission of the Church* (Ignatius, 2014). He is working on *Continuity or Rupture? A Study of the Second Vatican Council's Reform of the Liturgy.*

Christopher Smith is a native of Greenville, South Carolina. He was received into the Catholic Church at the age of 13. A graduate of Christendom College in Front Royal, Virginia, Smith entered priestly formation at the Pontifical Roman Major Seminary, the Pope's personal seminary, for service in the Diocese of Charleston. While there, he obtained a licentiate in dogmatic theology from the Gregorian University and also studied French at the Institut Catholique in Paris. Smith was ordained Deacon by Camillo Cardinal Ruini, Papal Vicar for the Diocese of Rome, in October 2004 and Priest by Bishop Robert Baker of Charleston in July 2005. Father Smith spent two years at St Mary's, Greenville as Parochial Vicar and then Administrator. He then was assigned to St Peter's, Beaufort and Holy Cross, St Helena's Island as Parochial Vicar and Administrator. He also spent two years at St Francis-by-the-Sea on Hilton Head Island. In all of his parishes, he had primary responsibility for Hispanic Ministry, chaplaincy and teaching in parochial schools, and apostolate to the sick. While in Beaufort and Hilton Head, Smith pursued the MBA at the Citadel.

In 2009, Bishop Guglielmone assigned Father Smith to the University of Navarre in Pamplona, Spain. He defended his doctoral dissertation in dogmatic theology on the thought of twentieth-century French Jesuit Henri De Lubac in June 2012, after which he received the degree of Doctor of Sacred Theology.

Father Smith speaks Spanish, Italian, French and some German. He is a member of the Church Music Association of America and the Catholic Theological Society of America. In 2011, Smith came to Prince of Peace Catholic Church in Taylors, SC, and was made Pastor there in 2015. In 2013 he was elected to the Society for Catholic Liturgy. In 2014 he was received into the Equestrian Order of the Holy Sepulchre of Jerusalem as a Chaplain.

Allan White joined the Dominican Order in 1973 having completed a degree in Modern History at Trinity College in the University of Oxford. After further philosophical and theological studies at Oxford and Edinburgh University he was ordained to the priesthood in 1979. He completed a doctorate in the history of the Scottish Reformation at Edinburgh and subsequently taught Church History and Liturgy at Blackfriars, Oxford, and Allen Hall, the Westminster diocesan seminary. He has served as chaplain in the universities of Edinburgh, Oxford and Cambridge, where he was also a member of the Divinity Faculty, and finally in New York University. He was Prior Provincial of the English Dominicans from 2000–2008 and assistant to the Master of the Dominican Order from 2008–2011. He presently lives and works in education in Southern California.

BEAUTY IN THE SACRED LITURGY AND THE BEAUTY OF A HOLY LIFE

Raymond Leo Cardinal Burke

1. *Introduction*

It pleases me to be able to address the topic of beauty as we seek to understand more completely the truth of our life in Christ, especially in its highest and most perfect expression: the Sacred Liturgy. The pursuit of truth is a particular challenge in our world which has, in great part, lost any sense of the truth and the source of the truth in God, the Creator and Savior of the world. It is my hope to offer some inspiration in pursuing faithfully the truth which alone opens up for us the sublime beauty of our life in Christ.

Above all, I hope that my words, in some manner, will lead us all to a deeper and more grateful appreciation of our life in Christ in His Mystical Body, the Church. There is nothing truer, better or more beautiful in all the world than the life of Christ within us through the outpouring of the Holy Spirit, especially by means of the sacraments. I hope that our time together will lift our hearts to contemplate the extraordinary nature of our ordinary daily life in Christ, informed by sound doctrine, nourished by the sacraments and by their extension in the life of prayer and the devotional life, and formed through the practice of the virtues.[1] Our Lord Jesus Christ is Truth, Beauty and Goodness Incarnate. Living completely and faithfully in Him, we encounter, especially in the Sacred Liturgy, the font of all that is true, beautiful and good.

Living in Christ, we live in communion with every member of the Church, in every part of the world and in every period of time. Truly, we participate in the Communion of Saints. Like Mary at Bethany, encountering the Lord alive for us in the Church, we desire to offer Him our

---

1. See: Ioannes Paulus PP. II, Epistula Apostolica *Novo Millennio Ineunte*, "Magni Iubilaei anni MM sub exitum," 6 Ianuarii 2001, *Acta Apostolicae Sedis* [hereafter *AAS*] 93 (2001), p. 288 n. 31.

worship. With all the saints, we wish to give glory to Him by means of the best which we have at our disposition (see: John 12:1–8). In truth, the Sacred Liturgy is the participation on earth in the heavenly Wedding Feast of the Lamb Who alone conquers the forces of evil and pours out in abundance upon the Church, His Bride, divine grace, communion with God—Father, Son and Holy Spirit—communion in Truth, Beauty and Goodness (see: Rev 19:7–10).

My considerations are based on the liturgical theology of Joseph Ratzinger, Pope Benedict XVI, who is a most faithful exponent of the Church's teaching in our time. First, I will present some philosophical principles on beauty and sacred art, and then I will reflect on beauty in the Sacred Liturgy. Finally, I will treat the ultimate beauty of holiness of life which has its source and highest expression in the Sacred Liturgy.

2. *Philosophical Principles*

In the Catholic tradition, beauty is understood as a metaphysical notion and, ultimately, as a theological one. The search for beauty has nothing to do with a mere aesthetic sensibility or with an escape from reason. From the divine perspective, beauty, together with truth and goodness, are manifestations of being and, ultimately, of the source of all being, God, Being Himself. God is Truth, Goodness and Beauty. In metaphysical language, truth, beauty and goodness are transcendentals, that is, those fundamental qualities of being which are in God in their fullness, in their perfection, but which are found in all being coming forth from the hand of God in Creation.[2] To the degree in which a creature participates in being and, therefore, in God's being, it is true, beautiful and good.

In his exposition of the natural law, Saint Thomas Aquinas relates the fundamental transcendental of being to the transcendental of goodness. His exposition is especially illuminating for us in the consideration of the beauty of both the Sacred Liturgy and of the good and holy life. He writes:

> Now a certain order is to be found in those things that are apprehended universally. For that which, before aught else, falls under apprehension, is *being*, the notion of which is included in all things whatsoever a man apprehends. Wherefore the first indemonstrable principle is that *the same thing cannot be affirmed and denied at the same time*, which is based on the notion of *being* and *not-being*: and on this principle all others are based, as is stated in *Metaph.* iv, text. 9. Now as *being* is the first thing that falls under

2. See: Battista Mondin, *Dizionario enciclopedico del pensiero di san Tommaso d'Aquino* (Bologna: Edizioni Studio Domenicano, 1991), pp. 610–11.

the apprehension simply, so *good* is the first thing that falls under the apprehension of the practical reason, which is directed to action: since every agent acts for an end under the aspect of good. Consequently the first principle in the practical reason is one founded on the notion of good, viz., that *good is that which all things seek after.* Hence this is the first precept of law, that *good is to be done and pursued and evil is to be avoided.* All other precepts of the natural law are based upon this: so that whatever the practical reason naturally apprehends as man's good (or evil) belongs to the precepts of the natural law as something to be done or avoided.[3]

What Saint Thomas Aquinas affirms regarding the transcendental of goodness apprehended by the practical reason applies also to the transcendental of truth apprehended by speculative reason,[4] and to the transcendental of beauty apprehended by the spiritual faculty of admiration for its integrity, its proportion and its splendor.

The *Compendium of the Catechism of the Catholic Church* expresses, in a clear manner, the Church's understanding of the transcendental of beauty, relating it directly to the Eighth Commandment of the Decalogue: "Thou shalt not give false witness." In response to question, "What relationship exists between truth, beauty and sacred art?" the *Compendium* declares concisely:

> The truth is beautiful, carrying in itself the splendour of spiritual beauty. In addition to the expression of the truth in words there are other complementary expressions of the truth, most specifically in the beauty of artistic works. These are the fruit both of talents given by God and of human effort.

3. "In his autem quae in apprehensione omnium cadunt, quidam ordo invenitur. Nam illud quod primo cadit in apprehensione, est ens, cuius intellectus includitur in omnibus quaecumque quis apprehendit. Et ideo primum principium indemonstrabile est quod *non est simul affirmare et negare*, quod fundatur supra rationem entis et non entis: et super hoc principio omnia alia fundantur, ut dicitur in IV *Metaphys.* Sicut autem ens est primum quod cadit in apprehensione simplicter, ita bonum est primum quod cadit in apprehensione practicae rationis, quae ordinatur ad opus: omne enim agens agit propter finem, qui habet rationem boni. Et ideo primum principium in ratione practica est quod fundatur supra rationem boni, quae est, *Bonum est quod omnia appetunt.* Hoc est ergo primum praeceptum legis, quod bonum est faciendum et prosequendum, et malum vitandum. Et super hoc fundantur omnia alia praecepta legis naturae: ut scilicet omnia illa facienda vel vitanda pertineat ad praecepta legis naturae, quae ratio practica naturalitur apprehendit esse bona humana." S. Thomas Aquinas, *Summa Theologiae,* I-II, q. 94, art. 2. English translation [hereafter: ET]: St Thomas Aquinas, *Summa Theologica,* Vol. 2, Iª-IIªᵉ (Westminster: Christian Classics, 1981), p. 1009, q. 94, art. 2.

4. See: Mondin, *Dizionario,* pp. 88–89, 610–11.

Sacred art by being true and beautiful should evoke and glorify the mystery of God made visible in Christ, and lead to the adoration and love of God, the Creator and Savior, who is the surpassing, invisible Beauty of Truth and Love.[5]

The text of the *Compendium* makes it clear that the beauty of sacred art is always the fruit of a more profound knowledge and love of God in Jesus Christ, the only-begotten Son of God, Who is All-Beautiful.

In the context of modern Western culture, it is precisely the transcendental dimension of beauty, inasmuch as it is essentially related with truth and goodness, which is disputed. According to the rationalistic thought which has strongly influenced contemporary western culture, beauty has been stripped of its metaphysical meaning. It has been "liberated" from the order of being and has been reduced to an aesthetic experience or even to something sentimental. The disastrous consequences of this revolution are not limited to the world of art. Precisely because we have lost beauty, we have also lost goodness and truth.

The good is now determined by what is pleasing to an individual or to the group in power, such that I determine whether a given thing is good according to my preference and convenience, even if it turns out to be destructive for the other or for the world around me. At the same time, there is the claim that each individual person determines what is good for him, such that the individual determines when human life begins or what constitutes marriage and the family.

One of the most painful consequences of the contemporary alienation of beauty from the good and the true is an aesthetics which denies any beautiful thing as a deception and maintains that only the representation of the crude, insofar as it is vulgar and base, corresponds to the truth. Beauty is suspect: it is considered to be inconsistent, superficial and incapable of revealing the truth. A similar aesthetics has also had an effect on the Sacred Liturgy, as well as on sacred art and sacred architecture. The great Catholic tradition of art, architecture, language, music and gesture, in which the traditional forms of prayer and worship are expressed, frequently collide with a similar lack of trust and with a true suspicion, even in the Church. It is not rare to hear it said that beauty is not an appropriate category of the worship of the Church.

---

5. *Catechism of the Catholic Church: Compendium* (Washington: United States Conference of Catholic Bishops, 2006), p. 150 n. 526, with reference to numbers 2500–2503, and 2513 of the *Catechism of the Catholic Church.*

In fact, on the basis of a false interpretation of the liturgical reform called for by the Second Vatican Ecumenical Council, one justified the destruction of beautiful altarpieces and statues in some parts of the Church, for example, not to mention what has happened to sacred music in the Postconciliar period. The corruption effected from such a mode of thinking seems to be a new manifestation of the perennial temptation to iconoclasm which has repeatedly assaulted the Church over the centuries. According to this way of thinking, that which is ugly attracts on account of its honesty and simplicity.

In an essay on beauty, written in 2002, Cardinal Joseph Ratzinger reflected on Psalm 44 [45], which "describes the wedding of the king, his beauty, his virtues, his mission, and then makes a transition to praise the bride."[6] He proceeds to explain:

> It is clear that the Church reads this psalm as a prophetic and poetic representation of the spousal relationship of Christ and Church. She thus acknowledges Christ as the fairest of men; the graciousness poured upon his lips refers to the inner beauty of his words, to the glory of his message. So it is not merely the external beauty of the Redeemer's appearance that is praised: rather, the beauty of truth appears in him, the beauty of God himself, who powerfully draws us and inflicts on us the wound of Love, as it were, a holy Eros that enables us to go forth, with and in the Church, his Bride, to meet the Love who calls us.[7]

It is the same Christ to whom the Church, remembering His Passion, applies the words of the Book of the Prophet Isaiah: "[H]e had no form or comeliness that we should look at him, and no beauty that we should desire him" (Isa 53:2). In the suffering Christ we begin to understand that "the beauty of truth also involves wounds, pain, and even the obscure mystery of death and that this can only be found in accepting pain, not

---

6. "…descrive le nozze del Re, la sua bellezza, le sue virtù, la sua missione, e poi si trasforma in un'esultazione della sposa." Joseph Ratzinger, *La bellezza. La Chiesa* (Castel Bolognese: Itacalibri, 2005), p. 11. ET: Cardinal Joseph Ratzinger, *On the Way to Jesus Christ* (San Francisco: Ignatius, 2005), p. 32.

7. "È chiaro che la Chiesa legge questo salmo come rappresentazione poetico-profetica del rapporto sponsale di Cristo con la Chiesa. Riconosce Cristo come il più bello tra gli uomini; la grazia diffusa sulle sue labbra indica la bellezza interiore della Sua parola, la gloria del Suo annuncio. Cosi non è semplicemente la bellezza esteriore dell'apparizione del Redentore ad essere glorificata: in Lui appare piuttosto la bellezza della Verità, la bellezza di Dio stesso che ci attira a sè e allo stesso tempo ci procura la ferita dell'Amore, la santa passione (eros) che ci fa andare incontro, insieme alla e nella Chiesa Sposa, all'Amore che ci chiama." Ibid., pp. 11–12. ET ibid., pp. 32–33.

in ignoring it."[8] Pope Benedict XVI speaks of a paradox of beauty which implies not a contradiction but a contrast.[9] The totality of the beauty of Christ is revealed to us when we contemplate the image of our crucified Savior, which shows His love "to the end."[10]

We therefore learn to contemplate the redemptive beauty of Christ, Crucified and Glorified, which is reflected with particular splendor in the lives of the saints and is also reflected in the works of art which the faith has generated. The great masterpieces of sacred art and sacred music have the potential to raise our hearts to things of heaven and to draw us out of ourselves to God Who is beauty itself. It is Pope Benedict's conviction that this encounter is "the true apologetics for the Christian message."[11]

3. *Sacred Art and the Sacred Liturgy*

For the Church, beauty is revealed most fully and most perfectly in the Sacred Liturgy, in the sacramental encounter with Christ Who lives in the Church through the outpouring of the Holy Spirit. Pope Benedict XVI, during his visit to the Cistercian Abbey of Heiligenkreuz in Austria, in September of 2007, exhorted priests and religious with the following words:

> I ask you to celebrate the Sacred Liturgy with your gaze fixed on God within the communion of the saints, the living Church of every time and place, so that it will truly be an expression of the sublime beauty of the God who has called men and women to be his friends![12]

His words are applicable to all who are called to life in Christ and, therefore, to worship God the Father "in spirit and truth" (John 4:23–24).

---

8. "...la bellezza della verità comprende offesa, dolore e, sì, anche l'oscuro mistero della morte, e che essa può essere trovata soltanto nell'accettazione del dolore, e non nell'ignorarlo." Ibid., p. 14. ET ibid., p. 34.

9. See: ibid., p. 13. ET ibid., p. 33.

10. "...sino alla fine." See: ibid., p. 14. ET ibid., p. 34. See: John 13:1.

11. "...la vera apologia della fede cristiana." Ibid., p. 21. ET ibid., p. 38.

12. "Ich bitte an dieser Stelle: Gestaltet die heilige Liturgie aus dem Hinschauen auf Gott in der Gemeinschaft der Heiligen, der lebendigen Kirche aller Orte und Zeiten so, daß sie zu einem Ausdruck der Schönheit und Erhabenheit des menschen-freundlichen Gottes wird." Benedictus PP. XVI, Allocutio "In visitatione Abbatiae 'Heiligen Kreuz', die 9 Septembris 2007, *AAS* 99 (2007), p. 855. ET: "Heiligenkreuz: Papal Address, Holy Cross Abbey, 9 September: Your Primary Service: Prayer and the Divine Office," *L'Osservatore Romano Weekly Edition in English*, 12 September 2007, p. 11.

Pope Benedict XVI reflected on beauty in the Sacred Liturgy in his Post-Synodal Apostolic Exhortation *Sacramentum Caritatis* of 2007. He wrote:

> This relationship between creed and worship is evidenced in a particular way by the rich theological and liturgical category of beauty. Like the rest of Christian Revelation, the liturgy is inherently linked to beauty: it is *veritatis splendor*. The liturgy is a radiant expression of the paschal mystery, in which Christ draws us to himself and calls us to communion. As Saint Bonaventure would say, in Jesus we contemplate beauty and splendour at their source. This is no mere aestheticism, but the concrete way in which the truth of God's love in Christ encounters us, attracts us and delights us, enabling us to emerge from ourselves and drawing us towards our true vocation, which is love. God allows himself to be glimpsed first in creation, in the beauty and harmony of the cosmos (cf. Wis 13:5; Rom 1:19–20). In the Old Testament we see many signs of the grandeur of God's power as he manifests his glory in his wondrous deeds among the Chosen People (cf. Ex 14; 16:10; 24:12–18; Num 14:20–23). In the New Testament this epiphany of beauty reaches definitive fulfilment in God's revelation in Jesus Christ: Christ is the full manifestation of the glory of God. In the glorification of the Son, the Father's glory shines forth and is communicated (cf. Jn 1:14; 8:54; 12:28; 17:1). Yet this beauty is not simply a harmony of proportion and form; "the fairest of the sons of men" (Ps 45[44]:3) is also, mysteriously, the one "who had no form or comeliness that we should look at him, and no beauty that we should desire him" (Is 53:2). Jesus Christ shows us how the truth of love can transform even the dark mystery of death into the radiant light of the resurrection. Here the splendour of God's glory surpasses all worldly beauty. The truest beauty is the love of God, who definitively revealed himself to us in the paschal mystery.[13]

13. "Relatio inter Mysterium fide acceptum et celebratum per theologicam liturgicamque vim pulchritudinis peculiari ostenditur modo. Liturgia quidem, sicut ceterum Revelatio christiana, intrinsecum habet nexum cum pulchritudine: est *veritatis splendor*. In liturgia paschale fulget Mysterium per quod ipse Christus ad se ipsum nos attrahit adque communionem vocat. In Iesu, sicut sanctus solebat adfirmare Bonaventura, pulchritudinem contemplamur atque originum fulgorem. Haec proprietas quam commemoramus non sola pulchritudinis est aestimatio, sed ratio qua veritas amoris Dei in Christo nos attingit, nos allicit rapitque, dum simul efficit ut ex nobis ipsis excedamus sicque attrahit ad germanam nostram vocationem: videlicet amorem. Iam in creatione Deus sinit ut in pulchritudine harmoniaque mundi conspiciatur (cfr *Sap* 13, 5; *Rom* 1, 19–20). Vetere denique in Testamento ampla invenimus signa fulgoris potentiae Dei, qui sua cum gloria manifestatur per prodigia inter populum electum acta (cfr *Ex* 14; 16, 10; 24, 12–18; *Nm* 14, 20–23). Novo in Testamento haec pulchritudinis epiphania absolute adimpletur in revelatione Dei in

In his work on the Sacred Liturgy, *The Spirit of the Liturgy*, then-Cardinal Ratzinger observed that there cannot be "completely free expression in sacred art,"[14] that is, an expression without reference to the objective order of things. He states: "No sacred art can come from an isolated subjectivity."[15]

Sacred art is at the service of the Sacred Liturgy and it is therefore fundamentally an expression of faith. I remember a visit I made to a cathedral built during the first years of the present century by a contemporary architect who seemingly had little or no appreciation of the distinct nature of sacred architecture. Concelebrating the Holy Mass in that cathedral, I was struck by the peculiarity of the various appointments in the sanctuary. Both the altar of sacrifice and the ambo seemed very strange to me in themselves and in their relationship to each other. After the Holy Mass, when I expressed my wonderment to an auxiliary Bishop of the diocese in question, he responded to me that I had to understand that the principle of the architecture of the cathedral was asymmetry. He assured me that my reaction was appropriate, because all the elements in the cathedral function, in accord with the principle of asymmetry, to induce disorientation. I could only respond that it seemed truly strange to me to use an architecture of asymmetry to erect a temple to the God of order and of harmony.

Iesu Christo: Ipse est plena gloriae divinae manifestatio. In Filii glorificatione elucet et datur Patris gloria (cfr *Io* 1, 14; 8, 54; 12, 28; 17, 1). Haec tamen pulchritudo non est simpliciter formarum convenientia; 'speciosus forma (…) prae filiis hominum' (*Ps* 45 [44], 3) est etiam arcanum in modum ipse cui 'non erat species (…) neque decor, ut aspiceremus eum' (*Is* 53, 2). Iesus Christus nobis demonstrat quomodo veritas amoris transfigurare valeat etiam obscurum Mysterium mortis in lucem fulgidam resurrectionis. Hic gloriae Dei splendor omnem superat intramundanam pulchritudinem, ut appellant. Vera pulchritudo est amor Dei qui se definitive nobis in Mysterio paschali revelavit." Benedictus PP. XVI, Adhortatio Apostolica postsynodalis *Sacramentum caritatis*, "de Eucharistia vitae missionisque Ecclesiae fonte et culmine," 22 Februarii 2007, *AAS* 99 (2007), pp. 133–34 n. 35. ET: Benedict XVI, Post-Synodal Apostolic Exhortation *Sacramentum Caritatis*, "On the Eucharist as the Source and Summit of the Church's Life and Mission" (Vatican City State: Libreria Editrice Vaticana, 2007), pp. 52–53 n. 35.

14. "…reine Beliebigkeit." Joseph Ratzinger, *Theologie der Liturgie. Die sakramentale Begründung christlicher Existenz*, Gesammelte Schriften, Band 11 (Freiburg: Herder, 2008), p. 121. ET: Joseph Ratzinger, *Theology of the Liturgy*, Collected Works, vol. 11 (San Francisco: Ignatius, 2014), p. 83.

15. "Aus der isolierten Subjektivität kann keine Sakrale Kunst kommen." Ibid., p. 121. ET ibid., p. 83.

In truth, it seems to me a profound injustice to ask an architect or an artist who does not enjoy a knowledge and appreciation of sacred architecture to design a Catholic church or its appointments. At the most, he could mechanically imitate the work of someone who does have the faith; at the worst, his art will express something other than the faith or even something contrary to the faith. In this regard, Cardinal Joseph Ratzinger wrote:

> Without faith there is no art commensurate with the liturgy. Sacred art stands beneath the imperative stated in the second epistle to the Corinthians. Gazing at the Lord, we are "changed into his likeness from one degree of glory to another; for this comes from the Lord who is the spirit" (3:18).[16]

Recognizing that sacred art is a gift that is received and not a product of the artist, he exhorts the church to "regain a faith that sees."[17]

The beauty of the Sacred Liturgy is given concrete expression by means of the objects and the gestures of which the person—a unity of soul and body—has need in order to be raised to the realities of faith which transcend the visible world. This means that sacred architecture and sacred art, including the sacred appointments, the vestments, the vessels and linens, must be of such a quality that they can express and communicate the beauty and the majesty of the liturgy as the action of Christ among us, uniting heaven and earth.

Pope John Paul II, in his last Encyclical Letter, *Ecclesia de Eucharistia* of 2003, recalled for us the biblical foundation of the concern the Church has for beauty in her worship, that is, the episode of the anointing of Jesus at Bethany:

> A woman, whom John identifies as Mary the sister of Lazarus, pours a flask of *costly ointment* over Jesus' head, which provokes from the disciples— and from Judas in particular (cf. Mt 26:8; Mk 14:4; Jn 12:4)—an indignant response, as if this act, in light of the needs of the poor, represented an intolerable "waste." But Jesus' own reaction is completely different. While in no way detracting from the duty of charity towards the needy, for whom the disciples must always show special care—"the poor you will always have with you" (Mt 26:11; Mk 14:7; cf. Jn 12:8)—he looks towards his

---

16. "Ohne Glauben gibt es keine der Liturgie gemäße Kunst. Sakrale Kunst steht unter dem Imperativ des Zweiten Korintherbriefs: Auf den Herrn hinschauend werden wir 'in sein eigenes Bild verwandelt, von Herrlichkeit zu Herrlichkeit, durch den Geist des Herrn' (3, 18)." Ibid., p. 121. ET ibid., p. 83.

17. "…einem sehenden Glauben." Ibid. ET ibid.

imminent death and burial, and sees this act of anointing as an anticipation of the honour which his body will continue to merit even after his death, indissolubly bound as it is to the mystery of his person.[18]

The episode illustrates, above all, that care for the beauty of churches and for all the things used in the Sacred Liturgy is a natural expression of love of God.

Even in those places in which the Church does not enjoy many material resources, this care should be a priority. In this regard, I refer to Pope Benedict XIV (1740–1758), one of the great Pontiffs of the eighteenth century, who wrote the following words in his Encyclical Letter *Annus Qui* which was dedicated to sacred music:

> We do not intend, with these words, to insist on sumptuous or majestic structures for sacred buildings, neither on rich and costly furnishings. We are conscious that these are not everywhere possible. That which we desire is fittingness and cleanness. These can accompany and be adapted to poverty.[19]

The history of the Church is, in fact, filled with examples of persons of modest economic means who made great sacrifices to provide for the construction of truly beautiful churches, with hand-carved statues in wood and marble, stained-glass windows, and vestments and linens of high quality.

18. "Mulier quaedam, a Ioanne uti Maria Lazari soror designata, infundit in Iesu caput vasculum *pretiosi nardi*, cum inter discipulos—praesertim in Iuda (cfr *Mt* 26,8; *Mc* 14,4: *Io* 12,4)—reclamationes excitaret, tamquam si actus ille, pauperum inspectis necessitatibus, «profusionem» intollerandam prae se ferret. At Iesu existimatio omnino alia est. Nihil quidem detrectans de caritatis officio erga indigentes, quibus discipuli se debebunt semper dedere—'semper pauperes habetis vobiscum' (*Mt* 26,11; *Mc* 14,7; see: *Io* 12, 8)—eventum potius Ipse respicit mortis suae et sepulturae imminentem et idcirco unctionem magni aestimat quae adhibita est ei tamquam illius honoris anticipatio quo corpus eius dignum esse perget etiam post obitum, ligatum vinculo indissolubili cum personae eius mysterio." Ioannes Paulus PP. II, Litterae Encyclicae *Ecclesia de Eucharistia*, "de Eucharistia eiusque necessitudine cum Ecclesia," 17 Aprilis 2003, *AAS* 95 (2003), p. 464 n. 47. ET: John Paul II, Encyclical Letter *Ecclesia de Eucharistia*, "On the Eucharist in Its Relationship to the Church" (Vatican City State: Libreria Editrice Vaticana, 2003), p. 58 n. 47.

19. "Hic autem adverti volumus, nos verba facere non de sumptuositate, et sacrorum Templorum magnificentia, nec de divite, ac pretiosa supellectili; non enim Nos latet haec non omnibus in locis haberi posse; sed decentiam, et munditiam desideramus, quas nemini detrectare licet, quia etiam cum paupertate bene convenire et componi possunt." Benedictus PP. XIV, Litterae Encyclicae *Annus Qui*, 19 Februarii 1749, *Sanctissimi Domini Nostri Benedicti Papae XIV Bullarium*, tomus III, vol. 7 (Mechliniae: P.-J. Hanicq, 1827), p. 36. ET by the author.

The "faith that sees" of Cardinal Ratzinger is essential for appreciating the immense treasure of beauty which previous generations have left us in splendid works of sacred art and sacred architecture. The cathedrals and the churches in all the world, for example, are not merely cultural monuments. Above all, they are testimonies of Catholic faith. In his masterpiece *The Spirit of the Liturgy*, Cardinal Joseph Ratzinger observed: "The great cultural tradition of the faith is home to a presence of immense power. What in museums is only a monument from the past, an occasion for mere nostalgic admiration, is constantly made present in the liturgy in all its freshness."[20]

During his Apostolic Visit to France, Pope Benedict XVI was inspired to give a similar reflection in his homily for Vespers on 12 September 2009, in the splendid Cathedral of Notre Dame in Paris, which he praised as a "living hymn of stone and light in praise of that act, unique in the annals of human history: the eternal Word of God entering our history in the fullness of time to redeem us by His self-offering in the sacrifice of the Cross."[21] The Cathedral of Notre Dame is truly a hymn of praise to the Mystery of the Incarnation of God the Son in the womb of the Blessed Virgin Mary. It is fitting to recall that it was in the same cathedral that the poet Paul Claudel (1868–1955) had a singular experience of the beauty of God, during the chanting of the Magnificat during Vespers on Christmas of 1886, which led to his conversion to the Catholic faith. It should not escape us that the *via pulchritudinis*, the way of beauty, is a most important and irreplaceable means of announcing God to a culture fraught with secularism and materialism.

20. "Zum einen wohnt der großen kulturellen Tradition des Glaubens eine ungeheure Gegenwartskraft inne: Was in den Museen nur nostalgisch bestauntes Zeugnis der Vergangenheit sein mag, wird in der Liturgie immer wieder frische Gegenwart." *Theologie der Liturgie*, p. 137. ET: *Theology of the Liturgy*, p. 97.

21. "...une vivante hymne de pierre et de lumière à la louange de cet acte unique de l'histoire de l'humanité: la Parole éternelle de Dieu entrant dans l'histoire des hommes à la plénitude des temps pour les racheter par l'offrande de lui-même dans le sacrifice de la Croix." Homilia "Lutetiae Parisiorum in Vesperarum celebratione apud Templum Cathedrale 'Notre-Dame'," 12 Septembris 2008, *AAS* 100 (2008), p. 692. ET: "The Holy Father's Vespers Homily on the Liturgical Experience and the Heavenly Jerusalem: In the Church Everyone Has a Place," 12 September 2008, *L'Osservatore Romano Weekly Edition in English*, 17 September 2008, p. 8.

For a study of the teaching of Joseph Ratzinger applied to sacred music, I invite you to read my presentation at the Third Fota International Liturgical Conference in 2010.[22] The Proceedings of the Conference are published under the title, *Benedict XVI and Beauty in Sacred Music*.

4. *The Beauty of a Holy Life*

The way leading to freedom and happiness is, for each of us, holiness of life, in accord with our state in life. Pope John Paul II, in fact, cast the entire pastoral plan for the Church in terms of holiness. He explained himself thus:

> In fact, to place pastoral planning under the heading of holiness is a choice filled with consequences. It implies the conviction that, since Baptism is a true entry into the holiness of God through incorporation into Christ and the indwelling of his Spirit, it would be a contradiction to settle for a life of mediocrity, marked by a minimalist ethics and a shallow religiosity. To ask catechumens: "Do you wish to receive Baptism?" means at the same time to ask them: "Do you wish to become holy?" It means to set before them the radical nature of the Sermon on the Mount: "Be perfect as your heavenly Father is perfect" (Mt 5:48).[23]

Pope John Paul II continued, making reference to the Second Vatican Ecumenical Council, by reminding us that "this ideal of perfection must not be misunderstood as if it involved some kind of extraordinary existence, possible only for a few 'uncommon heroes' of holiness."[24]

22. See: Raymond Cardinal Burke, "The New Evangelization and Sacred Music: The Unbroken Continuity of Holiness, Beauty and Universality," in Janet Rutherford (eds), *Benedict XVI and Beauty in Sacred Music: Proceedings of the Third Fota International Liturgical Conference, 2010* (Dublin: Four Courts, 2012), pp. 24–40.

23. "Re quidem vera, si pastoralis ordinatio sub signo sanctitatis statuitur, aliquid compluribus cum consectariis decernitur. Inde enim in primis firma aperitur sententia: si vera est Baptismus ingressio in Dei sanctitatem per insertionem in Christum ipsum necnon Spiritus eius per inhabitationem, quaedam repugnantia est contentum esse mediocri vita, quae ad normam transigitur ethnicae doctrinae minimum solum poscentis ac religionis superficiem tantum tangentis. Ex catechumeno quaerere: 'Vis baptizari?' eodem tempore est petere: 'Vis sanctificari?.' Idem valet ac deponere eius in via extremum Sermonis Montani principium: 'Estote ergo vos perfecti, sicut Pater vester caelestis perfectus est' (*Mt* 5, 48)." *Novo Millennio Ineunte*, p. 288 n. 31. ET: Pope John Paul II, Apostolic Letter *Novo Millennio Ineunte*, "At the Close of the Great Jubilee of the Year 2000," 6 January 2001 (Boston: Pauline Books & Media, 2001), p. 43 n. 31.

24. "...optima haec perfectionis species non ita est iudicanda quasi si genus quoddam secum importet vitae extraordinariae quam soli aliqui sanctitatis 'gigantes' traducere possint." Ibid, p. 288 n. 31. ET: ibid., p. 43 n. 31.

Pope John Paul II taught us the extraordinary nature of our ordinary life, because it is lived in Christ and, therefore, produces in us the incomparable beauty of holiness. He declared:

> The ways of holiness are many, according to the vocation of each individual. I thank the Lord that in these years he has enabled me to beatify and canonize a large number of Christians, and among them many lay people who attained holiness in the most ordinary circumstances of life. The time has come to re-propose wholeheartedly to everyone this *high standard of ordinary Christian living*: the whole life of the Christian community and of Christian families must lead in this direction.[25]

Seeing in us the daily conversion of life by which we strive to meet the high standard of holiness, the *"high standard of ordinary Christian living,"* our brothers and sisters will discover the great beauty of their own ordinary life in which God daily showers upon them his immeasurable and ceaseless love, calling them to holiness of life in Christ, His only-begotten Son. That beauty is most evident in our participation in the Sacred Liturgy.

Referring to the new evangelization of our culture, Pope John Paul II also observed that clearly, the "mending of the Christian fabric of society" can only come about by the remaking of "the Christian fabric of the ecclesial community," beginning with the individual in his family, at home.[26] The remaking of "the Christian fabric of the ecclesial community" has its inspiration and direction in the Sacred Liturgy which, at the same time, reflects the unity which necessarily marks the life of the Mystical Body of Christ.

Writing about our participation in the Sacred Liturgy, Cardinal Joseph Ratzinger wrote:

25. "Multiplices enim sanctitatis exsistunt viae atque cuiusque congruunt cum vocatione. Grates Domino referimus Nobis quod concessit his proximis annis tot christianos et christianas inter beatos adnumerare ac sanctos, ex quibus plures laici sanctimoniam sunt communissimis in vitae condicionibus adsecuti. Omnibus ergo tempus est iterum firmiter hunc proponere *'superiorem modum' ordinariae vitae christianae*: ad hanc namque metam conducere debet omnis vita ecclesialis communitatis ac familiarum christianarum." Ibid., p. 288 n. 31. ET: ibid., p. 43 n. 31.

26. "... consortium humanum spiritu christiano ubique denuo imbuendum est... *christianus commmunitatum ipsarum ecclesialium contextus.*" Ioannes Paulus PP. II, Adhortatio Apostolica *Christifideles Laici*, "De vocatione et missione Laicorum in Ecclesia et in mundo," 30 Decembris 1988, *AAS* 81 (1989), p. 455 n. 34. ET: Pope John Paul II, Post-Synodal Apostolic Exhortation *Christifideles Laici*, "On the Vocation and the Mission of the Lay Faithful in the Church and in the World," 30 December 1988 (Vatican City State: Libreria Editrice Vaticana, n.d.), p. 95 n. 34.

This *oratio*—the Eucharistic prayer, the "Canon"—is really more than speech; it is *actio* in the highest sense of the word. For what happens in it is that the human *actio* (as performed hitherto by the priests in the various religions of the world) steps back and makes way for the *actio divina*, the action of God. In this *oratio* the priest speaks with the I of the Lord—"This is my Body," "This is my Blood." He knows that he is not now speaking from his own resources but in virtue of the Sacrament that he has received, he has become the voice of Someone Else, who is now speaking and acting. This action of God, which takes place through human speech, is the real "action" for which all of creation is in expectation. The elements of the earth are transubstantiated, pulled, so to speak, from their creaturely anchorage, grasped at the deepest ground of their being, and changed into the Body and Blood of the Lord. The New Heaven and the New Earth are anticipated. The real "action" in the liturgy in which we are all supposed to participate is the action of God himself. This is what is new and distinctive about the Christian liturgy: God himself acts and does what is essential. He inaugurates the new creation, makes himself accessible to us, so that, through the things of the earth, through our gifts, we can communicate with him in a personal way. But how can we participate, have a part in this action? Are not God and man completely incommensurable? Can man, the finite and sinful one, cooperate with God, the Infinite and Holy One? Yes, he can, precisely because God himself has become man, become body, and here, again and again, he comes through his body to us who live in the body. The whole event of the Incarnation, Cross, Resurrection, and Second Coming is present as the way by which God draws man into cooperation with himself. As we have seen, this is expressed in the liturgy in the fact that the petition for acceptance is part of the *oratio*. True, the Sacrifice of the Logos is accepted already and forever. But we must still pray for it to become *our* sacrifice, that we ourselves, as we said, may be transformed into the Logos (*logisiert*), conformed to the Logos, and so be made the true Body of Christ. This is the issue, and that is what we have to pray for. The petition itself is a way into the Incarnation and the Resurrection, the path that we take in the wayfaring state of our existence... In the words of St. Paul, it is a question of being "united to the Lord" and thus becoming "one spirit with him" (1 Cor 6:17). The point is that, ultimately, the difference between the *actio Christi* and our own action is done away with. There is only *one* action, which is at the same time his and ours—ours because we have become "one body and one spirit" with him. The uniqueness of the Eucharistic liturgy lies precisely in the fact that God himself is acting and that we are drawn into that action of God. Everything else is, therefore, secondary.[27]

27. "Diese oratio—das eucharistische Hochgebet, der ‚Kanon'—ist wirklich mehr als Rede, is actio im höchsten Sinn. Denn darin geschieht es, dass die menschliche actio (wie sie bisher von den Priestern in den verschiedenen Religionen geübt worden war) zurücktritt und Raum gibt für die actio divina, das Handeln Gottes. In dieser

The objective reality of the Sacred Liturgy makes it the most perfect earthly encounter with God, the All-Beautiful, and, therefore everything about the Sacred Liturgy must reflect the incomparable beauty of the objective reality of the meeting of heaven and earth. At the same time, the Christian most perfectly sees the reflection of the incomparable beauty of his life in Christ through his participation in the Sacred Liturgy. For this reason also, the essential beauty of the Sacred Liturgy must be carefully served.

oratio spricht der Priester mit dem Ich des Herrn—'das ist mein Leib,' 'das ist mein Blut'—in dem Wissen, dass er nun nicht mehr aus Eigenem redet, sondern kraft des Sakraments, das er empfangen hat, Stimme des anderen wird, der nun redet, handelt. Dieses Handeln Gottes, das sich durch menschliches Reden hindurch vollzieht, is die eigentliche 'Aktion,' auf die alle Schöpfung wartet: Die Elemente der Erde werden um-substanziiert, sozusagen aus ihrer kreatürlichen Verankerung herausgerissen, im tiefsten Grund ihres Seins erfasst und umgewandelt in Leib und Blut des Herrn. Der neue Himmel und die neue Erde werden antizipiert. Die eigentliche 'Aktion' in der Liturgie, an der wir alle teilhaben sollen, ist Handeln Gottes selbst. Das ist das Neue und Besondere der christlichen Liturgie, das Gott selber handelt und dass er das Wesentliche tut: die neue Schöpfung heraufführt, sich selbst zugänglich macht, so dass wir mit ihm selber ganz persönlich, durch die Dinge der Erde, durch unsere Gaben hindurch kommunizieren können. Aber wie können wir denn an dieser Aktion teil-haben? Sind nicht Gott und Mensch völlig inkommensurabel? Kann der Mensch, der endliche und sündige, mit Gott, dem Unendlichen und Heiligen, kooperieren? Nun, er kann es eben dadurch, dass Gott selbst Mensch wurde, dass er Leib wurde und hier immer wider neu durch seinen Leib auf uns zughet, die wir im Leibe leben. Das ganze Ereignis von Inkarnation, Kreuz, Auferstehung, Wiederkunft is gegenwärtig als die Form, wie Gott den Menschen in die Kooperation mit sich selbst hineinzieht. In der Liturgie drückt sich das, wie wir schon gesehen haben, darin aus, dass zur oratio die Annahmebitte gehört. Gewiss, das Opfer des Logos *ist* immer schon angenommen. Aber wir müssen darum bitten, dass es *unser* Opfer werde, dass wir selbst, wie wir sagten, 'logisiert,' logos-gemäß und so wahrer Leib Christi werden: Darum geht es. Und das muss erbetet werden. Diese Bitte selbst ist ein Weg, ein Unterwegssein unserer Existenz in die Inkarnation und in die Auferstehung hinein… Für uns alle geht es gemäß dem Wort aus 1 Kor 6, 17 darum, 'dem Herrn anzuhangen und so eine einzige pneumatische Existenz mit ihm zu werden.' Es geht darum, dass letztlich der Unterschied zwischen der actio Christi und der unseren aufgehoben werde. Dass es nur noch eine *actio* gebe, die zugleich die seine und die unsrige ist—die unsrige dadurch, dass wir mit ihm 'ein Leib und ein Geist' geworden sind. Die Einzigartigkeit der eucharistischen Liturgie besteht eben darin, dass Gott selbst handelt und dass wir in dieses Handeln Gottes hineingezogen werden. Alles andere is demgegenüber sekundär." *Theologie der Liturgie*, pp. 148–49. ET: *Theology of the Liturgy*, pp. 107–8.

So often, today, a notion of tolerance of ways of thinking and acting contrary to the moral law seems to be the interpretative key for many Christians. This notion is not securely grounded in the moral tradition, yet it tends to dominate our approach to the extent that we end up claiming to be Christian while tolerating ways of thinking and acting which are diametrically opposed to the moral law revealed to us in nature and in the Sacred Scriptures. The approach, at times, becomes so relativistic and subjective that we do not even observe the fundamental logical principle of non-contradiction, that is, that a thing cannot both be and not be at the same time. In other words, certain actions cannot at the same time be both true to the moral law and not true to it.

In fact, charity alone must be the interpretive key of our thoughts and actions. In the context of charity, tolerance means unconditional love of the person who is involved in evil but firm abhorrence of the evil into which the person has fallen.

Fundamental to the Catholic life of virtue is the understanding of human nature and conscience. Critical to the deplorable cultural situation in which we find ourselves is the loss of a sense of nature and of conscience. Pope Benedict XVI addressed the question of the loss of a sense of nature and conscience, with respect of the foundations of law, in his address to the *Bundestag* during his Pastoral Visit to Germany in September of 2011. Taking leave from the story of the young King Solomon on his accession to the throne, he recalled to political leaders the teaching of the Holy Scriptures regarding the work of politics. God asked King Solomon what request he wished to make as he began to rule God's holy people. The Holy Father commented: "What will the young ruler ask for at this important moment? Success—wealth—long life—destruction of his enemies? He chooses none of these things. Instead, he asks for a listening heart so that he may govern God's people, and discern between good and evil (cf. 1 Kg 3:9)."[28]

The story of King Solomon, as Pope Benedict XVI observed, teaches what must be the end of political activity and, therefore, of government. He declared: "Politics must be a striving for justice, and hence it has to

---

28. "Was wird sich der junge Herrscher in diesem Augenblick erbitten? Erfolg—Reichtum—langes Leben—Vernichtung der Feinde? Nicht um diese Dinge bittet er. Er bittet: 'Verleih deinem Knecht ein hörendes Herz, damit er dein Volk zu regieren und das Gute vom Bösen zu unterscheiden versteht' (1 Kön 3,9)." Benedictus PP. XVI, Allocutio "Iter apostolicum in Germaniam: ad Berolinensem foederatum coetum oratorum," 22 Septembris 2011, *AAS* 103 (2011), p. 663. ET: *L'Osservatore Romano Weekly Edition in English*, 28 September 2011, p. 6.

establish the fundamental preconditions for peace… To serve right and to fight against the dominion of wrong is and remains the fundamental task of the politician."[29]

It is the same "listening heart" which leads us daily to turn to Christ in prayer and worship. In the incomparable communion of our hearts with the Heart of Christ in the Eucharistic Sacrifice, we know what is good and right, and are strengthened to do it. Referring to a text of Saint Paul's Letter to the Romans (2:14–16) regarding the natural moral law and its primary witness, the conscience, Pope Benedict XVI declared: "Here we see the two fundamental concepts of nature and conscience, where conscience is nothing other than Solomon's listening heart, reason that is open to the language of being."[30] It is through participation in the Sacred Liturgy that our reason is most fully opened to "the language of being," to the beauty of a life given completely to Christ in pure and selfless love.

Further illustrating the sources of law in nature and reason by making reference to the popular interest in ecology as a means of respecting nature, he observed:

> Yet I would like to underline a point that seems to me to be neglected, today as in the past: there is also an ecology of man. Man too has a nature that he must respect and that he cannot manipulate at will. Man is not merely self-creating freedom. Man does not create himself. He is intellect and will, but he is also nature, and his will is rightly ordered if he respects nature, listens to it and accepts himself for who he is, as one who did not create himself. In this way, and in no other, is true human freedom fulfilled.[31]

---

29. "Politik muss Mühen um Gerechtigkeit sein und so die Grundvoraussetzung für Frieden schaffen… Dem Recht zu dienen und der Herrschaft des Unrechts zu wehren ist und bleibt die grundlegende Aufgabe des Politikers." Ibid., p. 664. ET: ibid., p. 6.

30. "Hier erscheinen die beiden Grundbegriffe Natur und Gewissen, wobei Gewissen nichts anderes ist als das hörende Herz Salomons, als die der Sprache des Seins geöffnete Vernunft." Ibid., p. 666. ET ibid., p. 6.

31. "Ich möchte aber nachdrücklich einen Punkt ansprechen, der nach wie vor— wie mir scheint—ausgeklammert wird: es gibt auch eine Ökologie des Menschen. Auch der Mensch hat eine Natur, die er achten muß und die er nicht beliebig manipulieren kann. Der Mensch ist nicht nur sich selbst machende Freiheit. Der Mensch macht sich nicht selbst. Er ist Geist und Wille, aber er ist auch Natur, und sein Wille ist dann recht, wenn er auf die Natur achtet, sie hört und sich annimmt also der, der er ist und der sich nicht selbst gemacht hat. Gerade so und nur so vollzieht sich wahre menschliche Freiheit." Ibid., p. 668. ET ibid., p. 7.

In the beauty of the Sacred Liturgy the Christian sees the beauty of his own nature. Drawn to the worship of God "in spirit and truth" (John 4:24), the Christian understands the beauty of human nature made free to love God and neighbor by the immeasurable and unceasing grace which flows from the glorious pierced Heart of Christ, the "fairest of the sons of men" (Ps 45[44]:2) and "he had no form or comeliness that we should look at him" (Isa 53:2).

5. *Conclusion*

It is my hope that this modest study of the teaching of Pope Benedict on the beauty of the Sacred Liturgy and the beauty of a holy life has, first of all, made clear the most important and irreplaceable place of the Sacred Liturgy in the pursuit of holiness of life. The living of our faith finds its highest expression in the manner of our worship of God, in the various elements of the Sacred Liturgy.

Even as the first disciples were attentive to the worthy celebration of the Sacred Liturgy, as is, for instance, witnessed in the *First Letter to the Corinthians*, and even as the first missionaries were attentive, from the very beginning of their mission, to provide for the worthy and most beautiful possible celebration of the Sacred Liturgy, often at great sacrifice, so, too, must we be committed to the worthiness of our worship of God, so that it may be true worship of God and may, therefore, procure our sanctification and the sanctification of our world. Beauty is at the heart of worship of God and, therefore, leads us to ever greater holiness of life.

According to the ancient wisdom of the Church, the Sacred Liturgy is a "privileged witness of the apostolic tradition."[32] The Church's wisdom is expressed in an adage of Prosper of Aquitaine: "The law of praying establishes the law of believing."[33] We can add that the law of praying also establishes the law of acting. Since the Sacred Liturgy is the highest and most perfect expression of our life in Christ, we rightly turn to the sacred rites, in order to understand more deeply the holiness of the Christian life in its every aspect. The Sacred Liturgy remains the essential source of our understanding of the faith and of its practice in a good and holy life.

---

32. "…un témoin priviligié de la tradition apostolique." A. G. Martimort, *L'Église en prière: Introduction à la Liturgie*, 3rd edn (Paris: Desclée, 1965), p. 231. ET by the author.

33. "Legem credendi lex statuat supplicandi." Ibid., p. 231. ET by the author.

THE REFORM OF THE REFORM

Thomas M. Kocik

An examination of the nuanced language of the Second Vatican Council's Constitution on the Sacred Liturgy, *Sacrosanctum Concilium*, and the clarifications given during its debate at the Council,[1] shows that the Council Fathers intended a moderate reform of the liturgy of the Roman rite, one that would balance "sound tradition" and "legitimate progress" (n. 23).[2] Yet, as both the critics and the apologists of the reform acknowledge, the liturgical changes enacted in the wake of Vatican II went well beyond what Blessed Paul VI and the Council Fathers envisaged when the Constitution was promulgated on 4 December 1963.[3]

---

1. Discussion of the proposed Constitution continued through 15 general congregations from 22 October to 13 November 1962, with 297 written proposals and 328 verbal interventions before it was finally approved on 4 December 1963. For the development of the text, the interventions of the Council Fathers, and the clarifications provided by the conciliar Liturgical Commission, see: F. Gil Hellín, *Concilii Vaticani II Synopsis: Constitutio de Sacra Liturgia Sacrosanctum Concilium* (Vatican City: Libreria Editrice Vaticana, 2003).

2. We see this, for example, in the Constitution's treatment of the use of Latin. While Latin is to be retained in the liturgy, episcopal conferences may decide "whether and to what extent" the vernacular can be used (n. 36). Other examples include reception of Holy Communion from the chalice and the adaptation of the Roman rite to particular cultures or circumstances. Regarding the chalice, the Constitution states that while the discipline of Trent is to be retained (i.e., withholding the chalice from the laity), bishops may permit clergy, religious, and laity to receive from the chalice according to specifications made by the Holy See (n. 55). While the Council allows for "legitimate variations and adaptations to different groups, regions, and peoples," it stipulates that the "substantial unity of the Roman rite" be preserved (n. 38).

3. The primary reference is the candid memoir of Archbishop Annibale Bugnini CM (1912–1982), who from 1964 to 1969 served as Secretary of the *Consilium* (commission) for the implementation of the Vatican II Constitution on the Liturgy: *The Reform of the Liturgy 1948–1975* (Collegeville: The Liturgical Press, 1990; Italian original 1983). Bugnini recounts in detail the work of the *Consilium* from its establishment in 1964 to 1969, and the work for liturgical reform of the Congregation

The great question disputed today is not whether the post-conciliar liturgical reform was in some cases too hasty; it is the more profound question of whether the reform represents a development in substantial continuity with the received tradition, as the Council expressly desired.[4] If not, then it is possible to critique the products of the reform without calling into question the Council itself or the need for liturgical renewal that was obvious to virtually everyone at Vatican II.[5] One could even assert that justice to *Sacrosanctum Concilium* and to the Church's liturgical heritage demands such criticism, at the very least. That is the basis on which to consider the merits of a liturgical "reform of the reform."

for Divine Worship, of which he was Secretary from 1969 to 1975; inaccuracies present in the original Italian edition were corrected for the second Italian edition (1997). See also the more recent chronicle of Archbishop Piero Marini, former papal master of ceremonies (1987–2007), who while still a young deacon and priest served as Bugnini's protégé and secretary: M. Francis, J. Page, and K. Pecklers, eds, *A Challenging Reform: Realizing the Vision of Liturgical Renewal, 1963–1975* (Collegeville: The Liturgical Press, 2007). Employing a "good guy vs. bad guy" rhetoric, Marini documents the actions as well as the political intentions and maneuverings of the reformers, portraying conservative Curial opponents as reactionary, power-hungry, even theologically benighted. Monsignor Nicola Giampietro's study of the diaries and papers of Father Ferdinando Antonelli OFM, together with the recently published memoirs of Father Louis Bouyer, balance the received history of the post-conciliar reform with important historical details. See: N. Giampietro, *The Development of the Liturgical Reform: As Seen by Cardinal Ferdinando Antonelli from 1948 to 1970* (Fort Collins: Roman Catholic Books, 2009), and John Pepino (trans.), *The Memoirs of Louis Bouyer: From Youth and Conversion to Vatican II, the Liturgical Reform, and After* (Kettering: Angelico, 2015; French original 2014). Antonelli (1896–1993; created a cardinal in 1973) was a member of the Commission for Liturgical Reform established by Pope Pius XII, Secretary of the Vatican II Liturgical Commission, a member of the *Consilium*, and Secretary of the Sacred Congregation of Rites (1965–69). Bouyer (1913–2004) was a *peritus* at Vatican II and a consulter of the *Consilium* from 1966.

4. "...Finally, there must be no innovations unless the good of the Church genuinely and certainly requires them; and care must be taken that any new forms adopted should in some way grow organically from forms already existing," *Sacrosanctum Concilium* 23. See also n. 38 (the adaptation of the liturgy to particular cultures or circumstances should preserve the "substantial unity of the Roman rite") and n. 50 (the rites of the Mass are to be simplified but care must be taken to "preserve their substance").

5. *Sacrosanctum Concilium* was approved by an astounding vote of 2,147 in favor and only 4 opposed.

1. *The Reform of the Reform: An Agenda for Liturgical Renewal*

The phrase "reform of the reform" gained currency in the 1990s as a result of Joseph Cardinal Ratzinger's assessment of what went wrong (and what went right) with the liturgical reform pursuant to Vatican II. Himself an enthusiast for liturgical renewal as a young *peritus* at the Council, the future Pope Benedict XVI had suggested that some changes in the aftermath of the Council had the feel of being freshly manufactured in a liturgical factory. Specifically with regard to the Roman missal approved by Pope Paul VI in 1970,[6] he famously stated: "We abandoned the organic, living process of growth and development over the centuries, and replaced it—as in a manufacturing process—with a fabrication, a banal on-the-spot product."[7] As the context makes clear, Cardinal Ratzinger was not speaking of abuses in the celebration of the new rite of Mass, but of the manner in which Pope Paul's missal was prepared and abruptly imposed. We should note, however, that many other passages in Ratzinger's extensive corpus of writings on the liturgy point to features of the new missal, and of the liturgical reform in general, which he acknowledges with appreciation.[8] Taken together, these passages indicate

6. Although the complete *Missale Romanum* was published in March 1970, the new *Ordo Missæ* had already been promulgated in April 1969, taking effect on the First Sunday of Advent that year. The revised *Calendarium Romanum* and *Ordo Lectionum Missæ* had been published in March 1969 and May 1969, respectively.

7. This text appears on the back cover of K. Gamber, *The Reform of the Roman Liturgy: Its Problems and Background* (San Juan Capistrano/Harrison: Una Voce Press; Foundation for Catholic Reform, 1993), translating Ratzinger's text published in K. Gamber, *La Réforme Liturgique en Question* (Le Barroux: Éditions Saint-Madeleine, 1992), p. 8. The translation in the collected works of Joseph Ratzinger reads: "They [liturgists] no longer wanted to continue the organic *becoming* and *maturing* of something that had been alive down through the centuries, and instead they replaced it—according to the model of technical production—with *making*, the insipid product of the moment"; Joseph Ratzinger, *Theology of the Liturgy*, Collected Works, vol. 11 (San Francisco: Ignatius, 2014; German original 2008), pp. 537–38. (Although this volume is listed as vol. 11 of Ratzinger's collected works, it was the first volume to be published.) Monsignor Klaus Gamber (1919–89) was the founder and director of the Liturgical Institute in Regensburg, Germany. He maintained that Vatican II was justified in ordering a general reform of the liturgy but deemed Paul VI's missal a departure from the traditional Roman rite because in certain essentials it differs from what came before and did not develop organically from it.

8. Numerous citations are compiled in W. Johnston, "Pope Benedict XVI on the Postconciliar Liturgical Reform: An Essay in Interpretation," *Antiphon* 17 (2013), pp. 118–38. Here is a sampling: "There is no doubt that this new missal in many

an overall assessment of the reform as positive in many specifics, but often wrongly understood and carried out according to a "hermeneutic of rupture and discontinuity."[9]

Although Ratzinger himself did not employ the phrase "reform of the reform" during his pontificate as Benedict XVI (2005–13),[10] he did, in the late 1990s, express hope for "a liturgical reconciliation that again recognizes the history of the unity of the liturgy," indeed "a new liturgical movement," which will call to life the real heritage of the Second Vatican

respects brought with it a real improvement and enrichment," J. Ratzinger, *Milestones: Memoirs 1927–1977* (San Francisco: Ignatius, 1998), p. 148; "I am very grateful for the new missal, for the way it has enriched the treasury of prayers and prefaces, for the new Eucharistic prayers and the increased number of texts for use on weekdays, and so on, quite apart from the availability of the vernacular," J. Ratzinger, *The Feast of Faith: Approaches to a Theology of the Liturgy* (San Francisco: Ignatius, 1986), p. 87; with the new prayers accompanying the preparation of the gifts "a new treasure has entered the liturgy," J. Ratzinger, *God Is Near Us: The Eucharist, the Heart of Life* (San Francisco: Ignatius, 2003), p. 69. Some of Johnston's citations of Ratzinger, however, concern things that are not particular to the missal of Paul VI, such as congregational responses (J. Ratzinger, *The Spirit of the Liturgy* [San Francisco: Ignatius, 2000], p. 208), bringing the altar closer to the people (ibid., p. 81, albeit not for the purpose of celebrating Mass *versus populum*), and "a new sense of fellowship and of community participation in the eucharistic mystery" (*Feast of Faith*, p. 147). To these examples one could add the clear distinction (at all forms of Mass) "of the place for the Liturgy of the Word from the place for the properly Eucharistic liturgy" (*Spirit of the Liturgy*, p. 81).

9. In his address to the Roman Curia delivered on 22 December 2005, Pope Benedict XVI famously described two contrasting ways of interpreting the Second Vatican Council. The one is an erroneous "hermeneutic of discontinuity and rupture," which reads Vatican II as a mandate for radical change, even revolution, in virtually every sphere of the Church's life; the other is an authentic "hermeneutic of reform," which is attuned to the Church's tradition of teaching and worship as it has been handed on and its understanding faithfully developed over the centuries. The latter is also called the "hermeneutic of reform in continuity" and the "hermeneutic of continuity." See: *Acta Apostolicæ Sedis* 98 (2006), pp. 40–53 (46).

10. The phrase *was* used, however, by Archbishop Albert Malcolm Ranjith, Secretary of the Congregation for Divine Worship and the Discipline of the Sacraments from 2005 to 2009 and now Cardinal Archbishop of Colombo, Sri Lanka. In his Foreword to Monsignor Nicola Giampietro's important chronicle of the liturgical reform and of the Council itself, Ranjith states: "We need to identify and correct the erroneous orientations and decisions made, appreciate the liturgical tradition of the past courageously, and ensure that the Church is made to rediscover the true roots of its spiritual wealth and grandeur even if that means reforming the reform itself"; *The Development of the Liturgical Reform*, pp. xi–xvi (xvi).

Council."[11] The "reform of the reform" is best understood as a response to that call. Whether it is a movement or simply a precursory discussion, it comprises a loose affiliation of individuals and organizations dedicated to the process of liturgical renewal set in motion by Vatican II,[12] but implemented in a manner more consonant with tradition.[13] As such, it occupies a middle ground between an immobile traditionalism opposed to legitimate avenues of renewal and a progressivism inadequately attentive to the Church's doctrinal and liturgical traditions.

Under the umbrella of reforming the reform there exists a spectrum of opinions as to where to begin and how to proceed.[14] Some authors construe the reform of the reform as an alternative, less radical implementation of *Sacrosanctum Concilium* in line with the directives of the Council Fathers.

11. Ratzinger, *Milestones*, p. 149. But the idea of a new liturgical movement came with strength from Ratzinger's masterwork, *The Spirit of the Liturgy,* published in English by Ignatius Press in 2000.

12. For a detailed treatment of the movement's origins and representatives see: T. Kocik, "A Reform of the Reform?," in A. Reid (ed.), *T&T Clark Companion to Liturgy: The Western Catholic Tradition* (London: Bloomsbury/T&T Clark, 2016), pp. 317–38.

13. The general principles for the liturgical reform are enunciated in the first chapter of *Sacrosanctum Concilium* (nn. 5–46). Owing largely to the liturgical movement that arose in the early twentieth century, the Council emphasized the importance of liturgical theology and spirituality (n. 7). Since the liturgy is both "the summit toward which the activity of the Church is directed" and "the font from which all her power flows" (n. 10), "the faithful should be led to that fully conscious, and active participation in liturgical celebrations which is demanded by the very nature of the liturgy" (n. 14). In order to achieve this "aim to be considered before all else," pastors should become "thoroughly imbued with the spirit and power of the liturgy, and undertake to give instruction about it" (n. 14). Concerning the rites themselves, they "should be distinguished by a noble simplicity; they should be short, clear, and unencumbered by useless repetitions; they should be within the people's powers of comprehension, and normally should not require much explanation" (n. 34).

14. Various proposals for a structural reform of the reform appear as appendices in T. Kocik, *The Reform of the Reform? A Liturgical Debate: Reform or Return* (San Francisco: Ignatius, 2003). The most extensive reflection on future possibilities is L. Dobszay, *The Restoration and Organic Development of the Roman Rite* (London: T&T Clark/Continuum, 2010). On the basis of the liturgical books in force in 1962, Dobszay proposes a scheme for weaving a closer, more organic connection between the traditional and reformed liturgical rites, taking into consideration not only the Mass but also the Divine Office, the Roman calendar, and the rites of Holy Week. As for non-English-language publications of this kind, I know only of the work of the Italian priest Claudio Crescimanno, *La Riforma della Riforma liturgica. Ipotesi per un "nuovo" rito della messa sulle tracce del pensiero di Joseph Ratzinger* (Verona:

Others see it as a restructuring of the modern Roman rite so as to connect it more closely with the tradition it displaced. Both approaches have been described as reforming the reform, with the pre-Vatican II liturgy serving either as a point of departure or as a point of orientation. Such an endeavor faces considerable theoretical and practical challenges, which will be addressed here in due course. First, however, it seems logical to examine the premise on which the reform of the reform relies, namely, that the liturgy as revised after Vatican II represents a rupture from the ancient and organically developed Roman rite.

2. *The Central Question: Continuity or Rupture?*

The question of the Roman rite's identity is complex, and no precise set of criteria exists for determining which texts and ceremonies must be retained in any given reform if substantial continuity is to be preserved.[15] Some liturgists hold that what constitutes the "substance" of the Roman rite is not a particular set of components (texts, rites, rubrics, gestures) but, in the words of the Jesuit scholar Keith Pecklers, "its capacity to adapt and be shaped by the distinct cultures where it has been celebrated."[16] But this raises the question: What, then, is the "it" that adapts *itself* to particular cultural and historical circumstances? And what distinguishes *it* from any other rite of the Church?[17]

Fede e Cultura, 2009); this book carries a preface by Archbishop Albert Malcolm Ranjith, then-Secretary of the Congregation for Divine Worship and the Discipline of the Sacraments.

15. In scholastic terms, we are trying to distinguish between *accidental* and *substantial* change. A good comparison can be made with the human body, which changes considerably in appearance and in what it can physically manage over the years. Whatever these accidental changes, the person remains substantially the same, for the spiritual soul (with its powers of intellect and will), in tandem with bodily change, constitute the person and differentiate him or her from all others. So, too, by way of analogy, the Roman liturgy has its own "genius" or "native spirit" which differentiates it from others and preserves its identity across time. In a landmark essay "The Genius of the Roman Rite," Edmund Bishop (1846–1917), an English Catholic layman of considerable liturgical erudition, describes this genius as "simplicity, practicality, a great sobriety and self-control, gravity and dignity"; E. Bishop, *Liturgica Historica: Papers on the Liturgy and Religious Life of the Western Church* (Oxford: Clarendon, 1918), p. 12.

16. K. Pecklers, *The Genius of the Roman Rite: On the Reception and Implementation of the New Missal* (Collegeville: The Liturgical Press, 2009), p. ix.

17. An analogy can be made with respect to the Church's living Tradition, understood both as the specific content of the apostolic "Deposit of Faith" and as

Locating the essence of the rite somewhere other than within its components leads to the dubious view that new liturgical forms fabricated by an individual or committee can be *organically* related to ancient precedents. How so? Certainly not on the basis of uninterrupted historical continuance, but rather, as Rita Ferrone explains, because of "an inner logic that inspired both practices."[18] This seems to me a very loose application of the concept of organic development. Whatever merit it may have in this or other

the ongoing process of communicating or handing on that deposit. This multifaceted body of Christian doctrine has gradually come into being, and is still in the process of formation (and re-formation), through the complex interplay of Christian belief, teaching, and worship in changing historical contexts. This body of doctrine, accordingly, has a history of development, in which continuity has, on the whole, been more conspicuous than discontinuity. There *is*, in brief, a Deposit of Faith which throughout the centuries has constituted "*the* Tradition," despite perennial disagreements among Christians about various components of this Tradition. The mandate of *Sacrosanctum Concilium* was that the rites "be restored to the vigor they had in the tradition of the Fathers" (n. 50). Pope St Pius V used the same language in the liturgical restoration following the Council of Trent, when in the Apostolic Constitution *Quo Primum* (14 July 1570) he spoke of restoring the Roman missal "ad pristinam…sanctorum Patrum normam" (according to the pristine…norm of the holy Fathers"). For Pius V as for Vatican II, the issue was not a sort of antiquarianism, seeking to return to a mythical "golden age" of patristic liturgy. Rather, it was a matter of *ressourcement*, of scrutinizing the sources of Christian faith, especially in the first few centuries, for what could guide the Church in the present. On the relevance of *ressourcement* to twentieth-century liturgical renewal see: T. Kocik, "The 'Reform of the Reform' in Broad Context: Re-engaging the Living Tradition," *Antiphon* 12 (2008), pp. 26–44; a modified version appears in *Usus Antiquior* 3 (2012), pp. 102–14.

18. R. Ferrone, *Liturgy: Sacrosanctum Concilium* (New York: Paulist, 2007), pp. 41–42. By way of illustration, she relates the *Pascha antoninum* (the early Christian practice of commemorating the anniversary of baptism on or near the octave day of Easter by saying the Creed) to the renewal of baptismal promises practiced in the Easter Vigil as it was restored by Pius XII in 1951. Elsewhere she claims that the essence of the Roman rite cannot be found in liturgical books but is expressed, rather, in the liturgy's "dynamic relationship with what's outside the celebration, that is, the life of faith as immersion in the Paschal Mystery—the dying and rising of Jesus"; R. Ferrone, "The 'Substantial Unity' of the Roman Rite," *Pastoral Music* 39 (March 2015), pp. 13–16 (15). One is left to wonder what differentiates the Roman rite, so vaguely defined, from any other liturgical rite of the Church or, for that matter, from any non-liturgical Christian worship. David Power speaks in similar terms of "the organic workings of the rite as the rite of peoples, set in their given time and place, not simply the set of rituals and texts used"; D. Power, "Vatican Two and the Liturgical Future," *Antiphon* 5 (2000), pp. 10–18 (11).

contexts,[19] the fact remains: article 23 of *Sacrosanctum Concilium* stipulates that "any new forms adopted should in some way grow organically
from forms already existing." Which I take to mean: from forms existing
not simply on paper, in the ancient liturgical books of vanished rites,[20] but
in *extant* liturgical practice. It is on this point that the thesis of rupture, and
hence the case for reforming the reform, is strongest.

I cannot attempt an exhaustive review of the post-conciliar liturgical
reforms of the 1960s and 1970s here. Instead, I will highlight what I
consider the more salient changes made to the Roman liturgical books and
calendar. I am concerned for now with the material content of the reforms
as promulgated, not with popular perceptions.[21] The few areas of interest
that I have selected should suffice to demonstrate that "organic growth"
does not describe how the reformed liturgy came to be.

Until the introduction in 1969 of Pope Paul's New Order of Mass
(*Novus Ordo Missæ*), published in the Roman missal of 1970, the structure
of the Mass remained virtually indistinguishable from that of previous
centuries. Although the Council made possible some immediate changes
to the so-called Tridentine missal in its latest edition, that promulgated

19. If we apply the concept to another context, dogmatic theology, we can posit
a radical continuity between the dogma of the Immaculate Conception of the Blessed
Virgin Mary and the Christological teachings of the early ecumenical councils; there
is a certain logic in the development of doctrine that connects the whole. The Vatican
II reforms, like those of Trent, resulted from decisions about what should be done
on the basis of several factors, above all perceived pastoral need, and then finding
support in ancient precedents as interpreted in the light of those perceived present
needs.

20. Many of the proper prayers of the Roman missal of 1970 were drawn from
early Roman sources that were unavailable to the Tridentine reformers, especially the
Veronese collection of Mass formularies copied in the early seventh century (inaccu-
rately called the Leonine Sacramentary) and the Gelasian sacramentaries, the oldest
extant manuscripts of which date from the eighth century.

21. In the minds of most Catholics old enough to remember, the Vatican II liturgical reform was all about the replacement of Latin by the vernacular languages and
the "turning around" of the altars. Yet the Council Fathers did not desire an entirely
vernacular liturgy. To the contrary, "the use of the Latin language is to be preserved
in the Latin rites" (*Sacrosanctum Concilium* 36 §1), and "steps should be taken so
that the faithful may also be able to say or to sing together in Latin those parts of
the Ordinary of the Mass which pertain to them" (n. 54). Nor did they discuss, never
mind encourage or mandate, the celebration of Mass "facing the people." Mass in
the modern Roman rite may be celebrated wholly or partly in Latin (including the
readings), with the sacred ministers and assembly together facing *ad orientem*, toward
the liturgical "east" of the apse when praying to God.

by St John XXIII in 1962, these reforms did not touch on the essential content of the Order of Mass;[22] rather, they chiefly involved rubrical simplifications (e.g., fewer signs of the Cross, genuflections, and kisses of the altar) and the removal of some medieval accretions (e.g., the prayers at the foot of the altar were shortened and made optional, and the Last Gospel suppressed). By contrast, the 1970 missal contains significant additions to, and subtractions from, the missals in previous use. Two examples are especially noteworthy. The first is the replacement of the old Offertory prayers (dating to about the tenth century and of Gallican provenance) with new compositions derived in their main outlines from the table prayers of Israel.[23] The other is the addition of three newly composed Eucharistic prayers (approved in May 1968) for optional use as alternatives to the ancient Roman canon,[24] which hitherto had been the sole anaphora of the Catholic Church in the West.[25] These absolute innovations contradict the clear formulation of article 23 of *Sacrosanctum Concilium*.

22. These reforms resulted in the revised orders of Mass published in 1965 and 1967. See: A. Reid, "*Sacrosanctum concilium* and the Reform of the *Ordo Missae*," *Antiphon* 10 (2006), pp. 277–95.

23. This substitution has been one of the most controversial changes to the Roman missal, since it eliminates a series of rich, distinctively Catholic prayers using explicitly sacrificial language, invoking the Blessed Virgin and all the saints, and replaces it with a Jewish meal prayer. This was done out of the pastoral concern that the anticipatory references to Christ's Sacrifice in the traditional Offertory prayers would confuse the faithful about where the sacrificial oblation of the Eucharist is located. But in the tradition of the Church in both East and West, the Offertory prayers have always been conceived as an analogue of the Sacrifice of the Cross. See, for example, P. Tirot, *Histoire des prières d'offertoire dans la liturgie romaine du VIIe au XVIe siècle*, Bibliotheca Ephemerides Liturgicæ 'Subsidia' 34 (Rome: Edizione Liturgiche, 1985).

24. On the origins of these new Eucharistic prayers see: E. Mazza, *The Eucharistic Prayers of the Roman Rite* (New York: Pueblo, 1986; Italian original 1984); C. Folsom, "From One Eucharistic Prayer to Many: How It Happened and Why," *Adoremus Bulletin* 2, nos. 4–6 (1996), http://www.adoremus.org/9-11-96-FolsomEuch.html.

25. By the time the Roman missal of 1970 was introduced, it was in many places a relief from the preceding chaos, because it imposed a modicum of stability, for instance, with only four Eucharistic prayers in place of the hundreds that were in informal circulation. Additional Eucharistic prayers for use on special occasions were published in the second (1975) and third (2002) typical editions of the post-conciliar Roman missal. The marginalization of the Roman canon by other Eucharistic prayers has made it possible for priests seldom (if ever) to pray what had been a hallmark of the Roman rite for a millennium and a half.

Turning now to the propers of the Mass, many of the prayers of the 1970 missal were taken, either in whole or in some parts recycled, from early Roman sources that were unavailable when St Pius V, at the behest of the Council of Trent, codified the Roman Curial rite as the basis for the Roman missal of 1570. On these grounds the 1970 missal of Paul VI can be seen as a restoration of older elements and thus more "traditional" than the Tridentine missals of 1570–1962.[26] But it must also be noted that the scholars entrusted by Paul VI with revising the Roman missal after Vatican II used those ancient texts, as well as their own compositions, more often to *replace* the existing euchological material than to augment and enrich it. According to one study, only 17 percent of the proper prayers (collects, "secrets," post-communions) in the 1962 missal were carried over intact into the 1970 missal.[27]

The Council called for "the treasures of the Bible…to be opened up more lavishly" in the eucharistic liturgy, "so that richer fare may be provided for the faithful at the table of God's word" (*Sacrosanctum Concilium* 51). This directive resulted in the 1969 lectionary for Mass, with its biennial cycle for weekday readings and triennial cycle (with an additional reading) for Sundays. While the new order of readings certainly makes more extensive use of Sacred Scripture (especially the Old Testament), it abandons a very ancient annual Roman cycle of Sunday epistles and gospels. That discontinuity and loss was not necessary.

The Church's liturgical year has always been in need of periodic pruning. This process was achieved quite heavy-handedly in the 1969 reform of the Roman calendar. Many saints' feasts were either dropped or shifted, sometimes by only one day, for worthy reasons (e.g., to give priority to the ferial days of Advent and Lent), but, it is claimed, at the cost of weakening the link between the Gospel and culture.[28] Even more

---

26. Gamber opined that the restoration of earlier forms does not necessarily constitute a change in the rite, so long as it is done "on a case-by-case basis" and "within certain restraints"; *The Reform of the Roman Liturgy*, p. 31.

27. A. Cekada, *The Problems with the Prayers of the Modern Mass* (Rockford: TAN, 1991).

28. "A saint who had a feast for hundreds of years on one particular date found his or her day moved (sometimes by only a day), in the name of bringing about a greater correspondence between dates of death and liturgical observance. But what about people who had been named for such a saint because they were born on that day, or towns and villages named for a saint whose feast was now moved, thus breaking a wonderful and important link between faith and culture?" P. Stravinskas, "Epilogue," in Kocik, *The Reform of the Reform?*, pp. 105–12 (110–11).

disruptive was what befell the Proper of the Seasons. Many of its ancient features were abolished: the seasons "after Epiphany" (Epiphanytide) and "after Pentecost"[29] (Whitsuntide), the pre-Lenten season of Septuagesima,[30] Passiontide, the Octave of Pentecost, and Ember and Rogation days.[31]

If the Divine Office of the Roman rite "had sustained some significant damages" in St Pius X's reform of 1911,[32] "it actually died" after Vatican II. Its cause of death, says László Dobszay, was the rejection of its three constitutive elements: the structure and proportion of the hours, the distribution of the psalms, and the stock material of the antiphonary.[33] Consequently, the 1971 *Liturgia Horarum* marks a break with historic forms even more radical than the 1970 missal. Whether or not these structural changes were as radical as Dobszay claims is debated, just as judgments vary on so many other reforms.[34] But perhaps no other indictment of the post-conciliar

29. The Sundays "*post Epiphaniam*" and "*post Pentecosten*" were renamed Sundays "*per annum.*" This, together with the permission for certain major feasts to be moved to Sunday (e.g., Epiphany and Ascension), has destabilized the liturgical sanctification of time.

30. On Septuagesima see: L. Pristas, *The Collects of the Roman Missals: A Comparative Study of the Sundays in Proper Seasons Before and After the Second Vatican Council* (London: Bloomsbury/T&T Clark, 2013), pp. 95–111.

31. The traditional and universal observance of these days was abolished in the reform of the calendar, but they may be observed according to plans and times arranged by the conferences of bishops. On the question of their relevance today, see: E. Nickel, "Rogation Days, Ember Days, and the New Evangelization," *Antiphon* 16 (2012), pp. 21–36.

32. "Entailed in this reform was the loss of the *laudes*, psalms 148–50, as a daily component of Lauds — a rupture with a centuries-old, universal tradition"; S. Campbell, *From Breviary to Liturgy of the Hours: The Structural Reform of the Roman Office, 1964–1971* (Collegeville: The Liturgical Press, 1995), p. 17. Also: "For anyone with a sense of the history of the office, this was a shocking departure from almost universal Christian tradition"; R. Taft, *The Liturgy of the Hours in East and West: The Origins of the Divine Office and Its Meaning for Today*, 2nd edn (Collegeville: The Liturgical Press, 1993), p. 312.

33. See: Dobszay, *Restoration and Organic Development*, p. 49. Dobszay explores the reform of the Divine Office in depth in Chapter 15. It must be noted that *Sacrosanctum Concilium* itself mandated some of the more radical reforms that are reflected in the *Liturgia Horarum* of 1971, particularly the suppression of the Office of Prime (n. 89d) and the abandonment of the principle of the weekly recitation of all 150 psalms (n. 91).

34. The Jesuit liturgical scholar Robert Taft speaks of the post-Vatican II reform of the Roman Office as "even more radical than that of Pius X" but argues that "the

Office reform is needed than the fact that, for the first time in the history of Christianity, the "official prayer of the Church" does not contain the whole Psalter.[35]

A sound evaluation of the "continuity or rupture" question must take into account not only the different ritual elements of the reform but also the theological principles that guided the decisions about what was retained, expunged, or created for the revised liturgical books. The meticulous research of Lauren Pristas, involving careful linguistic and historical analysis of the collects of the Roman missal, supplies part of the answer.[36] Taken together with other studies, such as those on the revised Roman book of blessings[37] and the revised rite of major exorcism,[38] we find ample evidence of a radically different understanding of the nature of blessing and exorcism than that of the Catholic theological tradition. It is a serious matter when some "blessings" do not actually bless and "exorcisms" do not actually exorcize.[39]

basic structure of the Roman hours was more or less respected," with the exception of more Scripture and hymns moved to the opening of each liturgical hour; *Liturgy of the Hours in East and West*, p. 313.

35. The *Consilium* charged with revising the Mass and the Divine Office decided to omit certain passages deemed "extremely harsh and offensive to modern sensibilities"; A. Bugnini, *The Reform of the Liturgy*, p. 503. Many violent passages in the psalms (the "imprecatory" verses) and three entire psalms were removed from the Office; ibid., p. 511.

36. L. Pristas, *Collects of the Roman Missals*. Take, for instance, the complete overhaul of the corpus of Lenten collects. It might be claimed that article 109 of *Sacrosanctum Concilium*, which directs that the Lenten season's "twofold character" (penitential and pre-baptismal) be given greater prominence, justifies a revision of the Lenten formularies; but that makes all the more perplexing the absence of the baptismal elements from all of the new Lenten Sunday collects and of the penitential elements from most of them.

37. See: U. M. Lang, "Theologies of Blessings: Origins and Characteristics of *De benedictionibus* (1984)," *Antiphon* 15 (2011), pp. 27–46; D. Van Slyke, "The Order for Blessing Water: Past and Present," *Antiphon* 8 (2003), pp. 12–23.

38. See: M. Hauke, "The Theological Battle Over the Rite of Exorcism, 'Cinderella' of the New *Rituale Romanum*," *Antiphon* 10 (2006), pp. 32–69; D. Van Slyke, "The Ancestry and Theology of the Rite of Major Exorcism (1999/2004)," *Antiphon* 10 (2006), pp. 70–116.

39. Interview with Father Gabriele Amorth, "The Reform of the Rite of Exorcism," *30 Days* (June 2000), http://www.fisheaters.com/amorth.html. Father Amorth should know; he was for many years the chief exorcist of the Diocese of Rome.

The liturgy is of a whole with the Church's daily witness to the Gospel. *Lex orandi, lex credendi, lex vivendi*: how we worship shapes how we believe and thus how we live. If today many Catholics, including those who faithfully participate in the Church's liturgical life, regard certain truths of the Faith as quaint or *passé*—spiritual warfare, demonic possession, concupiscence, divine wrath, punishment of sins, the reality of purgatory and hell, the merits of the saints, the evils of heresy and schism—then we must ask whether this has something to do with the fact that the post-conciliar reformers systematically expunged or "softened" the prayers that expressed those ideas, in order to suit the modern mentality.

What all of this bears out is that the liturgical changes following the Second Vatican Council turned out to be more in the nature of revolution than renewal. To assert this is not to minimize the good fruits of the officially approved reforms. These include: the new relief provided to the ecclesial nature of the liturgy and hence to congregational participation; a wider allowance of the vernacular languages so as to enable worshipers to participate in a more direct way; the renewed articulation of the connection between liturgy and social action. Yet all of these pastoral advantages could have been achieved without radically recasting—nay, destroying[40]—the historic Roman rite.

3. *Reforming the Reform: What Is Presently Possible*

With Pope Benedict XVI's Apostolic Letter *Summorum Pontificum*, given motu proprio on 7 July 2007 and taking effect on 14 September of that year, the coexistence of "two forms of the same Roman rite" had begun.[41] In his letter to the world's bishops, accompanying and explaining *Summorum Pontificum*, the Pope expressed his desire for a positive, mutual influence or enrichment of the "forma ordinaria" (the 1970 missal of Paul VI; latest

---

40. Here is the evaluation of no less an authority than Father Joseph Gelineau SJ, one of the most influential members of Paul VI's *Consilium*: "We must say it plainly: the Roman rite as we knew it exists no more. It has gone. Some walls of the structure have fallen, others have been altered; we can look at it as a ruin or the partial foundation of a new building"; J. Gelineau, D. Livingstone (trans.), *The Liturgy Today and Tomorrow* (London: Darton, Longman & Todd; New York: Paulist, 1978), p. 11. The original French edition reads, "*Il est détruit*" ("It is destroyed," not "It has gone"); *Demain la liturgie* (Paris: Cerf, 1977), p. 10.

41. "...duo usus unici ritus romani"; Benedict XVI, Apostolic Letter *Summorum Pontificum* (7 July 2007), art. 1; *Acta Apostolicæ Sedis* 99 (2007), p. 779. I am inclined to accept László Dobszay's position that the formula "one rite, two forms" is legal and pastoral in nature, not liturgiological; *Restoration and Organic Development*, p. 50.

Vatican or "typical" edition, 2002) and the "forma extraordinaria" (the 1962 missal of John XXIII).[42] The faithful, he said, should be able to find in the ordinary form of the Mass that sense of adoration and transcendence ("sacrality") that attracts many people to the older rites. At the same time, he suggested that the extraordinary form could be enriched by the addition of propers for some of the saints canonized since 1962 and some of the new prefaces in the revised Roman missal.

Note the qualitative difference between these two directions of mutual enrichment as suggested by Pope Benedict. The extraordinary form's influence lies in its ethos or character (devotion, mystery, verticality), whereas the ordinary form's influence involves new texts. I do not think Benedict meant to imply that the ordinary form could not be improved by introducing into it elements now belonging strictly to the extraordinary form, or, on the flipside, that liturgical celebrations in the extraordinary form could not beneficially be imbued with the pastoral solicitude for "active participation"[43] and genuine human communication that is more popularly (though often superficially) identified with the ordinary form.[44]

What might be done, both in the short and long term, to foster a reconciliation of the "old" and "new" in Catholic worship? It is not unusual to hear the term "reform of the reform" applied to practices that amount to nothing more than the application of existing law: singing most of the Ordinary in Latin (the *Kyrie* is Greek); facing liturgical east while addressing God in

---

42. Benedict XVI, Letter (*Epistula*) "Con grande fiducia," *Acta Apostolicæ Sedis* 99 (2007), p. 797.

43. On the meaning of *participatio actuosa* (far from a new concept at the time of the Council) see: Ratzinger, *Spirit of the Liturgy*, pp. 171–77; M. Ranjith, "The Sacred Liturgy, Source and Summit of the Life and Mission of the Church," in A. Reid (ed.), *Sacred Liturgy: The Source and Summit of the Life and Mission of the Church* (San Francisco: Ignatius, 2014), pp. 19–39 (35–36); *Liturgy, Participation and Sacred Music: The Proceedings of the Ninth International Colloquium of Historical, Canonical and Theological Studies on the Roman Catholic Liturgy, Paris 2003* (London: CIEL UK, 2006).

44. "Not even the best celebration of the 1962 missal permits neglect or diminution of the participation of the faithful. This is the most important enrichment that the classical Roman rite has to gain from the Novus Ordo"; Dobszay, *Restoration and Organic Development*, p. 55. By "genuine human communication" I have in mind the various dialogues between the priest and people ("The Lord be with you," "Pray, brethren," etc.). The customarily engaging way in which the priest conducts the dialogues in the reformed liturgy seems more natural, more human (provided that "engaging" does not mean theatrical) than the rubrically mandated practice of keeping the eyes downcast when conducting those same dialogues in the extraordinary form.

prayer; placing a prominent crucifix at the center of the altar when Mass is celebrated *versus populum*; singing the Proper chants (entrance, offertory, communion) rather than "other suitable hymns."[45] These practices make the modern Roman rite more expressive of Catholic liturgical tradition and help restore a sense of the sacred. But they are "reform of the reform" practices only in a qualified sense because the reform of the reform, in its long term, seeks changes touching upon the material of the liturgical books: the texts, structures, and rubrics. That, of course, remains a task for the future.[46]

Setting aside for the moment the question of ritual reform, there are certain steps celebrants can take to maximize continuity between the traditional Latin Mass and its modern derivative, without need of special permission. As a general rule, whenever given a choice by the rubrics, preference should be given to that option which is most in continuity with the 1962 missal. As a corollary rule, too much variety should be avoided. With these principles in mind, I offer the following suggestions to priests who celebrate the ordinary form of Mass:

- At the principal Sunday Mass, instead of the Penitential Act, use the Rite for the Blessing and Sprinkling of Water, with its proper chants (*Vidi aquam* in Eastertide, otherwise *Asperges me*).[47] When the Penitential Act is used, choose the first option (i.e., the *Confiteor* and *Kyrie*).

45. In the United States it is permissible to substitute for any entrance chant, offertory chant, or communion chant in the Roman gradual "another liturgical chant suited to the sacred action, the day, or the time of year," provided it has been approved by the conference of bishops or the diocesan bishop. See: *General Instruction of the Roman Missal (Third Typical Edition)* (Washington: U.S. Conference of Catholic Bishops, 2011), nn. 48, 74, and 87; the precise wording used in the Latin typical edition is "alius cantus congruus."

46. See: http://www.newliturgicalmovement.org/2010/06/reform-of-reform-not-yet.html.

47. In the Roman rite's extraordinary form the ceremony of sprinkling the clergy and people with holy water takes place before the principal Mass on Sundays. Because this ceremony is not part of Mass the celebrant wears the cope instead of the chasuble and does not wear the maniple. In the ordinary form the ceremony may be done at any Sunday Mass. A rubric in the Roman missal of 1970/75 reads: "When this rite is celebrated it takes the place of the penitential rite at the beginning of Mass" ("Huiusmodi ritus locum tenet actus pænitentialis initio Missæ peragendi"), in which case the celebrant wears the chasuble. However, the corresponding rubric in the Roman missal of 2002 reads: "If this rite is celebrated during Mass, it takes the

- The antiphons which accompany the entrance, offertory, and communion processions can and in many cases should be sung.[48] "As chants, they are a sort of musical *lectio divina* pointing us towards the riches expressed in that day's liturgy."[49] These proper texts, which are often drawn directly from Scripture, are usually replaced by hymns that have little relationship to the texts proposed in the missal or the Roman gradual. Therefore, read aloud the entrance and communion antiphons, unless they are being read by the congregation or sung by a cantor or choir; since the offertory antiphon is not printed in the missal, have the cantor or choir sing it.[50]

- Sing the orations, the preface, and the Gospel[51] on Sundays and solemnities, at least at the principal Mass. By singing these texts as well as the proper chants, we are singing the Mass rather than merely singing at Mass.

- Incense may be used at any Mass in the ordinary form, whereas in the extraordinary form its use is limited to Solemn or Sung Mass. Use incense every Sunday and solemnity, at least at the principal Mass, and not only on "special occasions."[52]

place of the usual Penitential Act at the beginning of Mass" ("Si ritus intra Missam peragitur, locum tenet consueti actus pænitentialis initio Missæ"). The 2002 rubric implies that the ceremony may be carried out *before* Mass (in which case I do not see why the celebrant should not wear the cope), as would be more in keeping with tradition.

48. These are meant to be true processions. See: J. Burns, "The Processions of the *Ordo Missae*: Liturgical Structure and Theological Meaning," *Antiphon* 13 (2009), pp. 159–74.

49. A. Wadsworth, "Towards the Future—Singing the Mass" (keynote address to the Southeastern Liturgical Music Symposium, 21 August 2010), http://www.chantcafe.com/p/towards-future-singing-mass-by-msgr.html.

50. A useful resource for a single cantor or full choir is Adam Bartlett's *Simple English Propers: For the Ordinary Form of Mass Sundays and Feasts*, published in 2011 by the Church Music Association of America and available at http://www.musicasacra.com.

51. (That is, of course, when there is no deacon to sing it.) For Sundays and major feasts of the three-year cycle, see: E. Schaefer, *Evangelia Cantata: A Notated Book of Gospels* (Spokane: Priory, 2007); the English Gospel texts are set to the Gregorian formula for the solemn tone, Vatican square-note notation.

52. I recall having newly begun a parish assignment when, before Sunday Mass, I instructed the senior altar server to light charcoals for the thurible. Without hint of protest he asked, "What's the special occasion?" I replied, "It's *Sunday*."

- Omit the general intercessions on weekdays; I doubt they will be missed. Indeed, in some ways they duplicate the intercessions made in the Eucharistic prayer. When their use is required, borrow or craft the petitions from traditional models (say, from the Byzantine liturgy) and keep them brief and few.[53]
- Do the Preparation of the Gifts silently rather than aloud, even if there is no choral or congregation singing at the time. Silence has an important role in the liturgy, and here is one of the few places in the ordinary form of Mass where silence can be built-in rather than artificially imposed. In Masses celebrated *versus populum*, praying the prayers silently has the added benefit of underscoring the offertory as an act of worship directed to God.
- Do not neglect the Latin language. Not only is it the native language of the Roman rite, but it fosters a greater sense of the Church's universality.
- After a period of catechesis, begin celebrating Mass *ad orientem*. Advent suggests itself as the best time for this, as the Church awaits her coming Lord. (A popular Advent hymn enjoins us, "People Look East!" Amen, I say—including the priest!) In the interim, put a large crucifix at the center of the altar, flanked with the traditional six candles. Far from creating a barrier between the celebrant and the assembly, this serves as a reminder to everyone that the Lord is the center of the liturgy.
- Wear black vestments for funerals, All Souls Day, and other Masses for the dead. Considering that white vestments are worn on the feasts of Our Lord, Our Lady, non-martyr saints (i.e. confessors), and holy angels, the use of white vestments at Masses for the dead is an implicit canonization. In my opinion, the only time white vestments should be worn at funerals is when the deceased is a baptized child who died before attaining the age of reason, in which case we need not pray for divine forgiveness on the child's behalf, but rather for the consolation of the bereaved.
- Do not omit the optional sequences: *Lauda, Sion* (Corpus Christi) and *Stabat Mater* (Our Lady of Sorrows).
- Occasionally use the gradual chant instead of the responsorial psalm from the lectionary. I recommend doing this for funerals especially, when usually (and understandably) the only person inclined to sing is the one getting paid to sing.

53. I could recommend P. Elliott, *Prayers of the Faithful* (Totowa: Catholic Book Publishing, 2009).

- On weekdays when the liturgical calendar permits it, celebrate a votive Mass from time to time instead of the Mass of the previous Sunday, and requiem Masses (again: black vestments) during the month of November.
- Use the Roman canon (Eucharistic Prayer I) if not exclusively then at least on Sundays, the feasts of the apostles and saints named therein, the feasts related to the See of Rome,[54] and days for which a special *Communicantes* prayer is provided.[55]
- As indicated in the rubrics but seldom followed, bow your head at the mention of the three Divine Persons, the Holy Names of Jesus and Mary, and the name of the saint in whose honor the Mass is being celebrated.
- Although the Octave of Pentecost did not survive the 1969 reform of the calendar, there is nothing to prevent the offering of a Votive Mass of the Holy Spirit (hence, red vestments) on the ferial days of the week beginning Pentecost Sunday. Pentecost is too great and ancient a feast to confine to one day, and doing this would at least give the appearance of an octave.

Some of these suggestions are instances of extraordinary-form practices enriching the reformed liturgy in ways that the latter is not typically celebrated. Doubtless several other suggestions could be offered, and it would not surprise me to hear that many priests here are already doing these things. Again, they are already within the scope of existing liturgical norms and therefore require no permission.

What I have not yet addressed is the possibility of doing things beyond the existing norms. *Sacrosanctum Concilium* clearly states that no one, "even if he be a priest, may add, remove, or change anything in the liturgy on his own authority" (n. 22 §3). By this provision, no ritual changes are to be made, beyond those already provided for in liturgical law or rubrics. This rule applies not only in the ordinary form but in the extraordinary as well, as the 30 April 2011 Instruction of the Pontifical Commission *Ecclesia Dei, Universæ Ecclesiæ*, makes explicit, stating that the liturgical books of the extraordinary form "are to be used as they are" (n. 24).

---

54. Chair of St Peter the Apostle, 22 February; Sts Peter and Paul, 29 June; First Martyrs of the Holy Roman Church, 30 June; Dedication of the Basilica of St Mary Major, August 5; Dedication of the Lateran Basilica, 9 November; Dedication of the Basilicas of Sts Peter and Paul, 18 November.

55. These are: Christmas and throughout its octave, Epiphany, Holy Thursday, the Easter Vigil to the Second Sunday of Easter inclusive, Ascension Thursday, and Pentecost.

Nevertheless, it is not uncommon for traditionally minded priests (including an especially high-ranking, retired Bavarian bishop) to use prayers and ceremonial actions of the older liturgy when offering Mass in the ordinary form.[56] Some examples: saying the *sotto voce* prayers accompanying the censing of the gifts and altar; genuflecting *before* (as well as after) each elevation of the consecrated elements; keeping the thumbs and index fingers joined after the first consecration; crossing oneself with the Host and chalice when receiving Holy Communion. Yet when observance of existing norms remains the rule, the importation of elements from the older missal would seem to be illicit.[57]

But, as Father Timothy Finigan argues in the light of *Summorum Pontificum* and its accompanying Letter to the Bishops, the use of traditional gestures and prayers in the newer form of Mass is not to be viewed in the same light as liturgical abuses or impositions of the celebrant's personal whims. To the contrary, they are "part of what is 'sacred and great' for both previous generations and for us." The use of such elements "does not necessarily undermine the missal of Paul VI but can be seen as part of its historical pedigree and, for that reason not contradictory to it, nor harmful to its gradual organic development."[58]

Mutual enrichment happens first of all not at the level of the Holy See or the bishops' conferences but from the "ground up," in actual liturgical celebrations, to people and communities who have some experience worshiping in both forms of the Roman rite. William Johnston writes:

> "the formation of a liturgical custom typically begins by an unauthorized liturgical adaptation," whether beyond existing law (when the law says nothing about it one way or the other) or contrary to it (by not doing what the law prescribes, or doing what it prohibits). An incipient custom, if well and widely accepted in a community, may continue as a living part of that community's life. Practices that arise in this way can in time become

56. See: http://www.newliturgicalmovement.org/2008/08/assumption-in-maria-vesperbild-with.html.

57. In response to the question of whether Tridentine ceremonial could be used in the new rite of Mass, the Sacred Congregation for the Sacraments and Divine Worship replied: "Where the rubrics of the missal of Paul VI say nothing or say little in specifics in some places, it is not therefore to be inferred that the old rite must be followed. Accordingly, the many and complex gestures of incensation according to the prescripts of the earlier missal...are not to be repeated"; *Notitiæ* 14 (1978), pp. 301–2, http://notitiae.ipsissima-verba.org.

58. T. Finigan, "'Mutual Enrichment' in Theory and Practice," *Usus Antiquior* 2 (2011), pp. 61–68 (63–64); quotation from the Letter accompanying *Summorum Pontificum*.

binding practices: they can acquire the force of law, and they can eventually be approved by the legislator (a bishop or higher legislator)… It seems clear that mutual enrichment of the ritual form—more specifically, of the rubrics of the ordinary and extraordinary forms—will most naturally take place and is meant to take place primarily by way of custom.[59]

For Johnston, adopting the as-yet-unauthorized double genuflection at each consecration is an example of spiritually fruitful enrichment coming from one direction:

> This gesture was removed from the Mass because the council called for simplifying the rites and omitting duplications (*Sacrosanctum Concilium* 34, 50). Might newly experiencing this practice again in the [extraordinary form] reveal it to be, not a useless repetition to be removed (n. 34), but a meaningful repetition, a gesture of adoration worth appreciating again and adopting as a still effective way to manifest "worship of the divine Majesty" (n. 33), to offer "instruction for the faithful" (ibid.) regarding the mystery of the Eucharist, and to cultivate the "dignity, spirit of reverence, and sacred character" which "the [post-conciliar] rites must retain"?[60]

Coming from the other direction, experience of the ordinary form could lead to currently unauthorized, though not disruptive, practices in the extraordinary form. These might include the reception of Holy Communion under both species, the use of the vernacular beyond what is presently allowed,[61] the joint singing of the Lord's Prayer by the priest and assembly during Solemn or Sung Mass, or the observance of that provision of the first Instruction (1964) on implementing *Sacrosanctum Concilium*: "Parts belonging to the choir or to the people and sung or recited by them are not said privately by the celebrant."[62] These are speculations, obviously. My point is that adjustments conforming to the precepts of *Sacrosanctum*

59. W. Johnston, *Care for the Church and Its Liturgy: A Study of "Summorum Pontificum" and the Extraordinary Form of the Roman Rite* (Collegeville: The Liturgical Press, 2013), pp. 241–42, citing J. Huels, *Liturgy and Law: Liturgical Law in the System of Roman Catholic Canon Law* (Montreal: Wilson & Lafleur, 2006), p. 132.

60. Ibid., p. 243. The last two quoted phrases are from the Congregation for Divine Worship's third Instruction on implementing the Vatican II Constitution on the Liturgy, *Liturgicæ Instaurationes* (5 September 1970), n. 1.

61. *Universæ Ecclesiæ*, n. 26, permits the proclamation of the readings solely in the vernacular at low Mass.

62. Sacred Congregation of Rites, Instruction *Inter Œcumenici* (26 September 1964), n. 32. Reforms along this line had already been made before Vatican II. The 1962 missal ended the practice of the celebrant reading in a low voice the Epistle and Gospel while these are being sung at Solemn Mass.

Concilium are possible without causing major disruption to the Roman rite. Some of these adjustments occurred in the Order of Mass published in early 1965.[63]

Thus far we have considered the reform of the reform as it is already being done in many places, at ground level and within the context of the Church's existing liturgical life. Some of the liturgical initiatives popularly identified with the reform of the reform are simply applications of present legitimate options, while others constitute technically unauthorized additions. The reform of the reform as articulated by its early voices, however, proposes an authoritative revision of the liturgical *status quo*. Let us imagine now what an official reform of the reform might look like, and what interrelated theoretical and practical problems such an endeavor would face.

4. *Reforming the Reform: Theoretical and Practical Considerations*

In his Post-Synodal Apostolic Exhortation *Sacramentum Caritatis* (22 February 2007), Benedict XVI wrote: "The changes the Council called for need to be understood within the overall unity of the historical development of the rite itself, without the introduction of artificial discontinuities" (n. 3). These words, reflective of an evolutionary sensibility in liturgical reform, point to the best path ahead: the fundamental theological and liturgical principles of *Sacrosanctum Concilium*, interpreted by a hermeneutic of continuity.[64] As the history of the reform becomes clearer and more accessible, however, there is a growing awareness of problems inherent to some of those principles and the process by which the liturgical reform was conceived and implemented; these, too, must be taken into account. At the same time, as Dom Alcuin Reid suggests, it would be

---

63. Gamber judged this revised *Ordo Missæ* to be the last variant of the traditional Roman rite, appropriately reformed according to the Council's provisions. Significantly, Archbishop Bugnini dismissed the 1965 rite as insufficient because its alterations were merely "peripheral," whereas "a radical restoration" was necessary in order "to take an ancient building in hand and make it functional and habitable"; *Reform of the Liturgy*, p. 115.

64. The changes outlined in the Constitution are not doctrinal declarations, but certain sections of that document have been given an official interpretation either by papal teaching or by some other instrument of magisterial authority. See: C. Folsom, "The Hermeneutics of *Sacrosanctum Concilium*: Development of a Method and Its Application," *Antiphon* 8 (2003), pp. 2–9.

good to ask whether all of the subsidiary principles, contingent policies, and prudential decisions of the Constitution are helpful fifty-plus years later.[65]

Consider, for instance, this directive: "The rites should be distinguished by a noble simplicity. They should be short, clear, and free from useless repetitions" (n. 34). The broad rationale for this—indeed for all the changes made to the liturgy—is that great *desideratum* of liturgical reform: "full, conscious, and active participation" of the faithful in worship (n. 14). Are there other possible readings of noble simplicity than the predominantly rationalist reading which holds ritual repetition in suspicion? What might we discover if we set aside this predominant reading, and recall that repetition is "how we do our best learning," and how all human cultures and religions inculcate "a living sense of the sacred lore of a people"?[66] A different viewpoint emerges when we realize that mystery in the liturgy (in this case, *apparently* useless repetition) does not have to mean mystification. If the Church was not well served by noble simplicity, then this principle should be recognized for what it is— rationalist and prosaic—and quietly consigned to the annals of the 1960s.[67]

Distinguishing rock-solid fundamental principles from questionable subsidiary ones is a theoretical matter. There are also practical difficulties to consider. These revolve around a complex set of issues. One of them is the question of which form of the Roman rite, the ordinary or the extraordinary, should serve as the context for reforming the reform. I am personally convinced that the material disparity between the two orders of liturgy is so extensive that it is impossible to retrieve the tradition on the basis of the modern rites; that would be like trying to put Humpty-Dumpty

---

65. "It may be that some policies, whilst judged apposite fifty years ago, in the light of radically changed circumstances in the Church and world of the twenty-first century, can be seen today to be no longer as vital as they were thought to be in 1963. It may be that the intentions behind some policies were distorted in their implementation and in fact have brought about unhelpful results. It may also be that, with the advance of scholarship, the difference, if not the distance, between *Sacrosanctum Concilium* and the liturgical tradition it sought moderately to reform, and the rites produced by the *Consilium* charged with implementing the Constitution, has become more apparent"; Reid (ed.), *Sacred Liturgy*, p. 9.

66. C. Zaleski, "Worship and American Cultural Spirituality," *Antiphon* 4 (1999), pp. 5–13 (9).

67. See: A. Reid, "Noble Simplicity Revisited," in D. Vincent Twomey and J. Rutherford (eds), *Benedict XVI and Beauty in Sacred Art and Architecture* (Dublin: Four Courts; New York: Scepter, 2011), pp. 94–111.

together again. The extraordinary form must be the point of departure for any future organic development rooted in tradition.[68]

Another practical problem facing the reform of the reform is the diversity of opinions on what the re-reformed liturgy should look like. The "reform of the reform" thinkers all agree that the "real" Mass of Vatican II would be something much closer to the missal of 1962 than that of 1970, but with a fuller cycle of readings and, where opportune, priestly concelebration and Communion under both kinds. Beyond that, opinions differ on the details of the precise changes to be made. What one author deems a harmless simplification another deems an impoverishment.[69]

A third practical challenge comes from opposition based on various grounds: ignorance or misinformation ("Father wants us to sing the *Gloria* in Latin! He hates Vatican II!"), ideological resistance, and the corruptive influence of a consumerist and entertainment culture. Father Christopher Smith's observation captures it well:

> The reality of our ecclesiastical life is that what many of our parishioners experience in their parishes as the fruit of Vatican II is nothing like anything proposed by the [reform of the reform] advocates. As soon as a priest in a parish begins to implement these notions, no small amount of struggle invariably ensues. Parishes are divided, and the consumer mentality has taken over, with parishioners decamping to parishes where they feel comfortable. While veritable cases of [reform of the reform] liturgy have been created because of this, it has at the same time contributed to a further balkanization of Catholics along lines which critics of the [reform of the reform] are quick to deem ideological.[70]

68. See: http://www.newliturgicalmovement.org/2014/02/reforming-irreformable.html and http://www.newliturgicalmovement.org/2014/03/reforming-irreformable-postscript.html.

69. For example, concerning the prescription for ritual simplification (*Sacrosanctum Concilium* 50), Father Brian Harrison OS considers this met by the removal (beginning with the 1965 Order of Mass) of the double *Confiteor* and the Last Gospel; B. Harrison, "The Postconciliar Eucharistic Liturgy: Planning a 'Reform of the Reform,'" in Kocik, *The Reform of the Reform?*, pp. 151–93 (178). On the other hand, Fr Aidan Nichols OP favors the retention of the double *Confiteor* ("a beautiful expression of the sacramental fraternity of lay and ordained") and the Last Gospel ("a coda that sums up the meaning of the whole eucharistic action that has preceded it"); A. Nichols, "Salutary Dissatisfaction: An English View of 'Reforming the Reform,'" in Kocik, *The Reform of the Reform?*, pp. 195–210 (206–7).

70. "Is the Reform of the Reform Dead?," http://www.chantcafe.com/2014/02/is-reform-of-reform-dead.html.

Sudden liturgical change causes confusion, anger, and other problems which impede the Church's mission; therefore any introduction of change in the liturgy should proceed with prudence, even when it means the restoration of what should never have been cast aside. Such was Pope Benedict's approach. He did not impose the celebration of the traditional Latin rites on anyone; he allowed them for everyone. Neither did he impose the previous discipline of receiving Holy Communion kneeling and on the tongue; he simply introduced it as an exemplary practice at papal Masses.[71] And rather than decreeing a general return to the practice of celebrating the Eucharist *ad orientem*, he made use of the eastward-facing altar in the Sistine Chapel,[72] thereby signaling the legitimacy, even the aptness, of this option in the modern Roman rite, for: "Looking at the priest has no importance. What matters is looking together at the Lord."[73]

5. *Reforming the Reform: Groundwork and Possibilities*

As we look to the future, what might an officially sanctioned program to reform the reform look like? While it is impossible to foresee all the details, I can attempt to give its theoretical bases and broad outlines.

a. *Laying the groundwork*
First, before any revision of the rites, the future requires a more intense investment in the patient work of liturgical catechesis and formation.[74] This, the Council insisted, is an essential prerequisite to liturgical renewal and fruitful participation in the liturgy (*Sacrosanctum Concilium* 14). Cardinal Ratzinger reiterated the point when he stated that any new reform "ought

---

71. Beginning on the Solemnity of Corpus Christi, 2008.

72. On the Solemnity of the Baptism of the Lord, 2008 and on subsequent occasions.

73. Ratzinger, *Spirit of the Liturgy*, p. 81.

74. The challenge to formation in the true spirit of the liturgy was formulated by Father Romano Guardini, author of the now classic work, *The Spirit of the Liturgy* (1918). Writing in 1964, when the world was hurtling toward what is today called postmodernism, Guardini asked: Is modern man "capable of a liturgical act?" "A Letter from Louis Bouyer," *Herder Correspondence* Special Issue (1964), pp. 24–26 (26). The question has not lost its relevance. Are the impediments to worship—materialism, subjectivism, individualism—so severe as to render all but impossible the spiritual attitude required for genuine liturgical participation: humility, childlikeness, a desire for God on *His* terms? We have to hope otherwise. But in the absence of a felt need to be washed and reconciled and fed and anointed, no liturgy will "work," be it traditional, reformed, or re-reformed.

in the first place to be above all an educative process."[75] A significant step would be the creation of a General Directory for Liturgical Formation, akin to the general catechetical directories that were published by the Holy See in 1971 and 1997.[76] This directory would guide liturgical studies and practice in Catholic seminaries, colleges and universities, diocesan liturgical formation programs, as well as the production of catechetical materials for use in parishes. Such material would present the theological, liturgical, and pastoral justifications for reforming the reform, even if the phrase "reform of the reform" is not used.

In preparing for an official reform of the reform, it will also be necessary for Church leadership to encourage, possibly by means of ecclesiastical scholarships, further study of comparative liturgical history and theology, along the lines of the methodology adopted by Lauren Pristas in her comparison of the Sunday collects in the Roman missals of 1962 and 1970/2002. With few exceptions, critical evaluations of the liturgical reform are too often derived with the Mass alone in mind, and not the other liturgical rites. It would be good to have future discussion and evaluation take the wider view.

A third footing needed in laying the groundwork is greater attention to *Sacramentum Caritatis*, which brings together the deliberations of the 2005 Synod of Bishops on the Eucharist and the insights that Joseph Ratzinger has long advanced regarding liturgical renewal. To call it a *Magna Carta* for reforming the reform would be an exaggeration, but it does provide a lens through which to read *Sacrosanctum Concilium*. Pope Benedict's exhortation reiterates the importance of Latin and Gregorian chant, emphasizing that priests should be competent in both. In the liturgical celebrations of multilingual communities and at international gatherings, the universality of the Church should be underscored by the use of Latin (n. 62). The pope emphasizes, as he has before, that the Council's call to active participation in the liturgy does not mean busyness all the time; one is fully, actively, and fruitfully participating when engaged in silent contemplation (n. 52).

---

75. J. Ratzinger and P. Seewald, *God and the World: A Conversation with Peter Seewald* (San Francisco: Ignatius, 2002; German original 2000), p. 416. On the possibilities for liturgical education on the internet see: J. Tucker, "Liturgy, Liturgical Music and the Internet Apostolate," in Reid (ed.), *Sacred Liturgy*, pp. 337–54. On academic liturgical formation see, in the same volume: P. Gunter, "Academic Formation and the Sacred Liturgy," pp. 417–39.

76. These catechetical directories were published in accord with Vatican II's Decree on the Pastoral Office of Bishops in the Church, *Christus Dominus* (28 October 1965), n. 44.

Although *Sacramentum Caritatis* concerns the Eucharist, it contains treasures of relevance to Catholic worship in general. Benedict calls for a renewed understanding of "the rich theological and liturgical category of beauty" (n. 35). Accordingly, the reform of the reform should be stimulated by a new sense of beauty as perhaps *the* theological category from which all renewal flows.[77] Without a re-appropriation of liturgy as the mystery in which we encounter transcendent beauty, we are reduced to tiresome and jejune squabbles such as the value of contemporary "praise music" in place of plainchant and polyphony. The liturgy's ability to embody a sense of *doxa*, glory, eternal beauty—in music, art, and architecture—has historical models in abundance, and by no means only in the Christian East. Much good work has been accomplished in recent years by professionals who are inspired by and proud of the musical, artistic, and architectural heritage of the Western Church; the fruits of their labors deserve to be of a piece with reforming the reform.[78]

b. *Imagining an official reform of the reform*

Having established the groundwork, let us imagine what a papal motu proprio decreeing a reform of the reform might entail.[79] In its overall thrust, the document would establish the means by which the Roman rite's two forms would be brought, as closely as each form's structure and content permits, into line with the modestly renewed liturgy that was desired by the Fathers of Vatican II.

I argued above that the post-conciliar reform was so radical a deconstruction of the received liturgical tradition that the process of organic development cannot practically be restarted from within the framework of the reformed rites. That is not to say, however, that the modern Roman rite cannot be enriched with features of the traditional liturgy, or shorn of those changes introduced after 1970 that have weakened the bond between the *lex orandi* and the *lex credendi*. Toward that twofold end, our proposed motu proprio would immediately authorize the use in the modern Roman rite of specified gestures and prayers that did not survive the reforms of 1965–70. On the other hand, it would rescind the post-1970 permissions and indults derogating from the established liturgical norms. Let us consider these in brief.

77. See the collections of essays in Twomey and Rutherford (eds), *Benedict XVI and Beauty in Sacred Art and Architecture*, and J. Rutherford (ed.), *Benedict XVI and Beauty in Sacred Music* (Dublin: Four Courts, 2011).

78. For a good representation, see: the contributors and advertisers on the website New Liturgical Movement, http://www.newliturgicalmovement.org.

79. A motu proprio is a legislative decree issued by the Roman Pontiff on his own initiative.

First, the practice of receiving Holy Communion in the hand began

in flagrant violation of liturgical law [and] was "sanated" [legitimized] by Pope Paul VI in 1969, supposedly only for those places engaging in the abuse. Subsequently it spread like wildfire, with theological, historical, liturgical and pastoral implications well documented over the past forty-plus years, so that there is no need to "beat a dead horse" here, especially when the case against it has been so well made by Bishop Athanasius Schneider.[80]

Second, the administration of Holy Communion by non-ordained, "extraordinary" ministers was permitted by the Instruction *Immensæ Caritatis* of 1973. In many countries the "extraordinary" has become ordinary, in that lay ministers of Communion are a regular feature of liturgical life.[81] This undermines the Catholic theology of the ministerial priesthood and of the lay vocation.

Third, the *General Instruction of the Roman Missal* approved for the USA notes: "Besides the color violet, the colors white or black may be used at funeral services and at other Offices and Masses for the Dead in the Dioceses of the United States of America" (n. 346e). Father Peter Stravinskas observes: "While this concession was intended to make American liturgical practice supposedly correspond to contemporary social practice, it really does not since most mourners continue to wear black in varying degrees, thus rendering the celebrant out of step with all the other worshipers."[82] Noteworthy, too, is Bishop Peter Elliott's observation that "always wearing white and concentrating on the joy of eternal life has caused problems at some funerals. This approach can take away the right and the need to mourn, which is essential in certain situations."[83]

Lastly, while universal law allows for cremation, it does not permit cremation before the obsequies. That permission came by way of a letter

---

80. P. Stravinskas, "Brick by Brick: Modest Proposals for Liturgical Authenticity," *Antiphon* 14 (2010) pp. 301–11 (301–2), referencing Bishop Athanasius Schneider's *Dominus Est: Riflessioni di un vescovo dell'Asia Centrale sulla sacra Comunione* (Vatican City: Libreria Editrice Vaticana, 2008); English edn, *Dominus Est—It is the Lord!* (Mt Pocono: Newman House, 2009).

81. The interdicasterial Instruction *Ecclesia de Mysterio* (15 August 1997), approved *in forma specifica* by St John Paul II, acknowledges that "such...service is a response to the objective needs of the faithful," especially those of the sick and in the case of large liturgical assemblies, but insists that "the habitual use of extraordinary ministers of Holy Communion at Mass" is a source of "confusion" and should be "avoided and eliminated" (n. 8).

82. Stravinskas, "Brick by Brick," p. 302.

83. P. Elliott, *Liturgical Question Box: Answers to Common Questions About the Modern Liturgy* (San Francisco: Ignatius, 1998), p. 185.

from the Holy See to the bishops of the United States in 1997. It authorizes local Ordinaries "to permit that the funeral liturgy, including where appropriate the celebration of the Eucharist, be celebrated in the presence of the cremated remains instead of the natural body."[84] Despite the fact that this indult foresees an individual judgment on the part of the local Ordinary for each instance, I know of no diocese where that judgment has not been delegated to the parish priest. This puts strong pressure to allow the practice on any priest who deems it theologically, liturgically, and pastorally unsound. Moreover, the *Order of Christian Funerals* instructs that the cremated remains should be reverently buried or entombed in a cemetery or mausoleum. Yet it is not unusual for survivors to take the ashes home to keep on the mantel, or to scatter them over the waters, or to wear them in lockets or pendants. To ensure the observance of the norm according the mind of the Church, the conscientious priest must ascertain the place and time of burial or entombment before allowing the funeral liturgy in his church; of course it is only a matter of time before he gets a call from the chancery to discuss complaints received from families who could not have their way.

In addition to rescinding certain permissions which abet liturgical heteropraxis, the "reform of the reform" motu proprio would make the celebration of Mass *ad orientem* the preferred practice unless architecturally impossible, as a proven means of sustaining the transcendent power of the liturgy. That means more than where the celebrant stands; it means a sanctuary much more clearly defined than is now the custom, and a raised altar that permits the priest literally to "go up" to it.

The motu proprio would also authorize the production of a full ritual for papal celebrations in the major basilicas and "stational churches" of Rome. These liturgical books would include the necessary provisos for how these same rites would be celebrated outside of Rome, wherein the Pope, as supreme legislator, would resolve certain questions of ceremonial for himself and offer pilgrims a stellar example of moderate liturgical renewal in full continuity with the Roman tradition. A liturgical trickledown effect could result from bishops on *ad limina* visits taking these books home for use in their cathedrals.[85]

---

84. Congregation for Divine Worship and the Discipline of the Sacraments, Letter to Bishop Anthony Pilla (Prot. 1589/96/L), 21 March 1997, in *Thirty-Five Years of the BCL Newsletter: 1965–2000* (Washington: U.S. Conference of Catholic Bishops, 2004), p. 1535.

85. This particular proposal is not my own but was made by Archbishop Thomas Gullickson, papal nuncio to Switzerland and Liechtenstein. I thank His Excellency for his permission to incorporate it here.

Addressing two matters relative to the Church's pattern of fasting and feasting, the motu proprio would have solemnities kept at their proper times and not on the nearest Sunday, thereby upholding the liturgical symbolism of time. It would also restore the eucharistic fast to three hours, as it was from 1957 until 1964. This would be somewhat more physically demanding and thus more spiritually purposeful than the present one-hour fast, and might also lessen the instances of sacrilegious communions.[86]

Furthermore, some parameters would be restored to the practice of priestly concelebration, such as a limitation on the number of concelebrants, a requisite proximity to the altar, and a just cause.[87] The just cause should be more than simply the desire to take part in a Mass, which can just as well be done by assisting *in choro*.[88]

Some of these suggestions can be thought of as remote preparation for a fourth typical edition of the Roman missal, the vernacular editions of which, by mandate of the Holy See, would include the Latin texts in full. As to what kind of Mass this might be in specific terms, time allows for mention of just a few items on a list of what would be desirable:

- The ceremony of sprinkling of holy water takes place before Mass, as is traditional.
- There is no penitential rite, as this was never part of the Roman Mass until 1969. "One should have done one's penance before coming to join in the essentially post-penitential celebration of the Eucharist."[89] Before Mass there occurs the traditional prayers at the foot of the altar (possibly truncated, as in the 1965 rite) or a slightly revised version of the 1970 missal's penitential rite (first option).

86. See: E. Peters, "The Communion Fast: A Reconsideration," *Antiphon* 11 (2007), pp. 234–44; T. Kocik, "The Eucharistic Fast in Perspective," *The Catholic Response* (September/October 2010), pp. 26–29.

87. See the critical studies: J. de Sainte-Marie, *The Holy Eucharist—The World's Salvation: Studies on the Holy Sacrifice of the Mass, Its Celebration and Its Concelebration* (Leominster: Gracewing, 2015; French original 1982); G. Derville, *Eucharistic Concelebration: From Symbol to Reality* (Montreal: Wilson & Lafleur, 2011; Spanish original 2010).

88. The theological, canonical, spiritual, and pedagogical reasons why a priest might opt to assist at Mass *in choro* rather than concelebrate are presented in T. Kocik, "Preaching Through the Choir: The Merits of Assisting at Mass *In choro*," *Antiphon* 10 (2006), pp. 204–11.

89. J. Parsons, "A Reform of the Reform?," in Kocik, *The Reform of the Reform?*, pp. 211–56 (241).

In the latter case, once the priest and ministers have arrived at the altar, the priest begins with the Sign of the Cross, turns and greets the congregation, turns back toward the altar and says the invitation to public confession. Having said the *Confiteor* and absolution, he ascends the altar, kisses (and possibly incenses) it, and then says the introit (unless it is being said by the people or chanted by a cantor or choir), after which comes the *Kyrie*.

- Gone is the option of substituting hymns for the entrance, offertory, and communion chants. Appropriate hymns may be used in addition to, but not instead of, the Mass propers.
- Gone, too, is the directive that Mass should not be celebrated on an altar at which the Blessed Sacrament is reserved.[90] "This norm enshrines in liturgical law a very problematic concept, namely, that having the reserved Sacrament on the altar of sacrifice creates confusion between the so-called static and dynamic dimensions of the Eucharist."[91] Moreover, it conflicts with the Holy See's encouragement of the use, and even the existence, of only one altar in churches where the original altar with its tabernacle remains intact.[92]
- The ablutions must be done immediately after Holy Communion.
- The practice is restored of genuflecting whenever passing in front of the tabernacle, unless carrying an item that makes genuflection difficult.[93]

90. *General Instruction of the Roman Missal* n. 315.

91. P. Stravinskas, "Brick by Brick," p. 308. Pope Pius XII warned against this false dichotomy in an allocution to the International Congress on Pastoral Liturgy (22 September 1956): "To separate tabernacle from altar is to separate two things which by their origin and their nature should remain united"; *The Liturgy*, Papal Teaching Series (Boston: St Paul Editions, 1962), p. 512.

92. An editorial in the May 1993 issue of *Notitiæ*, the official publication of the Congregation for Divine Worship, affirmed: "Il principio dell'unicità dell'altare è teologicamente più importante, che la prassi di celebrare rivolti al popolo" (The principle of the unicity of the altar is theologically more important than the practice of celebrating facing the people); *Notitiæ* 29 (1993), pp. 245–49 (249).

93. Until the publication of the 2002 *editio typica* of the Roman missal all liturgical ministers were expected to genuflect whenever passing before the tabernacle unless carrying the processional cross or candles. That norm has been amended to read: "If, however, the tabernacle with the Most Blessed Sacrament is situated in the sanctuary, the Priest, the Deacon, and the other ministers genuflect when they approach the altar and when they depart from it, but not during the celebration of Mass itself"; *General Instruction of the Roman Missal*, n. 274.

- Double collects may be used when there are overlapping feasts, as is presently permissible in the Liturgy of the Hours during privileged seasons.[94] I grimace when a liturgical calendar informs me that "in other years" today is the feast of St Catherine (let us say), but not this year because it is Sunday. Must the saint be ignored altogether because her feast-day is outranked? Would precious time be lost by praying the saint's collect immediately after that of the Sunday?

These proposals for a "reform of the reform" motu proprio all involve the ordinary form. So, where does this leave the extraordinary form?

Recall that years of preparatory work involving careful reflection, liturgical formation, and critical scholarship would precede the proposed motu proprio. During this time, the problems inherent to *Sacrosanctum Concilium*—what Michael Davies calls "time bombs" built into the document by revolutionaries and concealed by orthodox padding in order to be exploited later,[95] and what Father Aidan Nichols calls the "seeds of its own destruction" encased in the innocuous language of pastoral welfare[96]—could be extensively discussed, published, and circulated. Possibly the idea of a "defused" *Sacrosanctum Concilium* is not so remote. Where the Constitution is ambiguous or pliable, this document would provide an explicit hermeneutic of continuity so as to safeguard the integrity of the traditional Roman rite and close the door to any of the "artificial discontinuities" with which we are familiar.

At some point the Pope would authorize this alternative implementation of *Sacrosanctum Concilium* and establish the official organs for such an undertaking. There would be a period of local use, *ad experimentum*, of a revised missal and lectionary. This alternative Mass "of Vatican II," if well received, could eventually be approved by the Holy See for use throughout the Church as the normative expression of the renovated Roman liturgy that the Council desired. By then, the process of mutual enrichment will have narrowed the gap between the Roman rite's ordinary and extraordinary forms. But there is no need to hurry.

94. See: the *General Instruction on the Liturgy of the Hours* (1971), n. 239b.

95. M. Davies, *Liturgical Time Bombs in Vatican II: The Destruction of Catholic Faith Through Changes in Catholic Worship* (Rockford: TAN, 2003).

96. A. Nichols, "A Tale of Two Documents," in A. Reid (ed.), *A Pope and a Council on the Sacred Liturgy* (Farnborough: St Michael's Abbey, 2002), p. 12.

6. *Conclusion*

In concluding, I would stress that without a solid liturgical foundation, nothing we undertake in the Church, no program of renewal *ad intra* and no "New Evangelization" *ad extra* will bear lasting fruit. Every aspect of the Church's life flows from and back to the saving action of Jesus Christ in the Sacred Liturgy. Therefore every effort to promote the correct, beautiful, and spiritually nourishing celebration of the liturgy, in any usage of any rite of the Church, is a good in itself and needs no justification.

Many people have criticisms and proposals, but commitment, *true* commitment: that requires sacrifice. In this connection I would offer a word particularly to my brother priests, deacons, and seminarians. In return for your dedication to the Church's demanding but richly rewarding liturgical heritage, be prepared to forgo ecclesiastical preferment, to be marginalized by your confreres, removed from parish assignments and blocked from becoming pastors. This is a sad state that continues today in places where any challenge to "how we do things here" is met with suspicion or worse. Over time, however, the "Benedict XVI Generation" will come into its own and set the tone for an increasing number of parishes, religious communities, and dioceses.

I am optimistic, overall, because the mood in the year 2015 about liturgical renewal and its success after the Council differs from that of the 1970s and 1980s. Thanks in no small part to the longstanding and well known views of Joseph Ratzinger, the liturgical reform has been reconfigured by a new theological and ecclesial climate. This signals some hope that the official reform of the reform may, in God's good time, come to pass, thus ending a long and tragic period of liturgical polarization. Much of what I have said may reflect wishful thinking or even naivety. But, as the promulgation of *Summorum Pontificum* and even the 2005 election of its author to the papacy attests, even wishful thinking is sometimes vindicated.

THE POST-VATICAN II REVISION OF COLLECTS: SOLEMNITIES AND FEASTS

Lauren Pristas

There are thirty collects assigned to the principal feasts that do not belong to proper seasons: the solemnity of the Most Holy Trinity, seven solemnities or feasts of the Lord, four of Our Lady, seventeen honoring angels and saints, and the feast of the Dedication of the Basilica of St John Lateran.

Our examination of texts proceeds according to type: days honoring our Lord, our Lady, and so forth—solemnities first, then feasts. The collects considered are those assigned to the aforementioned days in the last typical edition of the Tridentine missal and in the emended third typical edition of the Vatican II missal.[1] The discussion is based on the Latin orations. Unless otherwise indicated, the English translations presented here are my own.

This study makes ongoing use of three documents: (1) the unpublished schema that stipulates the principles for revising the Mass orations agreed upon by the *Consilium ad Exsequendam Constitutionem de Sacra Liturgia* members in September, 1966;[2] (2) a 1971 essay by Antoine Dumas, *relator* of the *Consilium* study group entrusted with the revision of the Mass

---

1. C. Johnson and A. Ward (eds), *Missale romanum anno 1962 promulgatum*, (Rome: CLV-Edizioni Liturgiche, 1994); *Missale Romanum ex decreto Sacrosancti Oecumenici Concilii Vaticani II instauratum, auctoritate Pauli PP. VI promulgatum et Ioannis Pauli PP. II cura recognitum*, editio typica tertia reimpressio emendata (Vatican City: Typis Vaticanis, 2008). With one exception, the collects examined here are the same in all editions of the post-Vatican II missals. The single exception, the alternate collect assigned to the feast of the Dedication of the Basilica of St John Lateran, is unique to the emended *editio tertia* published in 2008.

2. *Consilium ad Exsequendam Constitutionem de Sacra Liturgia, Schemata n. 186, De Missali* n. 27 (19 September 1966), pp. 2–4 and addendum p. 1. I gained access to all the unpublished *Consilium* documents cited in this essay through the kind generosity of the ICEL Secretariat in Washington, DC.

Consilium ad exsequendam Constitutionem de Sacra Liturgia, Elenchus membrorum - consultorum - consiliariorum coetuum a studiis (Vatican: Typis Polyglottis Vaticanis, 1964), pp. 9–14 indicates that in 1966 there were forty *Consilium* members, all but three

orations,[3] in which he discusses both principles that guided the work of redaction and the concrete ways in which the principles were applied, and helpfully provides specific examples;[4] (3) a list of the sources of the orations of the new missal that was compiled by Cuthbert Johnson and published in *Notitiae* in 1996.[5]

The principal goal of this study is to shed light on the editorial work that produced the set of collects assigned to solemnities and feasts in the Vatican II missals. The method is to present the pre- and post-Vatican II collects side by side and, when it is known that the revisers made use of a text other than the 1962 collect to produce the 2008 collect, to present that text as well. When the exact same collect is assigned to the same solemnity or feast in both missals it is neither presented nor discussed unless it is of interest because it comes under the rubric of one of the revision principles.

Reasons for particular changes are given when, and to the extent that, they are either explained by the revision policies agreed upon by the *Consilium* members at the start of the work or known from the published remarks of someone close to the work. It should be recognized from the start that the explanatory information, even when available, is extremely limited. For example, the policy decision that the texts of prayers will not be repeated in the revised missal may explain why a particular prayer was replaced, but does not explain how the revisers chose the replacement, or why they selected or composed the replacement that they did. For the most part, detailed records of particular decisions do not exist.[6]

of whom were bishops. Members were not responsible for producing the revised texts themselves, but for deciding matters of policy and approving the revisions proposed by the various study groups.

3. *Coetus* 18bis: De orationibus et praefationibus recognoscendis [Concerning the review prayers and prefaces]. See: *Elenchus*, p. 45.

4. "Les oraisons du nouveau Missel," *Questions Liturgiques* 25 (1971), pp. 263–70. The revision principles actually used by the revisers and those approved by *Consilium* members are not identical. See: Lauren Pristas, "The Orations of the Vatican II Missal: Policies for Revision," *Communio* 30 (2003), pp. 621–53.

5. C. Johnson OSB, "Sources of the Roman Missal (1975): Proprium de Tempore, Proprium de Sanctis," *Notitiae* 32 (1996), pp. 7–179.

6. C. Johnson and A. Ward, "The Sources of the Roman Missal (1975)," *Notitiae* 22 (1986), p. 454: "The material conserved in the Congregation's [Congregation for Divine Worship and Discipline of the Sacraments] archive documenting any particular text is uneven, depending on the work methods of a particular group (*coetus*) of revisers, the opportunities offered by distance and commitments to meet in person and so on. It should not be forgotten that all those involved were in some way experts in their field, many having worked for the best part of a lifetime with the texts in questions. Accordingly, there was often no need to prepare extensive written

Before beginning our examination of texts, a few words about Roman collects may be helpful. The Roman collect is always a single sentence. Collects have two parts. These are (1) the invocation, or direct address, which is usually accompanied by a statement of fact, and (2) the petition, which is almost always expressed in a dependent clause. The statement of fact mentions an attribute of God, or something he does or has done, which then provides the motive for the petition.[7] Thus the two parts of the typical Roman collect are thematically parallel. Recognizing the parallelism and its import are essential to full appreciation of the prayer.

1. *The Solemnity of the Most Holy Trinity*

Our first collect is that of the Solemnity of the Most Holy Trinity:[8]

1962: Most Holy Trinity	2008: Most Holy Trinity
Omnipotens sempiterne Deus, qui dedisti famulis tuis, in confessione verae fidei, aeternae Trinitatis gloriam agnoscere, et in potentia maiestatis adorare unitatem: *quaesumus; ut eiusdem fidei firmitate, ab omnibus semper muniamur adversis.*	**Deus Pater, qui, Verbum veritatis et Spiritum sanctificationis mittens in mundum, admirabile mysterium tuum hominibus declarasti**, da nobis, in confessione verae fidei, aeternae gloriam Trinitatis agnoscere, et Unitatem adorare in potentia maiestatis.

explanations, but simply to operate selections, and revisions of texts, the rationale of the details being more or less obvious to fellow specialists once broad policies had been defined. Let all users of this work be therefore assured that personal access to the official archival material would reveal no further information, except of the most incidental variety. Of what is available, the fullest use has been made."

7. The statement of fact is frequently expressed in a relative clause. Consider for example the collect for *Corpus Christi* which begins "Deus, qui nobis sub Sacramento mirabili passionis tuae memoriam reliquisti..." The invocation is "Deus" [God]. The statement of fact follows in the relative clause: "who in this wondrous sacrament have left us a memorial of your passion." After this comes the petition: "tribue, quaesumus, ita nos corporis et sanguinis tui sacra mysteria venerari; ut redemptionis tuae fructum in nobis iugiter sentiamus." Christ's gift of a sacrament that is a memorial of his redeeming passion inspires the petition: "grant us, we beseech you, so to venerate the sacred mysteries of your body and blood that we may ever experience in ourselves the effect of your redemption."

8. Throughout this study, likeness and difference in pre- and post-Vatican II collects for a particular liturgical day that share common text are presented as follows. Words that are the same in both collects appear in regular type. Words that are unique to the 1962 collect are italicized; words that are unique to the post-Vatican II collect appear in bold type.

Almighty, everlasting God, who have given your servants in confession of the true faith, to acknowledge the glory of the eternal Trinity, and to adore the unity in power of majesty: *we beseech you; that by steadfastness in the same faith may we ever be defended from all that opposes [us].*	**O God, Father, who sending the Word of truth and Spirit of sanctification into the world, have revealed your wondrous mystery to men**, **grant us**, in confession of the true faith, to acknowledge the glory of the Trinity and to adore the Unity in power of majesty.

The revisers made changes to both parts of the 1962 collect: they composed a new invocation and statement of fact, and they made the old statement of fact the new petition.

It is a curious redaction—unique, as far as I know. What the older prayer confesses God to have done, the new prayer asks him to do. In consequence, the request for firmness in faith and protection from adversity disappears. Another difference is that the new collect does not describe those who pray as God's servants.[9]

2. *Solemnities and Feasts of the Lord*

We move now to consideration of the days celebrating our Lord. There are four solemnities and three feasts. The solemnities celebrate the Annunciation, *Corpus Christi*, the Sacred Heart and Christ the King; the feasts are those of the Presentation, Transfiguration and the Exaltation of the Holy Cross.

a. *Solemnities of the Lord*

(1) *The Annunciation of the Lord.* In the 1962 missal, 25 March bears the title the Annunciation of the Blessed Virgin Mary, and the day is celebrated as a feast of Our Lady. The post-Vatican II missals celebrate 25 March as a solemnity of the Lord under the title of the Annunciation of the Lord—the same name given to the feast when it was first introduced in Rome in the seventh century.[10] The differences between the pre- and post-Vatican II collects are explained by the decision to celebrate the day as a solemnity of the Lord.

9. For a fuller discussion of the revision of this collect see Lauren Pristas, "Missale Romanum 1962 and 1970: A Comparative Study of Two Collects," *Antiphon* 7 (2002), pp. 29–33.

10. *Consilium*, Schemata n. 174, de Calendario 10-Addenda (August 1966), p. 2 and Schemata n. 188, de Calendario 11 (22 September 1966), p. 13.

The post-Vatican II collect is a new composition.[11] It combines words of the 1962 prayer, a phrase from a letter that Pope St Leo the Great wrote to the Empress Eudoxia,[12] and a clause composed by the modern editors.

1962: Annunciation of the BVM	2008: Annunciation of the Lord	Source: Pope St Leo I, Letter 123
Deus, qui *de beatae* Mariae Virginis utero Verbum tuum, *Angelo nuntiante,* carnem suscipere voluisti: *praesta supplicibus tuis; ut, qui vere eam Genitricem Dei credimus, eius apud te intecessionibus adiuvemur*	Deus, qui Verbum tuum IN utero Virginis Mariae VERITATEM **CARNIS HUMANAE** suscipere voluisti, **concede, quaesumus, ut, qui Redemptorem nostrum Deum et hominem confitemur, ipsius etiam divinae naturae mereamur esse consortes**	...qui ab unigenito Deo Vero negant IN utero Virginis matris VERITATEM CARNIS HUMANAE susceptam
O God, who willed your Word, *at the message of the angel,* to assume flesh in the womb of the blessed Virgin Mary; *grant to those humbly imploring you that we, who believe her truly to be the Mother of God, may be aided by her intercession in your presence.*	O God who willed your Word to assume THE REALITY OF HUMAN flESH in the womb of the Virgin Mary, grant, **we beseech you, that we who confess our Redeemer to be God and man, may be able also to be partakers of his divine nature.**	......who deny the REALITY OF HUMAN FLESH was assumed by the only-Begotten Word of God in the womb of the Virgin mother.

11. Johnson, "Sources," p. 113.

12. Ibid. Leo, Epistola CXXIII ad Eudociam Augustam De monachis Palestinis, Jacques Paul Migne (ed.), *Patrologia Latina* (Paris, 1841–1855), vol. 54, col. 1060–61 at 1061. The whole sentence from which the revisers took the phrase is: "Fides enim catholica sicut damnat Nestorium qui in uno Domino nostro Jesu Christo duas ausus est praedicare personas, ita damnat etiam Eutychen cum Dioscoro, qui ab unigenito Deo Vero negant **in utero Virginis matris veritatem carnis humanae** *susceptam*." [For as catholic faith condemns Nestorius who undertook to preach two persons in our one Lord Jesus Christ, so also it condemns Eutyches, with Dioscorus, who deny **the reality of human flesh** *was received* by the only-Begotten Word of God **in the womb of the Virgin mother**]. The footnote in J. P. Migne states the letter was written on 15 June 453; *Patrologia Latina*, vol. 54, col. 1059, n. 1.

The words that are the same in the two collects, whether or not they the serve the same purpose, appear in regular type—as do the words from Pope St Leo's letter that also appear in both prayers. Words that are unique to the 1962 collect are italicized; those which were introduced by the revisers are in bold type. Words and phrases in the text from Leo that the revisers adopted are in small caps and those not found in either collect are underscored. All that is new in the Vatican II collect, then, appears in bold-face type and the portion taken from Leo appears in bold-face small caps.

The verb *suscipio*, translated here as "assume," appears in all three texts. The collect employs the infinite form (*suscipere*). Leo uses the perfect passive participle (*susceptam*): "the real nature (*veritatem*: truth/reality/the true or real nature) of human flesh which the Word *assumed*."

The substantive differences between the old collect and the new are four:

1. The announcing angel disappears from the statement of fact.
2. The revised prayer places greater stress on the "reality" of Christ's human flesh.
3. There is a change in doctrinal emphasis: the 1962 prayer explicitly affirms Mary's divine maternity; the new prayer professes faith in Christ's possession of two natures.
4. The 1962 collect asks for the help of Mary's intercession; the new collect asks that we may become sharers of Christ's divine nature.

(2) *Corpus Christi*. In the post-conciliar liturgical reform, the name of the day was changed from the "the Most Holy Body of Christ" to the "Most Holy Body and Blood of Christ." No change was made to the collect:

Most Holy Body of Christ (1962) / Most Holy Body and Blood of Christ (2008)	
Deus, qui nobis sub Sacramento mirabili passionis tuae memoriam reliquisti: tribue, quaesumus, ita nos corporis et sanguinis tui sacra mysteria venerari; ut redemptionis tuae fructum in nobis iugiter sentiamus.	O God, who in this wondrous Sacrament have left us a memorial of your passion: grant us, we beseech you, so to venerate the sacred mysteries of your body and blood; that we may continually experience in ourselves the fruit/effect of your redemption.

In 1966, the voting members of the *Consilium* decided that, in general, the orations of the Roman missal would be directed to the Father.[13] The *Corpus Christi* collect, which is attributed to St Thomas Aquinas,

13. *Consilium*, Schemata n. 186, p. 4 and addendum p. 1.

addresses Christ as God and, as far as I know, is the only collect in the emended third typical edition of the Vatican II missal that addresses the Second Person of the Trinity. As we proceed with our examination we will encounter two examples of 1962 collects that address the Son which were replaced in the post-Vatican II reform.

In his 1971 essay, Dumas states that there were prayers that the revisers, while preserving the theme, so completely recast that the result was "tantamount to a new creation."[14] He gives no specific reason, but does name two examples. They are the two remaining solemnities of the Lord: the Sacred Heart and Christ the King.

(3) *The Most Sacred Heart of Jesus.* The old and new collects of the Sacred Heart are:

1962 and 2008 alternate: Sacred Heart	2008: Sacred Heart New Composition
Deus, qui nobis in Corde Filii tui, nostris vulnerato peccatis, infinitos dilectionis thesauros misericorditer largiri dignaris, concede, quaesumus, ut, illi devotum pietatis nostrae praestantes obsequium, dignae quoque satisfactionis exhibeamus officium.	Concede, quaesumus, omnipotens Deus, ut qui, dilecti Filii tui Corde gloriantes, eius praecipua in nos beneficia recolimus caritatis, de illo donorum fonte caelesti supereffluentem gratiam mereamur accipere.
O God who, in the heart of your Son wounded by our sins, mercifully deign to bestow upon us the infinite treasures of love, grant, we beseech you, that, as we present to him the devout homage of our piety, we may also offer the service [fulfill the duty] of fitting reparation.	Grant, we beseech you, almighty God, that we who, exulting in the heart of your beloved Son, reflect upon the extraordinary favors of [his] love for us, may be made worthy to receive overflowing grace from that fount of heavenly gifts.

The direct address of the 1962 collect is accompanied by a statement of fact which asserts that God mercifully continues to bestow (*largiri* is present tense) upon us the infinite treasures of his love in, or by means of, the heart of his Son which was wounded by our sins. The petition asks that, as we

---

14. Dumas, "Les oraisons," p. 269. For an English translation of Dumas's essay, see Lauren Pristas, "The Orations of the Vatican II Missal," pp. 629–39. Dumas's assertion that the recasting of certain prayers was tantamount to a new creation is found on p. 638 of the English translation. Hereafter the English translation of Dumas's essay is cited as: L. Pristas, "The Orations."

present to Christ the devout homage of our filial love [*pietas*], we may also fulfil the duty of making fitting reparation. Mention of sin, and of Christ's heart having been wounded, is absent from the new composition, which speaks rather of exulting in Christ's love and the extraordinary favors that flow from it. The petition to make suitable reparation is replaced by a request to be made worthy of overflowing grace.

The two prayers are quite different. It is important to note, however, that the new composition displaces, not replaces, the 1962 prayer which is retained in the Vatican II missals as the alternate collect of the solemnity.

(4) *Christ the King.* The last solemnity of the Lord is that of Christ the King. Pope Pius XI established the feast in 1925 and assigned it to the last Sunday in October, that which directly precedes the feast of All Saints. In the Vatican II missals, it is celebrated on the last Sunday of the per annum Sundays—that is, the one directly preceding the first Sunday of Advent.

1962: Christ the King	2008: Christ the King
Omnipotens sempiterne Deus, qui in dilecto Filio tuo, universorum Rege, omnia instaurare voluisti, concede propitius; ut *cunctae familiae Gentium, peccati vulnere disgregatae, eius suavissimo subdantur imperio.*	Omnipotens sempiterne Deus, qui in dilecto Filio tuo, universorum Rege, omnia instaurare voluisti, concede propitius, **ut tota creatura, a servitute liberata, tuae maiestati deserviat ac te sine fine collaudet.**
Almighty, everlasting God, who willed to restore all things in your beloved Son, the King of the whole world, mercifully grant that *all the families of Nations, rent assunder by the wound of sin, may be brought under his most sweet rule.*	Almighty, everlasting God, who willed to restore all things in your beloved Son, the King of the whole world, mercifully grant that **all creation, having been set free from slavery, may serve your majesty and praise you without end.**

Recasting this collect, the revisers retained the invocation and replaced the petition with a composition of their own. The substantive differences are three:

1. "All creation" replaces "all the families of Nations."
2. A request that all creation be "set free from slavery" and "serve your majesty and praise you without end" replaces the request that all nations become subject to the "sweet rule" of Christ the King.
3. The acknowledgment that sin is the cause of division among peoples is absent from the new collect.

On a literary level, the invocation and petition of the original prayer exhibit a parallelism not duplicated in the revised oration. The older collect asks "God, who willed to restore all things in his beloved Son," to fulfill his very own desire by bringing "all the families of Nations" under his Son's "most sweet rule."

b. *Feasts of the Lord*

The three feasts of the Lord are the Presentation, the Transfiguration and the Exaltation of his Holy Cross. Only the collects of the latter two feasts were revised. We consider them in order.

(1) *The Presentation of the Lord.* Previously celebrated as a feast of Our Lady titled the Purification of the Blessed Virgin Mary, 2 February is now celebrated as a feast of the Lord, titled the Presentation of the Lord, in the Vatican II missals.[15] No changes were made to the texts of the Mass.

Purification of BVM 1962 Presentation of the Lord 2008	Omnipotens sempiterne Deus, maiestatem tuam supplices exoramus, ut, sicut Unigenitus Filius tuus hodierna die cum nostrae carnis substantia in templo est praesentatus, ita nos facias purificatis tibi mentibus praesentari.	Almighty, everlasting God, we humbly implore your majesty that, as your Only-Begotten Son today, in the substance of our flesh, was presented in the temple, so may you grant us to be presented to you with minds made pure.

The Law of Moses commands that the first born son be consecrated to the Lord (Exod 13:2) and that a woman who has borne a male child present a sin offering to the priest on the fortieth day after giving birth—at the completion of the period stipulated for her purification (Lev 12:2–8). Mary and Joseph's obedience, and the events that occurred while they were at the temple in Jerusalem fulfilling these precepts of Mosaic Law, are reported in Luke 2:22–39 and commemorated liturgically each year by the Church on 2 February, the fortieth day following 25 December. For this reason, the day has always been something of a joint feast. The collect of the day, which has been in constant use in the Latin west from the eighth century,[16] mentions the presentation of the Lord explicitly,

---

15. *Consilium*, Schemata n. 188, de Calendario 11 (22 September 1966), p. 11.

16. Eugenio Moeller, Jean-Marie Clément and 't. Wallant Bertrandus Coppieters, *Corpus Orationum, CLX*, I–IX (Turnholt: Brepols, 1991–99), tomus VI, #3855.

and, in addition, employs language in the petition that alludes both to the presentation of the Lord and the purification of his Mother—for it asks that God grant us to be *presented* to himself with minds which have been *made pure.*

(2) *Transfiguration of the Lord.* To produce the revised collect, the editors omitted a phrase from the statement of fact of the 1962 prayer and composed a new petition.

1962: Transfiguration of the Lord	2008: Transfiguration of the Lord
Deus, qui fidei sacramenta in Unigeniti tui gloriosa Transfiguratione, patrum testimonio roborasti, et adoptionem filiorum perfectam, *voce delapsa de nube lucida,* mirabiliter praesignasti: concede *propitius; ut ipsius Regis gloriae nos coheredes efficias, et eiusdem gloriae tribuas esse consortes*	Deus, qui fidei sacramenta in Unigeniti tui gloriosa Transfiguratione patrum testimonio roborasti, et adoptionem filiorum perfectam mirabiliter praesignasti, concede **nobis famulis tuis, ut, ipsius dilecti Filii tui vocem audientes, eiusdem coheredes effici mereamur.**
O God, who, in the glorious Transfiguration of your Only-Begotten Son, confirmed mysteries of faith through the witness of the Fathers, and, *by the voice that came down from the bright cloud,* wondrously prefigured the full adoption of sons: *mercifully grant that you may make us coheirs with him, who is the King of glory, and may grant us to be partakers of the same glory.*	O God, who, in the glorious Transfiguration of your Only-Begotten Son, confirmed mysteries of faith through the witness of the Fathers, and, wondrously prefigured the full adoption of sons, **grant to us, your servants, that hearing the voice of him, who is your Only-Begotten Son, we made be made worthy to become coheirs of the same [Son].**

The revised prayer omits mention of the cloud and focuses on the instruction of the voice which came from it. Further, the "King" of the 1962 collect becomes the "Only-Begotten Son" in the edited text. The literary unity of the revised collect, constructed as it is on sonship—both Christ's and our own—is impressive. The literary unity of the older collect is considerably more subtle. Its source is the manifestation of glory in Christ's human body which both reveals his kingship and prefigures the glory that, in God's plan, awaits our own mortal flesh.

(3) *Exaltation of the Holy Cross.* The original and revised collects are:

1962: Exaltation of the Cross	2008: Exaltation of the Cross
Deus, qui *nos hodierna die Exaltationis sanctae Crucis annua solemnitate laetificas*: praesta, quaesumus; ut, cuius mysterium in terra cognovimus, eius redemptionis praemia in caelo mereamur.	Deus, qui **Unigenitum tuum** CRUCEM SUBIRE VOLUISTI, **ut salvum faceret genus humanum**, praesta, quaesumus, ut, cuius mysterium in terra cognovimus, eius redemptionis praemia in caelo **consequi** mereamur.
O God, *who make us joyful on this day in the yearly solemnity of the Exaltation of the Holy Cross*, grant, we beseech you, that we, who have known its mystery on earth, may be deemed worthy of the reward of its redemption in heaven.	O God, WHO WILLED YOUR **Only-Begotten Son** TO UNDERGO the **Cross so that the human race might be saved**; grant, we beseech you, that we, who have known its mystery on earth, may be deemed worthy **to attain** the reward of its redemption in heaven.

The first revision policy approved by the *Consilium* members in the Fall of 1966 was that the texts of orations would not be repeated.[17] Several collects assigned to various days in the 1962 missal have the same statement of fact accommodated to the day in question—that is, one which describes God as making us joyful in the annual celebration of a named solemnity.[18] In revising the collect of the Exaltation, the post-Vatican II revisers substituted a less generic statement of fact, and added the infinitive "to attain" to the petition. Cuthbert Johnson cites two Tridentine Holy Week collects as sources of the redacted invocation: those assigned to Palm Sunday and Wednesday of Holy Week.[19] These collects appear below with the adopted phrases indicated, as they are above, in small caps.

Palm Sunday (1962 and 2008)	
Omnipotens sempiterne Deus, qui humano generi ad imitandum humilitatis exemplum, Salvatorem nostrum carnem sumere, et CRUCEM SUBIRE fecisti: concede propitius; ut et patientiae ipsius habere documenta, et resurrectionis consortia mereamur.	Almighty everlasting God, who in order to give the human race an example of humility to imitate, has caused our Savior to take flesh and UNDERGO THE CROSS, mercifully grant that we may deserve to have both the lessons of his patience/endurance/suffering and fellowship in his resurrection.[21]

17. *Consilium*, Schemata, n. 186, p. 2.

18. Namely, the Vigil of the Lord's Nativity (24 December), Wednesday in the Pascal Octave, and the days celebrating St Agnes (24 January), Sts Philip and James (11 May) and Sts Cyriacus, Largus, and Smaragdus (8 August).

19. Johnson, "Sources," p. 140.

Wednesday of Holy Week (1962 and 2008)	
Deus, qui pro nobis Filium tuum crucis patibulum SUBIRE VOLUISTI, ut inimici a nobis expelleres potestatem: concede nobis famulis tuis; ut resurrectionis gratiam consequamur.	O God, who for our sake WILLED your Son TO UNDERGO the gibbet of the Cross, that you might drive from us the power of the enemy: grant to us your servants that we may attain the grace of resurrection.

4. *Solemnities and Feasts of Our Lady*

We come to the days honoring Our Lady. There are four that do not belong to proper seasons: the solemnities of the Assumption and the Immaculate Conception, and the feasts of the Visitation and the Nativity. In both the pre- and post-Vatican II missals, the Assumption has a vigil Mass.

The dogmatic definitions of Mary's immaculate conception and bodily assumption into heaven were declared in modern times. Subsequent to each definition a new collect was composed for the day Mass of the corresponding feast. The post-Vatican II revisers made no changes to these relatively modern compositions. On this account our considerations are confined to the collects assigned to the vigil of the Assumption, the Visitation and the Nativity.

a. *Solemnities of Our Lady*
(1) *The Vigil of the Assumption of the Blessed Virgin Mary.* The 1962 collect for this Mass is found in extant codices going back to the ninth century.[20] It addresses Christ as God (Deus). One of the revision policies agreed upon by the Consilium members, as we noted above, was that orations would, in general, be directed to the Father. The revisers did not retain the collect for use in the Assumption Vigil Mass, but assigned it to the Common of the Blessed Virgin used in Advent. Curiously, the version of the collect in the second typical edition of the Vatican II missal still addresses Christ, but as "Domine Iesu" [Lord Jesus], not "Deus" [God]. The prayer is otherwise unchanged. In the third typical edition the addressee of the collect is again "Deus," but now it is God, the Father, as other changes to the text make clear.[21]

---

20. Moeller et al., *Corpus Orationem*, vol. III, #2167.

21. **Deus**, qui virginalem aulam beatae Mariae, in qua **Verbum tuum habitaret**, eligere dignatus es, da, quaesumus, ut, eius nos defensione munitos, iucundos facias interesse eius commemorationi. [**O God**, who deigned to choose the virginal womb of the blessed Mary in which **your Word might dwell**, grant, we beseech you, that shielded by her protection, you may cause us to take part in her feast with joy.]

To replace the 1962 collect of the Vigil of the Assumption, the revisers selected the collect assigned to day Mass of the Assumption in the 1733 missal used by the monks of Cluny,[22] but edited it for use in the new missal.

1962: Vigil of the Assumption	2008: Vigil of the Assumption	*Missale Cluniacense (1733):* Assumption (Day Mass)
Deus, qui virginalem aulam beatae Mariae, in qua habitare, eligere dignatus es: da, quaesumus; ut, sua nos defensione munitos, iucundos facias suae interesse festivitati.	Deus, qui **beatam** Virginem Mariam, eius humilitatem respiciens, ad hanc gratiam evexisti, ut Unigenitus tuus ex ipsa secundum carnem nasceretur, et hodierna die superexcellenti gloria coronasti, **eius nobis precibus concede, ut, redemptionis tuae mysterio salvati,** a te exaltari mereamur.	Deus, qui Virginem Mariam, ejus humilitatem respiciens, ad hanc gratiam evexisti, ut Unigenitus tuus ex ipsa secundum carnem nascereretur, et hodierna die superexcellenti gloria coronasti: concede propitius, ut ejus precibis et imitatione, nosmetipsos in omnibus humiliantes, a te exaltari mereamur.
O God, who deigned to choose the virginal womb of blessed Mary in which to dwell: grant, we beseech you, that shielded by her protection, you may cause us to take part in [to enter into] her feast with delight.	O God, who, looking upon her humility, brought the **Blessed** Virgin Mary to this grace, that as your Only-Begotten Son was born from her according the flesh, and on this day have crowned her with surpassing glory, grant us through her prayers that, **having been saved through the mystery of your redemption,** we may be made worthy to be glorified/lifted up/ exalted by you.	O God, who, looking upon her humility, brought the Virgin Mary to this grace, that as your Only-Begotten Son was born from her according the flesh, and on this day have crowned her with surpassing glory: mercifully grant that as, through her prayers and in imitation of her, we humble ourselves in all things, we may be deemed worthy to be glorified/raised up/by you.

The significant differences among these three texts can be categorized and summarized as follows:

22. Johnson, "Sources," p. 135.

1. Between the 1962 collect and the others: the 1962 collect asks for protection and the others do not.
2. Between the Cluniac collect and that of the Vatican II missal: the Cluny collect links our being raised up or glorified by God in the next life to our humbling ourselves in all things in this life which we do in imitation of Mary and through her intercession; the Vatican II collect does not.
3. Between the Vatican II collect and the others: the new collect makes explicit mention to our being saved through the mystery of Christ's redemption and the others do not.

The reviser's decision to substitute "grant us through her prayers that, having been saved through the mystery of your redemption" for "for mercifully grant that as, through her prayers and in imitation of her, we humble ourselves in all things," produces a very different prayer in at least three important ways:

1. The statement of fact and petition are no longer parallel, for the parallelism of the Cluny prayer juxtaposes Mary's humility and our own.
2. Mary is no longer presented as an example for us.
3. There is no longer a reminder that the graced cultivation of humility prepares one to be raised up by God.

b. *Feasts of Our Lady*
(1) *The Nativity.* The two feasts of Our Lady that fall outside the proper seasons are the Visitation and the Nativity. The 1962 missal assigns the same collect to both feasts, changing only the name of the day according to the occasion:

1962: Visitation and Nativity of the Blessed Virgin Mary	
Famulis tuis, quaesumus, Domine, caelestis gratiae munus impertire: ut, quibus beatae Virginis partus exstitit salutis exordium; Visitationis/ Nativitatis eius votiva solemnitas, pacis tribuat incrementum.	Bestow, we beseech you, O Lord, the gift of heavenly grace upon your servants so that, as the labor of the Virgin appeared as the beginning of salvation, the longed-for solemnity of her Visitation/Nativity may grant an increase of peace to them.

The revisers retained this generic Marian collect and assigned it to the Nativity of the Blessed Virgin after making one change: they substituted the word "feast" for "solemnity," thereby bringing the wording of the collect into conformity with the rank of the day.

(2) *The Visitation.* Having assigned the collect formerly used on both the Nativity and the Visitation to the feast of the Nativity, the revisers composed a new collect for the Visitation that draws on the Visitation collect of the *Proprium Bracarense* 2.7.[23] The collect they chose is not unique to the *Proprium Bracarense*, but is also found in several fifteenth- and sixteenth-century codices.[24] The revisers altered the statement of fact of the original prayer and supplied a new petition.

Proprium Bracarense 2.7 and *CO* VI, #3936	2008: Visitation
Omnipotens, sempiterne Deus: qui ex *abundantia caritatis* beatam Mariam *tuo filio fecundatam* ad *salutationem* Elisabeth inspirasti, praesta, quaesumus, ut per eius *visitationem, donis caelestibus repleamur et ab omnibus adversitatibus eruamur.*	Omnipotens sempiterne Deus, qui beatam Virginem Mariam, **Filium tuum gestantem**, ad **visitandam** Elisabeth inspirasti, praesta, quaesumus, ut, **afflanti Spiritui obsequentes, cum ipsa te semper magnificare possimus.**
Almighty, everlasting God: who inspired the blessed Mary, *fruitful with your son*, to greet Elizabeth out of an abundance of love, grant, we beseech you, that *through her visitation we may be filled with heavenly gifts and rescued from all that opposes us.*	Almighty, everlasting God, who inspired the blessed Mary, **as she carried your Son, to visit Elizabeth**; grant, we beseech you, that **submitting to the inspiration of the Spirit, we may be able with her to magnify you always.**

Text common to both collects is in regular type, that which is unique to the original prayer is italicized, and what was supplied by the modern editors appears in bold-face type.

The revisers made three modifications to the statement of fact. First, they omitted mention of Mary's abundant charity. Second, they changed the participle modifying Mary. Variants appear in the ancient witnesses. Some, like the text above, describe Mary as *fecundatam*, fertile or fruitful, "with your son." Others say she was *impraegnatam*, or "pregnant with your Son." The revisers substituted *gestantem*, bearing or carrying. This necessitated rendering "your Son" in the accusative case.

---

23. Ibid., p. 120.

24. Moeller et al., *Corpus Orationem*, vol. VI, #3936. The prayer is also found in: *Missale Cisterciense* (1487), *Breviarium Cisterciense* (1494), *Breviarium Braccarense* (1494 and 1549) and *Missale Romanum* (1530 and 1540). I am indebted to James Monti for the information on the uses of the Cistercians, Braga and Rome. The last is also cited in Robert Lippe and Henry A. Wilson, *Missale Romanum Mediolani 1474*, vol. 2 (London: Harrison, 1907), p. 208.

The third change replaces the noun *salutationem* with the gerundive *visitandam*. In the original prayer God inspires Mary's *greeting* at which, when it reached Elizabeth's ears, the babe in her womb leapt and Elizabeth herself was filled with the Holy Spirit so that she responded: "Blessed are you among women, and blessed is the fruit of your womb! And why is this granted me, that the mother of my Lord should come to me?" (Luke 1:42–43, RSV). In the revised oration, God inspires Mary's *visit* to Elizabeth—the word from which the feast takes its name.[25]

The petition of the source prayer asks that, through Mary's visitation, we may be filled with heavenly gifts and rescued from all that is hostile to us or that opposes us *(omnibus adversitatibus)*. The newly composed petition alludes both to Mary's docility to divine inspiration (see the statement of fact) and to Luke's Gospel which tells us that Mary responded to Elizabeth's greeting with: "My soul magnifies the Lord..." It asks that we, like Mary, will be submissive to the promptings of the Holy Spirit and will, with Mary, magnify the Lord.

There are two things to note in this new petition. First, the prayer uses the words of scripture. In his essay, Dumas says that the revisers inserted words of scripture into new sanctoral compositions particularly when the saint in question was a New Testament figure.[26] Second, the prayer asks that we do what the saint did. We will see additional examples of both kinds of revision as we proceed.

4. *Solemnities and Feasts of Angels and Saints*

a. *Solemnities of Saints*

We come now to the solemnities honoring saints. There are four: All Saints, St Joseph, the Nativity of St John the Baptist, and Sts Peter and Paul. In both missals, the latter two are accompanied by vigil Masses. There was no change to the collect of All Saints, so we shall not discuss it.

(1) *St Joseph, Spouse of the Blessed Virgin Mary.* In his essay, Antoine Dumas states that new prayers were composed for the new missal when the texts in the former missal were particularly weak [particulièrement faible] and no fitting substitutes could be found in the old sacramentaries.

---

25. The version of the collect in *Missale Mixtum Toletanum 1499*, p. cccxxx, col. 1 substitutes *visitationem* (not *visitandam*) for *salutationem*. The volume is digitized by the Biblioteca Nacional as part of their digital collection, Biblioteca digital Hispanica, and is available at http://bdh-rd.bne.es/viewer.vm?id=0000176351&page=1. It is through the kindness of James Monti that I know of this.

26. Dumas, "Les Oraisons," p. 269; Pristas, "The Orations," p. 637.

In this context, he specifically mentions St Joseph.[27] Dumas does not say why the 1962 collect was judged to be so weak, but two of the 1966 policy decisions, that the texts of orations not be repeated and that prayers be addressed to the Father, required that revisers give attention to the prayer.

1962: Saint Joseph	2008: Saint Joseph New Composition
Sanctissimae Genetricis tuae Sponsi, quaesumus, Domine, meritis adjuvemur: ut, quod possibilitas nostra non obtinet, ejus nobis intercessionibus donetur.	**Praesta, quaesumus, omnipotens Deus, ut humanae salutis mysteria, cuius primordia beati Ioseph fideli custodiae commisisti, Ecclesia tua, ipso intercedente, iugiter servet implenda.**
May we be assisted, O Lord, we beseech you, by the merits of the Spouse of your Most Holy Mother: so that what we are not able to gain of our own power, may be given to us through his intercession.	**Grant, we beseech you, almighty God, that the mysteries of human salvation, whose beginnings you entrusted to the faithful protection of blessed Joseph, your Church may, through his intercession, ever preserve unharmed as they are being fulfilled.**

The two are altogether different prayers. The 1962 collect, addressed to Christ, is a straightforward request for St Joseph's intercession which includes a confession of our own weakness. It has exactly the same petition as the 1962 collect for St Matthew which, however, was not retained in the present missal.[28] The new composition also seeks Joseph's intercession, specifically on behalf of the Church, as she has been entrusted until the end of time with the task that God committed to Joseph at the beginning: custodial care of the "mysteries of human salvation."

27. Dumas, "Les Oraisons," p. 269; Pristas, "The Orations," p. 638.

28. I checked two concordances for the word "*possibilitas.*" The word is not listed in Thaddäus Schnitker and Wolfgang Slaby (eds), *Concordantia Verbalia Missalis Romani: Partes Euchologicae* (Münster: Aschendorff, 1983), p. 1898, which, however, was published before the appearance of the *editio tertia*. Toniolo Alessandro manages a website called liturgia.it (http://www.liturgia.it) at which there are links to concordances of the Tridentine and Vatican II missals, as well as to several ancient Latin sacramentaries. The concordance of the 2008 reprint of the third typical edition of the *Missale Romanum*, at http://www.rifugiodelleanime.org/m3/, shows no presence of the word *possibilitas*. The collect is not used in the Vatican II missals.

(2) *The Nativity of St John the Baptist.* The collect assigned to the Vigil Mass is the same in both missals. The collect of the day Mass, however, was edited. The redactors replaced the existing statement of fact with another—partly of their own composition and partly taken from the collect of the day Mass of the Nativity of John the Baptist in an ancient codex known as the Veronese or Leonine Sacramentary.[29]

1962: Nativity of St John the Baptist	2008: Nativity of St John the Baptist	*Veronense* 236: Nativity of St John the Baptist
Deus, qui *praesentem diem honorabilem nobis in beati Ioannis nativitate fecisti*: da populis tuis spiritualium gratiam gaudiorum; et omnium fidelium mentes dirige in viam salutis *aeternae*.	Deus, qui BEATUM IOANNEM BAPTISTAM suscitasti, ut PERFECTAM PLEBEM CHRISTO DOMINO PRAEPARARET, da populis tuis spiritalium gratiam gaudiorum, et omnium fidelium mentes dirige in viam salutis **et pacis**	Omnipotens et misericors deus, qui BEATUM BAPTISTAM IOHANNEM tua prouidentia destinasti, UT PERFECTAM PLEBEM CHRISTO DOMINO PRAEPARARET: da, quaesumus, ut familia tua huius intercessione praeconis et a peccatis omnibus exuatur, et [ad] eum quem profetauit inueniant
O God, who *have made the present day honorable for us in the nativity of blessed John*, grant to your people the grace of spiritual joys: and direct the minds of all the faithful into the way of *eternal* salvation.	O God, **who raised up BLESSED JOHN THE BAPTIST, THAT HE MIGHT PREPARE A PERFECT PEOPLE FOR CHRIST, THE LORD,** grant to your people the grace of spiritual joys, and direct the minds of all the faithful into the way of salvation **and peace.**	Almighty and merciful God, who, in your providence chose the BLESSED JOHN THE BAPTIST THAT HE MIGHT PREPARE A PERFECT PEOPLE FOR CHRIST THE LORD: grant, we beseech you, that your family, through the intercession of this herald, may be set free of all sins and find him whom he [John] foretold.

29. Johnson, "Sources," p. 24. The modern critical edition of the Veronese Sacramentary is Leo Cunibert Mohlberg, Leo Eizenhöfer and Petrus Siffrin (eds), *Sacramentarium Veronense*, Rerum Ecclesasticarum Documentas, Series maior, Fontes 1 (Rome: Casa Editrice Herder, 1956). The *Veronense* is also available at http://www.rifugiodelleanime.org/veweb/. Hereafter the Veronese Sacramentary is abbreviated *Ver.*

The revision introduces two paraphrases of Luke's Gospel: "…prepare a perfect people for the Lord" from Gabriel's words to Zachariah (Luke 1:17),[30] and "direct…into the way of peace" from Zachariah's canticle (Luke 1:79).[31]

(3) *Sts Peter and Paul.* A different, not a new, collect is assigned to the vigil Mass of Sts Peter and Paul, and the 1962 collect of the day Mass was edited.

(a) *Vigil Mass.* The 1962 collect for the vigil of Sts Peter and Paul was retained in the new missal but transferred to the feast of the Chair of St Peter. To replace it, the revisers chose a prayer that is found in codices that date from the sixth or seventh century and later, but used on the feast of St Andrew.[32] In some ancient codices a variant serves as a prayer honoring one or many (unnamed) apostles.[33] The collect does not seem to have been used in honor of Sts Peter and Paul before the post-Vatican II reform.

1962: Vigil of Sts Peter and Paul	2008: Vigil of Sts Peter and Paul	*Ver* 1219, Hadrianum 774: St Andrew
Praesta, quaesumus, omnipotens Deus: ut nullis nos permittas perturbationibus concuti; quos in apostolicae confessionis petra solidasti.	Da nobis, quaesumus, Domine Deus noster, **beatorum apostolorum Petri et Pauli** intercessionibus sublevari, ut, per quos Ecclesiae tuae superni muneris rudimenta donasti, per eos subsidia perpetuae salutis impendas.	Da nobis, quaesumus, domine deus noster, <u>beati apostoli tui·Andreae</u> intercessionibus subleuari; ut per quos aeclesiae tuae superni muneris rudimenta donasti, per eos subsidia perpetuae salutis inpendas

30. Vulgate: "parare Domino plebem perfectam" [to prepare for the Lord a perfect people].

31. Vulgate: "dirigendos pedes nostros in viam pacis" [our feet being directed in the way of peace].

32. Johnson, "Sources," p. 126 names *Veronense* 1219, *Hadrianum* 774. The modern critical edition of the Hadrianum is found in Jean Deshusses, *Le sacramentaire grégorien: ses principales formes d'après les plus anciens manuscrits*, 3rd edn (Fribourg: Éditions universitaires, 1992), vol. 1. Also at http://www.rifugiodelleanime. org/grh/.

33. Moeller et al., *Corpus Orationem*, vol. II, #993.

Grant, we beseech you, almighty God: that you may permit us, whom you have founded on the rock of apostolic faith, to be shaken by no disturbance.	Grant us, we beseech you, O Lord, our God, to be sustained by the intercessions **of the blessed apostles Peter and Paul**, so that, as you gave the beginnings of heavenly office to your Church through them, so may you through them extend the supports of everlasting salvation.	Grant us, we beseech you, O Lord, our God, to be sustained by the intercession of <u>your blessed apostle Andrew</u>; so that, as you gave the beginnings of heavenly office to your Church through them, so may you through them extend the supports of everlasting salvation.

The revisers made two changes to the ancient collect:

1. As required by the new setting, they rendered "blessed apostle" in the plural and substituted the "Peter and Paul" for "Andrew."
2. They removed the personal possessive pronoun "your"—that is, Peter and Paul are not described as "your" (God's) apostles.

Somewhat curiously, the plural pronouns of the dependent clause, "so that, as you gave the beginnings of heavenly office...<u>through them</u> [*per quos*], so may you <u>through them</u> [*per eos*] extend the supports..." appear in the ancient version of the collect which names only Andrew.

(b) *Day Mass*. Dumas, in a subsection of his essay entitled "Adaptation," states:

> ...one will note many transfers of orations from one Mass to another for the sake of a better fit. For example, the overflowing joy expressed in the former missal for a secondary apostle like Saint Bartholomew...is in a better place in the collect of the holy apostles Peter and Paul at whose solemnity the whole church rejoices.[34]

The pre- and post-Vatican II collects for the day, as well as the 1962 collect of the feast of St Bartholomew that Dumas mentions, are below:

---

34. "Les Oraisons," p. 268: On remarquera...plusieurs transferts d'oraisons d'une messe à l'autre pour une meilleure adaptation. Par exemple, la joie débordante exprimée dans l'ancien Missel pour un apôtre secondaire comme saint Barthélemy... est en meilleure place dans la collecte des apôtres saints Pierre et Paul, dont la solennité réjouit l'Église entière. See: Pristas, "The Orations," p. 636.

1962: Sts Peter and Paul	2008: Sts Peter and Paul	1962: St Bartholomew
Deus, *qui hodiernam diem Apostolorum tuorum Petri et Pauli martyrio consecrasti:* da Ecclesiae tuae, eorum in omnibus sequi praeceptum; per quos religionis sumpsit exordium	Deus, QUI HUIUS DIEI VENERANDAM SANCTAMQUE LAETITIAM IN apostolorum Petri et Pauli sollemnitate TRIBUISTI, da Ecclesiae tuae eorum in omnibus sequi praeceptum, per quos religionis sumpsit exordium.	Omnipotens sempiterne Deus, QUI HUIUS DIEI VENERANDAM SANCTAMQUE LAETITIAM IN beati Apostoli tui Bartholomaei festivitate TRIBUISTI: da Ecclesiae tuae, quaesumus; et amare quod credidit, et praedicare quod docuit
O God, *who made this day holy through the martyrdom of your Apostles Peter and Paul*; grant to your Church in all things to follow the bidding of them through whom she received the beginning of religion.	O God, WHO ON THIS DAY HAVE IMPARTED REVERENT AND HOLY JOY IN THE solemnity of the apostles Peter and Paul, grant to your Church in all things to follow the bidding of them through whom she received the beginning of religion.	Almighty, everlasting God, WHO ON THIS DAY HAVE IMPARTED REVERENT AND HOLY JOY IN THE feast of your blessed apostle Bartholomew: grant to your Church, we beseech you, both to love what he believed and proclaim what he taught.

As the statement of fact of the 1962 collect makes clear, this day commemorates the martyrdom of two saints who, although they did not die on the same day, "were as one"—as St Augustine puts it.[35] For the reasons Dumas gives, the revisers replaced the 1962 statement of fact about their martyrdom with a statement from the collect which, from at least the eighth century, had been prayed on the feast of St Bartholomew.[36] In addition, they made three other changes:

1. As required by the new setting, they rendered "blessed apostle" in the plural and substituted the "Peter and Paul" for "Bartholomew."
2. They again removed the personal possessive pronoun "your."
3. They brought the wording of the prayer into conformity with the rank of the day by replacing "feast" with "solemnity."

35. Augustine, *Sermo* 295.7, Migne, *Patrologia Latina*, vol. 38, col. 1352, quoted in Catholic Church, *The Liturgy of the Hours: According to the Roman Rite*, vol. 3 (New York: Catholic Book Publishing, 1975), p. 1504.

36. Moeller et al., *Corpus Orationem*, vol. VI, #3952B. Forty-two different codices dating from the eighth century to 1754 are listed.

b. *Feasts of Angels and Saints*

There are fourteen feast days honoring angels and saints. The number of days given to the archangels Gabriel, Michael and Raphael was reduced from three in the 1962 missal, in which they are honored individually,[37] to one in the Vatican II missals, in which they honored together in a single feast on 29 September. The collect assigned to the present feast is the same collect that is used in the earlier missals on the day dedicated to St Michael. No change was made to the prayer, so we shall proceed to the feasts honoring the saints.

Of the feasts celebrating saints, thirteen honor apostles and evangelists. A quick comparative examination of the collects assigned to these days in the two missals finds: that one collect, the one assigned to the feast of St Andrew, was left unchanged; that six collects were replaced with different prayers; and that only the petitions of the remaining six underwent substantive revision. The examination of collects assigned to feasts of apostles and evangelists that follows first considers the old and new collects of feasts to which a different prayer was assigned in the new missal and then examines the old and new texts of collects in which the only substantive changes were made to the petitions of the prayers.

(1) *Feasts of Apostles and Evangelists: entirely different collects*

(a) *The Chair of St Peter.* As we noted above, the 1962 collect of the Vigil Mass of Sts Peter and Paul is assigned to the feast of the Chair of St Peter in the revised missal.

1962: Chair of St Peter	2008: Chair of St Peter
Deus, qui beato Petro Apostolo tuo, collatis clavibus regni caelestis, ligandi atque solvendi pontificium tradidisti: concede; ut, intercessionis eius auxilio, a peccatorum nostrorum nexibus liberemur.	**Praesta, quaesumus, omnipotens Deus: ut nullis nos permittas perturbationibus concuti; quos in apostolicae confessionis petra solidasti.**
O God, who, in giving the keys of the kingdom of heaven to Peter your Apostle, entrusted [him with] the pontifical authority of binding and loosing: grant that through the help of his intercession, we may be set free from the entanglements of our sins.	**Grant, we beseech you, almighty God: that you permit us, whom you have founded on the rock of apostolic faith, to be shaken by no disturbance.**

37. The three are 24 March (Gabriel), 29 September (Michael) and 24 October (Raphael).

The two prayers are very different. The 1962 collect praises God for giving the power of the keys to Peter and asks that we may be set free from the entanglements of our sin. The Vatican II collect praises God for establishing us on the rock of apostolic faith, and asks that we may be shaken by no disturbance. The 1962 collect for this day was retained in the Vatican II missals where it serves as the collect for the votive Mass of St Peter.

(b) *St James, Apostle*. The revisers replaced the 1962 collect of St James with the collect assigned to the same feast in the *Missale Parisiense (1738)*,[38] which they edited slightly.

1962	2008	*Missale Parisiense (1738)*
Esto, Domine, plebi tuae sanctificator et custos: ut, Apostoli tui Iacobi munita praesidiis, et conversatione tibi placeat, et secura mente deserviat	Omnipotens sempiterne Deus, qui Apostolorum tuorum primitias beati Iacobi sanguine dedicasti, da, quaesumus, Ecclesiae tuae **ipsius** confessione firmari, et **iugiter** patrociniis confoveri.	Omnipotens sempiterne Deus, qui Apostolorum tuorum primitias beati Iacobi sanguine dedicasti, da, quaesumus, Ecclesiae tuae <u>ejus semper et</u> confessione firmari, et patrociniis confoveri.
Be, O Lord, the sanctifier and guardian of your people: so that defended by the protection of your Apostle James, they may please you with their manner of life and serve you with a steadfast mind.	Almighty, everlasting God, who consecrated the first fruits of your Apostles with the blood of blessed James, grant your Church, we beseech you, to be strengthened by his confession and **continually** supported by his patronage.	Almighty, everlasting God, who consecrated the first fruits of your Apostles with the blood of blessed James, grant your Church, we beseech you, both ever to be strengthened by his confession and supported by his patronage.

The 1962 collect has no statement of fact. The two-part petition, the request and the result of the request being granted, comprises the whole of the prayer. The logic of the collect is: if God sanctifies and guards his people, they will, defended by the protection of James, be able to please

38. Johnson, "Sources," p. 130. The modern critical edition is: C. Johnson and A. Ward, *Missale Parisiense anno 1738 publici iuris factum* (Rome: CLV-Edizioni Liturgiche, 1993).

him with their lives and serve him with steadfast minds. This collect, which was used on the feast of St James from the eighth century until the twentieth, was not incorporated into the Vatican II missal.[39]

The Vatican II collect is an entirely different prayer. The statement of fact recalls the tradition that James, head of the primitive Church in Jerusalem, was the first of the apostles to be martyred. The petition is a somewhat generic request that the Church universal be strengthened and supported by his heavenly patronage.

(c) *St Bartholomew, Apostle.* We saw above that the revisers took the invocation of the 1962 collect assigned to the feast of St Bartholomew and adapted it for use as the new invocation of the revised collect assigned to the Solemnity of Sts Peter and Paul. This having been done, the policy that texts of orations not be repeated required the revisers, at the very least, to supply a new statement of fact for the collect honoring St Bartholomew. They composed a new prayer.[40]

1962: St Bartholomew	2008: St Bartholomew New Composition
Omnipotens sempiterne Deus, qui huius diei venerandam sanctamque laetitiam in beati Apostoli tui Bartholomaei festivitate tribuisti: da Ecclesiae tuae, quaesumus; et amare quod credidit, et praedicare quod docuit.	**Robora in nobis, Domine, fidem, qua Filio tuo beatus Bartholomaeus apostolus sincero animo adhaesit, et praesta, ut, ipso deprecante, Ecclesia tua cunctis gentibus salutis fiat sacramentum**
Almighty, everlasting God, who on this day have given [us] reverent and holy joy in the feast of your blessed Apostle Bartholomew: grant to your Church, we beseech you, both to love what he believed and to proclaim what he taught.	**Strengthen in us, O Lord, the faith by which the apostle, blessed Bartholomew, clung to your Son with his whole soul, and grant that, through his prayers, your Church may become the sacrament of salvation for all nations.**

The new collect is another which is comprised, except for the invocation ("O Lord"), entirely of petition.

The most striking difference between the two prayers, indeed between the Vatican II collect for the feast of St Bartholomew and every other prayer we have considered here, is that the petition is not for something to

39. Moeller et al., *Corpus Orationem*, vol. V, #2445.

40. Johnson, "Sources," p. 137. The 1962 petition of the collect of St Bartholomew does not appear in the revised missal.

be given to us or to the Church, or accomplished in either or both, but for the Church itself to be something for the world—namely, the sacrament of salvation. Since Catholics understand the Church already to be the universal sacrament of salvation,[41] the intended meaning of the petition is not clear. Perhaps it is to be understood as a prayer for the sacrament of the Church to have its full effect.

(d) *St Matthew, Apostle and Evangelist.* Cuthbert Johnson identifies the collect assigned to the feast of St Matthew in the *Missale Parisiense (1738)* as the source for the Vatican II collect for the feast, which he describes as a new composition.[42]

1962: St Matthew	2008: St Matthew	*Missale Parisiense (1738)*: St Matthew
Beati Apostoli et Evangelistae Matthaei, Domine, precibus adiuvemur: ut, quod possibilitas nostra non obtinet, eius nobis intercessione donetur	Deus, qui ineffabili misericordia beatum Matthaeum ex publicano Apostolum es dignatus eligere, da nobis, eius exemplo et intercessione suffultis, ut, **te sequentes,** tibi firmiter adhaerere mereamur.	Deus, qui ineffabili misericordia beatum Matthaeum ex publicano Apostolum eligere dignaturs es, da nobis, eius exemplo et intercessione suffultis, ut, post te, relictis omnibus, ambulantes, tibi firmiter adhaerere mereamur.
O Lord, may we be helped by the prayers of the blessed Apostle and Evangelist Matthew: so that, what our own power is not able to obtain, may be given to us through his intercession.	O God, who, with ineffable mercy, deigned to choose the blessed Apostle Matthew away from tax-gathering, grant us that, supported by his example and intercession, we may cling to you steadfastly **as we follow you**.	O God who, with ineffable mercy, deigned to choose the blessed Apostle Matthew away from tax-gathering, grant us that, supported by his example and intercession, we may cling to you steadfastly as, having left everything, we walk behind/follow you.

As noted above, the petition of the 1962 collect of St Matthew is the same as that of the 1962 collect of St Joseph which was also replaced with a new composition.

41. *Catechism of the Catholic Church* n. 774.
42. Johnson, "Sources," p. 142. The prayer is *Missale Parisienne (1738)*, #3489.

The collect of the *Missale Parisiense* draws on Luke's presentation of Matthew. Most obvious is the mention of Matthew's former profession.[43] But the Parisian prayer also applies Vulgate description of what Levi/ Matthew did when Jesus called him, *relictis omnibus* [with everything having been left behind],[44] to those who make the prayer. The omission of this phrase from the revised version weakens the moral import of the prayer.

(e) *St Luke, Evangelist.* Cuthbert Johnson identifies the Vatican II collect for the feast of St Luke as a new composition.[45]

1962: St Luke	2008: St Luke
Interveniat pro nobis, quaesumus, Domine, sanctus tuus Lucas Evangelista: qui crucis mortificationem iugiter in suo corpore, pro tui nominis honore, portavit	**Domine Deus, qui beatum Lucam elegisti, ut praedicatione et scriptis mysterium tuae in pauperes dilectionis revelaret, concede, ut, qui tuo iam nomine gloriantur, cor unum et anima una esse perseverent, et omnes gentes tuam mereantur videre salutem.**
May your holy Evangelist Luke intercede for us, we beseech you, O Lord: who for the honor of your name continually bore in his own body the mortification of the Cross.	**O Lord God, who chose blessed Luke, that he might reveal in preaching and writing the mystery of your love for the poor, grant that they who already glory in your name, may persevere in being of one heart and one soul, and all nations may be deemed worthy to see your salvation.**

The 1962 collect is an unadorned request for St Luke's intercession that praises St Luke for his union with Christ in suffering. Used in the Latin West from the eighth century until the twentieth, it is not included in the revised missals.[46] The new composition does not seek Luke's intercession, but twice incorporates the words of his writings: "one heart and one soul"

---

43. Luke 5:27: et post haec exiit et vidit *publicanum* nomine Levi sedentem ad teloneum et ait illi sequere me (Vulgate). [After this he went out, and saw a tax collector, named Levi, sitting at the tax office; and he said to him, "Follow me." (RSV)].

44. Luke 5:28: et <u>relictis omnibus surgens secutus est eum.</u>

45. Johnson, "Sources," p. 148.

46. Moeller et al., *Corpus Orationem*, vol. V, #3180.

from Acts 4:32, and "see your salvation" from Simeon's canticle (Luke 2:30).[47]

(f) *St John, Apostle and Evangelist.* The last of the apostolic feasts to which a different collect is assigned in the new missal is that of St John, Apostle and Evangelist. The post-Vatican collect is a different, but not a new, prayer. It is a minimally edited version of an oration that was widely used in antiquity from at least the sixth or seventh century.[48]

1962: St John	2008: St John	*Ver* 1274 = *CO* III, #1981
Ecclesiam tuam, Domine, benignus illustra: ut beati Ioannis Apostoli tui et Evangelistae illuminata doctrinis, ad dona perveniat sempiterna	Deus, qui **per beatum apostolum Ioannem** Verbi tui nobis arcana reserasti, praesta, quaesumus, ut, quod ille nostris auribus excellenter infudit, intellegentiae competentis eruditione capiamus.	Deus, qui per os beati apostoli Ioannis evangelistae Verbi tui nobis arcana reserasti, praesta, quaesumus, ut, quod ille nostris auribus excellenter infudit, intellegentiae competentis eruditione capiamus.
Kindly illuminate your Church, O Lord: so that having been enlightened by the teaching of blessed John, your Apostle and Evangelist, she may attain unto everlasting gifts.	O God, who **through the blessed apostle John** disclosed the mysteries of your Word, grant, we beseech you, that we may grasp by instruction with proper understanding what he so excellently presented for our hearing/ to our ears.	O God, who through the mouth of blessed apostle John the evangelist disclosed the mysteries of your Word, grant, we beseech you, that we may grasp by instruction with proper understanding what he so excellently presented for our hearing/ to our ears.

The 1962 collect, which is not found in the revised missals, was widely used in antiquity from the eighth century.[49] Apart from the invocation, it is comprised entirely of the request and its desired result. Its ultimate object

---

47. Acts 4:32 Vulgate: Multitudinis autem credentium erat cor unum et anima una [Now the company of those who believed were of one heart and soul (RSV)]. Luke 2:30 Vulgate: …quia viderunt oculi mei salutare tuum […for mine eyes have seen thy salvation (RSV)].

48. Johnson, "Sources," p. 160 and Moeller et al., *Corpus Orationem*, vol. III, #981.

49. Moeller et al., *Corpus Orationem*, vol. IV, #2416c.

is that the Church attain "everlasting gifts." The new collect asks that we—that is, those who pray the prayer and those for whom it is prayed—may properly understand the teaching of the evangelist.

(2) *Feasts of Apostles and Evangelists: Different Petitions.* The remaining five festal collects of apostles, as well as that of the evangelist Mark, were edited. In every case the only substantive changes were to the petitions. Modifications to the invocations and statements of fact consisted of:

1. Omitting the possessive "your,"—for example, "your apostle" becomes "apostle";
2. replacing "solemnity," or the equivalent, with "feast," to make the wording of the collect conform to the rank of the day;
3. in one case, changing the invocation from "Lord" to "Almighty God," and omitting "we beseech you";
4. in the final case, omitting the names of the apostles from the statement of fact.

The new and revised collects for these six feast days are presented below with minimal comment.

(a) *The Conversion of St Paul*. The modern editors made no change at all to the invocation and statement of fact of the 1962 collect for this feast, but supplied a new petition.

1962: Conversion of St Paul	2008: Conversion of St Paul
Deus, qui universum mundum beati Pauli Apostoli praedicatione docuisti: da nobis, quaesumus; ut, *qui eius hodie Conversionem colimus, per eius ad te exempla gradiamur.*	Deus, qui universum mundum beati Pauli apostoli praedicatione docuisti, da nobis, quaesumus, ut, **cuius conversionem hodie celebramus, per eius ad te exempla gradientes, tuae simus mundo testes veritatis.**
O God who taught the whole world through the preaching of blessed Paul the Apostle, grant, we beseech you: that, *we who celebrate his Conversion today may, through his example, make our way to you.*	O God who taught the whole world through the preaching of blessed Paul the Apostle, grant us, we beseech you, that, **making our way to you through his example, we may be witnesses of your truth in the world.**

Without omitting the substance of anything in the 1962 prayer, the revision adds the request that we, like St Paul, may be witnesses of God's truth in the world. This change is somewhat like the change made to the source of the new Visitation collect whereby we ask that, submitting to the prompting of the Spirit, we may be able with Mary to magnify God always. Both changes are in service of producing prayers which ask that we may do what scripture tells us the saint did.

(b) *St Mark, Evangelist.*

1962: St Mark, Evangelist	2008: St Mark, Evangelist
Deus, qui beatum Marcum Evangelistam *tuum* evangelicae praedicationis gratia sublimasti: tribue, quaesumus; eius nos *semper et* eruditione proficere *et oratione defendi.*	Deus, qui beatum Marcum evangelistam tuum evangelicae praedicationis gratia sublimasti, tribue, quaesumus, eius nos **eruditione ita proficere, ut vestigia Christi fideliter sequamur.**
O God, who lifted up blessed Mark, your evangelist, through grace of proclaiming the gospel, grant us *always*, we beseech you, *both* to profit by his instruction *and to be defended by [his] prayer.*	O God, who lifted up blessed Mark, your evangelist, through grace of proclaiming the gospel, grant us so to profit by his instruction **that we may follow faithfully in the footsteps of Christ.**

The editors left the possessive pronoun (*your* evangelist) of the original statement of fact in place. The Vatican II request that we follow in the footsteps of Christ replaces the 1962 petition that we be defended by St Mark's prayer. The Vatican II petition posits a causal relationship between profiting from Mark's instruction and following Christ, and makes us active in a way that the 1962 petition does not.

(c) *Sts Philip and James.*

1962: Sts Philip and James	2008: Sts Philip and James	*Missale Parisiense (1738) 2555*
Deus, qui non annua Apostolorum *tuorum* Philippi et Iacobi *solemnitate* laetificas: *praesta, quaesumus; ut, quorum gaudemus meritis, instruamur exemplis.*	Deus, qui nos annua apostolorum Philippi et Iacobi festivitate laetificas, <u>da nobis, ipsorum precibus, in Unigeniti tui passione et resurrectione consortium,</u> **ut ad perpetuam tui visionem pervenire mereamur.**	Deus, qui nos annua apostolorum *tuorum* Philippi et Iacobi *solemnitate* laetificas, <u>da nobis, ipsorum precibus, in Unigeniti tui passione et resurrectione consortium, ut ad paratam in domo tua mansionem hereditate consequamur.</u>

O God, who make us joyful in the yearly *solemnity* of *your* Apostles, Philip and James, *grant we beseech you, that we may be instructed by the example of those in whose merits we rejoice.*	O God, who make us joyful in the yearly **feast** of the apostles Philip and James, grant us through their prayers a share in the passion and resurrection of your Only-Begotten Son, so that we may **be able to arrive at the everlasting vision of you.**	O God, who make us joyful in the yearly *solemnity* of *your* Apostles, Philip and James, grant us through their prayers a share in the passion and resurrection of your Only-Begotten Son, so that we may attain unto the mansion prepared in your house as an inheritance.

The 1962 collect has the same invocation and statement of fact, with the appropriate accommodation, as in the 1962 collect of the Exaltation of the Cross discussed above. The only revisions made to the first part of the collect, which is the same in both the Tridentine and Parisian missals, are those mentioned above: "your" is omitted from the Vatican II prayer, and the word "solemnity" is changed to "feast." The change that the revisers made to the petition substitutes a reference to the Beatific Vision ("everlasting vision of you") for the Parisian missal's mention of a heavenly mansion in the Father's house—an allusion to John 14:2, the verse in which Jesus tells his apostles he is going to prepare a place for them.

(d) *St Matthias, Apostle.*

1962: St Matthias	2008: St Matthias
Deus, qui beatum Matthiam Apostolorum *tuorum* collegio sociasti: *tribue, quaesumus; ut* eius interventione, *tuae circa nos pietatis semper viscera sentiamus.*	Deus, qui beatum Matthiam Apostolorum collegio sociasti, eius **nobis** interventione **concede, ut, dilectionis tuae sorte gaudentes, cum electis numerari mereamur.**
O God, who joined blessed Matthias to the company of your Apostles, *grant, we beseech you, that, through his intercession, we may ever experience the tender compassion [the bowels, viscera] of your mercy surrounding us.*	O God, who joined blessed Matthias to the company of your Apostles, through his intercession **grant us, that rejoicing in the lot/share of your love, we may be able to be numbered among the elect.**

Again the "your" is omitted from the statement of fact. The old petition asks that we may always experience the tender compassion of the Father's mercy round about us. The new petition, which seems to be a new composition, applies the language and imagery of Acts 1:26 to us. Acts 1 tells us that the apostles, after prayer, cast lots [*sortes*] to discover whom God had chosen [*eligo* = elect, choose] to replace Judas. The lot fell to Matthias. The revised prayer describes us as "rejoicing in the lot [*sorte*]" of God's love, and asks that we may be numbered among the "elect" or "chosen" [electis].

(e) *St Thomas.*

1962: St Thomas	2008: St Thomas
Da nobis, *quaesumus, Domine*, beati Apostoli *tui* Thomae *solemnitatibus* gloriari: ut eius semper et patrociniis sublevemur; *et fidem congrua devotione sectemur*	Da nobis, omnipotens Deus, beati Thomae apostoli festivitate gloriari, ut eius semper et patrociniis sublevemur, **et vitam credentes habeamus in nomine eius, quem ipse Dominum agnovit, Iesum Christum Filium tuum**
Grant us, we beseech you, O Lord, to glory in the solemnity of blessed Thomas your Apostle, that we may always be supported by his patronage *and with fitting devotion seek to imitate [his] faith.*	Grant us, almighty God, to glory in the feast of the apostle, blessed Thomas, that we may always both be supported by his patronage **and, believing, have life in the name of him whom Thomas confessed to be Lord, your Son, Jesus Christ.**

The revisers made three changes to the first part of the collect. First, they changed the invocation so that "Domine" [O Lord] of the Tridentine collect becomes "omnipotens Deus" [almighty God] in the Vatican II prayer. Second, they made the two changes in the statement of fact that we are accustomed to seeing: "your" was omitted, and "solemnity" substituted for "feast." Finally, the revisers omitted "we beseech you."

The change to the petition retains the request that we may always be supported by Thomas's patronage, but omits the request that we may seek to imitate his faith with fitting devotion. Instead the prayer asks that "believing, we may have life in the name of him whom Thomas confessed to be Lord, your Son, Jesus Christ." The revised petition takes its language from John 20, the New Testament chapter that presents the account of Thomas confessing the Risen Christ to be "my Lord and my God" and closes with the words: "Now Jesus did many other signs in the presence of the disciples, which are not written in this book; but these are written that you may believe that Jesus is the Christ, the Son of God, and that believing **you may have life in his name**" (John 20:30–31, RSV).

(f) *Sts Simon and Jude, Apostles.* Cuthbert Johnson lists the collects assigned to the feast of Sts Simon and Jude in both the *Misssale Romanum (1962)* and the *Missale Parisiense (1738)* as sources of the Vatican II collect.[50]

1962	2008	*Missale Parisiense (1738)* 3760
Deus, qui nos per beatos Apostolos tuos Simonem et Iudam ad agnitionem tui nominis venire tribuisti: da nobis *eorum gloriam sempiternam et proficiendo celebrare, et celebrando proficere.*	Deus, qui nos per beatos Apostolos ad agnitionem tui nominis venire tribuisti, **intercedentibus sanctis Simone et Iuda, concede propitius, ut semper augeatur Ecclesia incrementis in te credentium populorum.**	Deus, qui nos per beatos Apostolos tuos ad agnitionem tui nominis venire tribuisti: da nobis sanctorum tuorum Simonis et Iudae precibus, ut quod fides cognoscit, spes desideret, et caritas apprehendat;
O God, who through your blessed Apostles Simon and Jude have grant us to come to knowledge/confession of your name, grant us to celebrate the everlasting glory of these saints by advancing [in goodness, holiness, virtue], and by celebrating to advance [the more].	O God, who through the blessed Apostles have granted us to come to knowledge/confession of your name, **mercifully grant through the intercession of saints Simon and Jude, that the Church may always be strengthened through the increase of peoples who believe in you.**	O God, who through your blessed Apostles have granted us to come to knowledge/confession of your name, confer upon us through the prayers of your saints Simon and Jude that which faith knows, hope desires and love obtains.

The sole difference between the statements of fact of the 1962 and Parisian collects is that the latter does not name the apostles, but instead transfers mention of them to the petition which seeks the influence of their prayers. The revisers follow the Paris missal in this, except different words are used: "precibus" [through, or by, the prayers] becomes "intercedentibus" [interceding, a participle that modifies "saints"] and, additionally, the possessive pronoun "your" is omitted.

50. Johnson, "Sources," p. 150.

The request that the Church may also grow by increase in the people who believe in God seems to have originated with the Vatican II revisers. It replaces, on the one hand, the somewhat difficult 1962 petition that our advancement might celebrate the saints and that our celebration might advance us, and, on the other, that God may, through the prayers of Sts Simon and Jude, grant us the theological virtues and their proper effects: faith that knows, hope that desires, and love that obtains. The petitions of the source prayer seek goods for the members of the Church; the Vatican II petition is on behalf of the Church herself.

c. *The Feast of St Laurence, Deacon and Martyr*

The only saint on the universal calendar who is honored with a feast, but is not the Virgin Mother, an apostle or evangelist, is St Laurence. Until the Vatican II reforms, the feast of St Laurence was celebrated with a vigil, and, until about 1960, was also accompanied by an octave. St Laurence was given a new collect in the post-Vatican reform. The 1962 collect is not included in the new missals.

The *Corpus Orationes* index of first lines shows that the opening words of the Vatican II collect are those of a prayer that is found in a number of ancient codices, the oldest of which dates from the eighth century.[51] Johnson, who does not cite this prayer, names two other sources: the collect assigned to the octave day of St Laurence in the pre-1960 Tridentine missals and the preface for the feast of St Laurence in the Veronese Sacramentary.[52] The Vatican II collect is a centonized text which combines the opening words of the collect of St Laurence used in a number of ancient codices, an adaptation of the description of the saint presented in the Veronese preface and the closing words of the collect previously assigned to the octave day.

The pre- and post-Vatican II collects for the feast and the three source prayers are presented below. Each prayer is given its own print style: italics, bold, underscored, shaded and small caps. The entirety of the 2008 collect is in bold type and those sections of it which have been taken from, or have text adapted from, another prayer appears, additionally, in the type of that prayer. Likewise, the text which the revisers adopted or adapted appears in bold text in the source prayers.

---

51. Moeller et al., *Corpus Orationem*, vol. II, #1155.
52. Johnson, "Sources," p. 130. Johnson cites Veronese #740.

1962: St Laurence	2008: St Laurence	1962: Octave of St Laurence	*Ver* 740 Preface of St Laurence	*CO* II, #1155. Collect St Laurence
Da nobis, quaesumus, omnipotens Deus: vitiorum nostrorum flammas exstinguere; qui beato Laurentio tribuisti tormentorum suorum incendia superare.	**DEUS, CUIUS CARITATIS ARDORE BEATUS LAURENTIUS** servitio **claruit fidelis et martyrio gloriosus, fac** nos <u>amare quod amavit, et opere exercere quod docuit</u>.	Excita, Domine, in Ecclesia tua Spiritum, cui beatus Laurentius Levita servivit: ut, eodem nos repleti, studeamus **amare quod amavit, et opere exercere quod docuit**.	Uere dignum: praeuenientes natalem diem beati Laurenti, qui leuita simul martyrque uenerandus et proprio **claruit gloriosus** officio, et memoranda refulsit passione sublimis.	**DEUS, CUIUS CARITATIS ARDORE BEATUS LAURENTIUS** EDACES INCENDII flAMMAS CONTEMPTO PERSECUTORE DEVICIT, CONCEDE PROPITIUS, UT OMNES, QUI MARTYRII EIUS MERITA VENERAMUR, PROTECTIONIS TUAE AUXILIO MUNIAMUR.
Grant us, we beseech you, Almighty God, to extinguish the flames of our vices; who granted blessed Laurence to overcome the fires of his torments.	**O GOD, IN THE ARDOR OF WHOSE LOVE BLESSED LAURENCE** shone faithful in service and glorious in martyrdom, grant us <u>to love what he loved and practice in action what he taught</u>.	<u>Rouse, O Lord, in your Church the Spirit whom Blessed Laurence, the Deacon, served, so that we, having been filled with the same, may strive to love what he loved, and practice in action what he taught.</u>	[It is] truly fitting: anticipating the birth day of blessed Laurence, who is venerated both as deacon and martyr, and, **renown, was distinguished** in his own special service, and, exalted, has shone bright in suffering worthy of remembrance.	**O GOD, IN THE ARDOR OF WHOSE LOVE BLESSED LAURENCE,** HAVING DEFIED THE PERSECUTOR, OVERCAME THE VORACIOUS FLAMES OF THE CONFLAGRATION, MERCIFULLY GRANT THAT ALL WHO HONOR THE MERITS/ REWARDS OF HIS MARTYRDOM MAY BE DEFENDED BY THE HELP OF HIS PROTECTION.

St Laurence was grilled alive. The 1962 collect refers to this, as does the eighth-century source from which the opening words of the new collect were taken, but new collect does not. "O God, in the ardor of whose love blessed Laurence, having defied the persecutor, overcame the voracious flames of the conflagration," becomes "O God, in the ardor of whose love blessed Laurence shone faithful in service and glorious in martyrdom." The new prayer foregoes mention of Laurence's torments, of what fidelity required of him.

The petition of the 1962 collect asks God, who granted blessed Laurence to overcome the fires of his torments, to grant us "to extinguish the flames of our vices." These are not mentioned in the new collect. Further, the petition of the Vatican II prayer, that God grant us "to love what he [Laurence] loved and practice in action what he taught," is only part of the more comprehensive petition in the source prayer which asks that God rouse in His Church "the Spirit whom Blessed Laurence, the Deacon, served, so that we, having been filled with the same, may strive to love what he loved and practice in action what he taught." In consequence, the new petition asks for the same result, to love, etc., but not the means to love stipulated in the original text: "being filled with the Spirit whom Laurence served."

d. *The Feast of the Dedication of the Basilica of St John Lateran*

Our last feast celebrates the anniversary of the dedication of the basilica of St John Lateran. The same feast is named differently in the pre- and post-Vatican II missals, and this difference is reflected in the chart below. The Vatican II missals assign two collects to the Mass, neither of which is the 1962 collect of the feast, which was not incorporated into the new missals. The first Vatican II collect is an adaptation of the 1962 postcommunion prayer of the common of the dedication of a church. The second, or alternate, collect is composed of excerpts from a much longer oration that appears in numerous ancient codices. The four collects are below, with the alternate collect of the feast in the fourth column in shaded text. Its source is presented in the footnote with the adopted and adapted text shaded.

1962: Dedication of the Archbasilica of the Most Holy Savior	2008: Dedication of the Lateran Basilica	1962: Common of the Dedication of the Church, PC	2008: alt. Dedication of the Lateran Basilica
Deus, qui nobis per singulos annos huius sancti templi tui consecrationis reparas diem, et sacris semper mysteriis repraesentas incolumes: exaudi preces populi tui, et praesta; ut, quisquis hoc templum beneficia petiturus ingreditur, cuncta se impetrasse laetetur	**Deus, qui de vivis et electis lapidibus aeternum habitaculum tuae praeparas maiestati, multiplica in Ecclesia tua spiritum gratiae, quem dedisti, ut fidelis tibi populus in caelestis aedificationem Ierusalem semper accrescat.**	**Deus, qui de vivis et electis lapidibus aeternum maiestati tuae praeparas habitaculum:** auxiliare populo tuo supplicanti; ut, quod Ecclesiae tuae corporalibus proficit spatiis, spiritualibus amplificetur augmentis	Deus, qui Ecclesiam tuam sponsam vocare dignatus es, da, ut plebs nomini tuo inserviens te timeat, te diligat, te sequatur et ad caelestia promissa, te ducente, perveniat.
O God, who each year renew the day of the consecration of this your holy temple and ever bring us safely back to [these] holy mysteries: graciously hear the prayers of your people, and grant that, whoever enters this temple to beg favors may rejoice to have obtained all he sought.	**O God, who from living and chosen stones prepare an eternal dwelling place for your majesty, multiply in your Church the spirit of grace you have given, so that the people faithful to you may always increase by growth for the building up of the heavenly Jerusalem.**	**O God, who from living and chosen stones prepare an eternal dwelling place for your majesty,** help the people who humbly implore [you]; so that what advances your Church in physical spaces, may also be an increase in spiritual growth.	O God, who deigned to call the Church your bride, grant that the people devoted to your name may fear you, love you, follow you, and, with you guiding, attain the promises of heaven.[53]

53. Veronese #1576 served as an *oratio ad complendum* (post communion prayer) or *oratio super populum* (blessing over the people) of the Mass on the anniversary of the dedication of a basilica in a number of ancient codices dating from the eighth century and later. The text appropriated, by the revisers, even when adapted, appears in shaded type: "Deus, qui ecclesiam tuam sponsam vocare dignatus es, ut, quae haberet gratiam per fidei devotionem, haberet etiam ex nomine pietatem, da, ut omnis haec plebs, nomini tuo serviens, huius vocabuli consortio digna esse mereatur et ecclesia

The main difference between the 1962 collect for this feast and both of the new ones is that the older prayer asks God to attend to the needs of anyone who enters the church or basilica and begs for his help[54]—which everyone does, presumably, according to his particular situation at that particular time. The request evokes a sense of God's intimacy, and personal providential presence to each one of us, that the new collects, both of which look heavenward, do not. While the heavenly focus of the alternate collect is present in the source of the alternate prayer, it is not in the source of the other new collect which asks rather for spiritual growth in those who pray.

5. *Conclusion*

My goal has been to show what was done in the post-Vatican II revision of the collects of principal feasts, and, in those instances in which either a particular policy decision required the revision, or some explanation of it has been published by someone close to the work, to explain why. It is not possible to offer an overall evaluation for three reasons.

First, although we have considered a great many collects, we have given attention to a very small percentage of the collects in the revised missal. It is insupportable to generalize on the basis of such a small sampling. Second, while the category of *per annum* "solemnities and feasts" has the double advantage of focusing attention on important liturgical days and identifying a manageable number of texts, it has the disadvantage of separating some collects from others of their kind and of yoking unlike prayers together. For example, we considered a number of

tua, in templo, cuius natalis est hodie, tibi collecta, te timeat, te diligat, te sequatur, ut, dum iugiter per vestigia tua graditur, ad caelestia promissa, te ducente, pervenire mereatur." [O God, who deigned to call the church, your bride, so that whoever might possess grace through the devotion of faith, might also have mercy from the name, grant, that this whole people which serves your name may be made worthy by the fellowship of this appellation (name) and your church gathered to you in [this] temple, whose anniversary is today, may fear you, love you, follow you, so that as she walks constantly in your footsteps, may be deemed worthy, with you leading, to attain the promises of heaven.]

54. In this, the collect is similar to Solomon's prayer at the dedication of the temple in Jerusalem. See particularly, 1 Kgs 8:38–39: "…whatever prayer, whatever supplication is made by any man or by all thy people Israel, each knowing the affliction of his own heart and stretching out his hands toward this house; then hear thou in heaven thy dwelling place, and forgive, and act, and render to each whose heart thou knowest, according to all his ways (for thou, thou only, knowest the hearts of all the children of men)" (RSV).

sanctoral orations, but not all. And while it would not have been possible to do otherwise in the space available, it remains true that nothing much can be competently observed about the revision of the sanctoral orations without examining all of them. Third, with respect to our specific charge, we have not examined the collects which underwent no change at all— again for reasons of space. A responsible evaluation of the revision of even just these collects would necessarily include a consideration of the characteristics of the 1962 collects that the revisers incorporated into the new missal without emendation and assigned to the same setting. One goal of such a consideration would be to determine what distinguishes them from the collects that were replaced or revised.

It is possible, however, to offer some summary observations. Of the thirty-one collects we have considered, eight are assigned, without any alteration, to the same day in the new missals.[55] Of the remaining twenty-three, six underwent textual emendation in accordance with the revision principles approved by the *Consilium* members in 1966.[56] The remaining seventeen were revised, although nothing in the 1966 revision principles required their revision. Similarly, the source prayers of many of the new collects underwent revision prior to inclusion in the new missal, although nothing in the 1966 revision principles required that they be emended.[57]

In general, it is easier to present a quantitative description of the editorial activity than to explain its precise nature. The exceptions are the emendations that occur habitually and that we have noted throughout. The revisers always changed the wording of the collect to bring the language of the prayer into conformity with the rank of its day—"solemnity" becomes "feast" when the rank is feast. And almost always the revisers removed the possessive pronouns which indicate that the saint belongs to God—for example, "your apostle" in the original becomes "apostle" in the revised text.

---

55. One of these, however, the 1962 collect of the Sacred Heart, is the alternate collect in the Vatican II missals.

56. Exaltation of the Cross (repeats text), Vigil of Assumption (not addressed to Father), Visitation (repeats text), St Joseph (not addressed to Father and repeats text), St Barthomew (repeats text after its statement of fact was appropriated for Sts Peter and Paul). I also include the 1962 collect of the Annunciation in this category because the collect seems to have been revised because the day was made a solemnity of the Lord.

57. This is the case for the collects assigned to the Vigil of the Assumption, the Visitation, the Nativity of John the Baptist, and the feasts of Sts Matthew, John the Apostle and Evangelist, Philip and James, Simon and Jude. It is also true for the collect of the octave day of St Laurence which was used to confect the new collect for St Laurence.

There seems to be a tendency, at least in these prayers, to avoid mention of sin, our weakness and other sorts of unpleasantness. Sin is only mentioned in three prayers of 1962 corpus of collects considered here: one, the collect of the Sacred Heart, was demoted to an alternate collect; another, the collect of St Peter's Chair, was assigned to a votive Mass, and the last, the collect of Christ the King, was re-written. Additionally, the collect of St Laurence, which asks that our vices be extinguished, was replaced.

Weakness has many manifestations and, accordingly, is mentioned, presumed or alluded to in various ways in the collects. Certain requests for defense (1962 Trinity Sunday, Vigil of Assumption, St Mark) and for rescue from all that opposes us (source prayer for new Visitation collect) were not carried into the new missals. Other petitions which seek abiding spiritual assistance are no longer found in the collects or their replacements. These include requests for firmness in faith, to gain through the saint's intercession what we cannot through our own power, to please God with our manner of life and serve him with a steadfast mind, to make our way to God following the saints' example, to be instructed by the saints' example, for faith that knows, hope that desires and love that obtains (petitions of 1962 Trinity Sunday, St Joseph and St Matthew, St James, Conversion of St Paul, St Simon and James and the source prayer of the new alternate collect of the Dedication of the Church, respectively).

The new collects seem to present more petitions that we act. Examples are that we magnify God always, persevere in unity of heart and soul, follow Christ faithfully, proclaim God's truth in the world (Vatican II collects of the Visitation, St Luke, St Mark, Conversion of St Paul, respectively). Also, slightly more of the Vatican II collects ask that we attain heaven: the 1962 and 2008 collects of Transfiguration, Exaltation of the Cross and Nativity of John the Baptist all seek heaven; in addition the 1962 collect of St John the Evangelist asks that the Church may obtain everlasting gifts. The 2008 collect for St John ask that we may understand his instruction, but the 2008 petition of the Visitation (magnify you *always*), Sts Philip and James, and St Matthias are focused on eternity.

In the body of this chapter we called attention to the muting of the moral demands of the original texts from which the Vatican II collects for the Vigil of the Assumption and the feast of St Matthew were confected—respectively, the mention of humility and of leaving everything behind. Likewise, we noted that the new collect for St Laurence fails to include the request for the Spirit whom Laurence served while it retains the request that, in the original, was made possible through the gift of same Spirit. In the first instances, the moral force of the original prayers was weakened; in the latter instance, the Church's theology of grace made less apparent.

Lastly, we note again the limits of our study. It is a fairly easy matter to answer questions about what the revisers did, even when doing so involves identifying ancient and long unused texts of the Church's treasury which the revisers selected or excerpted for specific service in the new missal. What the present state of available documentation rarely enables us to do is explain changes that were made when the published revision policies did not require them.

The Ease of Beauty:
Liturgy, Evangelization, and Catechesis

Margaret I. Hughes

1. *Introduction*

Paul Claudel, whose conversion was famously prompted by the singing of the *Magnificat* at Christmas Day Vespers, writes about beauty, "One can resist force, skill, or self-interest. One can even resist Truth, but one cannot resist Beauty..."[1] He alights here on the reason that beauty, especially in the liturgy, is essential in evangelization and catechesis. There is no force or struggle in the perception of beauty: genuine beauty captures us freely, draws us in joyfully, and holds us there receptively so that we may respond with joy to the goodness of existence, to the goodness of the Creation and Redemption.

I would like to propose that the manifestations of the beauty of the liturgy in the sensible—in music, in art, in language, and in ceremony—allow us to approach the reality of the good of the liturgy receptively and with genuine joy, and so make the liturgy "easy" in a way that *Sacrosanctum Concilium* and the authentic anthropology assumed by the document prescribe. I will do so, first by considering why *Sacrosanctum Concilium* calls for ease in the liturgy, and then by examining the problems with considering ease only as "freedom from effort" in order to show that ease is in fact the intensification of activity that is for its own sake, and that this activity is contemplation. Then I will suggest that contemplation happens in the perception of beauty, so that implementing "ease" in the liturgy in fact means manifesting the beauty of the liturgy in all of its aspects.

---

1. P. Claudel, A. Sarment (ed.), Helen Weaver (trans.), *I Believe in God* (San Francisco: Ignatius, 1973), p. 102; from *L'Evangile d'Isaïe*, p. 316.

2. *Ease in* Sacrosanctum Concilium

In the Second Vatican Council's Constitution on the Sacred Liturgy, *Sacrosanctum Concilium* (4 December 1963), the word "easy"—*facile* or some related form—appears five times in order to describe the optimal relation between the faithful and the liturgy. For example, paragraph 21 states, "...texts and rites should be drawn up so that they express more clearly the holy things which they signify; the Christian people, so far as possible, should be enabled to understand them with ease and to take part in them fully, actively, and as befits a community," and paragraph 50 states, "The rite of the Mass is to be revised in such a way that the intrinsic nature and purpose of its several parts, as also the connection between them, may be more clearly manifested, and that devout and active participation by the faithful may be more easily achieved."

This prescription for "ease" points to the wondrous revelation of the Incarnation that God's love for human beings is without limit. Christianity is not a closed and exclusive mystery cult or gnostic religion, in which one's worth and participation is predicated on birth, or possessions, or intellectual ability. Christ reveals to us the depth and value of each person and the potential fulfillment of each person in the union with God in the beatific vision.

It is therefore appropriate that the "active participation by the faithful [in the liturgy] may be more easily achieved." This prescription recognizes that there is a good shared by all human beings because there is a shared human nature and that that good both lies in, and is foreshadowed by, participation in the Mass. The charity that is at the heart of the Christian life impels us to make that good accessible to as many human beings as possible, and so requires that the liturgy be approached with ease.

3. *The Modern Understanding of Ease and Its Problems*

It is tempting, however, to understand the "ease" for which *Sacrosanctum Concilium* calls according to the popular, contemporary notion of ease as simply freedom from effort. A brief survey of current English language dictionaries illustrates this conception: ease is freedom from labor and pain, freedom from concern and anxiety, freedom from difficult or great effort, freedom from financial need, freedom from stiffness and constraint. My suggestion is not that this definition of ease is wrong, but that it is incomplete, and that its incompleteness has dire consequences for human beings in general, and in particular when applied to the liturgy.[2]

---

2. This critique of ease follows from and is inspired by Josef Pieper's discussion of genuine leisure and its counterfeits. See, for example, *Leisure the Basis of Culture*

The popular notion of ease, freedom from pain and effort, is primarily understood as a subjective experience. We are at ease when we feel free from the pain of the strain and struggle of effort and labor. In order to be at ease it is necessary to pursue only those activities that bring immediate pleasure, or to not act at all. Ease, then, is a subjective state, but the pursuit of that state has consequences for what one chooses to do or not to do.

Ease understood as the subjective state of freedom from difficulty and effort follows from the privileging of human autonomy over all other goods, such that the individual's choice is the standard of good for that individual and, consequently, that the only good that all human beings have in common is the ability to choose. In order for the individual's choice to be the standard of what is good, it is necessary to be able to choose anything, regardless of the demands of reality. It seems, in fact, that this is precisely what so many of the technological innovations designed to make life easier actually do: they make it possible for us to live unencumbered by the limitations of reality. For example: refrigeration means that we can ignore the inevitable decay of the material world; electric lights mean that we can ignore the time of day; rapid travel and communication means that we can forget that we are bound by place and time. I do not mean to imply that things that make life easier in this way are bad—but do want to point out that it is important to be aware of how they shape the way in which we interact with the world, since these interactions, if we are not thoughtful about them, can lead us to a false understanding of reality.

If, however, we take ease to be freedom from effort and the demands of reality, then it appears that we are faced with a dichotomy: if ease is simply freedom from effort, then its only alternative is effort. Either we are at ease and inactive, or we are active in putting forth the effortful straining and striving of work. Underlying this idea of ease is the conception of a strained relation between the individual human being and the rest of reality: a human being can be at ease focused only on his subjective experience, or he can put forth effort and work to engage with things outside of himself and to shape them to his will, which means that the encounter with reality necessarily entails effort and pain. It seems we must opt either for the ease of inactivity and isolation from everything outside of us, or for the effort of the activity of shaping and molding reality.

That the human being's relation to reality is necessarily one of effort and work follows from the restriction of reason to discursive activity in modern philosophy. Discursive reason entails constantly advancing from one piece of knowledge to another, and, when the searched for knowledge

(South Bend: St Augustine's, 1998) and *In Tune with the World: A Theory of Festivity* (South Bend: St Augustine's, 1999).

is achieved, to move on to other pieces of knowledge and then to move on again to other discoveries, and so to be doomed to continuous effort and labor.[3] If we know reality through our reason, but the activity of reason is only effortful, then our relation with reality is necessarily and exclusively laborious.

But this view of man's relation to reality—either engaged and at work, or disengaged and at ease, leads to a conundrum. It sets reason and feeling at odds with each other. If the activity of reason is only discursive, then the activity of reason is only effortful, and so the activity of reason, it seems, cannot be done with ease. We can be at ease, or we can reason, but not both. On the one hand, we desire the pleasure of ease. But on the other hand, reasoning is hard work, and so lacks the pleasure of ease. This leads to a conviction that we must choose between pleasure and reason. In this understanding, pleasure and reason are pitted against each other. There is a divorce between subjectively satisfying experience and the activity of reason, which leads to knowledge of objective reality.

This conception of ease, and the dichotomy between the pleasure of not reasoning and the work of reasoning, seem to lead to two general ways in which *Sacrosanctum Concilium*'s prescription for ease in the liturgy has been applied. One is an emphasis on making the liturgy completely and totally graspable by reason, so that reason need do no work. If ease is only freedom from effort and the liturgy is to be approached with ease, but the engagement of reason requires effort, then it makes sense to try to present the liturgy in ways that appear to make it clearly and completely understandable, so that there is no effortful discovery still to make and the participants may be at ease. The other way to make the liturgy "easy," within this framework, is to emphasize the subjective experience of the liturgy by using devices to stir up the emotions, so that the liturgy is a subjectively satisfying experience without reference to reason.

But, I would like to suggest, these efforts to make the liturgy more easily accessible, while often done in good faith, fail because they do not reflect a full and authentic conception of reason, joy, and ease. This modern conception of ease, with its emphasis on human autonomy and on the split between reason and feeling, between the objective world and subjective experience, is profoundly harmful, in at least the following ways:

---

3. Josef Pieper discusses the relation between discursive reasoning and labor in "Philosophical Education and Intellectual Labor," in Berthold Wald (ed.), *For the Love of Wisdom* (San Francisco: Ignatius, 2006), p. 14.

To begin with, this understanding of ease is profoundly lonely. If there is no objective truth, or at least any that we can know, then I cannot communicate with you, nor you with me; there is nothing that we share, since your experience is yours and my experience is mine. Each person is isolated in his own world of subjective experience. This way of looking at and living in the world is deeply, desperately lonely.

Furthermore, this view of ease implies that life is devoid of meaning. It is devoid of meaning precisely because this position claims that each person chooses and constructs his own reality, and so is also the creator of his own good. But, if this is the case, then there is nothing that is actually good, prior to the individual's choice. The individual becomes responsible for creating all his own good, which means that there is nothing actually good already existing in the world, worth pursuing in-itself. And, if there is no good to which it is worth dedicating one's life, then life is meaningless.

If life is meaningless and there is no good that is not of our own construction, then all that we encounter as we live in the everyday world becomes banal. An emphasis on subjectively satisfying experience and aversion to all but the most pedantic reasoning leads to a lack of a sense of mystery. If all that we encounter in the everyday is simply a construction of our reason, then we understand it completely and totally. All that is real is what is immediately evident in the material world and so the world is flat.

When one sees the world as flat, real joy is impossible. Joy is a response to receiving what is good. If the world is meaningless and boring, then there is no good already existing and the world is joyless.

And this is the tragedy of a mistaken notion of ease, and the tragedy, not just of our own age, but of all those who have inherited Original Sin. It is the tragedy of losing sight of the fundamental goodness of the world whose existence is chosen, and so loved, by God. This is what Creation reveals to us and the Crucifixion reaffirms: that it is good to be, that there is something profoundly good about existing. Losing sight of the goodness of Creation leads to the subsequent loss of joy in any good. The remedy of this tragedy is at the heart of evangelization and catechesis. Evangelization, before all else, aims to reopen our eyes to what is genuinely good, so that we may, once again, rejoice in the real good that we have received in our creation and that we continue to receive in the fulfillment of that creation. And, in rejoicing in the real, objective good of Creation, we rediscover the harmony and fittingness of objective reality and subjective experience.

The New Evangelization is directed especially at those who have lost the ability to rejoice in the goodness of being. The re-evangelization of, as John Paul II writes, "the baptized [who] have lost a living sense of the faith, or even no longer consider themselves members of the Church, and live a life far removed from Christ and his Gospel" (*Redemptoris Missio*, 7 December 1990, 33) is aimed at those whose education and worldview have been steeped in the supposed divorce between subjective experience and objective truth, and the privileging of the former over the latter. Since this understanding of reality leads to a rejection of any claim to be able to know objective truth beyond what is measureable, it follows that religion cannot teach what is true; it can only be subjectively satisfying for some people.

In such a climate, the presentation of doctrine and an intellectual defense of Christianity, while important, is not enough, because the basis for this approach, reason, is already rejected.

Just as talking and lectures about Christ will not be heard by those who are resolutely convinced that religion offers no truth because reason cannot grasp the truth beyond the material, neither will a liturgy that attempts to be totally and completely graspable by reason be effective in manifesting the truth of Christ to those who reject reason.

But, at the same time, neither is a merely subjectively satisfying experience, especially of liturgy, enough. If the liturgy is easy in the sense of being only subjectively satisfying with no movement towards what is real and good outside of oneself, then as soon as it is no longer subjectively satisfying, it is no longer worthwhile. Such an approach robs those participating in it of the knowledge of the objective truth about Christ, a truth that does not change amidst the vagaries of subjective experience, and so robs them of knowledge that life is genuinely meaningful.

It follows quite plainly, I think, that the "ease" for which *Sacrosanctum Concilium* calls cannot be simply "freedom from effort." That the liturgy ought to be entered into with ease cannot mean that it is supposed to be immediately and completely graspable, or that it should be only subjectively satisfying. A liturgy that is easy in this sense does not allow for the full engagement of reason in receiving what is good, which results in joy, and so does not make evident the genuine good of the Creation and Redemption.

4. *Ease as the Activity of Rest*

Here I would like to suggest that there is an alternative to the dichotomy between reason and pleasure, between effortful activity and easy inactivity, and that this alternative is the real ease for which *Sacrosanctum Concilium* calls. We can find this alternative in a fuller understanding of reason. This notion of ease is the ease that comes with the activity that is the fulfillment of human nature, which is contemplation: the gazing on and rejoicing in what is good for its own sake. The gazing on and rejoicing in what is good is the perception of genuine beauty. Thus, the ease in the liturgy that *Sacrosanctum Concilium* requests is the ease of beauty. To defend this claim, I will consider this third alternative, which is the activity of rest in contemplation, and then show how this activity is also the perception of beauty.

When we must choose between only being inactive or working, life is meaningless because there is nothing that is pursued for its own sake. But, as Aristotle points out, there must be some good that we pursue for its own sake. If there were no good that we pursue for its own sake, then there would be no reason to act at all. All the other goods that we work towards would be in vain, because they would not lead to some final good, and so there would be no reason to pursue any of them. We do act, though. This means that there must be some good that we pursue for its own sake, some activity that is meaningful in itself.

That activity is rest, because it is an activity done for its own sake, and not in order to do something else. Although, when we first hear the word "rest," we may immediately assume that rest and being inactive are identical, I am suggesting that proper rest, the resting in what is good, is in fact our being most fully and appropriately active.

The restoration of this notion of rest restores also a more complete notion of the activity of reason. Whereas when reason is limited to discursive thought, the activity of reason involves only figuring out facts that can be manipulated, or what to do and how to do it—that is, reason is for the sake of doing other activities—when we consider rest as activity for its own sake, we see that the genuine rest of the human being is the activity of reason for its own sake, which is contemplation.[4]

Contemplation is not the cessation of reason. It is, rather, an activity of reason that is different from the activity of discursive thought. We can see this when we consider sight, which is analogous to knowing. Discursive thought is akin to the eyes glancing about, here and there, searching for an object on which to fix their gaze. Contemplation, on the other hand, is akin to the eyes' penetrating gaze. When the eyes rest on an object, they continue to see and to see even more intensely. In this way the activity of sight is realized in its openness and in its receptivity to taking in the object on which it rests. In the same way, the intellect's rest in knowing involves the activity of receptivity. The intellect rests when its proper activity has its proper object and so its activity may intensify. The proper object of the intellect is the truth, which is knowing reality as it really

---

4. Josef Pieper discusses contemplation in many of his works, but, perhaps most compellingly, in *Happiness and Contemplation* (South Bend: St Augustine's, 1998).

is. This intensification, though, is not an intensification of effort. It is an intensification of the activity of receptivity; of receiving reality as it is. It is most concentrated because it looks to nothing else and for no other purpose. Contemplation is a kind of knowing that is simply for the sake of knowing and so is good for its own sake.

The proper response to realizing the good is joy. Joy is not something that can be manufactured or forced. It happens to the subject; the subject feels joy as the result of receiving a good. Genuine joy that is indicative of the real human good is the result only of the possession of a genuine good that is actually good for the human being, which is the rest of the intellect in what is true, in knowing reality for its own sake.

In the genuine ease that is the human being resting in the intensification of the activity of reason done for its own sake, there is a harmonious meeting of objective reality and subjective experience. This is ease that is free from effort (although, certainly, reaching it may and often does require effort), but that is also much more than freedom from effort. It is also the fulfillment of the objective human good in gazing on reality for its own sake, and it is the subjective experience of joy. In contemplation, the subject and the object, the human being and the rest of reality, meet in a consonant, harmonious, and joyful manner.

5. *Rest in the Perception of Beauty*

It now remains for me to suggest that the ease that is the intensification of the activity of reason and its accompanying joy is the perception of beauty, and that the way to make the liturgy "easy" is to adorn it with beauty. In order to do this, I will draw on St Thomas Aquinas's well-known statement, "Beautiful things are those which please when seen" (*Summa Theologica*, Ia, 5, 4). These few, seemingly straightforward words contain a wealth of content on which to meditate as we look at what beauty is.

On the surface, it may appear that this definition of beauty endorses the notion that "beauty is in the eye of the beholder," and so that Aquinas is reducing beauty to mere subjective experience. A fuller examination of this statement, however, will demonstrate, I hope, that contemplation, which is a harmonious meeting of the objective and subjective that allows for the real ease that is the fulfillment of human nature, is also the perception of beauty.[5]

---

5. The following relies heavily on J. Aertsen, "Beauty in the Middle Ages: A Forgotten Transcendental?," in N. Kretzmann et al. (eds), *Medieval Philosophy and Theology*, vol. 1, (Notre Dame: University of Notre Dame Press, 1991), pp. 67–98.

The verbs "pleases" and "seen" establish that beauty involves a relation between an object and a subject. Beauty, then, consists in a specific relation between two things, one of which is capable of subjectivity. A subject sees and is pleased. But, and I hope that this will become clear, that does not diminish the objectivity of beauty. For the subject to be pleased and to see, there must be an object that is seen and that is pleasing.

Aquinas's statement, "Beauty is that which pleases when seen," expresses also the most important abilities of the rational animal: to know and to love. Because a human being is rational, he is able to know, and, because he can know, he is able to love. The ability to know is the intellect and the ability to love is the will. We are able to distinguish these two activities by that at which they are aimed. The aim of the intellect is the truth. The aim of the will is the good. The intellect and the will, then, are fully active and at ease when they are fully actualized in the possession of and resting in the truth and the good.

When a human being "sees," he perceives. He receives the world, reality, into himself. "Seeing" means not just the literal sensation of sight by way of the eyes, but any perception, especially intellectual perception. "See," in the statement, "Beauty is that which pleases when seen," refers to the relation formed between the knower and the thing known.

"Pleases" also refers to a relation. It is a sign of the will reaching its end. We are pleased when the pursuit of what we desire comes to an end, and we are able to rest in the possession of the good that we love.

In the perception of beauty, that "which pleases when seen," the intellect and the will are both engaged, and are brought into union with each other through their proper activities in relation to the same object. The intellect sees the object as it is and for its own sake: it sees the truth. That is, the intellect pursues the knowledge of what is, not in order to do something with it, or to make something, or even for its own satisfaction (although this satisfaction is the result of such seeing). Instead, the intellect gazes on the sight of the truth simply because it is good to know the truth, and so in seeing the truth for its own sake, the will is also satisfied. The intellect and will rest in seeing and enjoying the goodness of the truth, which is the goodness of reality.

The experience of beauty, then, is the subjective experience of actively resting in the objective good. It is not an experience manufactured by the work of the subject, but nor is it the subject simply inert, unbothered and unconnected to the world outside of himself. Instead it is the ever deepening sight of the good, in a movement that is at once determined by the objective state of things—by the reality of the nature of the human being that is fulfilled in knowing all that is, and the good that is there, in the world to be known—and yet is a free movement because it is in accord with the nature of the subject. Freedom, here, has a much more robust and classical meaning: freedom is freedom for something—freedom to pursue the good in which our fulfillment and delight rests.

Beauty, since it is the intellectual perception of the good and the consequent joy in that good, is essential to any catechesis or evangelization, since these endeavors are aimed, ultimately, at manifesting to human beings what is authentically good. Beauty conveys that it is good to exist, and so opens us to the appropriate, fitting joy in being, and being in the world. Joy is the only proper response to the gift of Creation and Redemption.

While there are many very nice consequences that follow from the perception of beauty—the development of skills, the knowledge of history and culture, and so on—these cannot be the primary motivation in perceiving or presenting beauty. As soon as there is some reason for presenting beauty other than the contemplation of the good for its own sake, then the sight of that good becomes obscured. The perceiver is no longer resting and delighting in the good for its own sake, because there is still some other purpose that he must continue to pursue. Beauty, therefore, belongs in evangelization and catechesis purely as a means of conveying and sharing in the joy of the goodness of Creation and Redemption—a joy so tragically lost when ease is "freedom from effort," but also so joyfully restored in the realization and experience of ease as "freedom for the contemplation of the good."

6. *Beauty in the Mass*

The greatest good for human beings, the locus of all of Creation and Redemption, is the Mass. As Cardinal Ratzinger writes, "The goal of worship and the goal of creation as a whole are one and the same—divinization, a world of freedom and love."[6]

The beauty of Mass is always there to be perceived, no matter the adornments that accompany its celebration, because it is an astonishing, overwhelming, and absorbingly mysterious revelation of the goodness of God. In response, we can do nothing more than to adore the God-Man whose generosity extends beyond even the gratuity of Creation to come to meet us and to catch us up into the contemplation of His goodness. In the Mass, we glimpse our final fulfillment in the Beatific Vision through adoring God made present under the appearance of bread and wine.

---

6. J. Ratzinger, *The Spirit of the Liturgy* (San Francisco: Ignatius, 2000), p. 28.

A mark of the beauty of the Mass is that it is for its own sake. While there are many consequences that come from participating in Mass—a sense of belonging, a connection with one's culture, religious instruction— these are not the aims of the Mass. The Mass is for the adoration of God, for gazing on the beauty of God which is beyond the material world and which we can do because we are intellectual creatures.

Even those who know this, who are well-formed, and who regularly enter into the beauty of the Mass, can lose sight of this beauty. We are easily distracted and wearied, so that even what we know intellectually does not always inform our will and passions. Just because we know that something is good does not mean that we always experience it as good and with the appropriate joy. For those who, as we discussed earlier, reject any objective truth about religion and who do not know what the Mass really is, it is almost impossible to catch even a glimpse of this intellectual beauty (leaving aside, of course, the possibility of the intervention of grace). Even instruction—which is, of course, very necessary—falls short, because it attempts, through propositions, to point to the beauty that is beyond propositions. But, if, as often happens, that beauty is not readily evident and experienced in the Mass, then those propositions and instruction simply add to the noisiness of the already noisy world. Consequently, something is needed to make manifest the goodness of the Mass and to remind us of its beauty, so that it can be entered into with joy, and so with the proper ease. What is needed is sensible beauty.

All knowledge, for humans, begins in the senses. Man, as a material being as well as a spiritual being, relies on his senses to first acquire information about the world. Based on what he has come to know and to the degree that he has come to know, he can begin to exercise his reason to learn more about material things and immaterial things. Without his senses, however, he would have no initial content for his inquiries and consequently would not be able to come to know anything. The senses and the intellect, then, are intimately connected. When the senses are engaged, the engagement of the intellect soon follows.

The senses, like the intellect and will, are activities, and, as activities, they reach out to their suitable objects. The object of seeing is the visible, the object of hearing is the audible, and so on. While, in general, what can be seen is suitable to seeing and what can be heard is suitable to hearing, some objects suit the natural inclination of the power, while others do not. For example, excessively soft or very loud music is not suitable to hearing; very bright or very dark light is not suitable to seeing. Each of the extremes is unsuitable for our sensation, whether because it fails to actuate the power, or because it does some violence to the power that it moves.

The senses, like the intellect and will, can rest in the intensification of activity in response to their appropriate objects. In the gazing on what appeals to the sight, the activity of seeing is intensified and rests. In the listening to what appeals to hearing, the activity of hearing is intensified and rests. The eyes and the ears can rest and delight in what is good for them, and, what is good for them is their appropriate object.

As the senses engage in this intensification of activity, their receptivity intensifies, and with the intensification of the receptivity of the senses comes the intensification of the receptivity of the intellect. In order for the senses to come to the stillness of receptivity, the intellect, too, must come to stillness. The eyes cannot absorb visible beauty, or the ears audible beauty, if the intellect is busy, jumping from one thought to another. For the senses to receive their proper object fully, the intellect must be at rest so as not to distract from the object on which the senses are focused.

But, as the intellect comes to rest in response to the rest of the senses, the intellect becomes more and more receptive, able to look beyond the visible beauty to focus on the intellectual beauty that is present. In the stillness of the senses, the intellect is not distracted, but instead, can gaze absorbingly on the intellectual beauty of the Mass. Therefore, when the Mass is adorned with sensible beauty, the whole of the human being is united in his intense gaze and openness to the mystery that is before him. The senses, the intellect, the will, and the passions are all bound together in the contemplation of the glory of God and the mystery of the Eucharist.

Of course, artistic beauty will always pale in comparison to the beauty of God, and manmade beauty, while it can be contemplated because it manifests genuine good, is not the final goal of contemplation. Rather, human contemplation is only fully complete in the contemplation of God. Sensible beauty is beautiful only in an analogous way to the beauty of God, and it is only genuinely beautiful when it points to the beauty of God.

I began with a somewhat dire diagnosis of the effects of a misconstrued ease on human beings. I would like to end by suggesting ways in which a more robust notion of ease—that of being fully active in the gazing on and rejoicing in the good for its own sake, which is the contemplation of beauty—applied to the liturgy offers a remedy to those effects.

The first is that sensible beauty in the liturgy, which engages the senses and the intellect together through their resting in the contemplation of the good, is profoundly communal. Whereas I suggested that the rejection of reason prohibits real communication and so is the cause of much loneliness, the shared experience of beauty together in the liturgy makes palpable a genuine communion that is beyond words. The perception of beauty of art, and especially music, leads to silence. Silence, as Josef Pieper observes, is different from being quiet. Being quiet is simply not making any noise, but being silent is listening, being open to receiving what is outside of us.[7] In the Mass, we are silent together. All together, we are bound up in openness to the reality of the Incarnation, the Cross and the Resurrection. This is most palpable, I think, at a solemn or sung Mass in the *usus antiquior*, when the last notes of the Sanctus are sung, and stillness hangs in the air, as everyone waits in poised anticipation for the arrival of Christ on the altar. We experience together the activity of reason that is beyond discursive thought, as expressed by our silence together. At such a moment, we experience the communion that is possible because we are subjective beings fulfilled by a shared objective reality.

And, in that silence, that attitude of receptivity to a good that is outside of and beyond ourselves, we rediscover the mysterious nature of the world. The experience of beauty, while joyful, is also painful. In the perception of beauty, as Cardinal Ratzinger writes, "…the wound of the arrow strikes the heart and in this way opens our eyes."[8] Even the experience of the most beautiful music and art, precisely because it is the most beautiful, leaves us both satisfied, but also unsatisfied, longing for more, longing for the beauty that is beyond even this most beautiful experience. And, in that longing, we see that all that is good in the world is a mere shadow of the good of the Beatific Vision. In the perception of beautiful art, the perceiver remembers that he is but a wayfarer on his journey to a much desired end and only when he reaches that end will he experience complete rest and happiness.

And so, in this experience of beauty, the perceiver discovers meaning. He discovers that he has an end, and an end that is given to him because his human nature is given to him. The beauty of the Mass, made palpable by sensible adornments, awakens in him the longing for that end, and so shows him that life is meaningful. In being wounded by the arrow of beauty, he comes to see that this life is a pilgrimage on the way to the Heavenly City.

Thus, as Claudel writes, we cannot resist beauty. We cannot resist beauty because our nature is such that we desire what is good, and the experience of beauty reveals that good to us. At this point, however, I

7. J. Pieper, *Only the Lover Sings: Art and Contemplation* (San Francisco: Ignatius, 1990), p. 55.

8. J. Ratzinger, "The Feeling of Things, the Contemplation of Beauty," *Message of His Eminence Card: Joseph Ratzinger to the Communion and Liberation Meeting at Rimini (24–30 August 2002)*, www.vatican.va/roman_curia/congregations/cfaith/documents/rc_con_cfaith_doc_20020824_ratzinger-cl-rimini_en.html.

must return to the quote with which I began and admit to quoting Claudel selectively. Claudel finishes the phrase, "One can resist force, skill, or self-interest. One can even resist Truth, but one cannot resist Beauty…" with the words "holding innocence in her arms." The beauty that Claudel is speaking of is the beauty of Our Lady, who is so perfectly receptive to the good that she receives Him into her so that we, too, may receive Him. It is she who shows us most clearly the fullness of charity by reflecting the glory of God and so making possible that we, too, enter into that glory. She shows us what the beautiful liturgy does because, as Gerard Manley Hopkins writes, she:

> Let all God's glory through,
> God's glory which would go
> Through her and from her flow
> Off, and no way but so.[9]

---

9. G. Manley Hopkins, "The Blessed Virgin Compared to the Air We Breathe," in John F. Thornton and Susan B. Varenne (eds), *Mortal Beauty, God's Grace* (New York: Vintage Spiritual Classics, 2003), pp. 41–45 (42).

ADDRESSING THE TRIUMPH OF BAD TASTE: CHURCH PATRONAGE OF ART, ARCHITECTURE, AND MUSIC

Jennifer Donelson

You might be expecting this chapter to be something it is not. You might be expecting this chapter to serve as an indictment of the failed artistic projects and styles of bygone generations, a description and denunciation of "wreckovation" projects and the ousting of choirs from the lofts of churches, a censure of terrible architectural, artistic, and musical experiments based on an even more terrible theology. While a critique of what has happened to sacred art in the recent past is indeed important (and it will, in fact, be addressed briefly), what will be offered instead is a sort of examination of conscience for those who ardently desire to offer their lives and work to Christ by renewing the Church's Sacred Liturgy and mission in the modern world, outlining principles for the sacred arts which must be considered in the path ahead.

Often, those who love the Church's liturgy and work daily for its re-beautification and re-sacralization hope to see old churches restored to their former glory, to hear, compose, or perform music suitable for the liturgy, and to find in their parishes liturgical furnishings and images which draw minds to God. Indeed, these are noble goals. Then about what should the well-intentioned person who sincerely desires to worship God in a fitting manner examine his conscience? Is what he is proposing, hoping to see, or doing *actually beautiful*? And, does the artistic language employed in the work of art fittingly accord with the theological reality?

In these matters, good intention alone is insufficient; even good theology is insufficient—though the former is helpful and the latter necessary. The stuff of art—the splendor, excellence, and perfection of its form, its manner of speaking, the materials with which it is made, the technique with which it is executed—actually matter and must be taken seriously.

The good and necessary work of critiquing ill-intentioned and heterodox principles and initiatives which undergirded over two generations of art in the liturgy after the Second Vatican Council has been done in other places, and what is presented here will not attempt to repeat or even summarize that work.[1] Instead, it is hoped that this examination of conscience will help us discover if we are doing what is necessary to renew sacred art in the Sacred Liturgy by means of sound artistic principles, language, and technique. These factors are the lynchpin missing in much of what has come before us and even what is going on now. This bears repeating: good theology and good intention by themselves are insufficient. What is needed is a triadic approach that adds artistic discernment to good theology and good intention. Let us begin by examining each of the elements in this triad to see why this is so.

1. *Good Theology*

Recent decades have produced theological confusion in many areas—doctrinal, ecclesiological, moral—and certainly each of these has had its own detrimental effects on the sacred arts. But to understand the question of art in the liturgy *per se*, we must start by understanding the role of the material in the Incarnation, and the subsequent problem of the role of matter in the worship of God.

These Christological questions were central in the first millennium of the Church's theological disputations, especially in the iconoclastic controversies of the eighth and ninth centuries which prompted the attention of St John Damascene and the Second Council of Nicea (787). The iconoclasm of these centuries was essentially rooted in the dualist heresy of the Paulicians (a sect of the Manicheans) who, viewing matter as evil, held that sacraments, rites, the veneration of relics, and reverence for holy images should be abolished.[2] The disdain of the Paulicians for

---

1. See, for example: M. Mosebach, *Heresy of Formlessness* (San Francisco: Ignatius, 2006); L. Dobszay, *The Bugnini-Liturgy and the Reform of the Reform* (Front Royal: Catholic Church Music Associates on Behalf of Church Music Association of America, 2003); U. M. Lang, *Turning Towards the Lord* (San Francisco: Ignatius, 2004); K. Gamber, *The Reform of the Roman Liturgy: Its Problems and Background* (Harrison: Foundation for Catholic Reform, 1993); W. Mahrt, *The Musical Shape of the Liturgy* (Richmond: Church Music Association of America, 2012); T. Day, *Why Catholics Can't Sing* (New York: Crossroad, 2013).

2. For more on the complex relationship between the Manicheans and Paulicians, see: S. Rossbach, *Gnostic Wars: The Cold War in the Context of a History of Western Spirituality* (Edinburgh: Edinburgh University Press, 1999), pp. 73–78.

ritual meant that they held meetings in "prayer houses" [*proseuchai*] rather than churches, thereby eschewing principles of church architecture built on the liturgy.[3] The heresy found muscle in the adherence of some Byzantine bishops and emperors, such as Leo III (the Isaurian) who "came to the conclusion that images were the chief hindrance to the conversion of Jews and Moslems, the cause of superstition, weakness, and division in his empire, and opposed to the First Commandment."[4] Leo III and a number of his successors actively persecuted those who held the orthodox view on the veneration of images, destroying many priceless images of Christ, the Blessed Virgin, and the saints in their wake.[5]

We see the heritage of this error in the wars waged on the exterior signs of the faith in the Protestant upheavals of the sixteenth century and the ruthless destruction of churches in the French revolution, but the political and cultural climate of the different outbreaks of iconoclasm evidences a slightly different motivation and emphasis in each. The destruction of images carried out in the ninth century at the command of the emperor by the military, though containing a political element, was at its root a misinformed concern for avoidance of the blasphemy of depicting that which was undepictable, a sort of respect for the divinity of Christ.[6]

In sixteenth-century England the misplaced iconoclastic concern for avoidance of superstition and ensuring the worship of God alone likewise resulted in the demolition of "shrines [...] pictures, [and] paintings"[7] in churches and homes.[8] As Eamon Duffy has shown, however, this ousting

3. See: A. Fortescue, "Paulicians," in *The Catholic Encyclopedia*, vol. 11 (New York: Robert Appleton, 1911), also: http://www.newadvent.org/cathen/11583b.htm.

4. See: A. Fortescue, "Iconoclasm," *The Catholic Encyclopedia*, vol. 7 (New York: Robert Appleton, 1910), also: http://www.newadvent.org/cathen/07620a.htm.

5. Ibid.

6. See: *Second Council of Nicea*, Philip Schaff and Henry Wace (eds), *Nicene and Post-Nicene Fathers*, Second Series 14 (Buffalo: Christian Literature Publishing, 1900), also: http://www.newadvent.org/fathers/3819.htm.

7. W. H. Frere and W. M. Kennedy (eds), *Visitation Articles and Injunctions of the Period of the Reformation*, vol. 2, p. 126, cited in: E. Duffy, *The Stripping of the Altars: Traditional Religion in England c. 1400–c. 1580* (New Haven: Yale University Press, 1992), p. 480.

8. See, for example, the woodcut from J. Foxe, *Actes and Monuments* (more commonly known as Foxe's *Book of Martyrs*), 1563 printing available online: http://www.bl.uk/learning/images/uk/crown/large2162.html. Other examples include that of the faces of Sts Augustine and Gregory, scratched out from the rood screen at Foxley in Norfolk (see: https://richardhaymanblog.wordpress.com/2015/03/26/the-tudor-reformation/); or the rood screen at Parracombe St Petrock in Devon, which was replaced by a boarded tympanum bearing almost exclusively text

was only sometimes the effect of a sincerely held Protestant desire to rid England of all memory of the ecclesiological and theological shadow of the Roman pontiff. Much of the whitewashing and destruction was instead the result of edicts of the English crown and much-resented by the faithful, carried out only in fear of penalties.[9]

The destruction of sacred art and churches during the French Revolution by the peasant *sans-culottes* and liberal intellectual *bourgeoisie* was the political fruit of seventeenth-century rationalism.[10] These ideas resonated with Protestant ideals both in their rejection of images as superstitious, distracting, idolatrous, and irrational, as well as in the populist rejection of the high culture (especially fine art), which was viewed as a tool and privilege of monarchical economic oppression and opulence.[11] The populist egalitarianism of the French Revolution was a political distortion of an authentic Christian anthropology—it gave exaggerated political implications to the notion of men as equals and unique individuals in the sight of God, and it rejected the legitimate Christian differentiation between men in terms of the scope of the exercise of authority and governance. This distortion at first led to the destruction of the art of the Church and nobility; the destruction was halted only by the moderating effect of those who viewed churches as the cultural monuments of France's past, a treasure of the people of the Republic to be preserved for their benefit.

This moderating influence had its price though, and that was the separation of the art created for the liturgy from the practice of the liturgy. It valued churches primarily for their aesthetic worth and as a monument to national brilliance rather than as a sacred locus consecrated to the glory of God and the celebration of the sacred rites of the Church. The Revolution also effected a disdain for spending money on art for purposes other than the glory of the Republic and the enjoyment of all its citizens. Domestic art reflected this "humility," prizing naturalness and a lack of artifice in depicting an idealized vision of the "common man" of France.

(the Ten Commandments, Lord's Prayer and Apostle's Creed)—the lone image is the Royal Arms (see photo: https://richardhaymanblog.wordpress.com/2014/06/21/rood-screens-catholic-heritage-in-anglican-churches/).

9. See: Duffy, *The Stripping of the Altars*, pp. 480–81.

10. Populist in origin, the populace quickly became the tyrannical ruling class. See: J. Noyes, *The Politics of Iconoclasm: Religion, Violence and the Culture of Image-Breaking in Christianity and Islam* (London: I. B. Tauris, 2013), pp. 97, 104–5.

11. Ibid., pp. 98–104. See, for example, the remains of a side aisle in the church at Cluny, attacked by Huguenots in the sixteenth century and ultimately mostly destroyed during the Revolution and its early nineteenth-century aftermath; see photo at: http://www.brynmawr.edu/cities/Cities/wld/01180/01180l.jpg.

The iconoclasm of the modern democratic era derives from the link between art and the secular, materialist state forged in the French Revolution. The nationalist movements of the nineteenth century evidence a preference for the "music of the people," favoring "simplicity," "naturalness," folk tunes, and the vernacular in the composition of art music and poetry, rallying behind artists of a shared ethnicity as emblems of national pride. This national and ethnic pride gained an importance in people's lives comparable to (or even surpassing) their religious identity, and this sense of identity prized art which reflected an idealized, egalitarian, non-pretentious, democratic state "of the people," eschewing any works which would remind people of economic inequalities, or art with religious subjects, subjects which were thought to cause friction and division.

Modern Americans and Western Europeans, as political children of rationalist and materialist ideas, are especially prey to this insidious connection since the way in which we've been taught the notion of the equality of all men before God and the importance of the individual person makes us wary of religious authority and leery of the artistic treasury of the age of opulent Catholic monarchs and churchmen. We are immersed in an environment that leads us to view the sacred arts with suspicion. In the model of Judas's reaction to the breaking of the jar of oil on the feet of Christ (John 12:1–8), we see art in the Sacred Liturgy as an unimportant frivolity, thinking money would be better spent on useful things, and the Church's funds better spent on providing food and medicine for the poor; we view an artistic masterwork used in the context of the liturgy as artificial or pretentious, as insincere and therefore untrue or unreal.

In the secular sphere, sacred art of the past must be admired only for its artistic technique and not the religious content it bears. Thus we have concerts of Palestrina Masses in concert halls and display altarpieces in art museums—we smile at them knowingly, appreciating their beauty and charm but reject their meaning because we are too sophisticated to be duped by the trappings of religion, which are a quaint appendage to the art. There is a cultural agnosticism that sets in, thinking that God is too sublime for our intellects to know, and, following the precepts of materialism, too uncertain or unreal to be conveyed by sound and light waves. Our desire not to offend the sensibilities of those who disagree with us means that we keep religious art at arm's length, indulging in it only when form and meaning have been divorced, so that we can claim to love the beauty of the work but show indifference or disdain towards its divisive religious content.

What does modern iconoclasm look like? Unfortunately the Catholic faithful know this all too well. Combined with a warped ecclesiology and a sense that bare brutalism evidences a sincere focus on what is essential, it looks like a recently constructed, nearly imageless "space" in the round with a wooden table at the center. Often the space eagerly hopes to embody utility with something like a baldachino of speakers. It may nod toward the liturgical year with some banners for color, and assert its devotion to music by erecting an organ façade on one wall in place of a high altar.[12] In older churches, it may take the form of whitewashed walls, dismantled high altars, removed communion rails, images, and stained glass, and chairs, a piano, and microphones in the sanctuary for the musicians who have abandoned the choir loft.

Indeed, iconoclasm has again wreaked havoc on the Church at the hands of those driven by erroneous theology. But the impact of iconoclasm on our aesthetic judgment, even as Catholics who desire to hold fast to orthodoxy and orthopraxis, is more detrimental than we might like to admit. It blinds us from seeing the importance of matter—of the physical world—in the worship of God and view of the world in general because it makes us feel guilty about lavishing resources and talents on creating artistic works of profound depth, intricacy, and beauty for the Sacred Liturgy. We are often shamed by others into thinking that intense interest in the beauty of the Sacred Liturgy is the result of a superficial faith which needs to be purified of material concerns so as to focus on spiritual things. In this way, modern iconoclasm inhibits our ability to pursue artistic excellence in renewing the Church's liturgical life and all the sacred arts, and ultimately it stunts our ability to draw souls to Christ because we choose sub-par art that fails to really speak to the modern world, a world which is, perhaps quite in spite of itself, still profoundly susceptible to the touch of beauty. To understand how this is so, let's look at the eloquent defense of the material world in St John Damascene's *Apologia Against Those Who Decry Holy Images*.

Like a true apologist, St John starts out by allaying the fears of those opposed to images: adoration (*latreia*) is given to God alone, and no one offends the first commandment by creating images of Christ, His mother, or his saints, or by venerating (giving *proskynesis* to) these images.[13] This is because the material world has been so elevated in Our Lord's Incarnation that we are compelled to honor it for the sake of Christ.

---

12. See, for example, the interior of St John the Evangelist Church, West Chester, OH, designed by Richard Vosko and John Ruetschle Architects (photo at: http://www.stjohnwc.org/st-john-photo-gallery.html).

13. See: St John Damascene, *On Holy Images* (London: Thomas Baker, 1898), p. 9.

> Of old, God the incorporeal and uncircumscribed was never depicted. Now, however, when God is clothed in flesh, and conversing with men, I make an image of the God whom I see. I do not worship matter, I worship the God of matter, who became matter for my sake, and deigned to inhabit matter. I will not cease from honoring that matter which works my salvation.[14]

In short, matter matters because God assumed a material body.

Matter matters so much that God compels the use of matter for the continuation of His working out of our salvation in the world. This is what the sacraments are all about, and so an attack on images is an attack not only on God Incarnate, but also on the way in which He continues to give grace to His Church. As St John says:

> If you say that only intellectual worship befits God, take away all corporeal things, light and fragrance, prayer itself through the physical voice, the very divine mysteries which are offered through matter, bread, and wine, the oil of chrism, the sign of the Cross, for all this is matter. [...] Either give up honoring these things as impossible, or do not reject the veneration of images.[15]

This iconoclastic rejection of matter is therefore a rejection of the sacraments, and a rejection of art in the liturgy. To understand the relationship between sacrament and art, we need to look at the physicality of sacraments.

At the apex of specificity, the Baltimore Catechism defines a sacrament as "an outward sign instituted by Christ to give grace."[16] More broadly, though, the Church has always understood a sacrament to be a type of sacred sign,[17] with the seven sacraments being a specific category of sign which, by virtue of their institution by Christ, effect the graces that they signify.[18] This definition is ornamented by the Church's notion of

---

14. Ibid., pp. 15–16.

15. Ibid., p. 35.

16. Confraternity of Christian Doctrine, *Saint Joseph Baltimore Catechism* (New York: Catholic Book Publishing, 1962), p. 144.

17. See: *Catechism of the Council of Trent for Parish Priests*, issued by Pius V (New York: Wagner, 1934), p. 143. "...[O]f the many definitions, none [is] more perspicuous than the definition given by St Augustine and adopted by all scholastic writers. A sacrament, he says, is a sign of a sacred thing; or, as it has been expressed in other words of the same import: A sacrament is a visible sign of an invisible grace, instituted for our justification." The last quotation is from St Bernard of Clairvaux. See also St Augustine, *De Civitate Dei* X, 5.

18. See: P. Pourrat, *Theology of the Sacraments: A Study in Positive Theology* (St Louis: B. Herder, 1910), p. 94.

a "sacramental";[19] things such as holy images, holy water, medals, or genuflection are instituted by the Church in their specificity and by virtue of the suitability of their symbolism to offer Christians means by which to "prepare for and prolong the sanctifying effects of the sacraments."[20]

The perceptible elements of a sacrament,[21] though together constituting a single sign, are in fact twofold. The first, *form*, is taken to mean the words of the rite (*verbum*); the second, *matter* (*res*), the sensible object like bread, water, or oil. The relationship between form and matter in forming a single sign, however, is of particular interest to our current topic. All natural or physical bodies are constituted by both an undeter-mined and potential principle (primary matter) as well as a determined and actualizing one (substantial form).[22] In a sacrament, both matter and form are individually constituted physical phenomena, each already consisting of its own matter and form. When, however, as St Augustine declared, "the word comes to the element," they form a new relationship and "a sacrament results."[23] In this new relationship, instituted by Christ and specified by the Church in its authority and tradition, the words of the rite, by virtue of the ability of language to bear more precise meaning, are able to specify the symbolic capabilities of the matter in a clearer manner and in a way that is analogous to the actualizing function of a substantial form in a physical body.

19. Per the definition of St Hugh of Victor as "those rites presenting an external resemblance to sacraments but not applicable to the sensible signs of Divine insti-tution." See: H. Leclercq, "Sacramentals," in *The Catholic Encyclopedia*, vol. 13 (New York: Gilmary Society, 1912), p. 293.

20. J. R. Quinn, "Sacramentals," in *New Catholic Encyclopedia*, vol. 12 (New York: McGraw Hill, 1967), p. 790.

21. I.e., the "signifier" in the symbolic equation in which a "signifier" symbolizes the "signified."

22. Moreover, these two are united and able to receive accidental characteristics which modify the substance, but without changing the nature of it. See W. A. Wallace, "Hylomorphism," in *New Catholic Encyclopedia*, vol. 7, p. 284. To illustrate, the *matter* of "wood" is that which can exist in the physical world and have the properties of mass and extension in space. The *form* of "wood" is that which determines matter to have the characteristics of being a plant material, being distinguishable from "dirt," etc. Wood, as a substance, then, might be shaped into a chair. The accidental properties of the wood in the chair distinguish it from some other wood that might be used for a table, but both secondary substances are made of the primary substance of wood. Applied by the medievals to the human person, the body is the matter and the soul is the form.

23. Quoted in J. R. Quinn, "Sacraments, Theology of," in *New Catholic Encyclopedia*, vol. 12, p. 808.

As in all effective symbols, the matter of a sacrament is not arbitrary. Water is not arbitrarily the matter of baptism—it is *fittingly* the matter because it symbolizes that which it effects. An example given in the *Catechism of the Council of Trent* illustrates this point: the water used in baptism is naturally symbolic both of washing and cooling. However, the words of the rite (that is, the form of the sacrament) specify the meaning of water in baptism as primarily that of cleansing, and even more specifically of a cleansing from sin. Thus, of all the symbolic possibilities of water, the words of the sacrament of baptism focus the signification and place it in the context of Christ's plan for salvation from sin.[24] In the same way, bread and wine are not arbitrarily the matter of the Eucharist; they are *fitting* insofar as they were really used by Christ at the institution of the sacrament, and they signify the spiritual nourishment given in the sacrament. Nor are the words of the rite, the form of the sacrament, arbitrary—they have an integral connection to the institution of the sacrament by Christ as handed down through the tradition of the Church.

In short, fittingness is essential when looking at the material world of the liturgy and the Church's rites and sacraments. Fittingness in the material world of the liturgy ensures that we are working for the coming of the kingdom of Christ in this world by more closely configuring the physical world to the liturgy of heaven. After all, we pray daily "thy kingdom come, thy will be done on earth as it is in heaven." Just as we seek to bring our lives into conformity with the will of Christ, so we seek to form the material world around us so that everything around us points towards Christ.

When we see art, architecture, and music at the service of the Sacred Liturgy as a type of sacred sign, we must expect *fittingness*. In the case of these signs, however, there is no word coming to the matter to forge a sacrament; rather they have a fitting artistic language that shapes the fitting physical matter of the art so that they speak of the mysteries they signify, and function as a symbol which opens the hearts of those who perceive them to God's grace, especially sacramental grace. This fittingness is part of how the artist has shaped the materials into the form

---

24. *The Catechism of the Council of Trent*, Part II (New York: Christian Press Association, 1905), p. 106. Certainly there are other symbolic meanings in the water of baptism, such as drowning and death, signifying our dying with Christ and rising with him as we rise out of the waters of baptism. In the comparison above, however, the Tridentine Catechism compares only two possible symbolic possibilities (cleansing and cooling) to show that one of the roles of the form of the sacrament is to favor one symbolism over the other.

of the artwork itself, and the physical materials used in the artwork have a dignity worthy of the Sacred Liturgy.

In the context of a holy image, the image must in some way be *fitting* to represent what it depicts—anyone who has studied the theology and symbolism of writing icons understands that the received traditions, symbolism, and artistic language have been honed through generations of holy hands so that this is indeed so. Even the physical materials from which the icon is made are fitting in how they point toward the reality depicted in the icon. Similarly, the architectural language and materials of a building must be *fitting* so as to convey the sacred nature of the rites that take place within its walls. Every nook and cranny, every structure and furnishing must speak of the heavenly liturgy come to earth in the Sacred Liturgy, and must be suitable for the noble celebration of the Church's rites. With regard to sacred music, the way in which the music itself speaks, along with the text it clothes, must point toward the reality they convey. The same is true of the poetry and style of the sacred texts of the Mass themselves, the vestments, the gestures—there must be a fittingness to the symbol so that the meaning of what they signify is not lost.

There is no arbitrariness in liturgical symbols and liturgical arts, though there is a legitimate diversity, as the diversity of rites which celebrate the same mysteries teaches us. Liturgical symbols develop within a rite through time as sturdy material representations of that which they signify; they move through time to different lands and to different people, proving that the way in which they signify the mystery is actually intelligible because the symbols speak in a way in which different men of different lands and times can understand. Such is the treasury of the gestures, vestments, images, architecture, and music that we have inherited from this process of development.

An example of the *unfitting* can prove this notion of fittingness and the necessity of organic development throughout time. A pastor could, for example, teach his people that when they come forward to receive Holy Communion, they are to jump before receiving the host so as to call to mind the humility necessary to receive Christ in the most holy Eucharist. The ineptitude of this symbol is apparent—there is a discontinuity between the gesture and that which is supposed to be signified. Despite what the pastor says about the gesture, nothing in how a jump looks, nor the spiritual and mental state of one jumping has anything to do with humility. The failure of the symbol explains the lack of any precedent for this symbol in the liturgy—there are no Church Fathers who encouraged the high lifting of the feet when processing to receive communion such that the gesture later developed into a jump. So too the failure to fittingly signify ensures that the symbol will not be transmitted to other liturgies, because doing so would require the same explanation by the pastor, and the same suspension of disbelief by the congregation so as to make the symbol persuasive. Thus, no matter the intention of the priest in instituting this symbol, it is ineffective and innately un-liturgical.

The opposite is true of the gesture of kneeling; there is an anthropological naturalness to the connection between kneeling and humility. The physical lowering of one's body indicates and engenders a lowering of one's self in submission; the physical vulnerability of one kneeling is greater than that of one standing, and so a physical vulnerability appropriately serves as a symbol of vulnerability of heart, a prime element of humility. Because of this naturalness, no substantial explanation is needed because the experience itself is pedagogical. Indeed, this gesture has been so used for centuries in the liturgy, and will continue to be used, since it is a highly effective material representation of a spiritual reality.[25]

In the sacred arts, there is a technical language of how to craft matter so that it bespeaks the divine mysteries. This technique may evolve through time, but in genuinely liturgical art it never does so in a total break from the past, even in the greatest strokes of genius, lest it become confusing and unintelligible to the people who view or hear it. And it is a technique honed in the hands of some of the greatest artists ever to have lived. In the traditional structures and proportions of architecture, in the received color and posture symbolism of figures in images, by the infusion of Gregorian chant (which is the native musical language of the Roman liturgy, indeed *the sung liturgy*) into new compositions—there is no arbitrariness. Works of art which have been found worthy of the liturgy in past generations have been found so because, through a well-crafted form which gives shape to fitting materials, they bespeak with every detail the mystery which they signify, and they are fitted to the liturgy so as to seem a natural embellishment of the reality of what happens at the liturgy.

Why stress this notion of fittingness of physical symbol? It is because modern iconoclasm thinks that *intention* trumps *fittingness*, and that the fittingness, especially of the form of the art, doesn't really matter as long as it fulfills a function or was crafted out of a sincere intention. Thus we come to the second part of our theology–intention–beauty triad: intention.

---

25. A good overview of the history of kneeling and genuflection in the Roman rite can be found in F. T. Bergh, "Genuflexion," in *The Catholic Encyclopedia*, vol. 6 (New York: Robert Appleton, 1909), also: http://www.newadvent.org/cathen/06423a. htm.

2. *Good Intention*

Good intention in this context could be thought of as personal holiness, practicing the faith, or at least having sympathy for and knowledge of the faith. But simply living a life of faith or even intellectually understanding the faith is insufficient in terms of artistic intention. Artists creating works for the Sacred Liturgy also ought to intend that their works glorify God, sanctify his people, and serve as a sacred window into the divine mysteries by means of a physically beautiful creation. To lack these latter elements in the intention would mean that, despite practicing or knowing the faith to some degree, the understanding of the role of sacred art in the Sacred Liturgy is deficient. Further, even having all these components in one's intention to create a work of sacred art is insufficient because a work of art requires both a well-formed creative idea in the artist's mind as well as skill-driven actions which manifest the idea in the physical world. Inadequate skills or lackluster ideas lead to works that are not as beautiful as they could be, or even as beautiful as the liturgy demands. Artists must possess sufficient skill to bring their intentions and creative ideas to fruition.

All too often in the modern world, iconoclasm takes the form of a parishioner or someone we know offering a work of art for the Sacred Liturgy that is bad in terms of artistic technique but sincerely donated or created, perhaps even for the right reasons. There are those plastic pink and blue angels on either side of the altar that Mrs. Smith gave in thanksgiving for the safe delivery of her children; the smiling Jesus with the wind-swept beach hair painted and donated by the parish school alumnus who thinks that students will find it touching if it is placed in just the right spot in the church; the emotionally and spiritually trite song a Catholic musician composed for Mass out of his devotion to the Holy Eucharist which uses wearied chord progressions, clichéd, syncopated melodies, and predictable, dull rhyme schemes in the text.

In these delicate situations, goodness of intention is mistaken for goodness of art, and insufficient distinctions are made in unraveling the link between the two because we don't want to hurt anyone's feelings, particularly the feelings of those who are sincere in their faith. When it comes to what God requires of us, Christ teaches us that the interior disposition is indeed the most important thing, since externals can be faked, but the heart, the inmost part of man, never deceives God. In the Gospel of St Matthew Christ says:

> Woe to you scribes and Pharisees, hypocrites; because you are like to whited
> sepulchres, which outwardly appear to men beautiful, but within are full
> of dead men's bones, and of all filthiness. So you also outwardly indeed
> appear to men just; but inwardly you are full of hypocrisy and iniquity.
> (Matt 23:27–28)

But we also know that because man is composed of body and soul,
physical and spiritual elements, that what happens in the body, in the
material world, affects the soul. For Christ also says earlier in that same
chapter, "All things therefore whatsoever they shall say to you, observe
and do: but according to their works do ye not; for they say, and do not"
(Matt 23:3). So, while the interior is most important, what is actually
asked of us is an exterior reality that conforms to the law and is supported
by a purity of heart and intention. To apply this principle to sacred art,
we can say that purity of artistic intention is important, but so too is the
creation of a work of art whose form is actually beautiful and possesses
true artistic merit.

3. *Artistic Technique and Beauty*

What is truly fitting for the Sacred Liturgy is something that is beautiful.
What is required is a truly beautiful work of art that stems from and
cultivates a holy life and right understanding of God. Excellent artistic
ideas incarnated by masterful artistic skills shape the material world into
beautiful forms which more adeptly call minds and hearts to God, as the
chapters by Cardinal Burke and Dr Hughes in this volume demonstrate
well. It is important that artists, as well as those charged with the care of
souls, be adept in making judgments of artistic merit so that sacred art
used in the Sacred Liturgy is beautiful.

Not possessing the ability to create beautiful art does not inhibit a soul
from entering heaven—after all, the Spirit does not distribute the same
gifts to all. It may also be said that the inability accurately to distinguish
between works of art of lesser or greater value is not morally wrong,
but this does not make it neutral or benign. This inability is, in fact, a
deficiency in human formation which affects one's ability to perceive
reality accurately, thereby dampening one's contact with goodness and
truth. Not being able to distinguish between, for example, real beauty and
shoddy work, or between something masterfully made and something
which is superficial or kitschy, means that one's apprehension of the world
is warped, corrupted, or unformed. And since God speaks to us through
the reality of the physical world that surrounds us, this deficiency cripples
our eyes, ears, and ultimately our heart from accurately perceiving God

to the fullest extent of our human faculties. We "have eyes to see and see not; and ears to hear, and hear not" (Ezek 12:2; see: Mark 8:18). The converse of this situation is also happily true: the artistic education of a man, the attuning of his senses to understanding and loving the fineness of an artistic masterwork, even if he never becomes a professional artist, makes him more susceptible to God's voice in the beauty of the things around him.[26]

For our purposes here, this deficiency in distinguishing between greater and lesser degrees of beauty is what is meant by the phrase "bad taste." It is true that those who are proficient in these matters of discernment may disagree about the goodness of some or other artwork in terms of personal taste and style—for example, someone who prefers the Romanesque to the Gothic—but it is unlikely that those disagreeing would say that the style they don't prefer lacks any artistic merit. Both would agree that there are excellent principles at work and excellent craftsmanship to be found in two well-executed churches of differing styles. This legitimate diversity in taste is not what is meant here.

Here the focus is the lack of artistic education which inhibits a person—especially a theologically well-formed and good-intentioned person—from perceiving accurately the difference between art made with real skill and art which is sub-par. This is not something taught in theology classes, or even automatically gained with a growth in personal holiness, though a growth in humility can make one more docile to learning these differences. The same is true in terms of creating art—just because someone is orthodox or intends that a work he creates glorify God doesn't mean that the thing he creates is actually a beautiful work of art. Indeed, a lack of artistic technique will probably mean that it is ugly, or at least possesses little beauty. It is his artistic skill that shapes the goodness or badness of a work of art as art, and good artistic skills are amplified in the hands of someone who, because he is orthodox and holy, has an easier time producing brilliant artistic ideas of profound theological insight. This is why the Church needs artists, and holy artists at that. As Pope St John Paul II reminds us in his *Letter to Artists*: "In producing a work, artists express themselves to the point where their work becomes a unique disclosure of their own being, of what they are and of how they are what they are" (4 April 1999, 2). If their being is conformed to Christ in a holy life and right manner of thinking, all the greater will be the art they make with honed skill.

---

26. See: John Paul II, *Letter to Artists*, 4 April 1999, n. 6.

4. *Problems Created by Bad Taste*

What are some common traps bad taste makes us fall into in the liturgy? One is that people who lack artistic discernment frequently confuse something that is emotional with something that is beautiful. While it is true that the apprehension of profound beauty is often (but not always!) accompanied by an emotional response, it is also true that works of art frequently pretend to be good by making cheap grabs at eliciting an emotional response from the relatively unformed viewer or listener, thereby tricking them into thinking that something is profoundly beautiful when in fact it is shoddily made and emotionally manipulative. This emotional manipulation leads souls to rely on emotion more than they should in the spiritual life, making them susceptible to temptation in periods of spiritual aridity—if the emotions disappear, so too does their faith. Pastors of souls and artists should want instead to form people in a faith that will withstand the inevitable periods of dryness. Excellent works of art which are beautiful touch the intellect and other dimensions of the person, serving as a remedy to the overreliance on emotion in the spiritual life.

Another common mistake of bad taste is to assume that when we perceive something to be theologically sound, we automatically think that it is a beautiful work of art. The good intention to respect the musical structure of the liturgy by the singing of the proper texts of the Mass becomes just as harmful as bad hymns when the texts are set to melodies which are forgettable and dull. Just because a piece of music is *a capella* with a text from the Gradual does not mean that it is good music! Similarly, not all churches which have a tabernacle at the center are truly beautiful! These are superficial assessments of the value of a work of art viewed through a lens of theology to the exclusion of an honest assessment of the complete reality. The result of this incomplete judgment is that we don't aim for what is best, settling instead for that which seems adequate or which fulfills a function—hardly a fitting way to worship the God who calls us to love Him with our whole heart, whole soul, and whole strength (see: Deut 6:5).

A third common mistake is exercising misguided charity. This problem occurs when thinking that if someone who is sincerely pious makes a work of art for the Sacred Liturgy that the art, by virtue of the good intention of its creator, is suited for the Sacred Liturgy. Think of the well-intentioned choir member who, no matter how hard she tries, makes the entire alto section flat or behind the beat, or the dedicated parish organist of 40 years whose playing is too slow and distracting to the congregation. Now, this is not to say that these people have absolutely no place offering something for the Sacred Liturgy—here prudence plays a role.

But prudence must be shaped by the recognition that the liturgy is a common, public act of worship in which one's deficiencies negatively affect others, and the concern must be not solely for the soul of the one offering the sub-par work, but also for the common good of all the souls in the parish. More on what to do in this circumstance below.

Finally, a common trap fallen into in Western Christianity by both those with good and bad taste alike is to boil everything in the liturgy down to validity and liceity in a sort of legalistic minimalism. We endure Masses in ugly churches with terrible music and cheesy ceremonial with the adage, "well, the Mass is the Mass," all the while downplaying the importance of the material world when surrounded by a material world which is unbelievably ugly. While it is true that Christ is truly present in the Eucharist in valid Masses, trite and beautiful alike, settling for this reality alone makes us tolerate all sorts of "deformations of the liturgy which [are] hard to bear."[27] Instead, an appropriate zeal for the worship of God should compel us to a more intelligent and active response. Settling for mere validity means deadening the ability of the liturgy to speak with every detail of the heavenly reality it signifies, and this deadening has a real consequence in the loss of souls.[28] This is because, in spite of the inadequate formation of so many in the Church in terms of the goodness and badness of art, beauty is such that it can break through even dulled senses and captivate them, drawing them out of their numbness into the infinite, into the perfection of God.[29] Offering a truly beautiful liturgy will touch even the hardest of hearts. Bad taste and bad art in the liturgy don't condemn a soul to hell, but they most certainly do stunt the ability of the liturgy to lead souls to heaven, and they also warp a person's ability to understand the underlying reality of the liturgy. If bad art adorns the liturgy, people may think that the reality of the liturgy is humdrum, unimportant, or even worse, a farce.

5. *A Better Way*

Having looked at the ways in which iconoclasm continues to affect us, and examined each of the parts in the theology–intention–beauty triad, and noting the consequences of some common pitfalls wrought by bad taste,

27. Benedict XVI, "Letter to the bishops on the publication of the apostolic letter motu proprio data 'Summorum Pontificum,'" 7 July 2007.

28. See: Martin Mosebach, *The Heresy of Formlessness: The Roman Liturgy and Its Enemy* (San Francisco: Ignatius, 2006), pp. 114–15.

29. See: The Second Vatican Council, Constitution on the Sacred Liturgy *Sacrosanctum Concilium*, 4 December 1963, n. 122.

we are now in a position to consider what ought to be done instead. These practical suggestions are not intended to be comprehensive, but rather seeds for the "firm purpose of amendment" necessary at the conclusion of our examination of conscience. What must the Church, as a patron of sacred art, do?

In order effectively to proclaim the Gospel to the world, the Church needs artists. And these artists must be excellent in their craft, well-formed theologically, and striving for holiness in order to accomplish the works of art which are most beautiful. How can the Church attract artists who strive to live up to this high calling?

It must put into practice its teachings on social justice, giving the artist a fair wage for his work. What is fair must take into account the time and effort spent in building mastery of skill. A sort of measuring stick might be the popular notion that 10,000 hours of practice are necessary to achieve mastery.[30] If one were to practice his art for 40 hours a week, it would take nearly five years of doing almost nothing else to achieve this, although we know that in reality the timeline looks different and usually encompasses most of the artist's life. The time and effort spent in honing artistic skills is part of a fair wage, so that one is paying not only for the work in the immediate moment, but also for all the work that has come before in making an artist capable of good work. Sit in on a choir rehearsal, watch an architect at the drafting table, observe an iconographer at work—these are not easy tasks which can be assigned to amateurs with the expectation that the product will be suitable for the liturgy. Skillful decisions are needed all along the way, as well as a masterful vision of the big picture. Plus, there is always administrative work, practice time, the money that went into that artist obtaining education, etc., etc., etc. We do not think twice about paying eighty dollars an hour for a plumber when the pipes are broken, making sure to look for someone who will do a good job, but how many pastors always look for someone who will play or sing for Mass free of charge, taking simply whatever can be gotten? This is not to say that the amateur has no place in the artistic life of a parish. If one implements a good wage for an artist in the parish, that artist can animate and educate volunteers within the parish into an artistic program of real excellence, truly worthy of the liturgy. But one needs at least one masterful artist to build such a program or project.

And what of ensuring the orthodoxy and suitability for the liturgy of the work of a masterful artist? We certainly know that not every talented artist produces works which satisfy these concerns. We can find directives for this matter in *Sacrosanctum Concilium*:

30. See: M. Gladwell, *Outliers: The Story of Success* (New York: Hachette, 2008).

Holy Mother Church has therefore always been the friend of the fine arts and has ever sought their noble help, with the special aim that all things set apart for use in divine worship should be truly worthy, becoming, and beautiful, signs and symbols of the supernatural world, and for this purpose she has trained artists. In fact, the Church has, with good reason, always reserved to herself the right to pass judgment upon the arts, deciding which of the works of artists are in accordance with faith, piety, and cherished traditional laws, and thereby fitted for sacred use. (n. 122)

As this paragraph points out, the Church has historically been the provider of education for artists. What are we doing in our parishes to provide for the training of children in the arts? Has artistic education been axed from our schools' curriculums because of budgetary or curricular concerns? Given what was said above about the role of artistic education in the life of the soul, this hardly seems appropriate. Has education taken a back seat to entertainment? Do we prefer that children sing for school "shows" rather than at the Sacred Liturgy? When children do sing at the Sacred Liturgy is it to show off to parents the skills learned in the classroom rather than to sing to the glory of God and for the sanctification of His people? Do we have curricula that ensures that students learn only to appreciate music and art rather than gain the real skills of doing music and art? Just think of the consequences we would face from parents if we implemented a "math appreciation" program in our schools: our children can't do math, but they sure appreciate fine arithmetic and geometry. Why do we dumb down arts curricula in this insane way? What better gift could be given to children than the skills of singing the liturgy in an artful way, or of approaching the sacred mysteries with an understanding and faith cultivated by the knowledge of sacred architecture and art? If the Church is tired of bad art, or of having art that seemingly pales in comparison to what the world offers, it should get rid of inadequate means of educating children.

An additional factor in the education of artists must be considered: Is the Church offering programs of artistic education that train artists in canonical techniques and traditional artistic language? In so many instances, artists come to the Church having been trained in artistic styles and grammars which are inimical to the faith. Consider, for example, the scarcity of programs which devote significant instructional and studio time to training architects in classical styles or artists in iconographic or realistic techniques. Most education programs are dominated by (post-)modernist, abstract, minimalist, brutalist, or "popular" styles that, when applied to the sacred arts, create terrible churches, furnishings, visual art, and music. The ubiquity of these styles in modern arts education, paired with a lack of training in aesthetic philosophy in arts programs, produces artists who may want to offer their work to the Church, but who may be completely unaware of the incompatibility of their training with the artistic language and canonical styles of the Church's sacred arts.

Sacrosanctum Concilium (n. 122) also calls for the Church to pass judgment upon a work of art vis-à-vis suitability for the Sacred Liturgy. This must be understood in light of what is required for a good judgment to be made. The good theology–good intention–beauty triad outlined here is a good frame for viewing this. Someone with authority in the Church to make this judgment—bishop, priest, director of the office of worship, etc.—must have a strong theological understanding of the faith in general and the role of the material in the salvific plan of the Father in particular. He must also be able to view a work of art in terms of its actual artistic merit, rather than constantly exercising a judgment clouded by a focus on the perceived good intentions of the artist or the work's functionality. Finally, he must have a refined taste which enables him to distinguish between good and less good and bad art. This taste can only be gained through regular contact with and an increasingly intelligent understanding of fine art.

Finally, there is the relationship between the artist and this legitimate authority of the Church. The authority which Christ gives His Church is not to be lorded over artists; instead, the authority must follow Christ's command to Peter: "Feed my sheep" (John 21:17). There exists in many corners of the Church today an antagonistic relationship between the Church and the artists who offer their work to Her. Priests often expect an amount of work from lay artists which mirrors their own celibate gift of life to the Church, not realizing that vocation for an artist is only analogous to the sacramental vocation, and so does not demand the total gift of self in the same way that the priestly vocation does. An artist cannot devote himself only to art in the same way that a priest devotes himself totally to Christ; for an artist to do so would be idolatry. In order to give spiritual sustenance to an artist, the Church must give him a legitimate artistic freedom governed by the bounds of orthodoxy and canonical artistic tradition.

A spiritual camaraderie should be developed between artist and priest as they strive to imitate Christ, each in his own way, and with the freedom of action appropriate to each. This camaraderie should be marked by mutual trust, not destroyed by the constant threat of termination of employment or refusal to give way to the other's legitimate concerns. The expertise of each is also respected in this camaraderie, and where one finds the other deficient in understanding his area of expertise, charity and truth demand an explication of expert knowledge, while humility demands that the wisdom of expertise is received. If the services of a Catholic artist are engaged, a pastor must not assume that this artist has no theological understanding. Likewise, if there is legitimate authority over a work of art exercised in the Church, the artist must not assume that the pastor has no artistic judgment. An antagonism built on the supposition of one's own total expertise has no place in a Church which needs art "in order to communicate the message entrusted to her by Christ" (John Paul II, *Letter to Artists*, 12).

In other words, and in summary, in addition to an understanding of the theological, intentional, and aesthetic issues at play here, there is required a true and sincere effort to understand the challenges and demands put upon artists in creating good and fitting works, and similarly, on the part of the artists, a true and sincere effort to render what is both fitting and beautiful, as well as the humility sufficient to accept the guidance of the Church. In charity and with prayer, these things are possible.

LITURGICAL MUSIC IS NON-NEGOTIABLE

Gregory Glenn

1. *Introduction*

The Madeleine Choir School, the parish school serving the Cathedral of the Madeleine in Salt Lake City, opened its doors for ministry in August of 1996. Beginning with just over one hundred students in grades four through eight, the school has grown to 400 students in pre-kindergarten through eighth grade, with the expectation that it will reach full enrollment in 2018 with 480 students.

A trend in the school's demographics has been the increase in school families identifying themselves as "nones." The percentage of families indicating they have no religion has doubled in the last ten years. In a recent conversation with a parent who self-identifies as a "none," he confided in me his unfaltering belief in and growing concern about the presence of evil in our world—while he could not endorse positions of faith in other matters beyond the natural, he was resolute in his belief in evil.

2. *The World Today*

This, of course, is not shocking at all. In 2015 five of the world's largest banks, four being from the United States, were fined 5.7 billion dollars, pleading guilty to criminal behavior which brought financial hardship and ruin upon countless fellow human beings. Amazingly these banks barely flinched at these staggering fines, and they continue to spend millions of dollars lobbying for the rejection of further regulatory controls.

A Tennessee man with ties to Utah and his family collected $187 million for cancer patients last year and then used much of the money collected to buy themselves cars, gym memberships and take luxury cruise vacations, pay for college tuition and employ family members with six-figure salaries. It was alleged that this is one of the largest charity fraud cases ever, involving all 50 states. Only 3% of the funds raised for the cancer patients from generous donors actually went to the patients while 97% of the funds were used for the family's leisure and entertainment.

64,000 women and young children with an average age of 6-and-a-half years crossed the USA border in the year 2014 looking for refuge from their countries and certain death at the hands of *pandillas* or gangs which control many of the poor and middle class neighborhoods in Honduras, El Salvador and Guatemala. The drug cartels throughout Central and South America continue to wreak havoc through killings and kidnappings.

In despair, we might give in to the philosopher Ernest Becker's horrific vision of the planet described in his last work *Escape from Evil* as a "theater for crawling life," or the more horrific assessment of the human as nothing more than a moving digestive tract with legs and appendages designed to stuff things down its gullet. Existence is reduced to a constant struggle to feed in which all animate species try to incorporate whatever other organisms they can fit into their mouths.[1]

We share a very different vision and hope for our world and for humanity. Our hope derives from our firm belief that while, at our beginning, something went dreadfully wrong one night at dinner, our final end is to be gathered at the great wedding banquet of the Lamb, a festal gathering with myriad angels and saints. We have come to know that the means by which we were released from that early tragic event at dinner and thus arrive at this festal gathering is the redemption wrought by our Savior Jesus Christ. It follows then that we are rightly concerned about the liturgy, because it is the liturgy "through which the work of our redemption is accomplished" (Second Vatican Council, *Sacrosanctum Concilium*, 4 December 1963, 2). In the liturgy, we are privileged to join the great prayer of Jesus Christ and his body the Church, addressed to the Father who is rich in mercy, and united in the commerce of their love in the Holy Spirit. We join our Savior's prayer of thanksgiving, sacrifice, remembrance, and intercession for the many needs of the Church and the world. It is in this sense that we can firmly assert just why we are so passionate about the liturgy: the liturgy advances the Kingdom of God and brings salvation and wholeness to our troubled world.

Our current age has such great need. Young people may rightly question what my generation has left to them: those of us who have gone before them have tried and failed in many ways to shape a just and fair society; we are rapidly consuming and poisoning the vast natural resources of our planet; we are seemingly powerless to fix the problem of famine and hunger for a billion fellow human beings, and standing by while the gap between the rich and the poor of the world continues to grow.

---

1. Ernest Becker, *Escape from Evil* (New York: Free Press, 1975), pp. 1–2.

Pope Benedict XVI wrote in his encyclical letter *Caritas in Veritate* that:

> The world's wealth is growing in absolute terms, but inequalities are on the increase. In rich countries, new sectors of society are succumbing to poverty and new forms of poverty are emerging. In poorer areas some groups enjoy a sort of "superdevelopment" of a wasteful and consumerist kind which forms an unacceptable contrast with the ongoing situations of dehumanizing deprivation. "The scandal of glaring inequalities" continues. (29 June 2009, 22)

In the last century we have barreled through a vast array of economic and political systems all derived from the great promise of the Enlightenment and human self-fulfillment: Communism, Fascism and other forms of bureaucratic societal organization have come and gone, tragically taking with them millions of human lives snuffed out in the name of their so-called progress. In the last century alone, we took the lives of over 200 million human beings by means of war. Our low regard for human life allows us to defend with the delight of political correctness the destruction of infants, the warehousing of the elderly, the harboring in the shadows of a permanent underclass to do our most oppressive acts of labor: for all the aforementioned, the suffering is very great indeed. While we are being "botoxed," coiffed, exfoliated and massaged, children are perishing in developing countries because of no access to the readily and easily available vaccine for pneumonia, and mothers are perishing at alarming rates in Africa because they do not have access to drugs which we know are certain to prolong the life of those who suffer the scourge of HIV infection.

With the failure of our systems, programs, ideologies and attempts at social reconstruction, what can be done to bring an end to this terror? What will inspire in us a greater commitment to the common good, the dignity of all human life and a sense of solidarity with our fellow humanity, especially the poor and the vulnerable? What is it that will save the world?

3. *Our Fundamental Response to the Situation of the World Today—Liturgical Prayer*

Again, from Pope Benedict's *Caritas in Veritate*:

> Development needs Christians with their arms raised towards God in prayer, Christians moved by the knowledge that truth-filled love, caritas in veritate, from which authentic development proceeds, is not produced by us, but given to us. For this reason, even in the most difficult and complex times, besides recognizing what is happening, we must above all else turn to God's love. (n. 79)

Pope Benedict continues:

> Development requires attention to the spiritual life, a serious consideration
> of the experiences of trust in God, spiritual fellowship in Christ, reliance
> upon God's providence and mercy, love and forgiveness, self-denial,
> acceptance of others, justice and peace. All this is essential if "hearts of
> stone" are to be transformed into "hearts of flesh" (Ezek 36:26), rendering
> life on earth "divine" and thus more worthy of humanity. (n. 79)

One of my true privileges in my work at the choir school is the teaching
of theology to the 7th and 8th grade classes. I have learned over the years
that when you speak to adolescents and young people, you have to really
focus your message. It is a great challenge and a rewarding exercise: your
communication must be succinct, compelling, comprehensive—and brief.

This was the case in Mexico some years ago when Pope Benedict
spoke to a large gathering of young people in León underneath a statue
of Christ the King-Cristo Rey—erected as a monument to the memory
of priests, religious and laity who had lost their lives in the Cristero
Rebellion that began in 1926. He had these profound words of advice for
the young people gathered: "If we allow the love of Christ to change our
heart, then we can change the world" (24 March 2012).

And so it is in changed hearts that true development, true change will
come to address the many horrors that cry to heaven from our planet, and
it is the liturgy, the great prayer of Christ and his Body the Church, by
God's grace, that will change hearts.

Caritas in Veritate insists:

> It is Christ's charity that drives us on: "caritas Christi urget nos." The
> urgency is inscribed not only in things, it is not derived solely from the rapid
> succession of events and problems, but also from the very matter that is at
> stake: the establishment of authentic fraternity. The importance of this goal
> is such as to demand our openness to understand it in depth and to mobilize
> ourselves at the level of the "heart," so as to ensure that current economic
> and social processes evolve towards fully human outcomes. (n. 20)

The Liturgy, this work of Father, Son and Holy Spirit, will bring salvation
to the world: it is this conviction that drives the passion among us for a
most noble, engaging and integral celebration of the Mass and the Liturgy
of the Hours. We respond to the injunction of the Apostle Paul, reminding
us that as often as we eat this bread and drink this cup, we proclaim the
Lord's death until he comes again in glory. In the prayer of the Church
we are taught and formed with the most fundamental attitudes and habits
needed for Christian living. It is the liturgy which invokes the adoption

of a particular logic for life: a kenotic, self-emptying which is the key to our human happiness and fulfillment. It is this logic for life that indicates the vocation of humanity will be realized only when all people learn to live together in self-transcending love. It is the logic for life articulated by Blessed Oscar Romero when he stated "We have never preached violence, except the violence of love, which left Christ nailed to a cross, the violence that we must each do to ourselves to overcome our selfishness and such cruel inequalities among us."[2] It is indeed a logic for life derived from the very heart of Jesus himself, a heart that is meek and humble.

4. *Liturgical Music*

My specific focus is the non-negotiable and essential role of music in this great work of the liturgy. *Sacrosanctum Concilium* begins its consideration of sacred music noting that it is a "…treasure of inestimable value, greater even than that of any other art" and affirming the unity of singing and the word as "…a necessary or integral part of the Sacred Liturgy" (n. 112). By qualifying the sung elements of the liturgy as integral, the Constitution on the Sacred Liturgy invites the Church seriously to reflect and deliberate on the institutions that provide formation for young people and adults in the Christian life, considering carefully the assignation of resources, personnel and pastoral prioritization that this important part of our common life receives. Given this assessment of the role of music in the liturgical prayer of the Church, it follows that liturgical music is a non-negotiable and essential element in our schools, houses of formation, pastoral institutes and educational initiatives.

Unfortunately, music has always been held in some suspicion when employed for religious purpose. In an ancient collection of sayings of primitive abbots and patriarchs we encounter the case of the Abbot Pambo, who was concerned about the musical innovations in the fourth-century church of Alexandria. Having sent one of the monastic brothers to the city, Abbot Pambo noticed that he was very disturbed upon returning to the monastery, and so he addressed him:

> "Son, I see that you are disturbed. Were you beset by temptation in the city?" The brother answered: "Father, we spend our days here serenely and we sing neither canons nor *troparia*. But when I came to Alexandria I saw the choirs in the church and how they sing, and I became very sad that we do not sing canons and *troparia*." Then the elder said to him: "Woe to us, my son! The days have come when monks turn away from the enduring nourishment which the Holy Spirit gives them and surrender themselves to singing. What

2. Óscar Arnulfo Romero, *The Violence of Love* (Maryknoll: Orbis, 2004), p. 25.

kind of contrition is that? How can tears come from the singing of *troparia*? How can a monk possess contrition if he stays in the church or his cell and raises his voice like the lowing of the cattle?"[3]

St Augustine also expressed concern about the role of music, noting the impact of the liturgical singing in Milan upon him. Referencing earthly pleasures, he writes "…sometimes, however, being too cautious of this very danger, I err by overmuch severity—so greatly in fact that I wish all the melodies of the sweet chants with which David's psalter is accompanied would be banished from my ears and from the Church herself."[4]

And much later in England, in 1572 a legislative group composed *An Admonition to Parliament* bemoaning the musical splendor of the cathedral churches:

> The dennes of all loitering lubbers, where master Deane…Canons…the cheefe chaunter, singing men…squeaking queresters, organ players…live in great idleness, and have their abiding. If you would knowe whence all these came, we can easely answere you, that they came from the Pope, as oute of Troian horses bellye, to the destruction of Gods kingdome. The churche of God never knewe them…[5]

Singing is among the most primal and elemental of all human forms of expression requiring no further medium than the human person. Given its crucial role in our prayer many of us are dedicated to promoting the use of proper texts so crucial to the liturgy, and preserving ordinary settings that are universally applicable both in performance while also being capable of transcending cultural diversity. We share a concern for the deracination that has occurred from the fount of our sacred music, and which remains a vital source for new musical development and composition. We mourn the loss of a vast treasury of musical prayer shelved and sidelined by a very narrow view of progress, perhaps too great a confidence in the social engineering of liturgical prayer, and a misplaced enthusiasm for the novel and the immediately satisfying and intriguing.

It is precisely these convictions and concerns that served as the inspiration for the founding of a choir school at the Cathedral of the Madeleine. The choir school was founded as one small agent of liturgical renewal and restoration, in service to the liturgy that is indeed the source and summit of

---

3. Cited in: Johannes Quasten, *Music and Worship in Pagan and Christian Antiquity* (Washington: National Association of Pastoral Musicians, 1983), p. 95.

4. Augustine, *Confessions* 10, 33 (Cambridge: Hackett, 2006).

5. Alan Mould, *The English Chorister* (London: Continuum, 2007), p. 96.

the life of the Church, advancing God's kingdom by the sanctification of souls and the changing of hearts, rendering sacrificial praise and thanksgiving to God.

The formation of young people in the work of the liturgy and the music essential to this work has a long and at times difficult history. From the households of the bishop committed to a routine of worship in Kent,[6] to the schools formed in the Carolyngian empire, described as "the envy of angels" by St Bernard,[7] places of education and formation which revolve around and find their reason for being from the Church's liturgy have made a lasting and profound contribution.

5. *A Roman Catholic Choir School in Salt Lake City, Utah? Really?*

I want to explore three fundamental questions about the choir school at the Cathedral of the Madeleine with hope that this will encourage the founding of additional choir schools to serve the liturgy and our respective ecclesial communities. They are: How did we get started? What does the choir school do? What are the critical lessons learned enabling the success of a choir school?

a. *How Did We Get started?*
In the Spring of 1990, we announced the opening of an after-school program for boys and girls that was to be housed at the cathedral known as the Madeleine Choir School. We conducted brief and simple auditions in the Catholic schools throughout the valley—if a child could negotiate the octave leap in the third phrase of "Happy Birthday" and go on to successfully sing the descending thirds and seconds, they were in! Invitation letters were distributed, and we were off to a start with roughly 35 boys and 35 girls in grades five through eight. We began with a weekly rehearsal, evolving to a twice-weekly rehearsal, and made very slow but real progress.

A critical feature of the early success of the ensemble was the annual summer camp where we were able over the course of a week to rehearse, instruct the students in music theory, sight-singing and ear training, basic principles of the liturgy and more. This week was always a huge success as we mastered the repertoire for the coming year and grew immensely

6. Ibid., p. 2.

7. See: Stephen Jaeger, *The Envy of Angels: Cathedral Schools and Social Ideals in Medieval Europe, 950–1200* (Philadelphia: University of Pennsylvania Press, 1994).

in our musical and liturgical knowledge. It prompted one of the parents to comment, "...the children learned more in one week's time than they accomplish after several months of weekly rehearsal." Ah ha!

1990 was also the year the cathedral was preparing to close for an eighteen-month period of restoration. In the discussions about the future work of the cathedral, Msgr Francis Mannion and I considered the "pipe-dream" of a choir school at the cathedral. While giving the matter a brief deliberation, we would generally chuckle at the overwhelming odds against such a thing and quickly return to our cocktails.

However, the dream remained alive and was soon to be taken up by parents who recognized the great value of this education with its musical and liturgical formation and performance experience. In fact, the summer camp comment began to take on a life of its own. In 1995 we appointed a committee and launched a feasibility study slated to review with detail the various aspects of a potential school: academics and curricula, financial viability, physical plant—could you really open a school in a basement? After months of work, we were somewhat surprised to discover that the results of the study were positive. In May 1996, the final review was submitted to Archbishop George Niederauer who on 26 May 1996 approved the opening of a new Catholic school at the Cathedral of the Madeleine. I remember vividly the response to this news of both Msgr Mannion and myself: Now what do we do?

With the announcement of the school's opening, a parent gathering was held, and the school was full in a matter of days. This was all rather shocking and a significant risk engaged by new parents: We did not have a Principal or a single teacher, there were no books, desks or other materials necessary to the proper functioning of a school. After a very hectic summer, the school opened on 26 August of that same year, with 108 students in grades 4–8. We were blessed with an outstanding faculty and staff in the beginning, and a very vibrant and supportive parent community who sacrificed and worked to get this fledgling school off to a great start.

We quickly realized that the basement was not a permanent home—work began on a capital campaign to enable the purchase of our current campus. In December of 2002, we moved from the tight quarters of the basement to the two-acre campus we have today. The new campus allowed us to begin expanding the student body, eventually including classes from pre-kindergarten through eighth grade. Enrollment continues to climb as we yearly add an additional classroom to a grade level—in August 2015 we welcomed approximately 400 students, and, given the current admissions trajectory, our projected full enrollment will finally be reached in 2018 with a student body of just under 500 young people.

b. *What Does the Choir School Do?*

Our first and most important work is to serve the public worship life of the cathedral. The choristers serve as the trebles for the cathedral choir. They do so in two groups: the boys and the girls. The cathedral choir assists at all Sunday Masses, and Masses on Solemnities and Feasts of the Lord throughout the choral term. The boys and girls alternate in joining the men of the choir, so that on a given Sunday or Solemnity it might be a choir of men and girls or a choir of men and boys. The choristers also assist at Mass Monday through Thursday at 5.15pm. The boys assist on Mondays and Wednesdays and the girls assist on Tuesdays and Thursdays.

What does Mass with the cathedral choir and choristers look and sound like? At the daily Masses the choir processes singing the proper Gregorian introit. The Ordinary of the Mass comes from one of the eighteen chant ordinaries or a treble setting of the ordinary, although I must admit—and I think my colleagues would agree—treble ordinaries get a bit tiresome. We look forward to the day that we will be able to staff the daily Masses with the men. Depending on the solemnity of the day, motets are sung at the preparation of the altar and at communion. Daily Mass concludes with the singing of the proper Marian antiphon before the shrine of Our Lady of Guadalupe.

Masses on Sundays and Solemnities also begin with the singing of the proper Gregorian introit, the ordinary in a choral setting ranging from Alonso Lobo to Francis Poulenc, proper motets as much as possible and the proper communion chant during Holy Communion.

Masses with the choir school as a whole occur regularly. The student body sings the ordinary in Latin depending on the season: Masses VIII, XI, IX and I are taught to all students. Any aversion to the Latin ordinary today is perplexing given the pastoral reality: there are just 283 words in the Latin ordinary, certainly manageable for young people today, and the recent document on liturgical music from the Bishops of the United States gently recommends that all of us know the *Kyrie* from Mass XVI, the *Gloria* from Mass VIII, the *Credo* III and the *Sanctus* and *Agnus Dei* from Mass XVIII.[8]

The choral term currently runs from the Sunday following Labor Day through the Solemnity of *Corpus Christi*, with the addition of the period of time extending from our Patronal Feast (22 July) through the Assumption of Our Lady. In addition to the Masses, the choir assists with vespers on Christmas Day, Easter and Pentecost, many other solemnities, the Sundays of the Advent and Christmas season, and the season of Easter.

---

8. *Sing to the Lord: Music in Divine Worship* (Washington: United States Conference of Catholic Bishops, 2007), n. 75.

What are the various ensembles that function at the cathedral? This is still a matter of development as we grow, but as mentioned above the two primary ensembles from the school are the boys' choir—the St Gregory Choristers—and the girls' choir—the St Cecilia Choristers. A group of our most qualified boys and girls come together in what is known as the schola. The schola performs with the men of the choir at major festivals and occasions. There is also a training choir known as the St Nicholas Choir. A subset of the boy choristers is made up of boys still in the school with changing or changed voices. They rehearse separately and are integrated into the service schedule. Additionally, we have a high school women's group made up of graduates that is beginning to take shape, and we have a high school young men's group, also made up of graduates. Both of these groups are integrated into the service schedule as well.

There are three other important elements of our work: the concert season, performance tours and collaboration with other professional arts organizations.

The choir has a regular concert season with 12–15 performances per year in which we celebrate that great treasury of sacred music. The concert season of the previous year included Howell's *Take Him Earth for Cherishing*, Britten's *St Nicholas*, Bach's *St John Passion* and Haydn's *Lord Nelson Mass*. Annually the choristers perform Britten's *A Ceremony of Carols* several times during the holidays and Pergolesi's *Stabat Mater* as a choral meditation on Good Friday afternoon. Other seasons have presented Britten's *Noye's Fludde*, Dvorak's *Stabat Mater*, Vaughan Williams's *Mass in G Minor* and Mendelssohn's *Paulus*. A personal high point was probably a performance of Messiaen's *Trois Petites Liturgies de la Présence Divine*—a truly remarkable and exhilarating work. The concert season is an opportunity for the choir school to provide a service to the larger community by offering free public performances of these great works of art. It has also been the primary way we have accessed the financial support of the larger community, and it drives a very successful annual appeal made each year.

The choir travels annually, with international tours alternating with tours within the Western United States. Every four years, the choir travels to Rome so that each child in the school will have the opportunity to experience this pilgrimage and performance opportunity. A recent tour traveled to Berlin, Leipzig, Prague and Vienna. Tours are great experiences in and of themselves, but they serve primarily for us as something of a choral boot camp: nothing whips a choir into shape as much as the pressures of a performance tour. And so, from a practical and musical standpoint, the tours are of great benefit to the work of the choir school.

Performances with professional arts organizations have been an invaluable experience for the children. Thanks in large part to my colleague Melanie Malinka, the choir school regularly supplies Utah Opera and the Utah Symphony with treble choristers whenever they are called for by the repertoire running in these organizations. In 2015 we prepared the boys for Utah Opera's *Tosca*, and have performed Mozart's *Magic Flute*, Puccini's *La Boheme* and *Turandot* and Britten's *A Midsummer's Night Dream*. The year 2015 marked the 75th anniversary of the Utah Symphony that involved the joint performance of the Mahler 8th and works of Orff and Ravel. In past years, we have also collaborated to a great extent with the Mormon Tabernacle Choir, including a once-in-a-lifetime joint performance of the Battle Hymn of the Republic at the reopening of our state capitol.

c. *What Are the Critical Lessons Learned Enabling the Success of a Choir School?*

While the cathedral was closed for restoration in the early 1990s, I was given the opportunity to travel to London's Westminster Cathedral and examine their choir school over a three-month period, where I was given the opportunity to experience the incredible musical and liturgical work of the choir. I was also able to travel to several other choir schools throughout England.

I was very keen to learn about the pedagogical techniques that produced these brilliant choirs, and what specific instruction was given to the boys in order to attain the great level of excellence with which they regularly performed. When I met with the various organists and choirmasters, my question was almost always met with a certain bewilderment. Generally, my questions produced puzzlement and mystification. I was greatly disheartened that there seemed to be no one who could articulate what it was that wrought these magnificent sounds.

Later, I realized the source of the bewilderment and perplexity: they did not have an articulated method of training choristers because the method has been in place in the daily routine of the cathedral and choir schools for centuries. While not being that long lived, the choir school at Westminster was a perfect example.

I propose the following critical factors that lead to the success of a choir school: first, the regular, daily assistance at the liturgy. A daily sung liturgy is crucial to the advancement of a choir, the development of a large body of repertoire and the maintenance of a high standard of performance. Building up to this can be painful—we've been through that pain—and a commitment of this kind can be vexing in our day and age as parents and children do not often take part in activities that are long term. It has taken a great deal of education and orientation. In the end, I have told our parents that we are actually "choir school lite" in that, between the boys and the girls, our choristers share the responsibility of the daily and Sunday Masses, and so perform only half the services of a typical choir school chorister. I have collected data from various cathedrals and choir schools detailing the service schedule, how often the choristers sing, etc., and put this in graphic form for parents to see. It is quite enlightening to them. Crucial to the development of the choir is the regular assistance at the liturgy.

Second: a clear sense of a deputed ministry. At Westminster Cathedral, the choristers are very charmingly vested as if they were diminutive miniature monsignors—however, this is not just for show. At Westminster, the choir is deputed by the cathedral's Chapter of Canons to perform the daily liturgies of the cathedral on its behalf. Because of this, the choir officially dons the vesture of the Chapter. There is a very clearly established and well-understood role for the choir—they have a very clear and engaged sense of the importance of their ministry. In the United States by Church law we do not have cathedral Chapters. This role is most often subsumed by the Diocesan College of Consulters.

Having some clearly defined sense of the ministerial role of the choir is crucial to its success. This is something children can really sink their teeth into—and it carries them through the demanding months of service they offer to the church. People need a sense of their place and role. While the full participation of the congregation remains a most important goal in our liturgical celebrations, the choir has suffered a tremendous loss in the understanding of its ministerial function. Cardinal Vaughan's vision for Westminster Cathedral originally included a community of Benedictine monks to be in residence, bearing responsibility for the daily office. A conflict about the pastoral leadership of the cathedral ensued and thwarted Cardinal Vaughan's vision, but the choir school and the choir have been able to perform a significant role in forwarding this vision.

Third: "event" versus "institution" models of formation. Everybody loves choristers around Christmastime. Inevitably, the major newspapers and television stations of Salt Lake City stalk around the cathedral for a photo shot of the choristers at Christmas. Everyone delights to the soaring descant topping off a lustily rendered singing of the First Nowell. But what about 21 February? We don't just remove the choristers from their closets, dust them off, and set them to singing the Christmas standards. What I have just described alludes to a greater challenge we face in church music today: the "event" versus the "institution."

I would argue that we need fewer events and more institutions. The event has become the model for formation: we go to great expense as a church to sponsor conventions, which gather like-minded individuals together for a hyper-intensive week of workshops, talks and unreal, perhaps unnatural ecclesial gatherings for worship.[9] Conventions are short-lived, often very minimal in their actual consequence and not terribly profitable for the parish or community they are intended to actually serve. You cannot ground adults in the chant and choral tradition of the Church, or give them the skills for new composition of quality, or advance their vocal production or choral technique greatly, or develop a healthy and sound liturgical spirituality in a weeks' time. We need fewer conventions and more schools.

This "event" versus "institution" challenge plays out in other ways as well. The direction for diocesan and cathedral liturgies is often not coming organically from the resident ensemble or body of musicians but rather from middle-level administrative offices—sometimes, cathedral musicians, who make music at the prayer in their buildings on a daily and weekly basis, are not involved at all in major diocesan events, as we witnessed a few years ago at the installation of an archbishop on the east coast. This is not to question the value of diocesan agencies in service to the larger Church, but a greater level of support for our choral founda-tions and institutions, especially in the cathedrals, would provide a more substantive and long-term solution to the challenges we face in celebrating these important gatherings of the local Church.

Institutions are often declared impossible and imprudent financial challenges, making events attractive in that they do not encumber a local church with long-term economic commitments. It should be noted that in many dioceses there is without question a far greater financial commitment made to high school athletics than there is to the musical and liturgical life of the cathedral church. I certainly espouse a both/and position when it comes to supporting the work of our Catholic high schools and the great value there is in young people participating in athletic activities. I would also propose that serious consideration be given to the financial support necessary for the formation provided in liturgy and music and the role of the cathedral church in any diocese.

9. I have to grant exception to the leaders and participants of *Sacra Liturgia* 2015 in New York City. They went to great lengths to prevent it from turning into the typical convention, and I believe that gatherings of this kind are very profitable.

6. *Conclusion*

In concluding I would like to offer a few further reflections on the value of a choir school. First: vocations to the priesthood and religious life. In October 2013, our first alumnus was ordained a deacon in Rome and then returned in the June 2014 for priestly ordination in our cathedral. This young man was trained at the choir school, continued service in the cathedral choir, knows the Gregorian propers and is versed in the church's vast musical tradition. His liturgical spirituality was planted and nourished at the choir school. I hope that he is the first of many.

Second, the choir school is in an interesting position with regard to a challenging pastoral reality of the cathedral and diocese: almost 70% of Catholics in Utah are Hispanic, the majority Spanish speaking, and largely comprised of more recent immigrants coming to Utah after the mid-1990s. The Hispanic population has led to the establishment of a second Sunday Mass in Spanish each weekend at the cathedral, and the community continues to grow. At the choir school, we have determined we must respond to this pastoral reality. In the last eight years we have enacted a scholarship program to begin the inclusion of children from the Hispanic community.

This has been no small challenge both financially and academically as we have had to strengthen our ability to properly engage these English Language Learners, and worked to ensure that these families are fully-incorporated in the school community. Most of the families have had little prior opportunity for instruction in music, although the majority of them have come from Mexico and Central America, where there is a stable body of repertoire with which they are all very familiar. It is a great challenge for the musicians at the cathedral to properly serve this community, as they often struggle in so many ways that liturgical music is not high on their list of concerns. However, the incorporation of these students, giving them musical and liturgical formation and experience with the great treasury, is proving highly successful and creating hope for a bright and promising future, albeit this is some way off. I count this work—and I know that my colleagues join me—as a particular blessing.

Finally, there is a great grace that I have discovered. The liturgy does not always constantly demand my vigorous leadership, or my strong intention or participation. I confess the possession of a slight, perhaps genetic, predisposition to semi-pelagianism. Sometimes I need to lead or participate most ardently. But other times the liturgy simply carries me, buoys me up and grants me the grace to stay at it. Perhaps we all need to call to mind the sobering diaconal admonition found in the Orthodox rites that proclaims at the outset of the liturgy that "Now is the time for God to work."

The liturgy will bring salvation to the world—in the liturgy that is the great song of the church: *Dilexisti iustitiam, Tibi dixit cor meum, Magnificat anima mea, Nos autem gloriari.* In this song God transforms and changes hearts and advances his kingdom, enabling us to build a civilization of love. Choir schools can do much to create this song.

As Pope Benedict XVI wrote: "The Church is to transform, improve, 'humanize' the world—but how can she do this if at the same time she turns her back on beauty, which is so closely allied to love? For together, beauty and love form the true consolation in this world, bringing it as near as possible to the world of the resurrection. The Church must maintain high standards; she must be a place where beauty can be at home."[10]

10. Joseph Ratzinger, *The Feast of Faith* (San Francisco: Ignatius, 1986), pp. 124–25.

Liturgical Leadership in a Secular Society: A Bishop's Perspective

Salvatore Cordileone

1. *Introduction*

In recent years we have witnessed a disturbing trend: many leaders in our country no longer speak about "freedom of religion," but "freedom of worship." There is a world of difference between the two. Freedom of *religion* was, of course, a founding principle of the United States of America, but this subtle change of nomenclature would indicate an attempt by some to construct an avowedly "secular society," with "secularism" as the new social religion whose doctrines must be inculcated upon the citizenry, even though individuals are allowed to conduct religious services within the walls of their houses of worship. At the outset of my reflections, I would observe that one problem affecting civil discourse is that people of various positions use the same terms, but often mean different things by them. So it is with the term "secular": what we mean as Catholics by this word is quite different from what many architects of a "secular society" do, and this is at the root of the difference between "freedom of worship" and "freedom of religion."

So, what does our secular society mean by "secular"? We can begin with the definition of the word found in the Merriam-Webster Dictionary:

1. Not spiritual: of or relating to the physical world and not the spiritual world;
2. Not religious;
3. Of, relating to, or controlled by the government rather than the Church.

In this understanding, religion has no place in the secular realm—it is a private set of beliefs which may be indulged like some hobby or craft, but must not extend its influence beyond the walls of a house of worship. This idea that freedom of religion can be reduced to freedom of worship cuts to the core of Catholic religion and Catholic liturgy. I would like to speak about this meaning of the word "secular" because it is part of the air we breathe; it exercises an influence on people, even those in the pews.

2. *The Historical Perspective*

We are children of the Enlightenment. One of the hallmarks of the so-called "Age of Reason" was the rejection of revealed truth. Two influential philosophical traditions flowed from the Enlightenment, empiricism and idealism. Each of these schools of thought has taken many forms; my concern here is not with these philosophical systems as such, but with certain tendencies or presuppositions they engender in contemporary culture.

Proponents of empiricism assert that only scientifically verifiable data can be objectively true. This approach undergirds the erroneous presumption that science and religion are inimical to one another. Idealism holds that objects of knowledge are dependent on the activity of the mind. Truth is subjectively determined: it is not something I recognize, it is something I manufacture. Very practical conclusions follow from these two approaches. For example, school children are given tests in which they are asked to distinguish between "fact" and "opinion." Statements of value, questions of moral right and wrong, are always placed in the category of "opinion." Apropos of this subjective and relativistic understanding of truth, I enjoy the response Francis Beckwith is reported to have given to a student in his philosophy class who asked, "Why is truth so important?" Professor Beckwith, I've been told, asked in turn, "Do you want the true answer or the false answer?"

This inheritance from the Enlightenment has created schizophrenia in our culture. On the one hand, there is the triumph of the (self-styled) scientific mindset: only scientifically verifiable claims can be considered "facts." By extension, only the physical, material world is real; thus the drive for as many physical pleasures and possessions as possible. On the other hand, there is an exaltation of the subjective perspective: something is true or not only if I think it is. This perspective trumps the scientific mindset if the former gets in the way of what I want. This has now even been enshrined in law. In finding for the constitutionality of Washington state's so-called "compassion in dying" legislation in 1996, the Ninth Circuit Court of Appeals asserted in its decision: "At the heart of liberty is the right to define one's own concept of existence, of meaning, of the universe, and of the mystery of human life." That the heart of liberty allows an individual the freedom to make decisions affecting the individual's own life, certainly, but to *define the meaning of the universe?* Really?

This schizophrenia continues to play itself out in more and more bizarre and tragic ways. For example, the most elementary knowledge of biology makes it clear that a child is the same organism, a human being, inside the womb or outside the womb. But this is, to borrow a phrase, "an inconvenient truth" for some, so the human dignity of the child becomes dependent on subjective judgment, not biological fact. Another example is what Pope Francis refers to as "gender ideology," the idea that one's biological sex and personal "gender identity" can be at variance with each other, with more and more different gender identities being invented beyond just male and female.

How does this state of affairs affect liturgy? If the physical universe is simply a mass of data, then there is no deeper meaning to creation, and certainly not what we would call a sacramental dimension to it. This strikes at the heart of our most fundamental Christian beliefs: that God is the Creator of the universe and that in the Incarnation of the second Person of the Holy Trinity, God Himself has entered into our material world and made it an instrument of our salvation. On the other hand, if truth is purely subjective, then the maxim, *"Lex orandi, lex credendi"* is watered down to refer to my beliefs, or those I share with like-minded people. Liturgy is valued for the feelings it generates, and it can be manipulated in order to produce an emotional experience. As I reflect on liturgical leadership in a secular society, I believe it is important to recognize the corrosive influence the secular meaning of "secular" has had, often unconsciously, on believers and unbelievers alike. More importantly, I believe that it is precisely a proper understanding of liturgy that can offer healing to the schizophrenia in our culture.

3. *The Catholic Perspective*

What is our Catholic understanding of "secular"? It is in fact rather complex, and the origins of that complexity can be found in the words of Our Lord and the writings of the inspired authors of the New Testament. "The world" has two very different meanings in St John's Gospel. We read in John 3:16 that "God so loved the world that He gave His only Son." And yet at the Last Supper Jesus says, "I am not praying for the world, but for those whom you have given me" (John 17:9). In fact, Jesus states that the world hates him and will also hate his disciples. Again, Jesus himself and the authors of the New Testament speak of an antithesis between "the flesh" and "the spirit"; and yet St John forthrightly teaches that anyone who denies that Jesus Christ has come in the flesh is the antichrist (1 John 4:3; 2 John 1:7).

These contrary connotations of words like "the world" and "the flesh" in Scripture come precisely from how the realities they describe are related to God. From a Catholic perspective, creation is good in itself and only becomes negative when it is viewed in isolation from God. In the words of David Fagerberg, "Creation does not contain its own end, and to treat creation as if it does changes the world into 'the world' about which Scripture warns us. When this happens, nothing in the world has changed, but everything about the world is different for us. Things are not wrong, but we have wronged things by loving them in the wrong measure."[1] Fagerberg goes on to state that the world's sacramentality will not be restored by information, but ascesis, because the ability to receive matter sacramentally requires a pure heart. This receptivity does not come from amassing more data, but by participation in the kenotic mystery of Christ's Incarnation and his death and Resurrection. There must be a pattern of conversion in our lives, of death and new life. To be a disciple demands discipline, and the fasts, feasts and rituals of the Church provide this discipline. By means of these we not only offer worship to God, we do so in the world and with the elements of the world.

Founded on the mystery of the Incarnation itself, the liturgy, then, is shaped by this sacramental principle, which I would define as "the invisible made visible through the physical." Both before and after his election to the See of Peter, Joseph Ratzinger wrote often and eloquently about this principle. His sensitivity to and encouragement of beautiful liturgy was not fueled by aestheticism, but by the conviction that the elements of creation are not just material for human labor, they are signs pointing beyond themselves to divine love. In an essay on the sacramental foundation of Christian existence written in 1965, the young theologian observed:

> "Water" is not just H_2O, a chemical compound that one can change by an appropriate method into other compounds and use for all sorts of purposes—in the water from a spring that the thirsty traveler encounters in the desert, something becomes visible of the mystery of refreshment that creates new life in the midst of despair; in the powerful waves of a river, on whose crests the brightness of the sun is reflected, something becomes visible of the might of the glory of creative love and also the deadly force with which it can hit the man who gets in its way; in the majesty of the sea glimmers something of the mystery that we designate with the word "eternity."[2]

1. David Fagerberg, *On Liturgical Asceticism* (Washington: CUA, 2013), p. 67.
2. Joseph Ratzinger, *Theology of the Liturgy*, Collected Works, vol. 11 (San Francisco: Ignatius, 2014), p. 161.

Some years earlier, C. S. Lewis made the same point in a more trenchant way in *The Voyage of the Dawn Treader*, one of the *Narnia* books. The rather troublesome young boy Eustace meets an exotic figure who tells him that he is a retired star out of the heavens. "In our world," Eustace says, "a star is a huge ball of flaming gas." And the character responds, "Even in your world, my son, that is not what a star is but only what it is made of."[3] We might say that, whereas contemporary secular education distinguishes between "fact" and "opinion," the Catholic education imparted by the liturgy distinguishes between "fact" and "meaning": what the sacramental principle yields is not "factual data" but "saving truth."

4. *The Sacramental Principle*

I would like to consider this sacramental principle from three angles: first, in terms of our church buildings themselves; second, in terms of what goes on in them when we gather for worship, with specific reference to the foundational meaning of marriage in liturgy and a vision for ongoing renewal; and finally, what happens when we leave them.

a. *Church Buildings*

Regarding church buildings, I would suggest that their very presence can be an actual grace, because they serve to remind all who see them of a higher reality. I suppose some people think of San Francisco as the consummate "secular city"—but within its forty-nine square miles there are at least fifty Catholic churches and chapels, and very beautiful ones at that, still intact—a testament to the faith of poor but intrepid Catholic immigrants who desired to build something beautiful for God and leave a legacy to later generations. There are beautiful houses of worship of many other religious traditions as well. I am happy to report that many Catholic churches are open daily, and I wish more were. An open church door is an invitation, and many a conversion has begun when some bereft individual found an oasis of prayer in the company of the saints, and in the presence (often without being aware of it) of our Eucharistic Lord. This is why the building of a Catholic church must never be reduced simply to providing a "gathering space" for a large number of people. Even apart from the liturgy, our places of worship should invite anyone who wanders in to experience something of God's beauty and the companionship of the saints.

---

3. C. S. Lewis, *The Voyage of the Dawn Treader* (New York: Scholastic, 1995), p. 209.

I would like to share an insight of Dorothy Day on this, especially in light of those who object to our expending resources on church buildings when there are so many poor people. The project to construct St. Mary's Cathedral in San Francisco began in 1963, and the project initially received enthusiastic support from all sides. By the time the cathedral was reaching completion, however, we had gone through the turmoil of "the sixties" and voices were raised to protest spending so much money on a house of worship. It happened that Dorothy Day took part in a meeting some months after the cathedral opened in the conference center under the church. One zealot complained of their meeting to discuss the needs of the poor in such an extravagant edifice. Many cheered him on, but Dorothy Day was not one of them. She forthrightly said:

> The Church has an obligation to feed the poor, and we cannot spend all our money on buildings. However, there are many kinds of hunger. There is a hunger for bread, and we must give people food. But there is also a hunger for beauty—and there are very few beautiful places that the poor can get into. Here is a place of transcendent beauty, and it is as accessible to the homeless in the Tenderloin as it is to the mayor of San Francisco.

b. *The Liturgy Itself*

Thus, we might see our church building as an act of worship expressed with the material realities of creation. The place where the Sacred Liturgy is carried out should be redolent of the sacred. But what of the liturgy itself? Gatherings such as the *Sacra Liturgia* Conference aim at helping us appreciate and foster the liturgical life of the Catholic Church. This liturgical life faces challenges on many fronts. Some of these are perennial. For instance, liturgy is about ritual; ritual is about repeated patterns; and repeated patterns can become a matter of routine, of "going through the motions." This was a problem in the pre-Vatican II days just as it is now. Bishop Francis Quinn, emeritus bishop of Sacramento, recalls being warned as a seminarian to beware of "the casual hand on the ciborium." The antidote to the sickness of routine is not frenetic novelty; it is a rather a matter of developing and nurturing a sense of reverence, and appreciating how part of the genius of Catholic worship is to combine an unvarying core structure with the changing vesture, prayers and ceremonies of the liturgical seasons of the year.

Other challenges we face are an inheritance from the liturgical changes enacted in the years immediately following the Council. Some of these changes represented an over-reaction to liturgical practices that were thought to create a chasm between the altar and the pews. It is no disloyalty to the Church to maintain that at times the "pruning" carried out by those responsible for implementing the decrees of the Second Vatican Council was excessive. In addition, those changes were made at a time when Western society itself was becoming very informal. Finally, the question of who does what in the liturgy led to "turf wars," and the social unrest surrounding accepted roles in our culture overflowed into the sanctuary. One bishop told me recently of a visit he made to a parish. Originally he was unable to attend the event, but a cancellation created an opening, and he was able to be present. He was not the principal celebrant, but did help distribute Holy Communion. The pastor told one of the Extraordinary Ministers of Holy Communion that the Bishop would take her place, and he asked her to direct him to his Communion station. When the time for Communion came, she told him, "You took *my* ciborium."

It is now fifty years since the conclusion of the Council. That may seem like a lifetime to many, but in fact it is a relatively short interval. The work of the Council may just be beginning. If I may draw an analogy with the Council of Trent, there was a remarkable blossoming of Catholic spirituality in France in the seventeenth century, but the decrees of Trent were accepted there only in 1615, fifty years after the close of that Council. We must continually return to the Constitution of the Sacred Liturgy promulgated in 1963, read it within the context of the liturgical movement that preceded it, and evaluate it in light of the whole body of subsequent liturgical legislation. This is what is meant by "the hermeneutic of continuity." Growth must be organic: it is artificial simply to excise what came before and replace it with something different— "change for the sake of change."

There is an inherent tension in Catholic liturgy between the world as the theatre of redemption and the world as a foreshadowing of the fullness of a Kingdom which is not of this world. The Cross is made up of both a vertical arm and a horizontal arm, and authentic worship oscillates between this world and the world to come. Our society is very pragmatic, and we need to balance this with liturgical worship that conveys a sense of transcendence. At the same time, the great fact of the Incarnation demands that the invisible become visible through the physical. Authentic Catholic worship must embrace "the secular"—that is, that which is of this world—and show how it points to "the sacred"—both in this world and beyond it.

(1) *Marriage and Liturgy.* To return to the question of the social schizo-phrenia we are witnessing due to the prevalence of the philosophies of empiricism and idealism, nowhere does this come more into conflict with the sacramental principle, with enormous consequences for the Church's understanding of liturgy, than with marriage. We are all well aware of the secular reasons why it is important to preserve the meaning and definition of marriage in the law, in that it protects the right of children to be reared by a father and a mother whenever possible, recognizing that principle of complementarity by which father and mother each makes a unique contribution that benefits the child in the child's maturing into adulthood. But the current debate about marriage redefinition, with the corresponding demise of the understanding of the sexual difference and complementarity of male and female, likewise corrupts our liturgical sense, and therefore our view of the universe, at the foundational level. This is because God has used marriage as the primary sacred sign of our relationship with Him, for the Incarnation is a marriage: God marries His divinity with our humanity in the Second Person of the Most Holy Trinity taking on our human flesh in order to redeem us. Marriage is about the two becoming one: they become one flesh in a comprehensive union of persons, while each retains their own identity. This corresponds to the ancient Church Fathers' teaching on "divinization," and why, for example, St Basil the Great could say something so bold as, "Through the Spirit we acquire a likeness to God; indeed, we attain what is beyond our most sublime aspirations—we become God."[4]

This mystery goes back to the very beginning, reflecting what is already obvious from physical observation of the world, that is, the secular realm: God made them male and female. This sets the pattern for all of revelation and the economy of salvation, for it is all the story of a marriage. As we know from the teachings of St John Paul II, the Bible begins and ends with a marriage: Adam and Eve, and the Wedding Feast of the Lamb. And it is replete with nuptial imagery throughout. God's Covenant with Israel is a *marriage* Covenant, so much so that when God's people violated the Covenant by worshipping the false gods of their pagan neighbors, the prophets excoriated them for being an unfaithful bride. This also explains how a book of love poems, that does not even mention the word God, was entered into the canon of Scripture. As Pope Benedict XVI explains in his first Encyclical, *God Is Love*:

---

4. Cited in the Roman Breviary, Office of Readings for Tuesday of the Seventh Week of Easter.

...the reception of the Song of Songs in the canon of Sacred Scripture was soon explained by the idea that these love songs ultimately describe God's relation to man and man's relation to God. Thus the Song of Songs became, both in Christian and Jewish literature, a source of mystical knowledge and experience, an expression of the essence of biblical faith: that man can indeed enter into union with God—his primordial aspiration. But this union is...a unity in which both God and man remain themselves and yet become fully one. As Saint Paul says: "He who is united to the Lord becomes one spirit with him" (1 Cor 6:17). (*Deus Caritas Est*, 25 December 2005, 10)

Is this nothing other than the nuptial mystery, that is, the two becoming fully one, yet remaining themselves, each retaining their unique individual identity?

In the New Testament, we have various sayings and parables of Jesus alluding to this imagery, such as the parable of the ten virgins (five wise, five foolish) who took lamps with them to *go out and meet the bridegroom* (Matt 25:1–13). It is also significant that Jesus chose the occasion of a marriage feast to perform his first miracle; his response to his mother, "My hour has not yet come," is a reference to the consummation of God's marriage to His people that will be accomplished by his death on the Cross. And of course, we are all familiar with Ephesians chapter 5, which explains that the prophecy from the creation account of Genesis, "For this reason a man shall leave [his] father and [his] mother and be joined to his wife, and the two shall become one flesh," is fulfilled in Christ and the Church.

It's all the story of a marriage: God's marriage Covenant with Israel is fulfilled in the blood of Christ on the Cross, establishing the new and eternal Covenant between him, the bridegroom, and his bride, the Church. This imagery is then taken over in the Christian liturgy, which traces its inspiration back to the Jewish liturgy in the Jerusalem Temple. There, the altar stood behind a veil marking off the Holy of Holies, where the priest would enter on the Day of Atonement (Yom Kippur) to offer sacrifice for his sins and those of the people. In his book, *Jesus of Nazareth, Volume II*, Pope Benedict speaks of how the definitive destruction of the Temple, and therefore of the Temple sacrifices, coincided with the precise moment that Christianity was established, and the Christians understood the sacrifice of the Eucharist as replacing the provisional Temple sacrifices, as the Eucharist is the re-presentation to us of the one, perfect sacrifice of Christ.[5]

---

5. See: Pope Benedict XVI, *Jesus of Nazareth, Holy Week: From the Entrance into Jerusalem to the Resurrection* (San Francisco: Ignatius, 2011), p. 36.

The Christian liturgy is, in fact, heavily influenced by this Temple theology. As the Jewish-Catholic art historian Helen Ratner Dietz explains, the "fourth-century Christian altar hidden by its canopy and curtains had a deliberately nuptial meaning...reminiscent of the Holy of Holies in the Jerusalem Temple."[6] Understanding their Covenant with God to be a marriage covenant, the canopy and curtains in the Temple represented for the Jewish people a "chuppah," the bridal chamber used in Semitic marriage rituals.

The Christian practice of hanging a curtain between the columns of the baldacchino to veil the altar continued throughout the first Christian millennium.[7] This served as a "sacred tent," sheltering the divine presence, harkening back to the Ark of the Covenant located within the Holy of Holies. The veil "sheltered" the divine presence. The purpose of a veil is to conceal. What is concealed is what is most sacred, and it is most sacred because it is most intimate—thus, the appropriateness of sheltering it.

Think about our human experience, keeping in mind here that revelation builds on what is already in the created order, it does not superimpose itself upon it: clothing is a veil, it shelters what is most intimate, that is, what is most sacred to us about our bodies, which is why we always keep that part of our body veiled. But the veil has to be removed—unveiled, revealed—in order for a marriage to be consummated. So we can understand the meaning of the veil in the Temple being torn in two from top to bottom at the moment of Christ's death (Matt 27:51): it symbolizes that, through the sacrifice of His Son, God has now revealed what before was concealed to us—His intimate, inner life—and has granted us access to it. The veil, then, conceals what is most intimate—and therefore most sacred—precisely so that it can be revealed to allow the nuptial communion of Christ and the Church. Extrapolating on this, we can see even more clearly the nuptial meaning of the sacrifice of the Eucharist: just as the consummation of a marriage is preceded by the unveiling of what is intimate and therefore most sacred to the spouses, so in the liturgy the marriage feast of the Lamb to his bride the Church is consummated by him giving us his flesh to eat and blood to drink, drawing us into a mystical nuptial union. The Church's insight into this truth can be seen from the Vulgate translation of the verse recounting Christ's last words on the Cross, "it is finished" (in Greek):

6. Helen Ratner Dietz, "The Nuptial Meaning of Classic Church Architecture," in Vincent Twomey and Janet Elaine Rutherford (eds), *Benedict XVI and Beauty in Sacred Art and Architecture* (New York: Scepter, 2011), pp. 122–42 (122).

7. Joseph Ratzinger, *The Spirit of the Liturgy* (San Francisco: Ignatius, 2000), p. 85.

consummatum est—literally, "it has been consummated." The drawing back of the curtain before Communion signifies this entering into nuptial union with Christ.

We learn from the Fathers of the Church that God's creation of a bride for His son Adam from Adam's side as he slept is a foreshadowing of God the Father's creation of a bride—the Church—for His Only-Begotten Son as he lay in the sleep of death on the Cross. Christ gives the seed of life to his bride, the Church, from the blood and water that flowed from his side on the Cross. The Church, as mother, receives it, generates new life for his Kingdom (the water of baptism) and nourishes that new life through the grace of the sacraments (his blood, the Eucharist) and by teaching the truth she received from him.

While the practice of the veil in front of the altar has been preserved in the liturgy of many of the Eastern rites of the Church, it has been extinct in the West for over a thousand years. However, the sense of the veil has been preserved in other—albeit diminished—ways up to recent times. Examples of this would be a veil placed in front of the doors of the tabernacle or immediately behind them inside the tabernacle, and the veiling and unveiling of the chalice during the celebration of the Mass. This also gives a deeper meaning to the old practice of women veiling their heads in church. In Christian liturgy, the sacred is veiled, and so again here there is a deeper, symbolic meaning: it is not just a matter of feminine modesty, but consideration given to women as having a special sacred status because they are the bearers of life.

All of this is indicative of a movement away from paganism toward worship of and allegiance to the one, true God; and, it is a movement that happens by way of marriage. As Pope Benedict XVI explains in *God is Love*, there is a connection between monotheism and monogamy evident at the beginning and determined by love as *eros*. He says:

> From the standpoint of creation, *eros* directs man towards marriage, to a bond which is unique and definitive; thus, and only thus, does it fulfill its deepest purpose. Corresponding to the image of a monotheistic God is monogamous marriage. *Marriage based on exclusive and definitive love becomes the icon of the relationship between God and his people and vice versa.* (n. 11, emphasis added)

Picking up on this theme, Helen Ratner Dietz explains it this way:

...as the ancestors of the Jews gradually emerged from paganism, God let them know that...polytheistic worship of nature deities was unacceptable to Him... [T]he God of Israel is hetero, "other." He is beyond and before the universe. His bride Israel yearns for Him because He is other. And God, in His own way, yearns for Israel in her earthliness because she, too, is hetero, other than Himself.

When King Solomon in his later years lapsed into the worship of Ashtoreth the earth goddess, thereby denying the oneness and otherness of the divinity, God let him know that there would be deleterious consequences in the next generation. It was with great effort that Israel emerged from pantheism.

Pantheism was like a vortex, tugging at Israel to suck her back in, *just as today pantheism is like a vortex tugging at the Church.*[8]

When you consider that the entire Judeo-Christian religious tradition is premised on the concept of sexual difference and complementarity in marriage, then you will understand that, if we lose that concept, nothing of our faith tradition will make any sense in the culture. Precisely because revealed truth is not super-imposed on nature but builds on it—that is, builds upon truths that are accessible to reason alone from the observation of nature—when the culture can no longer apprehend those natural truths, then the very foundation of our teaching evaporates and nothing we have to offer will make sense. The result is a societal reversion to the paganism of old but with a unique post-modern variation on its themes, such as the practice of child sacrifice, the worship of the earth goddess and other feminine deities, or the cult of priestesses. And in fact, just the other day a close collaborator of mine told me of a recent poll revealing that support for polygamy in the United States has increased from 7% to 16%.[9] Since the Church cannot but be immersed in the contemporary society, this is that pantheism tugging at her like a vortex to which Ratner Dietz refers.

(2) *Ongoing Renewal.* The truth that revelation builds upon what is in the created, physical order, just as grace builds on nature, will always be there, whether we notice it and thereby benefit from it or not. That, again, is why our practices of penance and spiritual discipline are so important: they will enable us to recognize it, receive it, and live it out in our lives. And this has to begin with our worship. A more generous availability of the extraordinary form of the Roman rite will help us to reclaim a

8. Dietz, "The Nuptial Meaning of Classic Church Architecture," pp. 141–42 (emphasis added).

9. This was revealed in a Gallup Poll published on 26 May 2015: http://www.gallup.com/poll/183413/americans-continue-shift-left-key-moral-issues.aspx.

heightened sensitivity to this sacramental reality, as well as provide a context for the liturgical renewal mandated by the Council with a sense of continuity with the liturgical movement of the last century-and-a-half. Devotional practices such as Eucharistic adoration and popular devotions to Our Lady and the saints, thoughtlessly abandoned immediately after Vatican II, are being rediscovered and provide enrichment to the liturgical life of the Church, not a distraction from it.

However, genuine liturgical renewal is not a matter of external ceremonies, new or old. Liturgical asceticism is a work of conversion, and conversion must not remain superficial. That is why the reclaiming of the practices of penance in the lives of individual believers is also so important, practices such as Friday fasting, fasting before Communion (one hour being understood as a minimum when necessary, not the norm to aim for), frequent Confession, a more serious and literal approach to fasting and other forms of self-denial during the season of Lent (people are told, instead of "giving something up" for Lent, to do something positive, but giving something up *is* doing something positive, precisely because it is something concrete and one can immediately feel the effect!), and observing penitential practices at other appropriate times of the year, such as Advent and 22 January (which the US bishops have proclaimed a day of penance in reparation for the sins against the sanctity of human life caused by abortion).

Educating our people to appreciate beauty and understand the deeper meaning of the Church's liturgy is also critical. As you may know, we have established in San Francisco the Benedict XVI Institute for Sacred Music and Divine Worship. Its purpose is to provide formation, not just training, for liturgical ministers, especially musicians and cantors. While in some cases liturgical ministers may have some training, what is really needed is formation, something similar, albeit not as extensive, to what those preparing for Holy Orders receive. In any discipline, one must know the tradition if one is going to excel. How can one be a competent liturgical musician if one is ignorant of the Church's millennial tradition of sacred music and hymnody, let alone what the Church is actually asking us to do based on the authentic documents on music in the liturgy? Even if a musician is providing a more contemporary style of Church music, this formation is necessary to guarantee that the music will serve the worship of God and not the exaltation of the singers.

While music is at the heart of this Institute, there is also envisioned formation for those who exercise other liturgical roles in the current form of the Roman liturgy. For example, it is not enough that lectors learn how to pronounce the words correctly. To proclaim the Word of

God effectively, the most important thing is to understand the meaning of the text. Thus, lectors need a deeper formation in biblical history and theology. Extraordinary ministers of Holy Communion should develop a particular Eucharistic spirituality. This is especially critical, for we can all share horror stories of things we've heard and seen when it comes to how the Blessed Sacrament is treated. Ministers charged with distributing Holy Communion who have developed a truly sacramental worldview and Eucharistic sensitivity do not need to be told what to do in every imaginable situation (e.g., someone walks off with the Host, or does not know how to receive); it will come as second nature to them.

c. *After the Liturgical Action*

Finally, let us consider what happens when we leave church after the liturgy. This is where Catholic worship should have its impact on "secular society." The most common name in the West for our Eucharistic celebration is "the Mass," from *Missa*, which implies that we worshippers are being sent forth. Far from separating us from the world, the Sacred Liturgy plunges us into the very heart of it and reveals its sacramental meaning. It is nothing short of blasphemous to allow us "freedom of worship" within the walls of our churches and prohibit "freedom of religion" in daily life.

When he was Archbishop of Munich, Cardinal Ratzinger gave a radio broadcast on the feast of Corpus Christi. He spoke of the symbolism of carrying the Blessed Sacrament out of the church; of a custom in Bavaria of reading from the four Gospels at various points in the procession; and imparting Benediction to the four points of the compass:

> [The four Gospels] are inspired, they are the breath of the Holy Spirit, and their fourfold number expresses the world-embracing power of God's word and God's Spirit... The world is thus declared to be the realm of God's creative word; matter is subordinated to the power of His Spirit. For matter too is his creation and hence the sphere of His gracious power. Ultimately we receive the very bread of the earth from his hands. How beautifully the new Eucharistic bread is related to our daily bread! The Eucharistic bread imparts its blessing to the daily bread, and each loaf of the latter silently points to him who wished to be the bread of us all. So the liturgy opens out into everyday life, into our earthly life and cares; it goes beyond the church precincts because it actually embraces heaven and earth, present and future. How we need this sign! Liturgy is not the private hobby of a particular group; it is about the bond that holds heaven and earth together, it is about the human race and the whole created world.[10]

---

10. Ratzinger, *Theology of the Liturgy*, pp. 415–16.

Christian life is inherently missionary. The risen Christ sent his disciples out to the ends of the earth, and he commissioned them not only to teach people, but to plunge them into the mystery of his life, death, and resurrection by means of a sacrament: "Go therefore and make disciples of all nations, baptizing them in the name of the Father and of the Son and of the Holy Spirit" (Matt 28:19). By using water for baptism, we are reminded that this element is not simply a commodity to be evaluated in terms of its necessity to human life and endeavors: it symbolizes in myriad ways our relationship to God, our Creator and Lord. Our interest in Catholic liturgy must be governed, not by aesthetical taste, but by the awareness that "the invisible becomes visible through the physical," so that we strive to use what is best in creation in our worship. We do this because God is deserving of the best we can offer Him, and also because as a priestly people we offer back to God the wonder of this world that He has first given us.

This Creator is not just some "force" or "energy"—the one God is a communion of Persons, and to be saved is to be brought into that communion. Just as liturgy reveals the sacramental reality of the world, so it destroys the imagined autonomy of the individual subject. We are created in communion, the union of man and woman in the marital act; and we are created for communion, by our second birth in baptism "in the name of the Father and of the Son and of the Holy Spirit." Hence, liturgy is not only the way we worship God within the walls of our churches, it is also the way that God heals wounds and restores harmony in the world beyond the walls of our churches.

5. Conclusion

In the face of those who would lock us up within our church walls, and in the face of those who feel that concern about the liturgy is unimportant compared to so many "practical" problems facing the Church, we can do no better than respond with words found at the beginning of *Constitution on the Sacred Liturgy* of the Second Vatican Council:

> For the liturgy, "through which the work of our redemption is accomplished," most of all in the divine sacrifice of the Eucharist, is the outstanding means whereby the faithful may express in their lives, and manifest to others, the mystery of Christ and the real nature of the true Church. It is of the essence of the Church that she be both human and divine, visible and yet invisibly equipped, eager to act and yet intent on contemplation, present in this world and yet not at home in it; and she is all these things in such wise that in her the human is directed and subordinated to the divine, the visible likewise

to the invisible, action to contemplation, and this present world to that city yet to come, which we seek. While the liturgy daily builds up those who are within into a holy temple of the Lord, into a dwelling place for God in the Spirit, to the mature measure of the fullness of Christ, at the same time it marvelously strengthens their power to preach Christ, and thus shows forth the Church to those who are outside as a sign lifted up among the nations under which the scattered children of God may be gathered together, until there is one sheepfold and one shepherd. (*Sacrosanctum Concilium* 2)

YOUTH AND THE LITURGY

Matthew R. Menendez

1. *Introduction*

This chapter will follow the life of a young Catholic I know very well, because it is me. As you might be able to guess, I am neither a published scholar nor a distinguished cleric. My invitation to contribute to this volume stems from an accident of my existence: I am young. After graduating from Harvard in 2014 with a degree in Renaissance Spanish and Italian Literature, I now work in the weapons industry, running an internal startup at TASER International, the world's top provider of public safety technology and non-lethal weapons.

The Church is in crisis. One in ten Americans is an ex-Catholic.[1] The median age when someone stops considering himself Catholic is 21 years old.[2] So with fewer people remaining Catholic and fewer children to be baptized, the number of practicing Catholic young adults is shrinking rapidly. In addition, statistics show that if we could just keep young people Catholic until age 30, the chances of them leaving are very slim.[3] After Vatican II we lost a third of the Mass-going Catholics, and we did even worse at convincing young men to devote not only Sunday, but every day, to Christ's Church as priests.

Perhaps we do not realize (or want to admit) the extent of the crisis; I myself was lied to by the generation that educated me. The post-conciliar period did not see a small drop in Catholic practice, but a precipitous fall: one that would be fatal to any other institution which does not share in our Church's curious, divine guarantee of victory. To illustrate: if we

---

1. G. Smith, *America's Changing Religious Landscape* (Washington: Pew Research Forum, 2015), p. 13.

2. M. Gray, *The Impact of Religious Switching and Secularization on the Estimated Size of the U.S. Adult Catholic Population* (Washington: Center for Applied Research in the Apostolate at Georgetown University, 2008), p. 6.

3. Ibid., p. 8.

lined up 20 seminarians studying for the priesthood in the United States in 1962, and wanted to adjust to 2002 levels, we would have to take 19 of the 20 and shoot them dead. We did not lose half of the seminarians; we lost over 90%.[4]

How can we draw young Catholics into the bosom of the Church? We must display something to the world that is worth fighting for, and be the heroic martyrs who fight for it. Given the fact that God only holds the attention of the average Catholic for a single hour on Sunday, the Mass becomes the only opportunity to evangelize and make present the beauty of the Faith. We cannot solve the apathy by adding programming to already over-stimulated lives.

My Uber driver on the way to the airport for the *Sacra Liturgia* Conference was a young man of about twenty-five, and we talked about the Church. But he said something that I think we should ponder: "You know, I'm more on the socially liberal side of things, but I just don't understand why the Church can't just be the Church. I mean I don't necessarily want to be Catholic, but it should just be there solidly for those who want it, not trying to cater to everybody."

To understand the importance of the liturgy in getting the Church to "just be the Church," one must begin by understanding the life of virtue, which is comparable to a shining castle atop a craggy mountain. It takes serious effort and willpower to make the treacherous climb to the top. The role of the liturgy should be to make the light from the castle shine more brightly so that the castle is more attractive and so that it more clearly illuminates the path upwards. Instead, however, we have put curtains over the windows and we have banalized the liturgy, making the faith lame, embarrassing, and undesirable to today's youth. I am one of the fortunate few who was guided to the top and found the hidden treasure.

I grew up, the fifth of six children, in Saint Louis, Missouri. My parish is representative of large suburban parishes anywhere in the United States. In my lifetime, there have been only two pastors, but a long series of ever-rotating Associates. They bring with them liturgical ups and downs, from Fr Chris skipping his sermon in favor of an *a capella* performance of "Cat's in the Cradle," to the most recent occupant who prefers the *usus antiquior*. Furthermore, there are several permanent deacons, who preach (rather unedifyingly) about once a month. The Mass schedule is the standard American offering: a brief hour of Saturday Confessions followed by a Vigil Mass, an early morning "Mass before the musicians

---

4. K. Jones, *Index of Leading Catholic Indicators: The Church Since Vatican II* (Fort Collins: Roman Catholic Books, 2003), p. 26.

wake up" (which even as a small boy I preferred over the hee-hawing of the choir Masses), then a series of Masses during the morning and early afternoon with various musical approaches, and finally in the evening a youth Mass, which almost certainly is affiliated with LifeTeen. LifeTeen was founded in Phoenix, Arizona, by the now laicized priest Fr Dale Fushek, as an attempt to make the Mass relevant for young people, while also providing material for bible studies and other events so that a lightly trained youth minister can easily craft a program for a parish.

2. The "Youth Mass"

The youth Mass (besides partaking in the odd suburban American expectation that all Masses must last for exactly one hour) has much to distinguish it from the others. In what follows, keep in mind the Church's axiom, *lex orandi, lex credendi*, that the law of praying is the law of believing. I think it is fair to assume that most young peoples' only experience with their faith is attendance at an hour-long Sunday Mass, i.e. no confession, devotions, or private prayer (although, given current events, I'm not sure whether I'm describing American teens or German priests).[5] Thus, the liturgy unfortunately becomes the only teaching opportunity available to most, and must be the point of departure for any attempt to save the Church.

The music of the youth Mass, written almost exclusively by heretics, ex-priests, and ex-Catholics, is performed on guitars, bongos, or, at the top of my list, the rain-stick. Children might be bringing canned goods to the altar, when they are not standing around it. Songs are meant for emotional soloists and are practically unsingable by the congregation.[6] The hymns are likely to have been chosen by a committee of young people, who will also write the general intercessions, unless it happens to be a day where congregants will be able to shout out their own needs, whether in sequence or all at the same time in a sort of glossolallic Babel. As a teenager, I was afraid of sleeping in and getting stuck going to a Mass that encouraged people to hold my hand and wave it in the air (as if throwing out antennas and adjusting them to try to get a good signal from divine radio). There is also often a feeling created that the evening Mass is not the main event, but rather a convenient meeting place before the bible study which will follow.

5. See data on the spiritual practices of German clergy collected between 2012 and 2014 and published early in 2015: http://rorate-caeli.blogspot.com/2015/04/the-german-catholic-collapse-priests.html.

6. For an amusing treatment of this subject, see: T. Day, *Why Catholics Can't Sing* (New York: Crossroad, 2013).

I was even more reluctant to attend these youth groups where I would be expected to share my feelings, or a retreat where the Mass was only a perfunctory necessity to be checked off the list, while the climax after three nights of keeping you up late and hyped-up on Coca Cola was a Circle of Truth, where you were supposed to break down emotionally and feel the warm welcome of the supporting community around you. Somehow this is supposed to create a long-lasting relationship with Jesus Christ. Instead youth groups are just that: something that ends with youth, and the most embarrassing part of any progressive youth liturgy is the average age which skews north because of the large number of elderly people stuck in the 1960s who cannot move on and who sometimes outnumber the youth.

And this is precisely the inherent flaw of the youth Mass: it is crafted for a very particular age group and setting. But what happens when those conditions no longer hold? Ultimately, the youth Mass is not directed with the worship of God foremost in mind, instead it is built for pedagogical purposes, for a form of active (activist?) participation, for congregational singing. Yet, because they have stripped divine worship from the Mass, none of these alternative things succeed: *nisi Dominus aedificaverit domum in vanum laboraverunt qui aedificant eam* (Ps 126:1).

3. *The Liturgy and the Catholic School*

My parish also had a Catholic school I attended. The same approach to the liturgy flowed over into the pedagogy. When we prepared for our first Confession we were subtly or not-so-subtly convinced that you only knelt behind the screen if you had been *really bad* and did not want the priest to know who you were. Instead, we should think of kneeling behind the screen looking at a crucifix as an important liturgical characteristic of the sacrament. In a visible way, it reminds us that we are not having a chitchat with Fr Bob, but rather are confessing to Almighty God who knows the hidden things of our hearts. In a similar way, Communion on the tongue was considered to be only for those kids whose parents were strict and old-fashioned. This anti-liturgical and anti-intellectual attitude permeates Catholic education at all levels and explains many of the difficulties in today's youth when it comes to the faith. In first grade, we learned "God loves you"; in fourth grade, "God loves you and Daniel and Mary"; and in eighth grade, "God loves you and Juan and Latoya and all the diverse peoples of the world." There is no substance. Even as we built more complexity on top of earlier foundations in math and foreign languages, we stagnated in religious studies.

Although I had already moved on to a Benedictine Abbey for middle school, I had to go back to my parish for confirmation classes, which were painfully dull and degrading. Even at the children's liturgies, I can hear the six-year olds moan as the permanent deacon talks down to them: "Hey, I'm not a baby! Stop treating me like I'm two."

There were certainly some good things going for me in liturgical formation—first of all, my parents. I remember being taught to genuflect every time I entered a church and to say an Our Father, a Hail Mary, and seven Glory Be's before ever sitting down. I cleaned the Church and prayed the rosary in the car with my mother. We went to Benediction with an ancient priest every Thursday in Lent and I understood that Mass was not just a thing for Sundays. As my father once said to a Lutheran friend, "Every day Catholics have a Holy Day of Opportunity."

In addition, the late Monsignor Joseph Pins, ordained in 1970 and one of the original "Ratzinger priests," was a wonderful influence. When *Redemptionis Sacramentum* rolled around—not that I knew what it was at the time—I remember him instructing us that from now on we would bow or genuflect before Communion and that the "resurrexifix" was going to be replaced with a suffering Christ on the Cross. Further, he handpicked a couple of us boys to teach to serve the Mass separately from the normal training, and this really was the beginning of my life as a man of the liturgy. It was little things like folding my hands that initially impressed upon me the sacred and set-apart nature of the liturgy. The other kids had their hands waving in the air singing a blessing for someone, but I was in a cassock holding a paten at Communion. The story of my faith is one of a growing understanding of the liturgy and can most easily be tracked through service at the altar. If you want to see a healthy parish, look to churches like Fr Richard Cipolla's in Norwalk or Fr Charles Higgins's in Newton with 45 altar servers at the *Missa cantata*.

The next thing to happen was that in seventh grade I enrolled at Saint Louis Priory, a school run by the English Congregation Benedictine monks of Saint Louis Abbey. A growing reform-of-the-reform community, the monks and the older altar servers were a great influence on me. My other siblings scattered to schools run by the Sisters of the Loretto, the Jesuits, the Christian Brothers, and the Marianists, but I got the Benedictines, for whom the liturgy was the center of their lives. We served the Abbey Masses as an invite-only squad and went on pilgrimages and retreats together. Contrary to popular opinion, good liturgy is not elitist; it is just elite. Young boys are idealistic, and so there is something terribly energizing when they feel they have discovered something special that not everyone knows about.

In 2007 Pope Benedict XVI issued *Summorum Pontificum*. I did not know what this all meant, but it changed everything. Benedict knew that freeing the Mass of the Ages would be important for young people, writing:

> Immediately after the Second Vatican Council it was presumed that requests for the use of the 1962 missal would be limited to the older generation which had grown up with it, but in the meantime it has clearly been demonstrated that young persons too have discovered this liturgical form, felt its attraction and found in it a form of encounter with the Mystery of the Most Holy Eucharist, particularly suited to them.[7]

People of my age came to our own when Benedict XVI was Pope and so his way of thinking seems perfectly natural to us, and not just a fluke of a single papal election.

Unbeknownst to me, Fr Bede Price of Saint Louis Abbey had been teaching me the motions of serving the Traditional Mass as he was adapting his *Novus Ordo* in preparation for the motu proprio. In addition, in our Church History class, he had us all recite the Prayers at the Foot of the Altar at the beginning of class. And so when the then Archbishop, Raymond Leo Burke, asked Saint Louis Abbey to found a parish for the extraordinary form, Fr Bede was assigned and he asked me to be his first server. I said I did not know how, but in an hour he had me memorize the *Suscipiat* and combine the actions and prayers—and I was ready.

Priests showed an interest in me and in my liturgical formation. Take note: one priest makes the difference. We may not be able to get all young people to stick around, but I challenge all priests to select at least a few promising young men and women and give them everything they need in those formative years to become leaders in the faith.

For me, *Summorum Pontificum* expounded a whole theory of evangelization. Imagine the Church as a giant room. After the 1960s, people were banging on the walls trying to get out, and we kept pleading with them and knocking down the walls and moving them further and further out, artificially keeping them within the confines of the Church. At the same time, there were others who were knocking on the door asking to come in (separated traditionalists, Anglo-Catholics, conservative Lutherans), but we were too busy catering to the loud liberals to let in these friends. Benedict XVI finally said, "Enough." He stopped moving the boundaries and making the concessions, and opened the door to these passionate

---

7. Benedict XVI, "Letter on the Occasion of the Issuance of the Motu Proprio *Summorum Pontificum*," 7 July 2007.

and committed Catholics and used them to build up the Church from the inside and make it more attractive. This metaphor guides my approach to the liturgy, and, indeed, to evangelization. Let us not keep adapting to the least common denominator, but rather let us do as Jesus did and provide everything, pure and unadulterated, to those who ask for it, and then these Apostles we form will go out and convert the others. In order words, focus at the top of the pyramid: trickle-down spirituality. As I said, one good priest changes everything.

Once I had come this far liturgically, it was clear that I was going to accept whatever I found to be true even if it meant I had to change a lot. Fr Bede and the younger monks had a clear trajectory worked out for my formation and in some sense we were all moving along together. The retreats improved liturgically as table grace moved into hieratic English and then into Latin, as reciting the Liturgy of the Hours gave way to Prime, Terce and sung Vespers from the traditional monastic Office, and as the day became scheduled around the Mass. We had readings from the martyrology at table. I had previously mocked Fr Bede for reading these things called blogs in the morning; now I read those same blogs and find myself publishing a paper on the liturgy!

At the Priory, we wanted to imitate the priests, most especially at Mass. They encouraged vocations. On the other hand, my dad and brother were educated by the Christian Brothers. In my dad's day, it was weird if one never considered being a priest. In 1965, there were 912 novices for the Christian Brothers in the USA, in 2000, there were 7.[8] I remember we used to have our retreats in their now-deserted novitiate. The barren wreckovated chapel was covered with blue carpet and had hanging above the altar a welded shrapnel crucifix that we nicknamed "the angel of death."

I ended up writing my senior thesis at the Priory school on the orientation of the altar, and this was when I first truly became involved in the liturgical debates. My advisor was ordained in the late seventies and the Abbey Church is one of the most famous early examples of a church in the round with the altar in the middle. He was unwilling to let me move forward with my conclusions when I presented my initial research. Later he became convinced and changed his mind, but do not underestimate the ability of people to ignore evidence. Old people making the argument for the liturgy will be dismissed as nostalgic, but young people are dismissed as naïve.

8. Jones, *Index of Leading Catholic Indicators*, p. 86.

The Saint Louis Priory provided the young men with one of the top ten theological educations of a high school anywhere in the world and a significantly above-average liturgical formation. Nevertheless, while many of us have gone on to be seeds of strong Catholic communities, many of my classmates have not persevered in their faith. This is an uphill battle. None of this is a magic cure; not because there is a better cure than the liturgy, but because there is no panacea. I still use the liturgy to evangelize my lapsed friends. When I return to St Louis, I organize singings of the traditional monastic Compline on campus for the alumni and then we talk and drink whisky.

4. *The Uphill Battle in the University*

After the Abbey, I enrolled at Harvard University for my undergraduate studies. Immediately, I had to confront a decision that is common to all committed Catholics going off to a mainstream college. There are three choices: first, suffer through the college chaplaincy with all of its problems and try to improve it; second, live a faith life separately, whether at the Opus Dei house, a traditional parish or somewhere else; or third, a mix of the two: the latter is what I chose.

When I arrived at Harvard the liturgical situation was bad. I promised myself that for the first semester, I would not meddle. But one day I was asked to come to training and be an Extraordinary Minister of Holy Communion. We had one of the girls teach us what to do if one of those dreaded "mouthers" came up and stuck their tongue out. Then, Father very nonchalantly taught us how to extend our hands and "bless" those who came up to communion and were not receiving. This was the bit where I had uncomfortably to ask him to clarify. Let us say I am not receiving communion. It would be just as reasonable for me to make the sign of the Cross over the Extraordinary Minister of Holy Communion as vice versa. This began a series of arguments with the chaplain that spanned many months and many topics and drew me in further to try to improve the situation at the Harvard chaplaincy.

There was an absolute refusal to teach or to have quality music in the liturgy because anything exalted would make the poorly formed students feel bad about themselves. This view of challenge is central to the youth Mass approach. One cannot use polysyllabic words like "ciborium" or "chalice," since not everyone knows those words and it would make them feel bad, so one must say "bowl" and "cup" and "bread" and "wine."

I once was leaving adoration with the chaplain and another student, Patrick. After the Blessed Sacrament was reposed, Patrick volunteered to put out the candles. After the altar candles, he asked Father if he should put out the candle glowing in the red glass holder. Father simply answered "no" with no further explanation. When I pressed him further, he said "because it's a symbol." I was furious because this question about the sanctuary lamp was an opportunity to teach Patrick about the Real Presence in the tabernacle and Father failed to take advantage of it. I will be bold here, and posit that the reason the priests are so anti-intellectual and afraid to teach is not that they do not know anything, but that they do not believe all of it anymore. The modern liturgy does not teach the real presence as explicitly as is necessary; nay more, it can seem at times visibly to teach the opposite! All a turnaround of the Church would really take is priests who really believe and therefore care about souls. Everything is about souls! We see people like Archbishop Salvatore Cordileone suffering to save souls. If only we could be like George Cardinal Pell, who when speaking in respect to the 2014 Synod on the Family remarked: "As Christians, we follow Christ... Some may wish Jesus might have been a little softer on divorce, but he wasn't. And I'm sticking with him."[9]

The dumbed-down Mass and sermons have left us with Harvard students who are perfectly capable of talking about the composition of neural cells or the effect of educational policies in Jakarta on economic mobility, but who can get through life without knowing the definition of a sacrament. The "old evangelization" was effective: a priest friend of mine was called into the hospital where a 90-year-old woman was dying. She had stopped practicing the faith, but her daughter insisted on a priest. Father went, but he could not get through to her. Finally, he started talking about her childhood and he asked her that classic question from the Baltimore Catechism: "Why did God make you?" She broke down crying and choked out the memorized answer; then made her confession, received communion, and died with the Last Rites. Our young people have not experienced anything like that today that they will be able to return to as a rock when times are tough.

Instead of a stable foundation, I found a hyper-relativized liturgy. One of the old priests who first agreed to offer Mass in the *usus antiquior* at Harvard would have been just as happy offering a clown Mass. There was a special Mass in one of the Harvard houses where Hosts were passed around in a basket, and another Mass in a meeting room next to the Church for the community service group. There was the early morning quick and quiet Mass for the athletes who were used to getting up early. There was the boys' choir *Novus Ordo* solemn Mass sung in the main Church with

---

9. See: Crux panel, "Francis: A Pope for the 21st Century," Rome, 8 October 2014. See: http://www.cruxnow.com/church/2014/10/08/cardinal-pell-on-divorce-im-sticking-with-jesus/.

Palestrina. There was the student Mass downstairs in the basement where no one knelt and the altar was on a cheap raised stage surrounded by a semi-circle of yellow plastic school-chairs. So many options!

Over the following years, I successfully managed several reform of the reform changes: getting students to kneel at the consecration, organically, through staging friends throughout the church who would kneel at the appropriate time, getting the tabernacle restored to the high altar, and having only men serving at the altar by volunteering to organize the servers and just not recruiting or scheduling women. The biggest change was moving the Mass upstairs from the unfinished basement into the Romanesque church, and that was done by vote of the students. The debate at the final meeting featured such silly excuses as "if we move it upstairs, I won't be able to find my friends" and "when I show up late, my heels clack on the wood floor."

In addition to my liturgical work, the new pastor brought in various groups of staff to aid evangelization efforts. However, most of these programs, though successful, are only partially so because they are built on faulty Protestant models of bible studies and social events. It is the Mass that matters, and if we do not get that right, what is the point? "Unless you eat my Body and drink my Blood, you have no life within you" (John 6:53).

After all this, it was clear that I wanted for my own sanity and for the health of souls to bring the traditional Mass to campus. I founded Juventutem Boston. Juventutem is an international group of young people dedicated to spreading the joy of the Church's traditional liturgy. We were the second chapter in the United States; the first was formed by another Harvard man, Paul Schultz, who converted 10 years earlier at Harvard and was received in the *usus antiquior*. None of us at Juventutem Boston really knew much about anything yet. We learned as we went, and started simply. I had never even been to a sung Mass until I planned one. I remember convincing Harvard's library to buy a whole section of books on liturgical ceremonies and serving Mass.

I had been warned that previous attempts to bring the traditional Mass to Harvard in 2007 had failed, and failed in a bad way. The parish council had brought liberal scholars to lecture the students, called the traditional students "the hands of the devil," and had them yelled at in private meetings with the priests. As a result, starting a group like Juventutem from scratch was made difficult because a significant part of the targeted membership were people so disaffected by the college Catholic programming that they pursued their religious life elsewhere. If one is hiding where does one find the other people who are also in hiding? Yet slowly, but surely they appeared. For instance, priests used to ask us if we had met so-and-so who had asked about a rosary group, and things to that effect, and thus these people would come on board.

I encourage priests, in their charity, to introduce young people to others of like mind. Many of my best friends are people I met through traditional Catholic apostolates, and they are from universities all over the country, from Princeton and Yale to Georgetown and Notre Dame to University of Dallas and Thomas Aquinas College. One friend said to me, "It's so wonderful that we have so many things in common." That is the beauty of clinging to the Truth. Great friendships can be based on sharing a common mission, as St Aelred taught.[10]

The main challenge Juventutem Boston faced was attempting to introduce traditional Catholic liturgy into an environment entirely dominated by the youth culture imposed from above. Young Catholics were never given a book full of worship music of every genre, from which they picked some Haugen and Haas ditties from the 1960s. On the contrary, these inane songs were forced on them. When you have been eating dog food for so long, you do not always know how to approach a filet mignon when they hand you the white napkin and the fork.

Obstacles abounded. When young and hopeful traditionalists meet the old and embittered traditionalists, bad things happen. Now, I am very understanding of the reasons why so many people are so upset. For years, they begged for crumbs from the clergy, and the best crumb they got was permission for Mass in the basement of the Cathedral. Oh wait, that is only because they showed up one Sunday for Mass to find their parish door locked, Mass cancelled, assets seized, and the priest reassigned. So certainly they have reason to be upset.

Yet, as a result, my first encounters with the old traditionalists were difficult. We relied on them for some amount of help, from borrowing vestments to assisting in training the altar servers to filling out the numbers in the *schola*. To be fair, young people like myself are also certainly rough around the edges and can be ideological, but years of lost political battles have not yet made us cynical or bitter. Our discovery of Tradition is qualitatively different from those who first encountered it before the year 2000. They had trauma. We have the Internet.

These difficulties and obstacles notwithstanding, I like a good fight and because there was a new pastor, I decided to have a go at founding Juventutem Boston and holding the first traditional Mass Harvard has enjoyed since the post-conciliar reforms. The pastor proved receptive to the idea, and we planned the whole affair in a matter of two weeks. It was

10. See: Aelred of Rievaulx, *Spiritual Friendship* (Kalamazoo: Cistercian Publications, 1977).

so unorganized that I did not even know who the celebrant was until the day before. Some begged that the first traditional Mass be a solemn Mass. In hindsight, I wish I would have taken this advice, but nevertheless, as I have already pointed out, the path to the liturgical tradition for youth is one that happens over time, not instantly. Despite all of this, a hundred people showed up for the Mass and it was all over the blogs as the first Mass in the Ivory Tower since the dark days descended.

Another frustration would soon plague me however: constant political trouble. If we are going to have Mass, we need a priest. The priest needs an altar. Altars are preferably in churches, and churches are run by bureaucrats. After founding Juventutem Boston, my co-founder Mary Curran and I took a 90-minute subway ride and walked 20 minutes to get to the chancery so that we could meet one of the auxiliary bishops. As a lay organization, Juventutem did not require anything from the bishop. I just thought it would be a good idea after several major events that we should introduce ourselves to the Archdiocese and let them know we were praying for the Cardinal and for vocations, and ask what we could do to help the Archdiocese further.

We entered the chancery with the bishop and his secretary and we sat down, and I told him our names and that we founded a group that has been organizing Masses for young people in the traditional rite with attendances in the hundreds. The bishop cut me off, "Why do you hate the new Mass?" I looked at Mary. After this point, she was so upset that she did not say a word the entire meeting. I attempted to explain to the Bishop that I do not hate the new Mass, and in fact I go to it 90% of the time, and that, besides, our apostolate had already brought back several non-practicing Catholics to Mass attendance. The rest of the conversation included such inane rebuttals as, "Well, why don't you just have pizza parties after the New Mass?," and "Obviously, you won't be getting anything from me."

I knew better than to argue with him on any of the points, and the secretary apologized profusely on the way out. The bishop's immediate vitriol seemed completely irrational, as he lashed into us before we even said anything, and it caused Mary to doubt the goodness and value of the work we were doing, as if we had done something wrong. We, of course, then sent the bishop a very nice spiritual bouquet thanking him for the "pleasant" meeting. A week later, I saw the Cardinal Archbishop on YouTube asking young Catholics in his diocese including those at some of the many universities "such as Harvard and Boston College" to get involved and volunteer ideas to help them in the evangelization of young people. The irony was too bitter to taste.

Fast forward to a couple months ago. I was travelling for work in a major city and went to Mass at the Cathedral. After spending 10 minutes asking various people where the Blessed Sacrament was (the "tabernacle"? The "Eucharist"? The "gold box"...?), I sat down for a rather disturbing Mass. At the time of communion, I walked over and got in the end of the line for the celebrant. Two summers ago, I had met Bishop Athanasius Schneider and read his booklet *Dominus Est* on the reception of Holy Communion. After that I decided I would always (not on a prudential basis, but always) receive communion kneeling and on the tongue.

This is one of the issues with dressing up the *Novus Ordo*. It involves prudentially adding in practices and accouterments, and this can be a temptation to pride. If one takes the strategy of the radical acceptance of the Truth, one just does it because it is right, not because one wants to— compromise with lots of people, but not with our Lord. So, no more not kneeling if I thought it would make a scene. Therefore, in this Cathedral, I knelt down in front of the priest...and nothing happened. Then, the priest said, "Stand up." I just looked at him. He said, "We don't do that here. You need to stand up." I asked him, "Are you going to deny me Communion simply because I am kneeling?" We had several more back and forths and I may have mentioned something about universal law trumping any particular legislation in this diocese and might have even made up a relevant paragraph number of *Redemptionis Sacramentum*. Intellectually, it was all simple, but in reality I was shaking and completely red and my heart was pounding. At this point, people were gathering around. Everyone else had already received, and it led to a standoff (or, rather, a 'kneeloff'). Then the priest said, "Are you trying to create a scene?" I politely answered, "No, I am trying to receive Communion." Then, after a few more mutterings, he exclaimed, "Boy! You need to learn some respect!" and threw the Sacred Host sideways into my mouth. I then awkwardly had to follow him halfway around the church to get back to the Blessed Sacrament chapel, where I parked myself and cried inwardly to God.

When the final blessing came, I crossed myself and ran for the door. I am no stranger to confrontation and I know all the details of the liturgical debate quite well, but this was emotionally traumatizing. I hobbled out and immediately texted my spiritual director, asking if I had somehow done something wrong. Did I do this to get attention? Did I want to make a scene? All sorts of devilish self-doubt took hold of me, and it really took me several hours to get over it. I texted another priest, and quite unintentionally it ended up all over the blogs with hundreds of comments and people writing to the Bishop of the Diocese. The point is that this priest was the same generation as the bishop in Boston and the same generation as the crotchety, bitter traditionalists.

5. *A Bit of Analysis*

The behavior of the bishop, the cathedral priest, and embittered tradition-alists can be explained, I think, by a single reason. All of these people lived through the traumatic days after the Council. Imagine if everything you held dear, from your Baltimore Catechism to your *Corpus Christi* proces-sions, were suddenly banned and you were told that it was repressive and part of a scheme to make clergy powerful at your expense. No matter how much you appeal it, the priests and bishops keep telling you that there is no going back.

Three reactions might arise from this experience of rupture:

1. leave the Faith completely: if it was wrong and needed to be changed, then the whole of Catholicism is a sham;
2. join some traditionalist movement with varying degrees of margin-alization; or
3. just agree with the priests and every time you remember those beautiful processions, repress that thought because it is not worth getting nostalgic about something that is wrong and forbidden.

The bishop and the priest who denied me Communion took option 3 and lied to themselves to handle the trauma. Then to see some young person come along with all that was taken away from them is unfair and upsetting. Today, the young people are encountering the liturgy like a treasure found in our grandparents' attics, but the problem is that when we bring it down, grandpa finds us admiring the jewelry of his deceased wife and gets quite upset. The traditionalist sacristan took the second option and grew bitter with constant persecution and separation from normal parochial life.

Pope Benedict XVI laid out the principle perfectly: "What earlier gen-erations held as sacred, remains sacred and great for us too, and it cannot be all of a sudden entirely forbidden or even considered harmful."[11] If we really got rid of the old liturgy, there is no truth in the faith. Or, more relevantly for people on college campuses, if the Church can change the essence of the Mass, the most noticeable thing for the average Catholic (short of rewriting the Hail Mary),[12] then why could she not change the teaching on gay marriage? And if she can and chooses not to, well then

11. Benedict XVI, "Letter on the occasion of the issuance of the Motu Proprio *Summorum Pontificum.*"

12. One shudders to think that Annibale Bugnini went as far as to propose exactly this, only to be overruled by Pope Paul IV. See: A. Bugnini, *The Reform of the Liturgy* (Collegeville: The Liturgical Press, 1990), p. 876.

she really is being mean and bigoted. That is the crux of the matter. That is why a restoration of the liturgy is so important for a coherent faith for today's youth. It is not about the vestments and the music. It is about the souls of millions of young people.

When we talk about souls, this radical commitment to the truth has other effects outside of the liturgy because it demands a cohesive faith. When I was a teenager, I used to blow out my birthday candles and wish that more of my friends would go to Confession. When we experience the traditional liturgy, we cannot help but notice what it is all about. If each little Crumb can save millions of souls, then we had better start kneeling in front of Our Lord, fasting and preparing for Communion, and making a good thanksgiving after. It also means that we have to confess our sins. The traditional liturgy creates frequent penitents. At Juventutem Boston, we always tried to find a priest to put in the confessional before and often during every Mass.

To realize that we are objectively sinners is similar to realizing that what looks like bread is objectively the Soul and Divinity of Jesus Christ. On the converse, the heresy of emotionalism that permeates youth Masses also affects confession. People only confess their sins when they "feel" sorry. Thank God the monks taught us that: "Boys, there will come a day when you do not 'feel' sorry, when you do not 'feel' like going to Mass. Those times are when you most need to attend weekly Mass and confess twice a month." Just as we see travesties committed in the liturgy of the Mass, so too do we find Confession destroyed. From confessing to Jesuits and hearing, "Oh, that's not a sin," to dubious absolution formulas and heretical advice, the confessional has become a joke—if the confessional is still even used as such and not as a closet for church cleaning supplies. Without young people confessing they are receiving communion unworthily and thus lying to themselves. I would suggest that most college students who leave their faith do it because they find themselves lying, and, really, it is always about sex. Here is the secret though. The answer is not to talk about sex.

The answer is to take that one hour we still have with them on Sundays and show them that there is something worth dying for and that God thought they were worth dying for. No one dies for something ambiguous. If recent liturgical scholarship has taught us anything, it has taught that the missal of Paul VI and the documents of Vatican II are full of ambiguities and debatable terms. Young people need clarity.

And so particular failures should not discourage one from trying to introduce the traditional traditional Mass anywhere, be it to a college campus or to a parish. One of the young men from the original group in 2007 was so traumatized, he vowed never to step foot in the Harvard Catholic Center again, and pulled away a growing contingent of ten key Catholic students with him to the traditional Mass downtown. When we had that first traditional Mass, he flew back in for it. At some point, the chaplains and bishops will have to realize that for pragmatic purposes they must give young people these things. The group I introduced to the traditional Mass revitalized Harvard Right to Life, which was almost dead, and also the Anscombe Society for Marriage. They revved up daily Mass attendance, and greased the wheels at the chaplaincy in general. By always worrying about scaring away the progressive crowds, chaplains tend to neglect and push away their greatest allies.

6. *Satanists in Harvard Square*

After I had retired as head of Juventutem and Harvard Right to Life and had finished my thesis, I had one last hurrah at Harvard: defeating the satanic Black Mass planned on campus. My best friend, the most recent President of Juventutem Boston, was walking around the Yard one day and saw a curious poster for a satanic ritual. After doing some investigating, we found that a student group at Harvard Extension School was planning to have a satanic group come to campus and perform the devilish ritual in the student pub under the freshman dining hall. I contacted the pastor, and since I only had one exam left and am quite suited to the role of crusader, I took charge in organizing resistance.

Late at night, I gathered together the core of the traditional Mass group, who of course then had become the core of all the Catholic apostolates on campus. Almost all of them had been introduced to the traditional liturgy for the first time at Harvard and fell in love with it after some time. I say some time because I require all people to try the ancient Mass at least three times before they can say they do not like it, and two of those three need to be sung or solemn Masses.

The satanic group announced they had in their possession a consecrated Host from a Catholic Mass. They had our Lord. They did not get Him by breaking into a tabernacle late at night, but almost certainly from just sticking their hand out and saying "Amen."

There were hence two prongs to the battle: political and spiritual. We drafted a petition which quickly gathered hundreds of thousands of signatures. I had people calling me all day and did radio spots and TV specials on NBC's Today Show. For a week we stayed up all night preparing the opposition. I even went to ecumenical charismatic prayer meetings (though while they were muttering, "Amen brother. Preach it!," I muttered, "Sancte

Raphael, ora pro nobis"). The devil was also palpably in the air as divisions brewed between myself and the pastor with regard to our different approaches. I remember I was so worn out that one night at 2am I made a split second decision and found four friends to get in a car at 4am and drive down to Norwalk to see Fr Richard Cipolla and Cardinal Burke (who was visiting), just so I could forget about it all for a bit and recharge. Driving back to Boston going 100 mph on the highway while doing an interview for the Harvard *Crimson* was interesting to say the least.

The Black Mass, like coming to an understanding of the traditional Mass, really drew a line in the sand. On which side do you stand? Is that a piece of bread or do they have my innocent Lord hostage? Do these Satanists have religious freedom or is this just wrong? In fact, I watched two of my mentors, a very well-known Catholic political philosopher and a legal scholar, refuse to sign our petition because they thought it would hurt ecumenical work. It was a hard time for us, but we stuck it out. We delivered hundreds of thousands of signatures printed on huge stacks of paper to the University President's office. The night before, several of us went and prayed at the pub. In fact, I dumped my entire stash of those scapulars, medals, and rosaries one gets in the mail when Catholic organizations are trying to get one's money all throughout the nooks and crannies of the space. I recently heard stories of people still finding miraculous medals and the like while drinking a beer in Memorial Hall.

Most important, we planned a procession in reparation scheduled at the same time as the satanic ritual. Enormous crowds showed up at MIT and I was the last minute Master of Ceremonies and coordinator for a huge Eucharistic procession down Massachusetts Avenue all the way to the Harvard Catholic chaplaincy. There has not been anything like that in Cambridge in decades. We then had a Holy Hour with the boys' choir and 2,000 people overflowing into the streets. During the middle of the Holy Hour, I got a text that, although the Satanists arrived, the Black Mass had been cancelled. We had people sending in prayers from all over the world, from busloads of people who drove in to Massachusetts from Indiana to the Monks at Norcia to parishes in Asia, and it worked. President Drew Faust of Harvard attended the Holy Hour. I spoke to her a week later during our Commencement and she told me that that Holy Hour was the most moving thing so far during her presidency of Harvard. Now, that is the power of the liturgy to move hearts.

7. *Conclusion*

We must, therefore, use the power of our ancient liturgical heritage. Today, children barely go to Mass. They do not want to go to some other program. An hour on Sunday is burdensome enough, so let us just do it right. Keep in mind that we do not want to fall into the trap of the reformers of using the Mass as a pedagogical tool. If we wish to do things right, we must focus on the Mass as an act of worship and allow its glory to shine forth—everything else will flow from that. At Juventutem Boston, we never had more than $100 in petty cash, and yet we managed to turn people to the Lord in a way that twenty years of programming and money from the diocese had failed to do. There were days when the servers greatly outnumbered the people in the congregation, but we persevered and hit numbers upwards of 250 in attendance and assisted a couple of universities and several parishes to celebrate their first traditional Mass and helped several priests learn the better half of the Roman rite.

When we introduce a liturgy that is so integral, so demanding, so rich, a real community can develop around an acceptance of the Truth aided by the authentic Christian culture that flows from the *cultus* innate to the *usus antiquior*. Along with our other Juventutem events, I hosted plenty of cocktail parties for first class feasts and we tried to grow in appreciation of good music and art. The liturgy is not only the apotheosis of Catholic life, but also its very beginning: both the *fons et culmen* (see: *Sacrosanctum Concilium* 10). When young people begin to ride the waves of this liturgical renewal, we will see a flowering of devotions, music, philosophy, and doctrine. And as we showed in Boston, young men and women formed by the liturgy can even rise up to defend Our Lord and our faith against the most hideous sort of blasphemy.

In the tech-world in which I work, we have a principle that you should never go into business unless you can be ten times better than your next competitor, and thus secure a monopoly. We need to stop trying to compete in the popular music space, or the Sunday evening entertainment space. Let us just focus on the thing the Catholic Church is the best at: Tradition! If we do that, how can we lose?

THE RENEWED UNDERSTANDING
OF THE LITURGY OF THE WORD
IN THE REFORMED LITURGY

Allan White OP

1. *Preaching: The State of the Question*

In 2013 the United States Conference of Catholic Bishops produced a document on preaching in the Sunday Assembly suggesting that all is not well in the ministry of the Word.[1] Priests may be preaching the truth but the question is: Is it doing anybody any good? They quote Pope Benedict in his letter following the Synod of Bishops on the Word of God *Verbum Dei*: "the quality of homilies needs to be improved" (30 September 2010, 59).[2] Pope Francis has also taken up this theme. He says in *Evangelii Gaudium* that he knows that the laity and the clergy both suffer from homilies, "the laity from having to listen to them and the clergy from having to prepare them" (24 November 2013, 135). The US bishops based their opinion on recent studies showing that many Catholics, for a variety of reasons, seem either indifferent to or disaffected with the Church and her teaching:

> We are also aware that in survey after survey over the past years, the People of God have called for more powerful and inspiring preaching. A steady diet of tepid or poorly prepared homilies is often cited as a cause for discouragement on the part of laity and even leading some to turn away from the Church.[3]

There you have it. You could be forgiven for thinking that this decline is the fault of those who preach. We are not giving the people what they want and what they so earnestly need, which is access to the living Word of God. Preachers are failing to edify, inform and entertain and our homilies

---

1. *Preaching the Mystery of Faith: The Sunday Homily* (Washington: USCCB, 2013).
2. See: ibid., p. 2.
3. Ibid.

are very possibly driving people out of the Church. Origen, amongst the greatest homiletic exegetes, warns us to be careful of presuming to speak about God: "It is dangerous to talk about God, even if what you say is true. And in fact, it is not only false ideas that are dangerous; even true ones are if they are not put forth at the right time."[4] In the matter of preaching Catholic truth as much harm can be done by telling the truth in wrong way and at the wrong time as being economical with truth.

2. *Liturgical Renewal and the Revival of Preaching*

From at least the 1930s onwards there were moves to revive the Church's life and mission through a renewal of her liturgy and a revitalization of the ministry of the Word. Those who advocated this renewal were convinced that the reassertion of the role of Scripture in the liturgy, particularly in the Mass, and its pastoral exposition in the preaching of the ordained ministry would unleash forces leading to the sacramental, ecclesiological, exegetical, catechetical and spiritual renewal of the Church. It would increase the active participation of the faithful in the Church's mission, and encourage a true devotion informed by the liturgy. The leaders of this movement operated against the background of the revival of patristic theology, and the reinvigoration of Scripture studies within the Catholic Church encouraged by Pius XII in *Divino Afflante Spiritu*.[5] For them the role of the living Word of God in gathering the Church and forming its ministry was of the utmost significance. At the same time there developed an intense questioning and even a rejection of the dominant neo-scholastic Thomist dogmatic system, which shaped so much of the clerical education and catechetical system of the time. It was thought to be excessively cerebral and arid in its lack of engagement with the devotional, affective and emotional sensibilities of the human being. The reigning manualist tradition in seminaries was decried in an effort to achieve a new doctrinal synthesis emphasizing the emerging disciplines of ecclesiology and litur- gical theology. Many of these strands of opinion came together at the Second Vatican Council having been prepared by an increasingly coherent liturgical movement in previous decades.[6]

---

4. Thomas P. Scheck (ed.), Origen, *Homilies on Ezekiel 1–14* (Washington: Catholic University Press of America, 2010), p. 40.

5. On Promoting Biblical Studies, commemorating the Fiftieth Anniversary of *Providentissimus Deus*, 3 September 1943.

6. An interesting and entertaining insider's memoir detailing some of these devel- opments may be found in Bernard Botte, *From Silence to Participation: An Insider's view of Liturgical Renewal* (Washington: Pastoral Press, 1988).

In the Constitution on the Liturgy, *Sacrosanctum Concilium*, promulgated by Vatican II, the idea of "liturgical preaching" began to emerge in a major way. A simple phrase in the Constitution states "the homily therefore is to be highly esteemed as part of the liturgy itself" (4 December 1963, 52). *Dei Verbum*, the Constitution on Divine Revelation, declares that "all preaching of the Church must be nourished and ruled by Sacred Scripture" (18 November 1965, 21). The Council thus set a course developed in subsequent documents for the exercise of the ministry of the Word in the Church. Preaching or proclamation was presented precisely as a "ministry" or a "service" of the living Word. It was at the service of Revelation. As the Constitution on the Church, *Lumen Gentium*, declares, "Christ is the light of the nations" (21 November 1964, 1). The Gospel, the Good News of Jesus Christ, is nothing other than the living Christ himself. He is the substance of "Revelation." Through his body the Church he continues his ministry of proclamation. It is to Christ that the Scriptures bear witness and this continuing living presence of Christ is made accessible to us in His Church pre-eminently by means of the Scriptures and the Eucharist. The Church channels or carries the scriptural revelation in preserving and venerating the texts and their interpretation through tradition. In handing it on the Church does not subdue it to its own purpose but is also subject to that same Word. It does not possess the Word. It cannot reify it. It cannot control it. The source of this revelation is neither a Book nor the Church but the one sent by God, Jesus Christ himself. This view was expressed by a decisively influential figure at Vatican II, Henri de Lubac (1896–1991), the French Jesuit, who wrote in his magisterial work: *L'Exégèse Médiévale*:

> Christianity is not, properly speaking, a "religion of the Book": it is a religion of the word (parole)—but not uniquely nor principally of the word in written form. It is a religion of the Word (verbum)—"not of a word, written and mute, but of a word 'living and incarnate,'" to quote St Bernard). The Word of God is here and now, among us, "which we have looked upon, and our hands have handled": the Word "living and active," unique and personal, uniting and crystallizing all the words which bear witness. Christianity is not the biblical religion: it is the religion of Jesus Christ.[7]

---

7. Henri de Lubac SJ, *L'Exegese Medievale* (Paris: Aubier, 1961), vol. 2/part 1, pp. 196–97. ET: *Medieval Exegesis*, 3 vols. (Grand Rapids: Eerdmans; Edinburgh: T. & T. Clark, 1998, 2000, 2009).

A similar emphasis on the dynamic character of the Word can be found in the work of Karl Barth. For Barth Revelation is always an event it is never something we can securely claim as our own possession.[8] Like Lubac and his contemporaries, Barth stressed that "God cannot be confiscated or put to work even by the church."[9] Revelation is not just an event, but also an action. It demands a response from the one who is acted upon. When God addresses us we are summoned to respond. As Pope Benedict wrote: "The faith that comes to us as a Word must also become a word in us, a word that is simultaneously the experience of our life."[10]

When the believer receives the Word he is not merely passive but is seized and held by it and drawn into the drama of revelation acting as its living witness. That witness, which is itself the work of the Holy Spirit, becomes part of that complex of revelation encountered in the life of the Church.[11] The same language of Revelation as event can be found in *Verbum Domini*, the post-synodal exhortation issued on 30 September 2010 by Pope Benedict.

3. *The Re-Birth of the "Homily" and the Concept of "Pastoral Liturgy"*

The emergence of the idea of liturgical preaching in the context of a new appreciation of the dynamism of Revelation can be traced in the work of two key characters who had a major influence on the composition of the Constitution on Revelation and the Constitution on the Liturgy: Henri de Lubac, the French Jesuit, and Josef Jungmann (1889–1975), his Austrian confrere.[12] The Constitution on the Liturgy, drawing partly on the work of these two scholars, stressed the ministry of the Word as an essential part of the Eucharistic liturgy. The warrant for this view was drawn from the first four centuries of the Church's practice. The change in emphasis or

8. Joseph L, Mangina, *Karl Barth: Theologian of Christian Witness* (Westminster: John Knox, 2004), p. 60.

9. Karl Barth, *Church Dogmatics*, vol. 1/part 1 (London: T&T Clark, 2004), p. 231.

10. Quoted in Scott Hahn, *Covenant and Communion: The Biblical Theology of Pope Benedict XVI* (Grand Rapids: Baker Brazos, 2009), p. 56.

11. The intellectual pedigree of this emphasis in the Reformed Tradition may be seen in Thomas F. Torrance, *Reality and Evangelical Theology: The Realism of Christian Revelation* (Eugene: Wipf & Stock, 2003), pp. 74ff.

12. For a useful treatment of the work of Josef Jungmann, see: Joanne M. Pierce and Michael Downey (eds), *Source and Summit: Commemorating Josef A. Jungmann SJ* (Collegeville: The Liturgical Press, 1999).

understanding of the act of liturgical preaching can be seen in a word change. The word "sermon" to describe the act of preaching appears only rarely in the liturgy Constitution—the preference is for "homily." The word "homily" was not in normal ecclesiastical usage before then.[13] We first encounter it in Origen, who described his 39 addresses on Luke's Gospel as "homilies."[14] By this time, Origen had largely undergone a substantial rehabilitation in scholarly circles. Henri de Lubac had already begun to salvage his reputation in his *History and Spirit: The Understanding of Scripture According to Origen*, originally published in 1950. In the last chapter of that work, "The Incorporations of the Logos," we can find elements of the theological groundwork for Vatican II's reassertion of the essential and intrinsic connection between the Liturgy of the Word and the Eucharist and the role of the homily as an exposition of the Scriptures in relation to the concrete circumstances of the particular congregation.

The Council's choice of the word "homily" was deliberate. Homilies, as seen in Origen's preaching and as described in Justin Martyr's account of the early Christian Eucharistic celebration, were always preached in a liturgical setting. They were prophetic in character with the preacher reflecting on the living word showing how it was present and active in the lives of his hearers. The homily presented a challenge to a joyful reformation of life on the part of all of those who heard it. It was not designed to encourage morose delectation. It usually took the form of a running commentary on a continuous reading of Scripture. It was assumed that the preacher, as well as the congregation, was subject to the discipline of the text. Since the preaching was shaped by continuous commentary the congregation was to be formed not by the choice of text of the preacher but by the Word itself. Both preacher and congregation stood under the judgment of the Word. Origen's tone and style was said to be distinctive and did not resemble that of other polished preachers. It was conversational, simple and accessible and devoid of the rhetorical flourishes of popular pagan oratory. The commentary on the text was an attempt to preserve the insight that it is God who first addresses us.

We cannot know God unless he first makes himself known to us. He reveals himself in his Word, that Word which is operative in creation and in the history of Israel even before the advent of the Logos in time. Revelation is a conversation that God inaugurates with humanity. The

13. Although the Encyclical letter *Mediator Dei* of Pius XII (20 November 1947) speaks of "the homily or sermon" as a *liturgical* practice of venerable antiquity (n. 21 of the Vatican edition).

14. Joseph T. Lienhard SJ (trans.), Origen, *Homilies on Luke* (Washington: Catholic University of America Press, 1996), p. xviii.

setting of the conversation God has with us is friendship. At Vatican II, during the debate on *Dei Verbum*, some Council Fathers were unhappy with the statement that God addresses us as friends (see n. 2). They thought that the word "friends" should be replaced by the word "sons." Their suggestion was rejected.[15] The Fathers did not opt for patriarchy and notions of filial obedience. They argued: was not Moses a friend of God? "And the Lord spoke to Moses face to face, as a man speaks to his friend" (Exod 33:11). With no one else had God shared his secrets: "And there arose not a prophet since in Israel like unto Moses, whom the Lord knew face to face" (Deut 34:10). We speak to our friends face to face. When we are ashamed, burdened with guilt, coming out with an untruth; we hang our heads; we cannot look up. We cannot show our faces, we cannot look our friends in the eye. Moses and the Lord spoke face to face, "as a man speaks to his friend." John tells us that at the Last Supper Jesus did not call his disciples servants, but friends (John 15:15). He speaks to them face-to-face, not man-to-man. Revelation is thus a conversation of God with humanity, a conversation in which God takes the initiative. It is an impulse of his love.

St John tells us we have seen, heard and touched…the word of life (see: 1 John 1:1). The revelation of the Holy Spirit in the divine conversation on which preachers are eavesdroppers takes place in word and gesture, language and signs. *Haec revelationis oeconomia fit gestis verbisqe intrinsice inter se connexis.* "This economy of revelation is achieved by deeds and words, which are intrinsically bound up with each other" (*Dei Verbum*, 2). At Vatican II, again in the debate on the Constitution on Divine Revelation, some Fathers wanted signs and gestures to be replaced by another word: the Latin word "factum" with its connotations of an action performed in the past and now over and done with; something which could be described and reported upon but which does not have the emphasis of something still living now. In this way the tradition could be wrapped, packaged and sealed, controlled and dispatched, consigned from hand to hand like a baton in a relay race. It was precisely this static notion of tradition from which some of those active at Vatican II wished to escape. The homily was seen to be a means of transmitting or channeling the still vital apostolic witness in the Church. The Ministry of the Word is an expression of God's continuous offer of friendship to humanity. This offer is continually actualized and rendered accessible in His Church.

15. Henri de Lubac SJ, *La Révélation Divine* (Paris: Cerf, 1983), pp. 36–38.

In Origen's writings Scripture and the Eucharist are closely associated. During the same liturgy the Bread of the Word is broken and the Body of Christ is distributed. Both of them should be the objects of the same veneration and reverence. Origen writes:

> You know, you who are used to assisting at the divine mysteries with such religious care, when you receive the Body of the Lord, you take care lest the least morsel fall from it... You would think yourselves blameworthy, and so you would truly be, if that were to happen through your negligence... Now how could it be less serious to neglect the Word of God than his Body?[16]

The life of the Church springs from one source, Christ himself, who is made present according to two modalities in the sacrament of the Word and the sacrament of the Eucharist. The same link is found in *Verbum Domini* where we read: "word and Eucharist are so deeply bound together that we cannot understand one without the other" (n. 55). The one who presides at the Eucharist and breaks the bread is the servant of the Church in that capacity so he is the servant of the Word. The two aspects of the one ministry go together. In Origen's view preaching was the actual advent of Christ in the midst of the assembly. His presence in the community of faith and worship was manifested in and through the ministry of the Word by the grace of the Holy Spirit.

The Church is the pre-eminent place of interpretation of the Word. The minister of the Word performs his particular task of interpretation and mediation of the Word in the midst of that fundamental hermeneutical community, which is animated by the Holy Spirit. Only those who have received the Spirit can understand the meaning of the Scriptures. Ignatius of Antioch and the later Fathers understood that it was the Church as whole that acted as the true representative of Christ on earth. As Gregory Dix wrote:

> The whole church prayed in the Person of Christ; the whole church was charged with the office of "proclaiming" the revelation of Christ; the whole church offered the Eucharist as the "re-calling" before God and man of the offering of Christ. All that which he has done once for all as the priest and proclaimer of the kingship of God, the Church, which is the fulfillment of Him (see: Eph. 1:23), enters and fulfills. Christ and his Church are one with one mission, one life, one prayer, one gospel, one offering, one being, one Father.[17]

16. *Homilies on Exodus* 13.3, Jacques Paul Migne (ed.), *Patrologia Graeca* (Paris, 1846–57), vol. 12 col. 1632.

17. Gregory Dix, *The Shape of the Liturgy* (London: Continuum, 2005), pp. 29–30.

The work of proclamation of the mystery of faith is the work of the entire body. Origen understood the work of preaching precisely in this way. It was a mutual search by the preacher and the congregation for the true voice of the one true God. Scripture was not a dead word imprisoned in the past, but a living word spoken and effective in the present.

4. *The Contemporary Homiletic Ministry and Its Roots in Word and Sacrament*

In Pope Benedict's Apostolic Exhortation *Verbum Domini* we read:

> The sacramentality of the Word can thus be understood by analogy with the real presence of Christ under the appearances of the consecrated bread and wine. By approaching the altar and partaking in the Eucharistic banquet we truly share in the body and blood of Christ. The proclamation of God's word at the celebration entails an acknowledgement that Christ himself is present, that he speaks to us, and that he wishes to be heard. (n. 56)

The Homiletic Directory issued by the Congregation of Divine Worship and the Discipline of the Sacraments (29 June 2014) reminds us that "it is because the homily is an integral part of the Church's worship that it is to be delivered only by bishops, priests and deacons. So intimate is the bond between the table of the Word and the table of the altar itself" (n. 5).[18] The homily is a ministry of pastoral proclamation but it is not only the work of the preacher, just as the celebration of the Eucharist is not entirely the work of the president of the assembly himself. In the Eucharist water, bread and wine become the stuff of the Eucharist. In the ministry of preaching, words, which take on life through the human instrumentality of the minister, are what constitute the preaching of the Word. The materials of the Eucharist are the elements of everyday life given to us by God, presented by the people for offering, which are then transformed by the Holy Spirit into the living Christ. In the Ministry of the Word the everyday words of the minister, the everyday experiences of the congregation are fashioned by the Holy Spirit, operating by his power in the midst of the community, into a real presence of Christ the Word. Through the operation of his Spirit God takes up temporal, everyday realities to be transformed into the means whereby his supernatural grace is channeled.

---

18. See also the Instruction of the same Congregation, *Redemptionis Sacramentum*, 25 March 2004, n. 161.

In this exchange both minister of the Word and those who hear him have a part to play. Preaching is not the task of the preacher alone. Proclamation is what the entire Church does as it gathers in a particular place to witness to him who is the way, the truth and the life. There are three characters at work in this sacred drama: the Holy Spirit, the preacher who disposes himself to be his instrument, and the congregation. The grace of baptism abiding in each member of the congregation enables it to receive actively the living Word as it is proclaimed to the assembly by the Church's minister. The witness of the Proclamation of the Mystery of Faith is the work of the entire assembly; it is more than the ministry of the president of the assembly alone. Just as the entire assembly shares in the liturgy of the Eucharist so it shares in the liturgy of the Word; both are acts of the Body and every member of the Body acts according to his own Order, having his own part to play. When true preaching takes place, the Holy Spirit, the preacher and the people of God are co-workers in the vineyard of Revelation. They co-operate in proclaiming not a dead Christ or a naked Christ but Christ in His Church clothed in his promises.[19]

5. *"Kerygmatic Theology"*

As we have said, an important influence on the renewed understanding of the Ministry of the Word, which featured at Vatican II, came through the Jesuit school of theology at Innsbruck in the 1930s. The principal actors in this renewal movement were the Jesuits Josef Jungmann, Hugo Rahner, the brother of the famous Karl, and Johannes Hofinger. All three were significant figures in what came to be known as the "kerygmatic movement" of the time, stressing preaching as the proclamation of the Good News given in Christ.[20] The Second Vatican Council, taking its inspiration from the Acts of the Apostles and the practice of the Church in the first four centuries, highlighted the "proclamation of God's wonderful works in the history of salvation" (*Sacrosanctum Concilium* 35). Renewal was to come about through *ressourcement*, a return to a renewed under-standing of the practice of the Church in the first four centuries of its existence.

---

19. In this section I am indebted to the work of Archbishop Donald Coggan, *Preaching: The Sacrament of the Word* (New York: Crossroad, 1988).

20. See: Aidan Nichols OP, *Catholic Theology Since the Enlightenment: A Survey* (Leominster: Gracewing, 1998), pp. 132–33.

Not all of the Conciliar bishops were happy with the notion of returning to the patristic understanding of the homily. Some regarded it as little more than pious antiquarianism with nothing to offer the circumstances of their time. For them the traditional "sermon" with its catechetical instructional nature was the paradigm.[21] The "sermon," which had been the dominant feature of the Church's approach since the Council of Trent, was designed to produce confident believers skilled in providing convincing apologetic answers to Protestant and secularist challenges. According to this view the sermon was not entirely integrated into the liturgical action, symbolized in the old liturgy by the priest's sometimes removing the chasuble and the maniple before proceeding to the pulpit to preach.[22] Put crudely it provided a useful opportunity for the priest to instruct the congregation before proceeding to the consecration. It was precisely this understanding that Jungmann and the members of the kerygmatic movement wished to escape.

Before joining the Society of Jesus, Jungmann had served as a pastor in Brixen, now Bressanone in the South Tirol. There he discovered that the Gospel was not "good news" for his parishioners. He kept notes of his experience there and what he described as the fear-laden piety of the local people that, in his assessment, contradicted the joyful nature of the good news he sought to preach. His experiences and the recollections they generated were recorded eventually in his influential 1936 work, *Die Frohbatschaft und unsere Glaubensverkundigung*, which only appeared in English translation in 1962 as *The Good News Yesterday and Today.*[23]

Jungmann believed that the style and methods of catechesis prevailing in the Church in his time were not only inadequate but also damaging, since they did not satisfy the deeper spiritual needs of the people. In his opinion the pattern of contemporary catechesis followed too closely the neo-scholastic manuals of theology dominating seminary life at the time. Clerical formation in the seminaries taught the clergy to fix their preaching in a defensive apologetic trajectory, instead of concerning themselves with the vital proclamation of a living faith; as a result, education in the faith

21. Rober P. Waznak SS, *An Introduction to the Homily* (Collegeville: The Liturgical Press, 1998), pp. ix, 1–30.

22. A norm redundant since at least *Mediator Dei*'s inclusion of the "the homily or sermon" as a liturgical practice (n. 21), and unjustifiable in celebrations of the *usus antiquior* today in the light of the Council's clarification of the nature of the homily in the life of the Church—which is valid whichever use of the Roman rite is celebrated.

23. Josef Andreas Jungmann SJ, *The Good News Yesterday and Today* (New York: Sadlier, 1962).

was too cerebral and too arid and based on rote learning.[24] A focus on what he considered as abstract theological questions divorced from the Christian experience of most people failed to nourish the people of God. The system concerned itself with historical questions, arid polemics and ivory-tower speculation. In Jungmann's view preaching should be motivated by a Christological dynamic, with the person of Christ at its center. He insisted that faith must not be abstract but must be founded on the overarching and unifying vision of Christ in whom all things hold together. Jungmann's belief was that catechesis and growth in the knowledge and love of God was not simply an intellectual process but should be directed towards the will and affections as well. The proclamation was to grasp and fulfill the whole person.[25] His vision was of a Christian community echoing the life and experience of the early Christians who were "exultantly happy and serenely confident in their whole-souled faith."[26] It was his Jesuit colleague Hugo Rahner who coined the phrase "Theology of Proclamation" and who wrote a book of the same name.[27]

In Jungmann's view the Church, especially in Europe, was marked by a strongly traditional and cultural conformity. In his scheme of things, Christians could be divided into conscious and unconscious Christians. Conscious Christianity was an active faith, moved by conviction, drawing the believer to build the kingdom of God by a dynamic engagement with the world. Unconscious Christianity on the other hand was passive and characterized by custom, habit, routine and duty. Unconscious Christians, distinguished as they were by the acceptance of the link between Christianity and society, came to see their faith as constituted by laws, rules and arid intellectual processes. Jungmann was deeply marked by his hostility to neo-scholasticism, but unlike the French Dominicans who challenged it directly and suffered for it, he simply ignored it.[28] He aspired to the development of an evangelical theology, which avoided purely speculative or scientifically based views.

Some of the theories of kerygmatic theology can be seen in the discussions and documents of the Council and in later catechetical documents, where the emphasis is on the paschal mystery of Christ as the fundamental axiom of faith and life. It is this mystery that is actualized in the

24. Ibid., pp. 27–37.

25. Ibid., pp. 94–97.

26. Ibid., p. 3.

27. Hugo Rahner SJ, *A Theology of Proclamation* (New York: Herder & Herder, 1968).

28. Jungmann, *The Good News Yesterday and Today*, pp. 28ff.

course of the liturgy. The liturgical reformers understood the liturgy not as a gathering of individuals but as a communal celebration offered by a communion of believers each according to his order but united in one body. Every celebration of the liturgical mystery of the death and resurrection of Christ was to be an exercise of the priestly office of Jesus Christ in his body the Church through head and members. All of those baptized into Christ exercised through their communion in the spirit the active participation in the celebration of that mystery.

Jungmann's influence on the development of the liturgy can be seen in many ways. At the heart of the liturgical year is the celebration of Easter. The Easter liturgy itself was reformed by a return to its primitive expression. The ancient structure of the liturgy of the Word and the liturgy of the Eucharist were restored. A more significant place was given to the proclamation of Scripture, the role of the homily in forming conscious Christians was stressed, the prayer of the faithful was restored and the integrity of the celebration during which the people were fed at the table of the word and the table of the Eucharist was recovered. In all of this the emphasis was on the pastoral. Jungmann's distrust of speculative theology as leading to useless and destructive controversy remained. As he wrote:

> It is here, however, that one finds the real difference between theology and the proclamation of the faith. Theology is primarily at the service of knowledge; hence it investigates religious reality to the outermost limit of the knowable (*verum*) and struggles here for the last little piece of truth that can be grasped without asking in each instance about the significance such effort may have for life. The proclamation of the faith on the other hand is entirely ordered towards life. Hence it considers this same religious reality wholly under the aspect of how it is a motivating goal of our efforts (*bonum*). From the wide assortment of matter offered by theological analysis, all that is mere knowledge falls outside its purview, and only that significance which offers guidance and leads to the goal, which corresponds to the demands and requirements of salvation.[29]

These are hard words for a Dominican—St Thomas does not recognize the distinction between theology and preaching and teaching. In his works he uses the words *praedicatio* and *doctrina* interchangeably.

Where can we go for enlightenment and encouragement on the subject of liturgical preaching? In his Apostolic Exhortation, *Evangelii Gaudium* (24 November 2013), Pope Francis devotes a section to the question of preaching. He situates the ministry of the Word firmly in the context of the Apostolic Tradition. Hugo Rahner in his *Theology of Proclamation*,

29. Ibid., p. 33.

published in 1938, envisages the Church as the continuum of the eternal Word, who proceeds from the mouth of the Father. The preachers stands in this living stream of continuity, modeling himself on the God who speaks. If he is to speak as his master speaks his preaching must be rendered dynamic and vital by an ever-renewed contact with the tradition as it is expressed in Scripture, the writings of the Fathers, the living liturgy and the writings of the saints in every century. He who proclaims does not simply announce but is himself drawn into the mystery and whose life and ministry becomes a sign of that same mystery.

6. *Pope Francis and the Pastoral Ministry of Proclamation*

In February 2015 Pope Francis had a meeting with the clergy of the diocese of Rome and talked to them freely about what was called the *ars celebrandi*, the proper way to celebrate Mass, and also on the subject of preaching.[30] He recommended two books: one was Rahner's 1968 *Theology of Proclamation*. One of the priests asked him what was the difference between Hugo and his brother Karl. The Pope answered "Hugo writes clearly." It seems to me that the influence of Hugo Rahner and of the kerygmatic movement led by Jungmann can be seen in this section on preaching in *Evangelii Gaudium*. The Pope begins by seeing the preacher as an instrument of God's divine Word disposing himself to be used as a personal mediation of the message of salvation. He then goes on to talk about the homily itself. It is not a place for meditation or catechesis but for dialogue between God and his people. The great deeds of salvation are to be proclaimed to stimulate the faith of the people and to bring them to participate actively in the celebration of the Eucharist in which the preacher is a mediator and interpreter. The ministry of the preacher is pastoral; he must know the hearts of his people and be moved by pastoral charity towards them. Preaching is not a form of entertainment. The preacher is not to be the center of attention. The style of his homiletic communication should be conversational, as when a mother talks to her children. Origen says, in reference to God's speaking to us, that he stoops down to our level and talks to us, as it were, in baby talk.[31] The preacher should be a listener, emphasizing dialogue much more than what he considers to be the simple communication of the truth. His homily should neither be doctrinaire, moralistic nor a lecture on biblical exegesis. All of this detracts from heart to heart communication.

30. See: *La Stampa*, 22 February 2015.
31. John Clark Smith (trans.), Origen, *Homilies on Jeremiah; Homily on 1 Kings 18* (Washington: Catholic University of America Press, 1998), Hom. 18, 4, pp. 198–99.

When grappling with the text he should strive to understand it in its original meaning and not project his own onto it. The Bible is to be read as a whole as interpreting itself, as Origen taught. The preacher must be personally familiar with the Word of God. People learn more by example than by precept, and as Paul VI wrote in *Evangelii Nuntiandi* (8 December 1975), the authority of an authentic witness is greater than one who is merely commissioned. His homily should be simple, accessible, brief and positive (see nn. 41, 76).

It is what Pope Francis says about the positive nature of the Gospel message and how it is communicated that gives some insight into how he understands his ministry. It should not be concerned with pointing out what should not be done but with suggesting what we can do better. The presentation of a positive vision of human life in response to Christ is more helpful than the negative. People often live down to our expectations of them. If we have to be negative it should be balanced with a positive and attractive value, lest we come across as always complaining, reproaching, lamenting or criticizing.

Positive preaching offers hope. It points to the future. The core of the Christian kerygma is the proclamation that God has come amongst us in Christ and he has shown us how much he loves us. This is most important aspect of all Christian preaching. In an interesting phrase Pope Francis says: "We must not think that in catechesis the kerygma gives way to a supposedly more 'solid' formation. Nothing is more solid, profound, secure, meaningful and wisdom-filled than that initial proclamation" (*Evangelii Gaudium*, n. 165). Our preaching should be marked by joy in its execution and in its effect. We should not reduce preaching to a few philosophical doctrines, which are at times more philosophical than evangelical. The preacher should be characterized by approachability, readiness for dialogue, patience and warmth, and offer a welcome that is non-judgmental.

You might say that all of this is all very well, but the Catholic faith is an articulated whole. Conversion involves a change of life. *Metanoia*, at which all proclamation aims, means a change of *nous*, a change of mind of attitudes and of habits. We know from our own experience as well as by accompanying others that this is not easy. We must stress the joy of the Gospel but this involves the way of the Cross and the taking up of the Cross. The risen and glorified Christ, in whose life we share through the Holy Spirit, is the central mystery of our faith; we must never fail to preach that. Believing in the hierarchy of truths that not everything teaching is of equal importance does not mean that some things are of no importance.

7. *Conclusion*

How do we communicate the hard sayings of our moral tradition, which seems so much at odds with the beliefs of those amongst whom we live? Pope Francis says we must stress the attractiveness of our way of life. Rather than being experts in dire predictions, dour judges, bent on rooting our every threat and deviation, we should appear as joyful messengers of challenging proposals, guardians of goodness and beauty which shine forth in a life of fidelity to the Gospel. It seems to me this is as close as it gets to a pastoral manifesto of the Pope so far. It seems to describe his own strategy and understanding of his mission rooted in the experience of the *Theology of Proclamation* and the liturgical reforms of the Second Vatican Council. If I may sum it up in the words of William Wordsworth, the English Romantic poet, "what we have loved, others will love and we will teach them how."[32] As Blessed Pope Paul VI wrote,

> It will be useful to stress this point: that in the Church the witness given by a life truly and essentially Christian and which is dedicated to God in an indissoluble union which is likewise dedicated with the utmost fervor of soul to our neighbor is the primary organ of evangelization... The men of our day are more impressed by witness than by teachers and if they listen it is because they also bear witness. (*Evangelii Nuntiandi*, 41)

The most powerful sermon we ever preach is the sermon of our own lives.

---

32. William Wordsworth, *The Prelude*, lines 446–47.

THE FORMATION OF PRIESTS IN "THE SPIRIT AND POWER OF THE LITURGY" (*SACROSANCTUM CONCILIUM* 14)— OBSERVATIONS ON THE IMPLEMENTATION OF THE CONSTITUTION AND PROPOSALS FOR THE LITURGICAL FORMATION OF PRIESTS IN THE TWENTY-FIRST CENTURY.

Kurt Belsole OSB

1. *Introduction*

I would like to mention the following story, both as background as well as an example of well-celebrated liturgy. Part of my position at the Pontifical North American College, the American seminary in Rome, is that I am responsible for arranging the diaconate ordinations at St Peter's Basilica. Usually we have between 40–50 students being ordained each year, with one or two cardinals present, 10–20 bishops concelebrating, about 250 concelebrating priests, 20 deacons and about 1,500 faithful. It is no small undertaking.

One of the most rewarding e-mails regarding the 2013 ceremony came from one of the newly ordained deacons. He wrote:

> The evening of the ordination, at the reception that we had at a local restaurant, a family friend in his 60s, a husband and father of two, got up to speak. He is a man who can command a presence and the room went silent. I had never known him to speak of the faith personally, and we were very surprised at what he said. You could tell that he was choosing his words carefully, and it seemed that something extraordinary was happening. He said: "Today, our family was very, very privileged to be at Matt's ordination. And I have to say, seeing all those priests, and everything about the ceremony, *for a moment the veil was lifted*...(he began to get red in the eyes and fight back tears)... *and my faith was renewed.*" Then he sat down, and the atmosphere was heavy with the supernatural. It was extremely moving.[1]

---

1. Matthew Dalrymple, "Comments After Ordination at St. Peter's," e-mail message to the author 3 March 2015 (emphasis in the original).

The veil was lifted, my faith was renewed, and the atmosphere was heavy with the supernatural. That speaks volumes on what liturgical renewal and the formation of priests means for the Church.

2. *The Promotion of Liturgical Instruction and Active Participation in* Sacrosanctum Concilium *14*

In the Second Vatican Council's Constitution on the Sacred Liturgy, *Sacrosanctum Concilium* (4 December 1963), 14 we read:

> Mother Church earnestly desires that all the faithful should be led to that fully conscious, and active participation in liturgical celebrations which is demanded by the very nature of the liturgy. Such participation by the Christian people as "a chosen race, a royal priesthood, a holy nation, a redeemed people" (1 Pet. 2:9; cf. 2:4–5), is their right and duty by reason of their baptism.
>
> In the restoration and promotion of the Sacred Liturgy, this full and active participation by all the people is the aim to be considered before all else; for it is the primary and indispensable source from which the faithful are to derive the true Christian spirit; and therefore pastors of souls must zealously strive to achieve it, by means of the necessary instruction, in all their pastoral work.
>
> Yet it would be futile to entertain any hopes of realizing this unless the pastors themselves, in the first place, become thoroughly imbued with the spirit and power of the liturgy, and undertake to give instruction about it. A prime need, therefore, is that attention be directed, first of all, to the liturgical instruction of the clergy.

Consequently, what kind of priest does the Council expect?

1. Priests who lead the faithful to full, conscious, and active participation—who is to lead them to this if not the priest?
2. Priests who make it possible for the faithful to enjoy the rights of full, active, and conscious participation in the Sacred Liturgy as well as priests who present this as one of the duties of the faithful, and who do not make it seem optional for them.
3. Priests who fulfill their responsibility that the faithful experience the full and active participation in the Sacred Liturgy as the primary and indispensable source from which the faithful are to derive the true Christian spirit.

4. Priests who themselves are thoroughly imbued with the spirit and power of the liturgy and undertake to give instruction about it.
5. Priests who are docile to the prime need of the liturgical instruction of the clergy.

3. *Observations on the Implementation of the Constitution*

Sacrosanctum Concilium was implemented in various ways, and here I limit myself to the Council's directives for the celebration of the Eucharist, and their implementation, which we find mainly in *Sacrosanctum Concilium* 50–57:

1. The treasures of the Bible have been opened up more lavishly with the three-year cycle of the lectionary which appeared after the Council.
2. The homily is seen as part of the liturgy itself.
3. The vernacular has come to be used in the celebration of the liturgy.
4. The faithful frequently receive from the same sacrifice as the one that they participate in.
5. Communion is often given under both kinds.
6. Permission for concelebration has been extended.

Although the theological liturgical vision of the Council has not always been implemented, it is significant that the Mass rite has become more participatory, that the treasures of the Bible have been opened up more lavishly, that the homily is understood as part of the liturgy, that people receive from the elements consecrated at that Mass, that they sometimes have the opportunity to receive under both kinds, and that concelebration has been extended. These are significant ways in which the vision of the Council was implemented.

4. *Fourteen Proposals for the Liturgical Formation of Priests in the Twenty-first Century*

During his visit to the Cistercian abbey of Stift Heiligenkreuz outside of Vienna on 9 September 2007, Pope Benedict XVI said:

> Your first service for this world must, therefore, be your prayer and the celebration of the liturgy. The disposition of every priest and of every person who has been consecrated to God must be "to prefer nothing to the work of God" (*Rule of St Benedict* 43,3). The beauty of such an outlook will express

itself in the beauty of the liturgy, so that where we gather together to sing, to praise God, to celebrate, and to adore, a part of heaven becomes present on this earth.[2]

Before we move to specific proposals, I would just like to mention that these proposals are directed towards the veil being lifted, faith being renewed, and heaven becoming present on this earth. Also, I do not know if this needs to be said, but one must love and be patient with today's seminarians when it comes to the liturgy. They have much good will, but their experience of the liturgy has sometimes not been the most reverent or the most devout and so they may not understand or appreciate what happens at the liturgy.

(1) *Embrace the Teaching of Vatican II,* Sacrosanctum Concilium, *and the subsequent exposition of the Sacred Liturgy in the* Catechism of the Catholic Church: *the Sacred Liturgy is the font and summit of the Christian life, and it is a public work done by Christ in his paschal mystery, a work done for the people, in which we are privileged to participate.*

My first proposal is theological and is at the heart of the liturgical life of the Church. *Sacrosanctum Concilium* 10 calls the liturgy the *culmen et fons* of the life of the Church: "(T)he liturgy is the summit toward which the activity of the Church is directed; it is also the font from which all her power flows." Again, the Dogmatic Constitution on the Church of Vatican II, *Lumen Gentium* (21 November 1964) 11, states: "Taking part in the Eucharistic Sacrifice, which is the fount and apex of the whole Christian life (*totius vitae christianae fontem et culmen*), they offer the Divine Victim to God, and offer themselves along with It."

Seeing the liturgy as the *culmen et fons* of Christian life is essential in the formation of priests. *Nemo dat quod non habet,* and unless priests really believe that the liturgy is the source and summit of Christian life, from the time of one's baptism into the life of the Father, the Son, and

---

2. Benedict XVI, Visit in the Abbey of Heiligenkreuz, Address, 9 September 2007, "Euer erster Dienst für diese Welt muß daher Euer Gebet und die Feier des Gottesdienstes sein. Die Gesinnung eines jeden Priesters, eines jeden gottgeweihten Menschen muß es sein, 'dem Gottesdienst nichts vorzuziehen.' Die Schönheit einer solchen Gesinnung wird sich in der Schönheit der Liturgie ausdrücken, sodaß dort, wo wir miteinander singen, Gott preisen, feiern und anbeten, ein Stück Himmel auf Erden anwesend wird."

the Holy Spirit, until the time when they receive their Savior in *viaticum*, their priesthood will be impoverished and not correspond to the teaching of Vatican II.

The *Catechism of the Catholic Church* teaches as well in n. 1069: "The word 'liturgy' originally meant a 'public work' or a 'service in the name of/on behalf of the people.' In Christian tradition it means the participation of the People of God in 'the work of God.'" That seminarians understand the Sacred Liturgy as a public work is essential. The basic etymology is from the Greek word *leitourgia*, a word already used by the pagan Greeks to denote a public action usually with civil, military, or religious overtones, basically a public act or work that benefits the people. Christ is the liturgist, and his paschal mystery is the work done for the very salvation of his People. He is the primary agent and we are the beneficiaries. In the sixth century, St Benedict in his *Rule* referred to the liturgy as the *opus Dei*, the *work of God*.[3] Much damage has been done by the overly facile and untheological etymology that claimed that the liturgy is the work of the people, deriving the word from *laos* and *ergon*. Unless seminarians get beyond that they will have a flawed idea of the Sacred Liturgy.

(2) *Develop a liturgical vision: it is essential to embrace, and if necessary to recover, the theological liturgical vision that gave birth to* Sacrosanctum Concilium.

If the liturgical vision of the Fathers of Vatican II is to be fruitful, there is a desperate need for the recovery of the liturgical vision that gave birth to *Sacrosanctum Concilium*. We are well aware that an historical-critical reading of scripture must take into account the historical, social, and theological contexts in which the text developed. Unfortunately, we have not been applying the same healthy historical-critical reading to *Sacrosanctum Concilium*. By and large the names and persons who were so important in the movement that gave birth to the conciliar document are forgotten today. A very partial list might include Prosper Guéranger, Columba Marmion, Lambert Beauduin, Romano Guardini, Odo Casel, Jean Daniélou, Cipriano Vagaggini, and Louis Bouyer. The pastoral liturgical perspective could also include such personages as Virgil Michel, Martin Hellriegel, Clifford Howell, and Pius Parsch.[4] But who today has

3. See: *The Rule of St Benedict*, 7,63; 22,6; 22,8; 43,6; 43,10; 43, title; 43,3; 44,1; 47, title; 47,1; 50,3; 52,2; 58,7; 67,2; and 67,3.

4. Works that remain foundational for a theological vision of the liturgy and which, therefore, continue to be of great value today are: Virgil Michel (trans.), Lambert

read them, has imbibed their theological vision, and has incorporated the pastoral consequences? This leaves unmentioned the great encyclicals *Mystici Corporis* and *Mediator Dei* of Pope Pius XII. I tend to agree with Keith Pecklers where he writes at the conclusion of his book, *The Unread Vision: The Liturgical Movement in the United States of America: 1926–1955*: "Perhaps the liturgical movement needs to be re-founded, and a sense of the Church as the Mystical Body of Christ retrieved. What is clear is that the vision to which the liturgical pioneers gave their lives remains unread, unfulfilled."[5]

Social consciousness, social justice, and social action as well are key to a good liturgical formation. One cannot be concerned about what goes on in the sanctuary without being touched by the plight of the members of the Mystical Body of Christ and even simple human solidarity. One need only recall that Lambert Beauduin was a member of a fraternity of priests who served as labor chaplains before he entered Mont César and that Virgil Michel not only founded the Liturgical Press but was also involved in the National Catholic Rural Life Conference and various social questions of his day.[6]

(3) *Distinguish between liturgy and ceremonies: ceremonies are not liturgy—although they are important. Liturgy embraces the whole of life; ceremonies go on, by and large, within the sanctuary.*

To cling to the external form without fostering the internal element is to ignore the divine mysteries in which we are called to live and move and have our being.

Beauduin, *Liturgy: The Life of the Church*, 3rd edn (Farnborough: St. Michael's Abbey, 2002); Odo Casel, *The Mystery of Christian Worship and Other Writings* (London: Darton, Longman & Todd, 1962); Charles Davis, *Liturgy and Doctrine* (London: Sheed & Ward, 1960); as well as Clifford Howell, *Of Sacraments and Sacrifice* (Collegeville: The Liturgical Press, 1952)—a book that some eighth graders in the United States were using as a textbook in the early 1960s. An application of the place of the paschal mystery and Caselian sense of liturgical mystery to the parish can be found in Henri Oster, *The Paschal Mystery in Parish Life* (New York: Herder, 1967). A very helpful book that takes one through the patristic typology of the Fathers in regard to the Sacred Liturgy is Jean Daniélou, *The Bible and the Liturgy* (Ann Arbor: Servant Books, 1979), originally published by the University of Notre Dame Press in 1956.

5. Keith Pecklers, *The Unread Vision: The Liturgical Movement in the United States of America: 1926–1955* (Collegeville: The Liturgical Press, 1998), p. 287.

6. See: ibid., pp. 124–37; Jeremy Hall, *The Full Stature of Christ: The Ecclesiology of Dom Virgil Michel* (Collegeville: The Liturgical Press, 1976), pp. 177–99.

A further distinction must be made between liturgy and ceremonies. Liturgy is more than ceremonies. To believe or act otherwise would be at best ritualism or at worst rubricism. Liturgy is about the theological realities of Trinity, Incarnation, and Church and our participation in the very life of God. It is supernatural and involves God's condescension and our participation in divine life—through the sacred mysteries—in the celebration of the rites of the Church. Key to the liturgical formation of seminarians is the liturgical theological vision and reality which the ceremonies are meant to serve. Anything less is poor, shabby, and insufficient. Unfortunately, after Vatican II, the reforms were implemented as a cosmetic change rather than a theological paradigmatic shift. It is one thing to issue a conciliar constitution, it is quite another to have its theological vision implemented throughout the world, especially when not everyone was prepared for it theologically.

As Pope Pius XII wrote in his Encyclical on the liturgy, *Mediator Dei* (20 November 1947): "The universal worship rendered by the Church to God must be, in its entirety, interior as well as exterior... The chief element of divine worship must be interior... The Sacred Liturgy requires, however, that both of these elements be intimately linked" (nn. 23–24).

At this point, I would urge most ardently that seminarians enter into the contemplative dimension of the liturgy. By that, I mean a true *lectio divina* on the liturgical texts. My work has shown me that it is essential to teach seminarians to pray the Mass—but not in a way that turns the liturgy into a holy show. If people are subjected week after week to priests who speak the liturgical texts without being struck by the fact that their priest is actually praying the liturgical text—a very personal, intimate, and truly awe-inspiring act—the liturgical life of the Church is stifled. A true *lectio divina* of liturgical texts involves *lectio, meditatio, oratio*, and *contemplatio*. It means that the priest, and hopefully his people and ministers, spends time in prayer with the texts of the Sacred Liturgy.

I will limit myself to two examples, *In the name of the Father, and of the Son, and of the Holy Spirit*. What we are about to do in Mass is in the names of the three divine persons, it is an act that has its roots in the very life of God and by which we participate in divine life. The Sign of the Cross is not just a formula to be got through before we do the rest of the Mass. A second example would be an expression that appears at the conclusion of all of the Easter prefaces: *profusis paschalibus gaudiis— overcome with paschal joy*. Participating in the paschal mystery is the very vehicle by which the joy of Christ's passion, death, resurrection, and ascension—which takes our breath away—colors all of our life and by which we enter into the great Christian perspective of *apatheia*.

(4) *Live the Faith and the Tradition of the Church: It is in the Sacred Liturgy, above all, that the tradition is passed down.*

The liturgical formation of priests for the 21st century has to take seriously the fact that it is the liturgy itself that not only passes down the faith but also forms in the faithful the true Christian spirit. As *Sacrosanctum Concilium* 14 states: "In the restoration and promotion of the Sacred Liturgy, this full and active participation by all the people is the aim to be considered before all else; for it is the primary and indispensable source from which the faithful are to derive the true Christian spirit."

Regarding the liturgy passing down the Christian faith, the great Dominican theologian who served on the Doctrinal Commission at Vatican II, Yves Congar, in his masterful work, *Tradition and Traditions*, considers the Church's liturgy as a *locus theologicus* and treats it first among the principal monuments or witnesses to the tradition, even before the Fathers of the Church, and certainly before the ordinary expressions of the Christian life. There Congar notes:

> We are not here concerned with the liturgy as a dialectic arsenal…but as the expression of a Church actively living, praising God and bringing about a holy communion with him: the covenant as fulfilled in Christ Jesus, its Lord, Head and Spouse…the voice of the loving, praying Church, doing more than merely expressing its faith: hymning it, practising it, in a living celebration, wherein too, it makes a complete self-giving.[7]

The importance of the Sacred Liturgy is once again emphasized when Congar, in considering *legem credendi statuit lex orandi*, writes: "Thus the liturgy is the privileged *locus* of Tradition, not only from the point of view of conservation and preservation, but also from that of progress and development."[8] Again, Congar approvingly cites Dom Prosper Guéranger's *Institutions liturgiques* in the text below where he writes:

> Because of all this, *"the liturgy is the principal instrument of the Church's Tradition."* "It is in the liturgy that the Spirit who inspired the Scriptures still speaks to us; the liturgy is tradition itself at its highest degree of power and solemnity." The liturgy acts according to the general manner of Tradition, and since it is endowed with the genius of Tradition, it fills Tradition's role in a superlative way.[9]

---

7. Yves M.-J. Congar, *Tradition and Traditions* (London: Burns & Oates, 1966), pp. 427–28.

8. Ibid., p. 429.

9. Ibid., pp. 434–35.

Proposition 35 of the members of the 13th Ordinary General Assembly of the Synod of Bishops meeting from 7–28 October 2012 on the New Evangelization for the Transmission of the Christian Faith, states:

> *The worthy celebration of the Sacred Liturgy, God's most treasured gift to us, is the source of the highest expression of our life in Christ* (cf. *Sacrosanctum Concilium* 10). *It is, therefore, the primary and most powerful expression of the new evangelization.* God desires to manifest the incomparable beauty of his immeasurable and unceasing love for us through the Sacred Liturgy, and we, for our part, desire to employ what is most beautiful in our worship of God in response to his gift. In the marvelous exchange of the Sacred Liturgy, by which heaven descends to earth, salvation is at hand, calling forth repentance and conversion of heart (cf. Mt 4:17; Mk 1:15). Evangelization in the Church calls for a liturgy that lifts the hearts of men and women to God. The liturgy is not just a human action but an encounter with God which leads to contemplation and deepening friendship with God. In this sense, *the liturgy of the Church is the best school of the faith.* (emphases added)

(5) *The Liturgy is a given; it belongs to the Church, and the faithful have a right to the celebration of the liturgy according to the rites of the Church: the Sacred Liturgy does not belong to the priest, and he has a sacred obligation to celebrate the liturgy that the Church provides. Today's priests and tomorrow's priests are stewards of the sacred mysteries and that means that they are given the care of something that they did not create and which does not belong to them.*

Sacrosanctum Concilium 22 states that the regulation of the Sacred Liturgy depends solely on the authority of the Church, that is, on the Apostolic See and, as laws may determine, on the bishop. It allows for the regulation of the liturgy within certain defined limits by competent territorial bodies of bishops, but then states that no other person, even if he be a priest, may add, remove, or change anything in the liturgy on his own authority.

Also given the fact that law is often made to protect the weak since the stronger can enforce their will by strength, it is helpful to note that canon 846, §1 of the *Code of Canon Law* states that the liturgical books approved by the competent authority are to be faithfully observed in the celebration of the sacraments; therefore no one on personal authority may add, remove or change anything in them. In addition, the *responsum ad dubium* published in *Notitiae*, the journal of the Congregation for Sacraments and Divine Worship, in 1978 is instructive:

> It must never be forgotten that the Missal of Pope Paul VI, from the year
> 1970, has taken the place of that which is improperly called "the Missal of
> St Pius V" and that it has done this totally, whether with regard to texts or
> rubrics. Where the rubrics of the Missal of Paul VI say nothing or say little
> in specifics in some places, it is not therefore to be inferred that the old rite
> must be followed.[10]

Finally, St John Paul II, Pope Benedict XVI, and Pope Francis did/
do not make a habit of inserting the rubrics of the 1962 missal into their
celebration of the ordinary form. They strike me as good models to follow.

Interestingly, Joseph Ratzinger, when he was Archbishop of Munich,
in his *Silvesterpredigt* on 31 December 1979 observed that the Tradition
is not given over to the one who is baptized; rather the one baptized is
given over to the Tradition. The Tradition does not belong to him as his
possession that he can shape at will. Rather, he comes to belong to the
Tradition. It (Tradition) is the greater pattern by which he is formed and
not vice versa.[11] I would say that the same is true of the Sacred Liturgy.
When we are baptized, the liturgy is not given over to us, we are given
over to the liturgy.

The faithful have a right to the rites of the Church. These rites belong
to the Church, not to the priest, and most of us are probably familiar with
the saying: "Say the black, do the red." That is true; it is a place to begin.
But it is not sufficient. It will not take us where we want to go. To say
the black and to do the red is insufficient. First of all, the priest should
not *say the black* but *pray the black*. His interior disposition and his mind
should conform to the black. Nor is good liturgy robotic. It is neither the
ars celebrandi of the tin soldier nor that of the grizzly bear—but more on
that below.

The priest also needs to have good taste (or listen to others who do) and
understand and apply the principle of progressive solemnity. It does not
hurt if he also has a good voice, or at least one that is good enough. More
priests can sing than actually do. Good singing takes time and practice, but
that is part of progressive solemnity, and it is time well spent. Nonetheless,
good speaking is better than bad singing.

10. *Notitiae* 14 (1978), pp. 301–2.
11. Joseph Ratzinger, Silvesterpredigt, "Was ihr von Anfang an gehört habt soll in
euch blieben" (Munich: Herausgegeben vom Pressereferat der Erzdiözese München
und Freising, 1979), p. 12: "Nicht die Tradition wird dem Täufling übergeben, sondern
der Täufling der Tradition. Sie wird nicht sein Eigentum das er beliebig gestalten kann,
sondern er wird ihr Eigentum; sie is die grössere Form, die ihn gestaltet und nicht
umgekehrt."

Archbishop Alexander Sample, when he was Bishop of Marquette, also made a very helpful distinction between planning the Mass and preparing to celebrate the Mass. In his pastoral letter on sacred music in divine worship, "Rejoice in the Lord Always," Archbishop Sample wrote:

> It is important to keep in mind that we do not *plan* the Mass; the Church has already provided us with a plan. We *prepare* to celebrate the Mass. This is a subtle yet important distinction. The plan is found in the liturgical calendar and the official liturgical books: the ordo, the missal, the lectionary and the graduale. Our celebrations should carry out the Church's plan as far as we are able, according to the resources and talents of the community, formed by the knowledge of the norms and the Catholic worship tradition.[12]

(6) *The liturgy enables the Christian to enter into the true Christian spirit: the true Christian spirit is imbibed by entering fully into the Sacred Liturgy rather than by any other means.*

In *Sacrosanctum Concilium* 14 we read:

> In the restoration and promotion of the Sacred Liturgy, this full and active participation by all the people is the aim to be considered before all else; *for it is the primary and indispensable source from which the faithful are to derive the true Christian spirit*; and therefore pastors of souls must zealously strive to achieve it, by means of the necessary instruction, in all their pastoral work. (emphasis added)

Already in the preamble to *Tra le sollecitudini* (22 November 1903), St Pius X had written:

> Therefore, as it is our most ardent desire that the *true Christian spirit* blossom again in every way and be preserved in all of the faithful, it is necessary to provide above all for the holiness and the dignity of the church, where the faithful themselves gather to draw exactly this spirit from its first and indispensable fountain, which is the active participation at the most holy mysteries and from the public and solemn prayer of the Church. (emphasis added)[13]

---

12. Alexander Sample, Pastoral Letter "Rejoice in the Lord Always" (21 January 2013), p. 11, http://www.dioceseofmarquette.org/UserFiles/Bishop/PastoralLetter-RejoiceInTheLordAlways.pdf.

13. "Essendo, infatti, Nostro vivissimo desiderio che il vero spirito cristiano rifiorisca per ogni modo e si mantenga nei fedeli tutti, è necessario provvedere prima di ogni altra cosa alla santità e dignità del tempio, dove appunto i fedeli si radunano per attingere

Consequently, I would say that the formation of seminarians demands that they imbibe deeply of the true Christian spirit, which I understand as participation in the life of Christ and his mysteries, what it means to live *in Christo*. This includes the participation of the baptized in the incarnation, passion, death, resurrection, and ascension of the Lord. As the passages above indicate, the true Christian spirit is derived above all from the Sacred Liturgy.

That would indicate that there is a primacy to the liturgy that no other activity of the Christian possesses, including the praiseworthy practice of Christian devotions. The December 2001 *Directory on Popular Piety and the Liturgy* of the Congregation for Divine Worship is helpful in this regard. In article 11 of that document one reads:

> History shows that, in certain epochs, the life of faith is sustained by the forms and practices of piety, which the faithful have often felt more deeply and actively than the liturgical celebrations. Indeed, "every liturgical celebration, because it is an action of Christ the Priest and of his Body, which is the Church, it is a sacred action surpassing all others. No other action of the Church can equal its efficacy by the same title or to the same degree" (*Sacrosanctum Concilium* 7). Hence, the ambivalence that the Liturgy is not "popular" must be overcome.

And it continues:

> The faithful should be made conscious of the preeminence of the Liturgy over any other possible form of legitimate Christian prayer. While sacramental actions are necessary to life in Christ, the various forms of popular piety are properly optional. Such is clearly proven by the Church's precept which obliges attendance at Sunday Mass. No such obligation, however, has obtained with regard to pious exercises, notwithstanding their worthiness or their widespread diffusion.

The same document, in the same paragraph, adds: "The foregoing requires that the formation of priests and of the faithful give preeminence to liturgical prayer and to the liturgical year over any other form of devotion."

Seminarians are, therefore, called upon to derive the true Christian spirit from the Sacred Liturgy above all. Liturgy and liturgical prayer need to be recognized as taking primacy over all devotions. That is not to imply that devotions are not important, it simply means that devotions

tale spirito dalla sua prima ed indispensabile fonte, che è la partecipazione attiva ai sacrosanti misteri e alla preghiera pubblica e solenne della Chiesa." http://w2.vatican.va/content/pius-x/it/motu_proprio/documents/hf_p-x_motu-proprio_19031122_sollecitudini.html.

must flow from and lead back to the liturgy.[14] Adoration of the Blessed Sacrament, *lectio divina*, private mental prayer, the rosary, devotions to the Sacred Heart, Divine Mercy, or the Immaculate Heart of Mary are not to be discounted in seminary formation. They simply may not replace the liturgy as the *culmen et fons* of the Christian life. Otherwise, when devotions replace the liturgy as the source of the true Christian spirit and the *culmen et fons*, one falls into devotionalism, a surrogate for liturgy, where what is mainly subjective and emotive replaces the objective and *logikos* as the font of the true Christian spirit.[15]

Seminary formation must recognize the primacy of the liturgy in the seminarian's spiritual life. At the same time, however, the liturgy does not embrace the whole of the Christian's spiritual life, nor was it intended to. Nonetheless, it is important to recognize that the liturgy never interrupts one's prayer, and if one thinks that it does, one has a false sense of what Christian prayer is.

14. Examples of how liturgical spirituality affects the whole of Christian life can be found in the retreat conferences given by Odo Casel. See: Odo Casel and Burkhard Neunheuser (eds), *Vom Wahren Menschenbild* (Regensburg: Pustet, 1953). Another pastoral resource would be Pius Parsch's *Das Jahr des Heiles*, which underwent eleven printings by 1934 and was translated into various languages in the course of over twenty years. See: Pius Parsch, *Das Jahr des Heiles*, 11th edn, 3 vols. (Klosterneuburg: Volksliturgisches Apostolat Klosterneuburg, 1934); ET: *The Church's Year of Grace*, 5 vols. (Collegeville: The Liturgical Press, 1954–59); Spanish translation: *El Año Litúrgico* (Barcelona: Herder, 1957). Parsch's *Das Jahr des Heiles* was republished by Echter Verlag, Würzburg, in 2008 with a new introduction by Harald Buchinger. Nonetheless, it remains based on the pre-Vatican II calendar.

15. On objective and subjective piety see Gabriel Braso, *Liturgy and Spirituality* (Collegeville: The Liturgical Press, 1971), pp. 209–37. On pp. 235–36 one reads: "In order to be *public* worship, liturgical worship requires an active, communitarian celebration. But in so far as it is *worship*, it requires interiority and personal assimilation of that which is celebrated outwardly… If the liturgy 'is the summit towards which the activity of the Church is directed and at the same time the font from which all her power flows' (*Sacrosanctum Concilium* 10) there is no doubt that a spiritual life which tries to tend toward this summit, following the Church and which loves to drink from this fountain, will arrive at the idea of Christian perfection and even of infused contemplation more surely in this way than in any other." See also: Burkhard Neunheuser, "Objektive Frömmigkeit: Ein Beitrag zur Geschichte und Systematik dieses Begriffes," in Giustino Farnedi (eds), *Paschale Mysterium: Sudi in Memoria dell'Abate Prof. Salvatore Marsili (1910–1983)* (Rome: Studia Anselmiana, 1986), pp. 97–114. Fr Neunheuser, for example, after recommending the rosary in his article, writes on p. 11: "Marienverehrung aber ist vor allem zu pflegen im Rahmen des Kirchenjahres, in der Feier ihrer Hochfeste, ihrer Feste und Gedächtnistage, in der Votivmesse der freien Samstage, in den Marienantiphonen nach der Komplet."

Finally, it is helpful to think and speak theologically rather than devotionally of liturgical feasts, e.g., the Second Sunday of Easter is the Sunday within the octave celebration of the resurrection of the Lord. To call it Divine Mercy Sunday puts it in the context of a certain devotion rather than in the theological context of the paschal mystery. The *editio typica* of the *Missale Romanum* lists it as *Dominica II Paschæ seu de divina Misercordia*, and the English translation refers to it as the Second Sunday of Easter (or of Divine Mercy). The subsequent days of that week are listed as *In Feriis Post Dominicam II Paschæ* or *Weekdays after the Second Sunday of Easter*. They are not presented as days after Divine Mercy Sunday.

(7) *Seminarians need to be schooled in the* ars celebrandi. *Without a clear and defined* ars celebrandi, *which involves not only the priest, but all of the ministers, the liturgical celebration will be radically deficient.*

Pope Benedict XVI wrote in *Sacramentum Caritatis* (22 February 2007):

> While it is true that the whole People of God participates in the eucharistic liturgy, a correct *ars celebrandi* necessarily entails a specific responsibility on the part of those who have received the sacrament of Holy Orders. Bishops, priests, and deacons, each according to his proper rank, must consider the celebration of the liturgy as their principal duty. (n. 39)[16]

Already in article 38, Pope Benedict had defined *ars celebrandi* as the art of proper celebration, but in article 40, he becomes more explicit. There one reads:

> The *ars celebrandi* should foster a sense of the sacred and the use of outward signs which help to cultivate this sense, such as, for example, the harmony of the rite, the liturgical vestments, the furnishings and the sacred space. The eucharistic celebration is enhanced when priests and liturgical leaders are committed to making known the current liturgical texts and norms... Equally important for a correct *ars celebrandi* is an attentiveness to the various kinds of language that the liturgy employs: words, and music, gestures and silence, movement, the liturgical colours of the vestments. By its very nature the liturgy operates on different levels of communication which enable it to engage the whole human person.[17]

16. This states the same as what Pope Benedict mentioned later on that same year in his address at Stift Heiligenkreuz on 9 September 2007, cited above.

17. It is also not insignificant that the Pope mentions here that the eucharistic celebration is enhanced when priests and liturgical leaders are committed to making known the current liturgical texts and norms. On *ars celebrandi* see also: Alcuin Reid, "From Rubrics to *Ars Celebrandi*—Liturgical Law in the 21st Century," *Antiphon* 17 (2013), pp. 139–67.

Two things regarding *ars celebrandi* that need to be stressed to seminarians are first of all that it is not enough for the priest to have a good *ars celebrandi*. The *ars celebrandi* must include as well the deacons, acolytes/ servers, lectors, musicians, and congregation. It is insufficient for the priest to have a good *ars celebrandi* if what he does is basically undone by people not showing up for their assignments, performing them poorly, or not knowing what is expected of them. Secondly, a good *ars celebrandi* means that everyone ministering in the liturgy not only knows what they are doing, but also look like they know what they are doing. The Sacred Liturgy will not look splendid if we allow it to look haphazard.

(8) *The vernacular language may make the liturgy accessible, but that presumption needs to be understood more deeply than it usually is. In some ways, the accessibility of the liturgy is much less than one thinks.*

The use of the vernacular in the Sacred Liturgy has been seen as a tremendous blessing, and I believe that it is. Nonetheless, this does not mean that it is without its challenges. The most significant challenge is that because the liturgy is in the vernacular, e.g., English, we think that we understand it. That presumption needs to be both challenged and addressed. The challenge would be that I think that it is simply untrue. I will give some examples:

    i.   In the penitential act, the priest addresses the assembly asking all to acknowledge their sins, and so prepare themselves to celebrate the sacred *mysteries*. What, I ask, do the Christian faithful understand by the liturgical *mysteries*? I tend to think that a *mystery* might make them think of a novel, a television show, a movie or anything else that is unknown or needs to be solved. I doubt that they know much of the paschal mystery or mystery theology, but if they do not, I would suggest that they be educated so that they can understand the basics of the mystery of Christ and the Trinity into which they have been baptized.

    ii. The creed confesses that the Son is *consubstantial* with the Father. I remember one conversation that I had when the new English translation came out with an educated person, although not philosophically educated, who objected to the word *consubstantial*. She said that she did not know what that meant. In a round about way, I ended up mentioning to her, referring to the previous translation, that in light of Greek philosophy neither did she know what *one in Being* meant either.

iii. Or when the lector/reader concludes the first reading at Mass saying that it is *the word of the Lord*, what does that mean? Do people really think, as Vatican II teaches, that when the Sacred Scripture is read in the Church that Christ really speaks to them? (*Sacrosanctum Concilium* 7) Do they think that God just spoke to them—which he did—or do they think that Mary or John or whoever just read a passage from some book of the Bible?

iv. Or when the Church prays in her liturgy for *eternal rest* for those who have passed from this life, what is the understanding that those at Mass have of *eternal rest*? Does *requies æterna/eternal rest* conjure up in their minds the *requies/after-rest* that is related to recreation and relaxation, or the *somnus/sleep* which is more related to slumber, drowsiness, inactivity, or idleness? My own image of *requies æterna* is the eternal weekend, the beginning of a Friday afternoon, when a lot of the pressure comes off—and then in eternity, Monday never comes!

These are just a couple of examples of how the vernacular can hide the fact that we do not really understand all of the words or expressions of Christian prayer, and of how those who are charged with responsibility for the Sacred Liturgy cannot ignore that. Liturgical mystagogy or doctrinal preaching needs to take that into account.

Finally, although I love Latin but am by no means fanatical about it, I believe that a disregard for Latin, and Gregorian chant, is an impoverishment of the Catholic liturgical tradition.[18] I would no more want to abandon Latin in the Ordinary of the Mass than I would want to give up the words: *amen, abba, hosanna,* and *alleluia* because they are not originally English words. They have become too closely intertwined with the Catholic liturgical tradition for them to be abandoned.

(9) *It is important for seminarians to learn to foster the Ordinary Form with reverence and dignity rather than the Extraordinary Form of the Roman rite; to learn the art of proper celebration, the* ars celebrandi *of the Ordinary Form, corresponds to the expectations of both the Second Vatican Council and Pope Benedict XVI.*

Joseph Cardinal Ratzinger, in the year 1999, wrote in his preface to *The Spirit of the Liturgy*:

18. See: Pope Benedict XVI, *Sacramentum Caritatis* 42; *Sacrosanctum Concilium* 116.

We might say that in 1918, the year that Guardini published his book (*The Spirit of the Liturgy*), the liturgy was rather like a fresco. It had been preserved from damage, but it had been almost completely overlaid with whitewash by later generations. In the missal from which the priest celebrated, the form of the liturgy that had grown from its earliest beginnings was still present, but, as far as the faithful were concerned, it was largely concealed beneath instructions for and forms of private prayer. The fresco was laid bare by the liturgical movement and, in a definitive way, by the Second Vatican Council. For a moment its colors and figures fascinated us. But since then the fresco has been endangered by climatic conditions as well as by various restorations and reconstructions. In fact, it is threatened with destruction, if the necessary steps are not taken to stop these damaging influences. Of course, there must be no question of its being covered with whitewash again, but what is imperative is a new reverence in the way we treat it, a new understanding of its message and its reality, so that rediscovery does not become the first stage of irreparable loss.[19]

What I am to say now should not be understood as feeding into the dichotomy of "before Council bad, after Council good." Nor would I be one to foster the idea that there is no place in the Sacred Liturgy for reverence or devotion. Nor do I think that a lack of care for the Sacred Liturgy is a good thing. Nor would I maintain that everything that came after the Council was proper and helpful. People who are devoted to the extraordinary form are often devoted to that form because they find reverence, devotion, and a respect for the sacred in the priests and communities who celebrate according to that form. Nonetheless, the extraordinary form can be celebrated sloppily as can the ordinary form.

The fact is clear that the Second Vatican Council in *Sacrosanctum Concilium* 21 asked for a general restoration of the liturgy.[20] In addition, article 25 asked that the liturgical books be revised (*recognoscantur*).[21] Again, article 50 decreed that the order of the Mass was to be revised.[22] That brings us to a theological issue. Since an Ecumenical Council confirmed by the Pope is the highest teaching authority of the Catholic

19. Joseph Ratzinger, *The Spirit of the Liturgy* (San Francisco: Ignatius, 2000), pp. 7–8.

20. "Pia Mater Ecclesia, ut populus christianus in sacra Liturgia abundantiam gratiarum securius assequatur, ipsius Liturgiae generalem instaurationem sedulo curare cupit."

21. "Libri liturgici quam primum recognoscantur, peritis adhibitis et Episcopis consultis ex diversis orbis regionibus."

22. "Ordo Missae ita recognoscatur, ut singularum partium propria ratio necnon mutua connexio clarius pateant, atque pia et actuosa fidelium participatio facilior reddatur."

Church, it follows that for one to be a Catholic one must accept the decision of the Council Fathers and the Holy Father himself in teaching that the liturgy was to be restored and the liturgical books were to be revised. This is not to argue that everything that happened in the liturgical books after Vatican II was the decision of the Council. Nonetheless, it is clear that the Roman Missal of 1962 was the missal that the Council said needed to be revised.

Consequently, I am convinced that the instruction of seminarians must be according to the mind of the Council and consistent with the reform that it called for. When Pope Benedict XVI issued *Summorum Pontificum* on 7 July 2007, in article 1 of that document he stated that the use of the *Roman Missal* promulgated by Pope Paul VI constituted the ordinary form of the Roman rite and that use of the Roman Missal of 1962 to offer Mass constituted the extraordinary form.[23] Again in the same article of *Summorum Pontificum* he stated that it was permissible to celebrate Mass according to the Roman Missal of 1962 (*celebrare licet*).[24] It is helpful to make the distinction here between what the Church permits and what the Church recommends. While *Summorum Pontificum* permits celebration according to the Roman Missal of 1962, the phrase *celebrare licet* is totally neutral. The document neither recommends it nor discourages it. It simply permits it.

The letter which Pope Benedict XVI addressed to the bishops of the world on the same day that he issued *Summorum Pontificum* states the same, i.e., that the *Roman Missal* promulgated by Pope Paul VI is the ordinary form, and the Roman Missal of 1962 is the extraordinary form of the Roman rite.[25]

23. "Missale Romanum a Paulo VI promulgatum ordinaria expressio 'Legis orandi' Ecclesiae catholicae ritus latini est. Missale autem Romanum a S. Pio V promulgatum et a B. Ioanne XXIII denuo editum habeatur uti extraordinaria expressio eiusdem 'Legis orandi' Ecclesiae et ob venerabilem et antiquum eius usum debito gaudeat honore."

24. "Proinde Missae Sacrificium, iuxta editionem typicam Missalis Romani a B. Ioanne XXIII anno 1962 promulgatam et numquam abrogatam, uti formam extra-ordinariam Liturgiae Ecclesiae, celebrare licet."

25. Pope Benedict XVI, *Letter of His Holiness Benedict XVI to the Bishops on the Occasion of the Publication of the Apostolic Letter "Motu Proprio Data" Summorum Pontificum on the Use of the Roman Liturgy Prior to the Reform of 1970*, 7 July 2007: "In this regard, it must first be said that the missal published by Paul VI and then republished in two subsequent editions by John Paul II, obviously is and continues to be the normal Form—the *Forma ordinaria*—of the Eucharistic Liturgy. The last version of the *Missale Romanum* prior to the Council, which was published with the authority of Pope John XXIII in 1962 and used during the Council, will

Finally, I do not find it either accurate or helpful to speak of the ordinary form of the liturgy as the *forma recentior* or of the extraordinary form as the *forma antiquior*. I realize that Pope Benedict in his letter of 7 July 2007 refers once to the extraordinary form as the *forma antiquior*, but I see that as simply meaning that it is the older of the two forms in chronological sequence. I do not find any official document where he refers to the ordinary form as the *forma recentior*. Besides, if one considers the placement of the readings and communion antiphons of cycle A of the lectionary during Lent for the ordinary form, it turns out that the so-called *forma recentior* is *antiquior* than the so-called *forma antiquior*.[26] In short, while it does not exclude seminarians from being trained in the extraordinary form, the ordinary form of the Roman rite is the rite that they will find celebrated in most parishes by most Catholics, and it is incumbent on seminarians to learn to celebrate the ordinary form in a manner that is valid, licit, and beautiful.

(10) *Liturgy must be beautiful.*

Pope Benedict XVI wrote in *Sacramentum Caritatis* n. 41 that everything related to the Eucharist should be marked by beauty. He notes here as well that special care must be taken of vestments, furnishings, and sacred vessels and also comments that by their harmonious arrangement they will foster awe for the mystery of God, manifest the unity of faith, and strengthen devotion. Proposition 35 from the 2012 Synod on the New Evangelization (cited above) also spoke of beauty in the liturgy

---

now be able to be used as a *Forma extraordinaria* of the liturgical celebration." See also the interview that Pope Benedict gave as he was on his way to France on 12 September 2008: *Fr Federico Lombardi, SJ, Director of the Holy See Press Office: What do you say to those who, in France, fear that the "Motu proprio" Summorum Pontificum signals a step backwards from the great insights of the Second Vatican Council? How can you reassure them?* Benedict XVI: Their fear is unfounded, for this "Motu Proprio" is merely an act of tolerance, with a pastoral aim, for those people who were brought up with this liturgy, who love it, are familiar with it and want to live with this liturgy... In this sense, it seems to me that there is a mutual enrichment, and it is clear that the renewed liturgy is the ordinary liturgy of our time." (http://w2.vatican.va/content/benedict-xvi/en/speeches/2008/september/documents/hf_ben-xvi_spe_20080912_francia-interview.html).

26. For a comparison of the two forms of the Roman rite, see: Patrick Regan, *Advent to Pentecost: Comparing the Seasons in the Ordinary and Extraordinary Forms of the Roman Rite* (Collegeville: The Liturgical Press, 2012).

in terms of the New Evangelization. There, we read that the worthy celebration of the Sacred Liturgy is the source of the highest expression of our life in Christ and, therefore, the most powerful expression of the New Evangelization. The same proposition continues by stating that God desires to manifest the incomparable beauty of his immeasurable and unceasing love for us through the Sacred Liturgy and that we, for our part, desire to employ what is most beautiful in our worship of God in response to his gift. Then again in Proposition 20 of the same synod, one reads that in the New Evangelization particular attention should be paid to the way of beauty. Christ is seen as the beautiful revelation in sign, pouring himself out without measure. The same proposition continues by stating that in the formation of seminarians, education in beauty should not be neglected, that beauty attracts us to love, and that it is necessary that the church be vigilant in caring for and promoting the quality of art in sacred spaces reserved for liturgical celebrations.[27]

Seminarians, therefore, if they are to be fruitful stewards of the sacred mysteries, are called to provide the People of God with a beautiful liturgy, a liturgy that attracts, draws them in, and leaves them longing for more—in part at least—simply because they enjoy being there. To be surrounded by beauty means that time passes all too quickly, and a silent period of thanksgiving afterwards becomes the prolonging of an awe-inspiring celebration. I think that it is worthwhile asking if in the celebration of the Sacred Liturgy priests allow the paschal mystery to shine forth in all its splendor. In *Evangelii Gaudium* (24 November 2013) article 145 Pope Francis states quite forcefully that a preacher who does not prepare himself for preaching is "dishonest and irresponsible"; then in article 151

---

27. "In the New Evangelization, there should be a particular attention paid to the way of beauty: Christ, the 'Good Shepherd' (cf. John 10:11) is the Truth in person, the beautiful revelation in sign, pouring himself out without measure. It is important to give testimony to the young who follow Jesus, not only of his goodness and truth, but also of the fullness of his beauty. As Augustine affirmed, 'it is not possible to love what is not beautiful' (*Confessions*, Bk IV, 13.20). Beauty attracts us to love, through which God reveals to us his face in which we believe. In this light artists feel themselves both spoken to and privileged communicators of the New Evangelization.

In the formation of seminarians, education in beauty should not be neglected nor education in the sacred arts as we are reminded in the teaching of the Second Vatican Council (see: *Sacrosanctum Concilium* 129). Beauty should always be a special dimension of the new evangelization.

It is necessary that the Church be vigilant in caring for and promoting the quality of the art that is permitted in the sacred spaces reserved for liturgical celebrations, guarding both its beauty and the truthfulness of its expression."

he calls him a "false prophet, a fraud, a shallow imposter." I wonder if the same could be said for the priest who fails to provide the faithful with a well-prepared and beautiful liturgy that draws them ever more deeply into the sacred mysteries.

Seminarians need to know that as young priests, if the liturgy is not beautiful, they can make it so, but only slowly, perhaps very slowly, leaving the people wanting more, not taking them to a place that they are not prepared for and to which they do not want to return again. Nonetheless, it is indeed gratifying when the liturgy is beautiful and people describe it as splendid because it enabled them for a moment to touch the Beauty—ever ancient, ever new—which is God.[28]

(11) *The Sacred Liturgy has a formative quality in itself and one learns by doing it. The liturgy is a harsh mistress. She reveals her secrets only to those who are going to trust her and to spend time with her.*

The 3 June 1979 *Instruction on Liturgical Formation in Seminaries* from the Congregation for Catholic Education states in article 33:

> Full and perfect formation of the students requires that, throughout their years of preparation in the seminary, they experience the richer and more developed forms of the liturgical celebrations of the seasons and solemnities of the liturgical year. Since after their ordination to the sacerdotal ministry they will be directing the liturgy, and feast day solemnities will increase their apostolic activity, they will be obliged to repeat these celebrations in various places, oftentimes in more simple form, as provided for in the liturgical books. Thus it is clear that the way the students experience the liturgy in the seminary will be an example for them on which their future pastoral ministry will be based, as well as the foundation for their meditation on and knowledge of the liturgical year.

28. Here I am reminded of the report of the envoys of Vladimir in the *Chronicle of Nestor*: "Then we went to Greece, and the Greeks led us to the edifices where they worship their God, and we knew not whether we were in heaven or on earth. For on earth there is no such splendor or such beauty, and we are at a loss how to describe it. We only know that God dwells there among men, and their service is fairer than the ceremonies of other nations. For we cannot forget that beauty." Samuel Hazzard Cross and Olgerd P. Sherbowitz-Wetzor (trans. and ed.), *The Russian Primary Chronicle: Laurentian Text* (Cambridge: The Mediaeval Academy of America, n.d.), p. 108.

Again, article 32 of the same document mentions that the whole liturgical year should be not only a liturgical celebration, but a way of life, in the manner of a spiritual journey, in which the mystery of Christ is communicated. Seminarians consequently are expected to live the liturgy, as is made clear in article 32. The liturgical year is not simply made up of celebrations, but is itself a way of life, a spiritual journey in which one participates in the very mystery of life in Christ. Seminarians are, at the same time, in the course of their seminary formation to experience the richer and more developed forms of the liturgical celebrations of the seasons and solemnities of the liturgical year. Once they are ordained priests, seminarians will necessarily be challenged to adapt these celebrations to the capacities of the various parishes to which they are assigned, and it would be generally unreasonable to expect that the resources that are available in a seminary will be available in any parish. Finally, it is important to note that, as the Congregation states, celebrations in the seminary are to be celebrated in their "richer and more developed forms" since seminarians can adjust to more simple forms as necessary, but they cannot adjust to "richer" forms if they have never experienced them.

The trust in formation that the seminarian brings to the liturgy is significant. Seminarians need to be formed in the liturgy as much as they are in other dimensions of the spiritual life, academics, apostolic endeavours, pastoral life, and human formation. The liturgy, either its celebrations or the spiritual journey spoken of by the Congregation, will not be able to work its effects if there is not a hermeneutic of trust. A hermeneutic of suspicion, an attitude of judgment, a stance of critique and suspicion which either approves or condemns will not serve the seminarian in his liturgical formation. Such a mindset indicates that one is not handing himself over to the liturgy. He is standing on the margins and looking at it as a judge who either approves or condemns.

Finally, sometimes seminarians might want to ask why the seminary liturgy does not reflect the liturgy that they found in their parishes or the liturgy that they grew up with. Since they come from so many different parishes, to answer this would be an impossible task. It is important that the seminary liturgy reflect the current liturgical texts and norms. If seminarians want to know why their parish liturgy does not reflect that, it is best that they ask their pastors. As one young priest expressed it, the seminary liturgy is in many ways like the encyclopedia: if you want to know how it should be done, you only need to remember how it was done in the seminary.

(12) *The homily is an integral part of the Mass and not extrinsic to the liturgy.*

The readings of the liturgy are not simply to be given some kind of general moral application. The homilist needs to see the constellation of the readings, prayers, and prefaces of the Sacred Liturgy as crucial to his interpretation of the Word of God and his subsequent preaching. The Word of God is part and parcel of the celebration of the paschal mystery of Christ—the homily is not simply an exposition on the moral teaching of the Church.

Pope Benedict XVI in his Post-Synodal Apostolic Exhortation *Verbum Domini* (30 September 2010) 52 wrote that when one considers the Church as the home of the Word, attention must be given first of all to the Sacred Liturgy since the liturgy is the privileged setting in which God speaks to us in the midst of our lives. Consequently, since the liturgy is the privileged setting of the Word, I believe that seminarians must first be led to an understanding and appreciation of the use of Sacred Scripture in the liturgy. Only after that can they be led to understand the Word in *lectio divina*, exegesis, and imaginative prayer. The Church assigns certain readings to certain seasons and certain feasts and solemnities. Pope Benedict wrote as much when in *Verbum Domini* 52 he remarked that he encourages the Church's pastors and all engaged in pastoral work to see that all the faithful learn to savor the deep meaning of the Word of God which unfolds each year in the liturgy, revealing the fundamental mysteries of our faith. Then he concluded by saying that this is the basis for a correct approach to Sacred Scripture.

My point here is that homiletics is impoverished if the homily is treated as something extrinsic to the liturgy—or prepared as something extrinsic to the Church's celebration of the paschal mystery. Pope Benedict had already called for a homiletic directory in *Verbum Domini* 60 and the Congregation for Divine Worship and the Discipline of the Sacraments issued its *Homiletic Directory* in 2015. The document is remarkable for its integration of Sacred Liturgy and Sacred Scripture. I suggest only a couple of texts. In article 1 in the introduction, it notes that just as the Catholic liturgical movement that began in the late nineteenth century sought to re-integrate personal piety and liturgical spirituality among the faithful, so there were efforts to deepen the integral bond between the scriptures and worship. In article 4 the *Homiletic Directory* speaks not only of how listening to God's Word culminates in the sacrificial offering of Christ to the eternal Father, but it also goes on to consider how the homily is an act of worship and how many of the homilies of the

Fathers concluded their discourse with a doxology, recognizing that the purpose of the homily was not only to sanctify the people, but to glorify God. Moreover, the homily is a hymn of gratitude for the *magnalia Dei*. Finally, in article 11, the *Directory* points out that the homily is based on the sacred text, which refers to both the biblical passages and the prayers used in a liturgical celebration.

Consequently, seminarians need to understand that all homilies are liturgical acts and not just some other kind of moral instruction or a conference of sorts. In addition, in the preparation of their homilies, seminarians obviously need to consult the Sacred Scriptures being proclaimed, but that is radically insufficient. They must, as well, be guided by consulting the prayers and the prefaces, especially during the strong seasons of Advent, Christmas, Lent, and Easter, as well as the solemnities and feasts of the Church year. To preach on the paschal mystery, they need to celebrate what the Church celebrates. Especially in the strong seasons and on the great feasts, the readings do not appear at random. They are chosen for a specific purpose. Seminarians are often taught that their homilies should flow into the Eucharist. If that is so, I would maintain that a successful homily would make the people thankful for the *magnalia Dei* that they are celebrating. It would also inflame their hearts to burn within them as the marvelous works of God are sung about in the preface.[29]

29. "The post-conciliar liturgical reform has enabled preaching on a richer collection of biblical readings during Mass. But what to say about them? In practice, the homilist often answers this question by consulting biblical commentaries to give some background on the readings, and then offers some kind of general moral application. What is sometimes lacking is sensitivity to the unique nature of the homily as an integral part of the Eucharistic celebration. When the homily is understood to be an organic part of the Mass, it becomes clear that the preacher is asked to see the constellation of the readings and prayer of the celebration as crucial to his interpretation of the Word of God." Congregation for Divine Worship and the Discipline of the Sacraments, *Homiletic Directory* 16. See also: Jorge Mario Bergoglio, "Come si tiene un'omelia: Poco e bene," *L'Osservatore Romano*, 20 February 2015, p. 6. On 1 March 2005, the Cardinal Archbishop of Buenos Aires spoke to the plenary assembly of the Congregation of Divine Worship and the Discipline of the Sacraments reflecting on this aspect of the *ars celebrandi*. This text was chosen by Pope Francis as the basis of reflection when he met with the clergy of Rome on the morning of 19 February 2015 in the Paul VI Audience Hall.

(13) *Liturgy costs time and money. It is not free: budgets, whether of time or money, disclose what we truly value; we must allow the liturgy to look like it is worth being taken seriously; it needs to have experiential credibility.*

Values emerge in various ways, and one way can be found in how people choose to spend their time and money. In an age when resources of personnel and finances seem to be stretched thin, there is usually the need to see where one can cut from the budget. It is a time of scarce resources, and I would ask people to reflect on what they really value and how their budgets both of time and money reflect the importance of their participation in the paschal mystery.

Sometimes it seems that people act as if the Sacred Liturgy is almost free, and if one just makes sure that there are sufficient hosts and wine, the Mass will be valid, and it will all be fine. I would maintain that it will cost in both time and money. Good art costs, and it is no different with the *ars celebrandi*. That means that somebody will need to train the deacons, the altar servers, the lectors, the cantors, and the organists, and will have to intervene when things go awry—pastorally and sensitively—but still intervene. Cowardice or low energy might be reasons for putting this off, but one needs to ask if this is helpful in the long run. Finally, parish liturgy committees must be taught to read the documents of the Church pertaining to the liturgy. They have the right and duty to think with the Church, and their decisions need to be informed by what the Church has written concerning the Sacred Liturgy.

Financial costs include not only constructing worthy churches, but also keeping them in good repair and clean. Books must be bought and replaced or rebound. Musicians need to be paid. Music has to be bought and rehearsed. Vestments need to be dry cleaned/washed and repaired. Sacred vessels and thuribles need to be cleaned and polished. Sacristy laundry has to be done, candles have to be replaced, and flowers need to be arranged. I would maintain that the Sacred Liturgy needs to be valid, licit, beautiful, and fruitful. That all costs. So often priests comment that they have only a short window of time to instruct their people in the homily. I would respond that the homily is not the only liturgical act that teaches. The whole liturgy does—without at all intending it to be didactic. Liturgy teaches because of the priest truly praying it, because care is obviously being expended on the sacred rites, and because the furnishings of the Sacred Liturgy are well maintained.

On 12 May 2015 the Pew Research Center published the study "America's Changing Religious Landscape: Christians Decline Sharply as Share of Population; Unaffiliated and Other Faiths Continue to Grow."[30] This study indicates that in 2007 23.9% of the American population identified themselves as Catholic. It also indicates that in 2014 only 20.8% of Americans identified themselves as Catholic—a 3.1% drop in seven years. One might ask if the manner of how important the liturgy is treated is not one element contributing to that. I know of one young priest who lamented the fact that he could not convince people that Sunday Mass was the most important thing that they did all week. One might be tempted to ask if it is treated as important—not by him, but in general.

Basically, we must allow the liturgy to look like it is worth being taken seriously. It needs to have experiential credibility. We cannot make liturgy look like something that is not or cannot be taken seriously or people will vote with their feet and find something else to do with their Sunday mornings. We would not accept sloppiness in the hard sciences, or a military exercise, or professional sports with the same attitude with which it is sometimes tolerated in the liturgy. For example, if an athlete in a football game kept just missing catching the ball, the coach will take him out of the game. Similarly, the ritual of the army Sentinels at the Tomb of the Unknown Soldier in Arlington National Cemetery in Virginia, marching back and forth, what is known as Walking the Mat, would certainly seem less important if at some point the formality there became sudden informality.

The *culmens et fons* of Catholic life dare not be treated flippantly. It is there that we are baptized into the life of the divine Trinity, where heaven is wedded to earth, and where we are nourished with no less than the very Body and Blood of the Lord. There, God breaks into our life. Seminarians must be trained not only to know what they are doing, but also to look like they know what they are doing. The Sacred Liturgy has been given to us by the Son of God himself, and has effects in both time and eternity. Catholics treat it as unimportant to their own detriment.

---

30. Pew Research Center, "America's Changing Religious Landscape: Christians Decline Sharply as Share of Population; Unaffiliated and Other Faiths Continue to Grow," 12 May 2015. http://www.pewforum.org/2015/05/12/americas-changing-religious-landscape/.

(14) *The music of the liturgy is given to us from the tradition of the Church. The paschal mystery of Christ will be much more evident in the Sacred Liturgy if the faithful are presented with texts and music that is inspired by and true to the expressions of the tradition.*

In *Verbum Domini* article 70, Pope Benedict XVI, in writing about the liturgy as "The Privileged Setting for the Word of God," states:

> As part of the enhancement of the Word of God in the liturgy, attention should also be paid to the use of singing at the times called for by the particular rite. Preference should be given to the singing which is of clear biblical inspiration and which expresses, through the harmony of music and words, the beauty of God's word. We would do well to make the most of that singing handed down to us by the Church's tradition which respects this criterion. I think in particular of the importance of Gregorian chant.

Years before, already in 1969, the Congregation for Divine Worship, when asked if the Instruction of 3 September 1958 which allowed for the singing of four vernacular hymns during a recited Mass still applied, responded as follows:

> That formula has been *superseded*. What must be sung is the Mass, the Ordinary and the Proper, and not 'something,' *no matter how consistent*, that is imposed on the Mass. Since the *liturgical action* is one, it has a single countenance, one motif, and one voice: the voice of the Church. To continue to sing motets, even if they be reverent and devout…but extraneous to the Mass, *in place of the Mass of the day that is being celebrated*, amounts to continuing an unacceptable ambiguity: it is like giving the people bran instead of the finest wheat, and a lesser type of wine diluted with water instead of a truly fine wine.
>
> Liturgical song involves not mere melody, but words, texts, thoughts, and sentiments clothed in poetry and melody. Thus, these texts must be those of the Mass, not others. Singing, therefore, means singing *the* Mass and not just singing *during* Mass.[31]

---

31. *Notitiae* 5 (1969), p. 406 (emphasis original). This text, generally as translated above, was quoted over twenty years later in the NCCB's *Committee on the Liturgy Newsletter*, August/September 1993, p. 2, in the article "Rereading the Constitution on the Liturgy (art. 112–121)." In that article, the text quoted above was preceded and introduced by the following: "In spite of these efforts to promote the sung liturgy, preference continues to be given to singing *during* the Mass instead of singing the Mass. In fact many of the faithful interpret singing the liturgy to mean singing hymns or songs. Thus those involved in liturgical preparation oftentimes confine themselves to the selection of hymns as their first priority and neglect the singing of ritual texts.

Finally, Pope Benedict XVI in *Sacramentum Caritatis* article 42 writes that in the *ars celebrandi*, liturgical song has a pre-eminent place. In the same paragraph, he also says that in the course of her two-thousand-year history, the Church has created, and still creates, music and songs which represent a rich patrimony of faith and love, and then he goes on to comment that this heritage must not be lost. But, contrary to the wishes of Pope Benedict, has our heritage been lost? How much of what Catholic parishes sing has been composed before 1965? Have Catholics been trained to sing at Mass or to sing the Mass?

5. *Conclusion*

In conclusion, I admit to being, as Cardinal Ratzinger wrote in *The Spirit of the Liturgy*, one *who has been and remains fascinated by the colors and figures of the fresco that is the liturgy*. I give thanks to God for this

---

Likewise many composers give preference to the composition of hymns and other sacred songs rather than to the ritual texts of the liturgy" (emphasis original). Regarding the pace of liturgical renewal, it is not insignificant that a text that was written by the Consilium over twenty years before still needed to be cited by the Committee on the Liturgy in 1993. In addition, the United States Conference of Catholic Bishops in *Sing to the Lord: Music in Divine Worship* (2007) states: n. 76 "The assembly of the faithful should participate in singing the Proper of the Mass as much as possible, especially through simple responses and other suitable settings" (*Musicam Sacram*, 33); n. 117 "Proper antiphons from the liturgical books are to be esteemed and used especially because they are the very voice of God speaking to us in the Scriptures. Here, 'the Father who is in heaven comes lovingly to meet his children, and talks with them. And such is the force and power of the Word of God that it can serve the Church as her support and vigor, and the children of the Church as strength for their faith, food for the soul, and a pure and lasting fount of spiritual life' (Vatican Council II, *Dei Verbum*: *Divine Constitution on Divine Revelation*, 1965, 21). The Christian faithful are to be led to an ever deeper appreciation of the psalms as the voice of Christ and the voice of his Church at prayer"; n. 144 "The text and music for the Entrance song may be drawn from a number of sources: a. the singing of an antiphon and psalm during the entrance procession has been a long-standing tradition in the Roman Liturgy. Antiphons and psalms may be drawn from the official liturgical books—the *Graduale Romanum*, or the *Graduale Simplex*—or from other collections of antiphons and psalms; b. Other hymns and songs may also be sung at the Entrance, providing that they are in keeping with the purpose of the Entrance chant or song. The texts of antiphons, psalms, hymns, and songs for the Liturgy must have been approved either by the United States Conference of Catholic Bishops or by the local diocesan bishop"; n. 192 "As a processional piece, the Communion chant or song presents particular challenges... In order to foster participation of the faithful with 'unity of voices,' it is recommended that psalms sung in the responsorial style, or songs with easily memorized refrains, be used."

unmerited grace and marvel that we have been given the opportunity in this age to do our best to transmit to coming generations the gift that we have inherited—so that the seminarians of today may become exemplary stewards of the sacred mysteries—and that for the People of God, at least on occasion, for a moment, the veil between heaven and earth may be lifted—and faith may be nourished—and, if necessary, be renewed.

Liturgy as the Source of Priestly Identity

Richard Cipolla

1. *Introduction*

It is impossible for me to approach my topic as something merely objective and in the end having nothing to do with me as a priest. Therefore I must ask your forbearance so that, while not disregarding the objective and scholarly information that comes to bear on any explication of this most important subject in the life of the Church, I cannot pretend to an impassive objectivity given the precarious state in which the Church finds herself, precarious with respect to the antagonism of the world as conceived in the Gospel of John and as experienced at this present time. The thesis I shall advance is that the identity of the Catholic priest has been severely obscured by the near loss within the Church of the understanding of the Eucharist, the Mass, as a sacrifice and therefore the priest as the one who offers sacrifice. This loss of priestly identity is part of the crisis in which the Catholic Church has found herself for the past fifty years at least.

I could end immediately by just stating that when a young man comes to me and tells me that he may have a vocation to the priesthood, I say nothing except this: "Read this book, take your time reading it, and if it says anything to you, then come back and we will talk. But remember to return the book, please." That book, which is a novel, is the *Diary of a Country Priest*, which was made into a remarkable film by Robert Bresson.[1] Most of these young men who have read or tried to read this novel have not come back to talk, but they all have given me back my not in good shape copy of it.

---

1. Georges Bernanos, *The Diary of a Country Priest* (New York: Macmillan, 1937).

2. *The Priesthood and the Eucharist in Catholic Tradition*

We begin in a rather prosaic way with a reference to the meaning of the English word, priest. The etymology of the word is mildly controverted. The Oxford English Dictionary, the self-styled arbiter in these matters, traces the word back to the Greek *presbyteros*, meaning elder, elder both in the sense of having lived many years and elder in the honorific sense, the latter meaning being difficult for us to comprehend in a society that defines elders as senior citizens who are entitled to cut-rates on means of transportation and movie tickets. Others, not intoxicated by the dreaming spires of Oxford, claim that this English word comes from the Vulgar Latin *prevost*, "one put over others," from Latin *praepositus*, a person placed in charge, from the past participle of *praeponere*. Whichever etymology one chooses, the meaning is essentially the same: the one who is the leader of an action, of an assembly.

But it is quite clear that by the early patristic era the word *presbyteros*, used to describe the man who led the nascent Christian cult, acquired sacrificial overtones, evoking the Latin word *sacerdos*, and the Greek word *hieros*, both of which refer to those who make things holy by sacrifice. I cannot help at this point to offer what is probably a totally irrelevant aside to cite John Milton's famous words to the enforcers of the Long Parliament: "New Presbyter is Priest written large."

Sergio Bianchini, in his fine work, *Il Sacerdozio Cristiano*,[2] the Sacred Priesthood, traces the shift from *presbyteros* to *sacerdos*, and he does so in the context of the expanding Church from St Paul to the beginning of the patristic era. I quote in my translation from Italian:

> The spiritual cultus of the Christians, to which the proclamation of the Word gives rise, reaches its climax in the *fractio panis*... The sacrificial interpretation of the death, resurrection and ascension of Christ, already present in the New Testament, was made present also in this new rite and gave it its meaning. It seems that it was in this way that the sacerdotal interpretation of the ministry of the presbyter gained ground gradually, until it became the lynchpin of theological reflection on the priesthood.[3]

Bianchini goes on to say:

> If the Eucharist is not only the remembrance of the "Supper of the Lord," but the memorial of the Sacrifice of Christ Priest and Victim, one understands how its ministers, likened to the priest of the old *cultus*, came to be seen as

2. Sergio Bianchini, *Il Sacerdozio Cristiano* (Torino: Marietti, 1973).

3. Ibid., p. 21.

the minister of Christ the High Priest... This change, already in place by the end of the second century, could not but be consolidated in the succeeding centuries. This process...is fully legitimate...and therefore the translation of *presbyteros* as Priest in the Acts of the Apostles and the Pastoral Epistles is fully justified.[4]

By the end of the fourth century and the beginning of the fifth century, often considered as the gold part of the patristic age, the process was quite advanced, as we see in these quotes from St Ambrose, who is not one for hyperbole, and from St John Chrysostom, who is one for hyperbole, but remember that hyperbole can point back to truth.

From St Ambrose's *Commentary on the Psalms* 38:25:

We saw the Prince of Priests coming to us, we saw and heard Him offering his Blood for us. We follow, as much as we are able, being priests; and we offer the Sacrifice on behalf of the people. For even if Christ is not now seen as the one who offers the Sacrifice, nevertheless it is He Himself that is offered in sacrifice here on earth when the body of Christ is offered. Indeed, to offer Himself He is made visible in us, he whose word makes holy the Sacrifice that is offered.[5]

And from St John Chrysostom's *On the Priesthood* III, 4:

For when you see the Lord sacrificed and laid upon the altar, and the priest Standing and praying over the victim, and all the worshipers empurpled with that precious blood, can you then think that you are still among men and standing on the earth? Are you not, on the contrary, straightway translated to heaven, and casting out every carnal thought from your soul, do you not with disembodied spirit and pure reason contemplate the things which are in Heaven?[6]

I would venture to say, with little fear, that the venture will be not obviously consonant with reality—and this is important, for the Catholic faith is a realistic faith—that St John Chrysostom's understanding of the Eucharist as sacrifice and the role of the priest in the Sacrifice is not consonant with the present understanding of the Mass as celebrated in the great majority of Catholic parish churches throughout the world today.

---

4. Ibid., pp. 22ff.

5. W. A. Jurgens, *The Faith of the Early Fathers*, vol. 2 (Collegeville: The Liturgical Press, 1979), p. 150.

6. Ibid., p. 925.

I will not go on—in imitation of Cicero's predilection for use of *preteritio*—to offer a catena of patristic citations while protesting that it is not necessary to show clearly that the Fathers understood the Eucharist as the re-presentation of Christ's Sacrifice on the Cross in such a sense that the Eucharist is not merely a memorial of that event—here even allowing the strongest possible meaning for "memorial"—but is in fact a sacrifice in and of itself.

The medieval period saw a deepening in Eucharistic theology which is often accompanied by vigorous if not actually acrimonious debates on the nature of the Mass as sacrifice and on the Real Presence of Christ in the Eucharist. St Thomas Aquinas, that coolly passionate expositor and summator, says in the *Summa Theologiae*: "There is but one victim, namely that which Christ offered and which we offer" (III, 83,1). And again: "Hence in one of the Sunday Secrets we say: 'Whenever the commemoration of this sacrifice is celebrated, the work of our redemption is enacted...(thus) it is proper for Christ to be sacrificed in its celebration" (III, 83,1,c).[7] As a side note here, the thought of anyone today using one of the Prayers over the Gifts in the *Novus ordo* rite to prove a theological point boggles the imagination.

It is the formidable Council of Trent that solidifies the understanding both of the Mass as a proper sacrifice and the priest as offering that sacrifice. The three relevant thundering anathemas read as follows:

> If anyone says that in the Mass, a true and proper sacrifice is not offered to God or that the sacrificial offering consists merely in the fact that Christ is given to us to eat, let him be anathema.
>
> If anyone says that by the words "do this in remembrance of me" Christ did not make the apostles priests or that he did not command that they and other priests should offer his body and blood, let him be anathema.
>
> If anyone says that the Sacrifice of the Mass is merely an offering of prayers and of thanksgiving or that it is simply a memorial of the Sacrifice offered on the Cross and not propitiatory or that it benefits only those who communicate and the Mass should not be offered for the living and the dead for sins, punishments and satisfactions and other necessities, let him be anathema.[8]

---

7. The English translation of the *Summa* used here is from the translation of the English Dominican Province (www.newadvent.org/summa/).

8. J. Waterworth (trans. and ed.), *The Canons and Decrees of the Sacred and Oecumenical Council of Trent* (London: Dolman, 1848), pp. 158–59.

These are strong words—not likely to be uttered in the present climate in Rome—and the harshness of these words are understandable in a time of crisis as the Church's answer to Luther, Calvin, Zwingli and the other Protestants' denial of the sacrificial nature of the Mass and the reality of the Christian ministerial priesthood. But we can also say that Trent was the means by which important elements of the Catholic faith, especially the liturgy, and more specifically the Mass, were deep frozen, were placed in aspic, as a defense against the radical and un-Catholic revisions by the Protestant reformers of the Christian faith as it had developed for 1,500 years. While we can and should have sympathy for what Trent did, we may still question the effect of the stifling of the ongoing organic development of the liturgical rites.

When things are frozen for a long time, things that were alive, there is often a messy puddle when they melt. That messy puddle is the post-Second Vatican Council era in which we still live. *Quamdiu, Domine! Quamdiu!* But we must note that the Second Vatican Council itself affirmed the traditional teaching, echoing Trent, on the Mass as a proper Sacrifice and on the priest as offering the sacrifice. In *Lumen Gentium* 28 we read: "Through the ministry of the priests, the spiritual sacrifice of the faithful is made perfect in union with the Sacrifice of Christ. He is the only mediator who in the name of the whole Church is offered sacramentally in the Eucharist and in an unbloody manner until the Lord himself comes." And in the document on the priesthood, *Presbyterorum Ordinis*, we read: "They exercise their sacred function especially in the Eucharistic worship or the celebration of the Mass by which acting in the person of Christ and proclaiming His Mystery they unite the prayers of the faithful with the Sacrifice of their Head and renew and apply in the sacrifice of the Mass until the coming of the Lord the only sacrifice of the New Testament, namely that of Christ offering Himself once for all a spotless Victim to the Father."

If we look back to that first quote from St John Chrysostom we see clearly that the identity of the priest is deeply linked to his role at the altar, as the one who offers the awesome and Unbloody Sacrifice that is the Mass. And if Chrysostom's treatise *On the Priesthood* sometimes reads as an over the top adulation of the priest, it is because of the awesome act he performs as the priest at the altar offering the Holy Sacrifice. In this way if the priest forgets who he is and what he is doing at the altar, if he forgets he is the *alter Christus offerens Christum* to use another idiom, then his very identity comes under attack, his very identity is at stake. Chrysostom and the many other commentators on the priesthood understand that the priest is not merely the one who offers sacrifice. They do not deny the priest's pastoral and administrative roles. But the latter roles do not define his identity, as does his role at the altar. In saying this, I am not denying the larger evangelical context of the priest's role and essence. To locate the priest's essence and identity merely in cultic terms would be an error. But nevertheless, his cultic role in offering the Unbloody Sacrifice of Christ to the Father is at the heart of what it means to be a priest.

3. *The Current Crisis and Its Causes*

Now suppose the sacrificial nature of the Eucharist is denied or obscured within the Catholic Church. Then it is obvious that the identity of the priest is if not denied then surely obscured. But how can this happen if as we said before the Documents of the Second Vatican Council repeat and affirm the traditional, that is, definitive, teaching of the Church on the Mass as a sacrifice and the priest as he who offers the Sacrifice? And, if one examines the four general Eucharistic prayers in the Pauline missal, there is reference to a sacrifice that is being offered. One should note, however, that only the Roman canon, now so-called, has this understanding at its very heart, for it combines language with sound and style in stark reference to the Sacrifice: *hostiam puram, hostiam sanctam, hostiam immaculatam*, that alliteration besounded by assonance that is part of what it means.

One should note as well that in the most used Eucharistic prayer, Eucharistic Prayer II (of the origin of which we know more after the recently published memoirs of Louis Bouyer),[9] the sacrificial nature of the Eucharistic action is not as obvious. If I were a liturgical scholar and had the credentials of such a lofty personage, I would—all this in the subjunctive of course, whose loss in English is to be lamented deeply—I would point out that the removal of the traditional offertory prayers with their specificity about the sacrifice to be offered in the traditional Roman rite and their replacement with the prayers based on Jewish thanksgiving prayers in the Pauline missal—for the reason given that prolepsis creates problems for the people's understanding of the Mass—has weakened to a great extent the obvious understanding of the Mass as a sacrifice.

On the imagined difficulty an anxiety that a proleptic prayer is claimed to produce in the faithful, I am sure that, just like W. G. Ward, an Anglican convert at the time of Newman and Faber—who in a wonderful burst of ultramontanism exclaimed that because of his Catholic faith, he would

9. See: J. Pepino (trans.), *The Memoirs of Louis Bouyer* (Kettering: Angelico, 2015), pp. 220–22.

be happy to swallow a papal bull every day with his coddled eggs at breakfast—we, men and women armed with intelligence and imagination, would be happy to listen to a proleptic prayer every day without fear of mental indigestion or spiritual reflux that would require the suppression of a spiritual burp. In fact, if an objective reader examined Eucharistic Prayer II, he could plausibly arrive at the conclusion that what is being done is to offer God bread and wine. But I am not a liturgical scholar or professional theologian. I am merely a priest who says Mass, so who am I to make any judgment about these things?

I will move on to questions of praxis, praxis being a hot topic in the Church right now, and I am qualified to speak of praxis as a parish priest of some years. Some will insist that one cannot separate the liturgical texts from the praxis. To some extent that is true. But it is a fact that if one wants to change someone's understanding of a particular action or event that uses a text, one does this by the way the action or event is presented. The medium is the message.

In Shakespeare's *A Midsummer Night's Dream* the tragic text of *Pyramus and Thisbe*—translated by generations of Latin students from Ovid's text—is transformed into comedy by its setting and how it is presented. And along with setting and presentation, this transformation of meaning can bring about the invention of new language, new terms to describe the action or event. Thus came about the liturgical new-speak of the '70s and '80s. The man at the altar at Mass is no longer called a priest but declared to be a presider, or the president of the assembly, and his chair is declared to be the president's chair. And everyone else around him is declared to be a minister. I remember the first time I heard this language. In one of my first parish assignments I was assigned to be the clergy liaison—a phrase to reckon with in itself as new-speak—to the Liturgical Committee. I could not understand why we would have such a thing in a Catholic church. I could understand the Presbyterian church down the road having such a thing because they have no liturgy. During the meeting the woman who was the head of the committee kept talking about the presider. I finally asked her who this person is. She looked amazed at such a question. And she said: "the one who is celebrating the Mass." I won't go on with the rest of that conversation—it would be too painful—but I know that many of a certain age have had experience with liturgical new-speak whose Orwellian purpose was, and still is, to advance a novel understanding of the Mass as a communal meal-assembly with the presider president presiding and wearing funny clothes.

To reduce the priest to the presider surely does harm to the priest and certainly undermines his true identity. The question or element of sacrifice does not even enter into the picture of the presider, who for me, from the sound of the word, always has had overtones of a character in an Arnold Schwarzenegger movie. But the greatest blow to the priest's identity was the introduction of the table altar where the priest was made to face the people at Mass. It is one of the greatest mysteries in the history of the Church how this revolutionary and totally untraditional practice was carried out in a short time as if it had been mandated by the Second Vatican Council. Its history lies not so much in the early Church—and, *pace* the liturgical experts, we know very little in specifics about how Mass was celebrated in the early Church—but rather in liturgical experimentation in the 1930s and 1940s in some parts of Europe.

One of the men I admire greatly, Romano Guardini, was involved in this experimentation whose aim was to make the Mass more accessible, real, relevant, especially to young people. I call him one of my heroes certainly not for his liturgical experimentation but because he is the author of one of the very greatest commentaries on the Roman Mass ever written, *The Spirit of the Liturgy*.[10] It is significant that Guardini, seemingly in the vanguard of the liturgical reform that characterized the post-Vatican II years, came to the conclusion in his last writings that modern man is incapable of the liturgical act, of worship.[11] That is a true dead end for liturgical reform.

What were the effects on the priest's identity by putting him in a presider's chair and facing the people across a table? Most priests had to abandon entirely the traditional understanding of the priest as *sacerdos*, the one who makes holy by sacrifice. The contradiction in what they thought they were and the role in which they found themselves in was too much to bear. And so they either left the priesthood, or they became leaders of the Mass, much like their Protestant counterparts who lead Sunday services. They became 'Mother Mary Principal' presiding over a high school assembly, where everyone has a part to play. They understood that now the Mass depended on them, that their personality was one of the important ingredients in making the Mass a successful event, an event

10. Romano Guardini, *The Spirit of the Liturgy* (New York: Sheed & Ward, 1937).

11. "Would it not be better to admit that man in this industrial and scientific age, with its new sociological structure, is no longer capable of a liturgical act?" Cited in: Robert Barron, *Bridging the Great Divide* (Lanham: Rowman & Littlefield, 2004), p. 53. For the philosophical and theological bases underlying this statement see also: R. Guardini, *The End of the Modern World* (Wilmington: Intercollegiate Studies Institute, 1998).

that would capture the people's attention so they would not be bored. So the telling of jokes in the homily became a widespread phenomenon along with folksy banter. Music was introduced into the Mass that was an imitation of what can be vaguely called popular music, and a bad imitation at best. The text of the Mass, the introductions, prayers, even the Eucharistic prayer were now within the presider's purveyance to alter at will. And all this made sense, because his job was to engage the people, and if there were words and phrases that the people might not understand, then he as the presider, the facilitator, had to find other words more accessible to the people. And to avoid the obvious contradiction in claiming to be talking to God in the prayers while facing the people, many presiders said the prayers as if they were indeed talking to the people. A common practice still seen today is the priest saying the words of consecration directly to the people and looking at them while holding the host.

Other priests tried their best to manage somehow the contradiction they found themselves in. They tried to restore a sense of reverence to the Mass, a sense of the role of beauty in the Mass, but this always at great cost to themselves, for their sense of reverence was too often interpreted by their people as not engaging with them. The mass exodus of priests from the Church in the 1960s and '70s surely is one of results of the loss of identity of the priest that was the mark of those decades. And this continues down to this very day.

It may be obvious that the return to the traditional posture of the priest at the altar, *ad orientem*, facing liturgical East with his people, his people with him as he as priest offers the Holy Sacrifice, is an important first step in the process of the regaining of the identity of the priest as priest. But what stands in the way of this return to liturgical sanity is liturgical and doctrinal positivism that marks the hierarchy and the professional *periti* who serve them. This brand of positivism is marked by the attitude that what has happened in the Church for the past fifty years is good just because it happened. And it is the Church's job to justify what has happened in whatever way possible and continue on a path that objectively would seem problematic to say the least.

The rabid and opportunistic ultramontanism that has gripped the Church since the Second Vatican Council is one of the biggest problems facing the Church today. This is exactly what Newman feared would happen if the infallibility of the Pope were defined, although he assented fully to the definition in 1870. Newman understood that everything that the Church believes does not need to be defined. And he was prescient in what was to come: even though the definition of infallibility of the Pope was defined in what many thought were minimalistic terms, that doctrine can be used and has been used to advance theological positions that are quite debatable but are declared to be beyond debate because of the positivistic attitude that whatever happens in the Church is the work of the Holy Spirit acting through the Pope and the Magisterium and the matter is closed.

The "Bologna school" of interpretation of Vatican II is an example of the production of baloney and declaring it to be prosciutto. This illogical and unrealistic positivism masquerading as faithfulness to the Council and the Magisterium has caused great damage to the Church especially in her liturgical life. My first academic training is in the physical sciences, and I must admit that compared to the doctrinal and liturgical positivists in the Church today, Bertrand Russell looks pretty good. The continuing reign of this liturgical positivism in the face of objective data that is in direct opposition to the presumption of this positivism is both amazing and depressing.

Many know of the May 2015 Pew Research report on the state of Christianity in the USA.[12] It came as no surprise to anyone except to the positivists. The news is bad. There is an ever-decreasing number of people in this country who call themselves Christians. And Catholics are included in this decline. Where are Catholics going? Some are becoming Evangelical Protestants, because they find a more real faith community there. But most are opting out entirely, becoming nothing, no religion, vaguely religious but having no religious commitment. And it is in this situation that the presider is expected to minister to his flock with his identity as priest sucked out of him and to try to continue to go down a path that objectively is a failure in a time of crisis.

Of course it is true that the rapid secularization of our society has made being a priest and being a Catholic more difficult. But even in this society the search for the sacred exists, for the search for the sacred is the search for ultimate meaning of life, of existence. And the sacred will not be found in places where presiders sit behind tables not knowing who they are or what they are supposed to be doing.

Our priests have become clergymen, who dress in suits of black color and with clerical collars. The Italians call these suits "clergyman" in contrast with the soutane, the cassock, which is the ordinary dress of the priest. The priest has become a religious functionary, in the end indistinguishable from other clergyman other than the black suit with the special collar, which collar, if in the tab form, can be taken out on hot days and

12. Pew Research Center, "America's Changing Religious Landscape: Christians Decline Sharply as Share of Population; Unaffiliated and Other Faiths Continue to Grow," 12 May 2015. http://www.pewforum.org/2015/05/12/americas-changing-religious-landscape/.

put into the shirt pocket. There are those who declare that the wearing of the cassock is a barrier to the people. Tell that to St John Vianney or to St John Bosco or to Guareschi's Don Camillo. I have written elsewhere about what I call the devirilization of the Mass and the accompanying devirilization of the priest,[13] and this devirilization of the priest, the taking away of his manliness, is certainly part of the tragedy of the sexual abuse scandals of the post-conciliar years. The liminal nature of the cassock is part of the sacred identity of the priest.

4. *Towards a Resolution of the Crisis*

Where does the spiritual strength of a priest come from, the strength to be a priest who offers the only acceptable sacrifice to God? It comes from his encounter with God, his contact with God. This encounter, this contact surely is found in the priest's prayer life, a life of prayer that is absolutely necessary for the priest to be priest. The Daily Office is an example of prayer as office, as obligation, and this obligation has always been indeed difficult, but it is more so now, for the post-conciliar Divine Office is burdened with the Grail psalms that cannot be sung except with great difficulty and the disappearance of the soaring beauty of the traditional Office hymns, replaced by bowdlerized Protestant hymns and bad 1960's Catholic songs. But all of this assumes that the priest is living a life of sacrifice that is an imitation of the life of Christ.

But the most intimate contact with God surely is when the priest stands at the altar to offer the Sacrifice, which offering includes and assumes the consecration of the species of bread and wine to become the body and blood of Christ to be offered in sacrifice and then to be given as heavenly food to the people. From the time of consecration to the reception of Holy Communion is for the priest the *communio* with God, of which the deepest communion is his reception of the Body and Blood of Christ that consummates the Sacrifice for which he is sacramentally consecrated to offer. This is the source of his identity in the most existential sense. This is where doctrine, teaching on the priesthood, must become real. If it does not become real at this point, then the priest becomes merely the presider who is the clergyman leading a service.

For this to happen the priest must give himself over to what he is doing. He must conform, in the deepest etymological sense of that word, to the One in whose place he stands, the One he represents in the re-presentation of Calvary. But this conformation is possible only if he is able to do this

13. See: http://rorate-caeli.blogspot.com/2013/06/the-devirilization-of-liturgy-in-novus.html.

by the given-ness of the liturgy, by something he enters into, something that is already there. There must be at this moment a loss of the priest into the action of the Sacrifice, a giving of himself over to what he is doing and who he is representing and what he is re-presenting. At this moment the priest must no longer be the focus, no longer seen by his people at the Mass. The people must see through him to Christ. This is part of the priest's own sacrifice, to get out of the way, to point to the ultimate reality, just as in all the early icons Mary points to her Son and is never depicted alone. The priest becomes the *theotokos* in the spiritual sense by uttering mystically the words of Mary: "Let it be done to me according to thy word" (Luke 1:38), *Hoc est enim corpus meum*, and "the Word became flesh and dwelt among us" (John 1:14), as the incarnation of the bread and wine in the Mass echo the mystery of Christmas that is a divine dagger into the warp and woof of space and time.

But this is impossible to do as a presider. It is impossible to do if the priest is facing his people and is deemed to be responsible for making this real and meaningful, if his personality is what is driving the event, driving the moment. In this position he is not with his people offering sacrifice. He is obliged to try to make sense of all of this to his people who are looking to him to make it happen. There is no given-ness except what is written in the missal, but there is no deep and existential given-ness that alone is able to allow the priest and people to lose themselves in order to find themselves in the awesome presence of God. Lest anyone think I am indulging in mysticism here, I would say that even at the low Mass of yesteryear, celebrated with little style and perhaps even hurriedly, there was a sense of this given-ness on the part of both the priest and the people that made them aware of something more than what they saw and heard.

This given-ness is not merely objective, although it is and must be if it participates in truth. Kierkegaard's famous and misunderstood phrase, "Truth is subjectivity," is relevant here. What Kierkegaard meant by this, which meaning one can easily understand by a close reading of this essay, is that the subject, the person, has the solemn obligation to acknowledge truth, which does not depend on him and in this sense is objective, and to make this truth his own, and in this way defining him as subject. The great irony is those who are known as existentialists, like Camus and Sartre, turned this insight on its head and made the subject person the arbiter of truth and so helped to usher in the age of radical individualism, the age of the selfie. The very idea of the liturgy of the Mass as the place and time and action in which there is an encounter with the ultimate truth who is the Word of God is foreign to the contemporary Church for which the Mass is didactic in essence and experience and is grounded in this time and place.

This given-ness of the Mass, which is vital to the priest's identity and to the people's participation in the act of the Sacrifice of the Mass (which is what *participatio actuosa* means in English), is also a product of organic growth. The gardener who loves his or her garden and his or her calling to garden, loves the sheer wonder of how things grow, how tomato flowers appear, and soon there are tiny tomatoes and then in late summer there are tomatoes which can be pulled off the vine, sliced open, a little salt added, and the flavor explodes in one's mouth, a flavor that is the product of millennia of organic development, unlike the hot-house tomatoes that tempt one in the winter by their red color but taste of absolutely nothing.

So this given-ness of the Mass is a gift that is given through the distillation of unseen and unknown elements that have little to do with the actual liturgical books that scholars pore over and comment upon. Scholarship is always *ex post facto* and this is especially true of a living organism like the liturgy, especially the Mass. One must always beware of labeling something as an early Eucharistic prayer by Hippolytus and using this assumption to build a liturgical theology and then find out, again through scholarship, that this may not have been a Eucharistic prayer at all by Hippolytus. Tomatoes with wonderful flavor are not products of committees, *consilia* or analysis of documents. They are products of organic development that includes serendipity, mistakes, oddities, brilliance, local and universal. This is not to in any way disparage liturgical scholarship and theology. They are necessary and vital. We see this in Dr Lauren Pristas's scholarly work on the collects of the Pauline missal,[14] the results of which should give bishops, the guardians of the liturgy, great pause. But liturgical scholarship can never be the basis for the liturgical life of the Church.

If the Eucharistic liturgy, the Mass, is to provide that deep and lasting identity for the priest who celebrates this liturgy so that he can be fully priest—the one who offers sacrifice, pastor and man of the Church—and if he is going to encounter the person of Jesus Christ who is the priest and victim of the Sacrifice, then he must have the opportunity of this encounter in this celebration of Mass. It is not enough to enter into the given-ness, the gift of the Mass, although this is a *sine qua non*. What is necessary for encounter with God is an absence of distraction, an ability to focus, focus not in some artificial and contrived sense, but focus as looking and seeing with the eye of the mind, heart, body and soul, and for this silence is needed, the silence of contemplation. And this can never

14. See: Lauren Pristas, *The Collects of the Roman Missals: A Comparative Study of the Sundays in Proper Seasons Before and After the Second Vatican Council* (London: Bloomsbury, 2013).

happen if the priest is the presider or the clergyman or the maker of the liturgical event. This does not mean that the Mass is to be identified with contemplative prayer. But it should be identified with contemplation in the sense that the priest opens himself up to the presence of God and lets himself be transformed by that presence.

The priest at the altar is always alone. It is true that he is surrounded and supported by his people who stand with him in support of his offering of the Sacrifice. But yet, he is alone like Christ, bearing in his heart, in the words of Romano Guardini, "la tristezza così perenne,"[15] the sadness that never goes away, that self-identification of himself with the aloneness of Christ on the Cross, and this despite the real presence of the love of his Mother and St John, despite the love and support of those who join his offering with him at the Mass, that *tristezza* that is the mark of his identification with the Crucified Lord, that *tristezza* that is the other side of the golden coin that bears the image of the risen Lord.

Silence. There is nothing else to do at this point. There are various reasons offered by liturgical scholars for the development of the silent canon of the Mass. It has always made perfect sense to me from the vantage point of a priest: at this moment of offering, offering for the people, for the world, for those who do not believe or have a clue, this moment of offering that is also the moment of actualization of the priest's identity with the Holy Victim that is being offered, there can be nothing but silence, not in earthquake, wind or fire, but in that small whispering sound that can be barely heard. I have always been amazed that this was so deeply understood by the Unitarian hymn writer, John Greenleaf Whittier, who cuts through the chatter of Catholic piety to say this in his hymn, "Dear Lord and Father of all mankind":

O Sabbath rest by Galilee!
O calm of hills above,
Where Jesus knelt to share with Thee
The silence of eternity
Interpreted by love!

With that deep hush subduing all
Our words and works that drown
The tender whisper of Thy call,
As noiseless let Thy blessing fall
As fell Thy manna down.

15. Romano Guardini, *The Church and the Catholic and the Spirit of the Liturgy* (New York: Sheed & Ward, 1935), p. 52.

Drop Thy still dews of quietness,
Till all our strivings cease;
Take from our souls the strain and stress,
And let our ordered lives confess
The beauty of Thy peace.

Breathe through the heats of our desire
Thy coolness and Thy balm;
Let sense be dumb, let flesh retire;
Speak through the earthquake, wind, and fire,
O still, small voice of calm.

5. *Conclusion*

In the end I come back to Bernanos and his little country priest. Bernanos was a remarkable man of deep faith and love for the Church and was strongly anti-clerical. And he was anti-clerical because he loved the Church, and he loved the priesthood.

It is significant that the greatest scene in *The Diary of a Country Priest* has nothing to do with the priest's celebration of Mass. The scene of the priest's encounter and conversation with Mme la Comtesse in the château, a world so far removed from his own personal world and yet so full of grace, is a scene the equal of anything in Dostoyevsky in its power to depict the action of grace and redemption. And yet in the novel as well as the film, there is no specific mention of the priest saying Mass except in a purely factual way, as what the priest does every day in the early morning. There are no liturgical ecstasies, no mention of hours spent before the Blessed Sacrament.

There was no mention because there was no need. For the essence of this country priest was his state of conformity to the Sacrifice of the Mass, his conforming to the suffering and death of the Lord—that was it, and then he went forward, forward never sure where he was going, but always conformed to the Cross. In one of his essays Bernanos rails against well-meaning pious people who try to turn his little priest into a saint, to make him into one of the awful late nineteenth-century French holy cards.[16]

He dies, the country priest, he dies of stomach cancer in ambiguous and, shall we say, secular surroundings. These are the last words he wrote in his diary: "How easy it is to hate oneself! True grace is to forget. Yet

16. George Bernanos, "Christianity and the Writer's Task," *Communio* 28 (2001), pp. 202–10.

if pride could die in us the supreme grace would be to love oneself in all simplicity—as one would love any one of those who themselves have suffered and loved in Christ."[17]

The man in whose house the priest died writes to the Curé de Torcey, a priest from a neighboring parish who knew the little country priest, to express his regret that the priest he summoned never arrived before the country priest died. This is what he says:

> The priest was still on his way, and finally I was bound to voice my deep regret that such delay threatened to deprive my comrade of the final consolations of Our Church. He did not seem to hear me. But a few moments later he put his hand over mine, and his eyes entreated me to draw closer to him. He then uttered these words almost in my ear. And I am quite sure that I have recorded them accurately, for his voice though halting was strangely distinct. "Does it matter? *Tout est grâce.* All is grace. Grace is everywhere.[18]

17. Bernanos, *Diary of a Country Priest*, p. 296.
18. Ibid.

Holy Week Reforms Revisited—Some New Material and Paths for Further Study

Alcuin Reid

1. *Introduction*

My first Holy Week in sacred orders found me assigned to a new parish in suburban Melbourne, Australia. On Palm Sunday the Pastor blessed palms before the principal Mass at the front of the temporary hall-church without attempting any form of procession. On Holy Thursday the sanctuary (in fact the stage of the hall) was curtained off and all present sat at specially arranged trestle-tables so as to imitate the Last Supper. We were "back on stage," as it were, after that, and indeed did not move from it: the paschal fire consisted of methylated spirit applied to cotton wool sitting in a portable barbecue base, lit and blessed, again at the front of the church hall under the glare of fluorescent lights at the usual Saturday evening Mass time. I was instructed that if I really *must* sing the Exsultet, it had to be the short form and I had to sing it quickly![1]

Seminary formation had prepared me somewhat for such eventualities—an Easter Vigil where the parts of the rite had been rearranged into an order the celebrant thought would be more meaningful, and the desire for everyone to sit at long tables on Holy Thursday, various forms of hand and foot washing, and other "creative" liturgical arrangements, were amongst my most formative liturgical experiences in the celebration of the rites of Holy Week and beyond.[2] Some of my seminary formators were inspired by a spirit often associated with the Second Vatican Council, but which was in reality of little if any connection with it.

---

1. Holy Week at the Parish of St Thomas the Apostle, Greensborough North, Archdiocese of Melbourne, Australia, 1990. Pastor: Fr Kevin McIntosh.

2. Corpus Christi College, Archdiocese of Melbourne, 1982–84 and St Francis Xavier Seminary, Archdiocese of Adelaide, 1987–89. For more on the liturgical practices of the Corpus Christi College, Melbourne, see: Michael Gilchrist, *Rome or the Bush: The Choice for Australian Catholics* (Melbourne: John XXIII Fellowship, 1986).

The minimalism with which the (new, twice reformed) great rites of Holy Week were celebrated in the parish to which I had been assigned suggested that "the spirit and power of the liturgy," the promotion of which was at the heart of the classical liturgical movement, and the formation in which the Second Vatican Council asserted as the *sine qua non* of the liturgical renewal it sought to achieve, had not permeated the liturgical life of this parish.[3] I suspect that the unreformed rites would have been celebrated just as perfunctorily were it to have been thirty or fifty years earlier.

We have come a long way since that cotton wool paschal fire was lit. Today it is far more widely possible to assist at Holy Week rites celebrated according to the *usus recentior* with that *ars celebrandi* so eloquently proposed by Pope Benedict XVI,[4] although a YouTube search will reveal the continuing existence of a boastful "creativity" well beyond the bounds permitted by even the modern liturgical books. And liturgical sloth and minimalism still weighs too many parishes down. So too, today, it is possible to participate in the rites of Holy Week according to the *usus antiquior*. Officially this is permitted according to the reformed rites contained in the *Missale Romanum* of 1962, though the celebration of the pre-1955 Holy Week rites occurs in some places, without due authorisation and based solely on private judgement—a stance that is very difficult to reconcile with traditional Catholic ecclesiology.

I do not need to explain why a cotton wool paschal fire is an utter travesty of the Sacred Liturgy, unworthy of God or man, in what should be the greatest liturgical rite of the Church's year. Rather, I suggest that what is necessary is to revisit the twentieth-century reforms of Holy Week—the experimental reform of 1951, the definitive reform of 1955, the modifications to the rites of Holy Week of 1965 and those promulgated in the *Missale Romanum* of 1970—and to ask whether it is possible to find sound tradition being retained and legitimate progress being made.[5]

---

3. See: *Sacrosanctum Concilium* 14; also: Alcuin Reid, "Thoroughly Imbued with the Spirit and Power of the Liturgy—*Sacrosanctum Concilium* and Liturgical Formation," in A. Reid (ed.), *Sacred Liturgy: The Source and Summit of the Life and Mission of the Church* (San Francisco: Ignatius, 2014), pp. 213–36.

4. See: Apostolic Exhortation *Sacramentum Caritatis*, 22 February 2007, nn. 38–42.

5. See: *Sacrosanctum Concilium* 23; also: Alcuin Reid, "*Sacrosanctum Concilium* and the Organic Development of the Liturgy," in Uwe Michael Lang (ed.), *The Genius of the Roman Rite: Historical, Theological, and Pastoral Perspectives on Catholic Liturgy* (Chicago: Hillenbrand, 2010), pp. 198–215.

This is no easy or simple task. It requires a very detailed and careful study making many distinctions—an excellent doctoral dissertation or a number of careful volumes of analysis would be required to do it justice. Here, alas, it is only possible to look at some newly available material to see what light it sheds on the various reforms of Holy Week, and to suggest some pathways for further study. I hope that this will be of help to students and researchers in this field, and indeed to others, in identifying what has happened, for good or for ill, in recent Holy Week reforms and in developing a reasoned and critical stance in respect of them. Before doing this, however, a brief *excursus* on one aspect of liturgical reform is necessary.

2. *Excursus—Liturgical Development and Reform Is Possible*

Some years ago a then colleague insisted that, in any solemn celebrations of the *usus antiquior* for the society he organised, the celebrant must read the epistle and gospel, even though these were, of course, sung by the deacon and subdeacon. Since the 1960 rubrics had explicitly abolished this practice,[6] (extending the provision first introduced in the 1951 experimental paschal vigil and subsequently widened to all of Holy Week in 1955),[7] and given that I had found nothing other than positive reactions to this reform from the 1950s and beyond, I looked into the origin of the celebrant himself reading the readings whilst other ministers sang them.

It would appear that this practice emerged in the sixteenth or early seventeenth century. Its precise origins and motivation are unclear.[8] From what is known I would hypothesise that it found its way into the rubrics

6. See: Sacred Congregation for Rites, Decree, *Novum Rubricarum*, 26 July 1960, n. 473.

7. See: 1951 *Ordo Sabbati Sancti*, n. 15; Instruction accompanying the 16 November 1955 Decree of the Sacred Congregation of Rites, *Maxima Redemptionis Nostrae*, n. 6. In a chapter dense in its description of the 1955 reform, P. Goddard dedicates almost an entire page to this minor reform describing it as a "change of profound significance," without, however, explaining why; Philip J. Goddard, *Festa Paschalia: A History of the Holy Week Liturgy in the Roman Rite* (Leominster: Gracewing, 2011), p. 269. Goddard's work is certainly helpful in its historical descriptions, though its treatment of the 1955 and 1970 reforms does not engage in detailed analysis or with a large body of contemporary literature.

8. See: A. Bugnini CM and C. Braga CM, *Ordo Hebdomadae Sanctae instauratus commentarium*, Bibliotheca Ephemerides Liturgicae Sectio Historica 25 (Rome: Edizioni Liturgiche, 1956), pp. 44–46; Archdale A. King, *Liturgy of the Roman Church* (Milwaukee: Bruce, 1957), p. 249. King is in error when he states that "no such regulation is found in the missal of Pius V (1570)."

as a result of the regarding of low Mass as normative and of viewing activities at solemn Mass, such as those of the deacon and subdeacon, as ceremonial "extras" to the "integral" Mass *said* by the priest.[9]

It seems to me that the removal of the requirement that the priest himself read the readings when they are sung by another minister in the facultative 1951 reform, the widening of this to all of Holy Week in 1955 and its extension in 1960 to the whole liturgical year, was nothing other than a sane return to liturgical authenticity, indeed genuine progress, underlining the important realities that solemn Mass is the norm both historically and liturgically, and that the functions of its other ministers are not simply ceremonial or ornamental additions to a "base-rite" of low Mass but are in fact themselves integral parts of the liturgical rite itself. It partially corrected what Dom Lambert Beauduin had described in 1920 as "a truly regrettable anomaly."[10]

The colleague who had prompted my enquiry was not moved. As far as he was concerned priests read the readings before 1960 and that was that. Because it was done then it should be done now, regardless of the fact that its origins are unclear and its meaning liturgically doubtful, or indeed regardless of the fact that competent authority had ruled on the matter in a manner utterly consonant with sound liturgical principles. For him, it seemed, all possibility of change, development or reform beyond a given date was excluded.

In discussions of such questions the word "custom" is often invoked. Apart from the fact that those invoking custom in this way are often seeking to revive practices that have long since ceased to be observed (and sometimes, if not often, with good reason) and which are therefore in no sense customary, we would do well to ponder the maxim of St Cyprian

---

9. The *Ritus Servandus in Celebratione Missarum* of the *Missale Romanum* of St Pius V always gives the rubrical directions for low Mass first. In respect of the epistle, it adds: "Si sollemniter celebrat, legat demissa voce cum ministris. Similiter Graduale et Evangelium"; M. Sodi and A. M. Triacca (eds), *Missale Romanum Editio Princeps 1570* (Vatican City: Libreria Editrice Vaticana, 1998), p. 12. As King notes, some French missals of the following centuries did not impose this "new" practice and allowed a choice here; see: *Liturgy of the Roman Church*, p. 249.

10. Lambert Beauduin OSB, "Messe basse ou Messe solennelle," *Les Questions Liturgiques et Paroissiales* 5 (1920), pp. 90–97 (90). Beauduin's article argues for "un retour à la vraie tradition romaine" (p. 97), including the priest listening to and not himself reciting the Ordinary or Proper of the Mass, something not achieved in the Pian reform of Holy Week or indeed in the rubrical reform of St John XXIII (25 July 1960). Accordingly, the rubrics of the *Missale Romanum* 1962 require that the priest recite the Ordinary and Proper of the Mass at a sung or solemn Mass.

of Carthage (†258): *Consuetudo sine veritate, vetustas erroris est*—a custom without truth is simply error grown old. Without truth, without authenticity, customs hold little importance—above all for the Sacred Liturgy.

I raise the spectre of such uncritical liturgical intransigence because where it exists it is utterly futile to engage in an examination of the reforms of Holy Week or of any other rites. Liturgical "intransigists" draw their line in the sand according to their own private judgement or simple preference.[11] Nothing further can be said. Unsound tradition is idolised and legitimate progress is excluded *a priori*.

Certainly, the second half of the twentieth century saw much violence done to received liturgical tradition, officially and authoritatively (before anyone mistranslated or abused the new rites), and that is *the* big issue. But not everything in the reforms of the 1960s or the 1950s was unwise, imprudent or plain wrong. We simply cannot exclude liturgical reform and development *a priori*. Reactionary intransigence does not provide a legitimate response to the grave problems of some twentieth-century liturgical reform or to the widespread state of the liturgical life of the Western Church at the beginning of the twenty-first century. To adopt such a position is both a-historical and is to condemn the Sacred Liturgy to become an archaic museum exhibit rambling throughout history not capable of the appropriate, proportionate, indeed organic, development which is integral to the living organism that is the liturgy of the Roman rite.[12]

11. One must once again underline the distance of this stance from traditional Catholic ecclesiology and state clearly that such exercise of private judgment by clergy or laity in matters liturgical is more akin to Protestantism than Catholicism—regardless of whether it is used to bring about more purportedly "traditional" or more "modern" liturgical celebrations. Catholics are obliged to follow the law of the Church in respect of the celebration of the Sacred Liturgy. This is applicable in respect of which Holy Week rites are celebrated, how many *Confiteors* are used at Mass, and so on, no matter what arguments can be advanced in respect of the respective reforms. We are simply not free, as Catholics, to make these decisions ourselves. See: canons 834–39 of the Code of Canon Law, and canon 846 §1 which reflects the norm promulgated by the Second Vatican Council in *Sacrosanctum Concilium* 22 §3: "Therefore no other person, even if he be a priest, may add, remove, or change anything in the liturgy on his own authority." For an excellent recapitulation of the authority of the Bishop in respect of the Sacred Liturgy see: Alexander K. Sample, "The Bishop: Governor, Promoter and Guardian of the Liturgical Life of the Diocese," in Reid (ed.), *Sacred Liturgy*, pp. 255–71.

12. See: Alcuin Reid, *The Organic Development of the Liturgy*, 2nd edn (San Francisco: Ignatius, 2005). In "Reflections on *Summorum Pontificum*," *Worship* 83 (2009), pp. 98–112, John Baldovin SJ asserts that the thesis of *The Organic*

Accordingly, at the outset, I submit that we must reject out of hand any fetishisation of a given date in respect of liturgical reform in general and of the reform of Holy Week in particular, be that 1950, 1955, 1962, 1965 or 1970, regardless of whether one looks only forwards or backwards from it. Our task as critical students of the liturgical reforms of the particularly charged and indeed challenged decades in the middle of the twentieth century is not to dig a trench from which to throw grenades, but to weigh the historical, ritual, theological and pastoral questions with clarity and equanimity. With such an approach it should be possible to be able to indicate areas in which the various Holy Week reforms can or even ought to be authoritatively revisited for the good of the Church today.

3. *The Reforms of Pius XII*

Some are, perhaps, not that accustomed to regarding Pope Pius XII as a liturgical reformer, but a significant liturgical reformer he was. In 1946 he established a Commission for Liturgical Reform,[13] the first public fruit of which was a restored rite of the paschal vigil promulgated by a decree of the Sacred Congregation of Rites dated 9 February 1951. The reform was facultative. The experimental *Ordo Sabbato Sancti* appeared less than a month before Easter of that year.[14]

In his account of the liturgical reform from 1948–1975, Archbishop Bugnini states that this "elicited an explosion of joy throughout the Church. It was a signal that the liturgy was at last launched decisively on a pastoral course."[15] Similarly, the definitive reform of Holy Week promulgated by a decree of the Sacred Congregation of Rites dated 16 November 1955 was described in February 1956 by Fr Ferdinando Antonelli OFM,

---

Development of the Liturgy is "manifestly not the case" (p. 99), basing his assertion on the *quantity* of liturgical reforms catalogued by Martin Klöckener and Benedikt Kranemann's *Liturgiereformen: Historische Studien zu einem bleibenden Grundzug des christlichen Gottesdienstes*, 2 vols. (Münster: Aschendorff, 2002). Klöckener and Kranemann's demonstration that there has been a good deal of liturgical *change* in liturgical history does not, however, take away from the thesis that authentic liturgical development in such change is in fact organic. See further: Martin Klöckener, "Liturgical Renewal through History," *Studia Liturgia* 44 (2014), pp. 13–33, which fails to engage with the thesis advanced in *The Organic Development of the Liturgy*.

13. See: Reid, *The Organic Development of the Liturgy*, pp. 150–64.

14. See: ibid, p. 172.

15. Annibale Bugnini CM, *The Reform of the Liturgy 1948–1975* (Collegeville: The Liturgical Press, 1990), p. 10. On pastoral liturgy see: Alcuin Reid, "Pastoral Liturgy Revisited," in A. Reid (ed.), *T&T Clark Companion to Liturgy* (London: Bloomsbury, 2016), pp. 341–63.

Relator Generalis of the Historical Section of the Congregation for Rites since 1935, as "the most important event in the history of liturgy since the time of St Pius V."[16]

Pius XII's reform of Holy Week is sometimes called "the Bugnini Holy-Week." In revisiting it, it is important that we be good historians and not fall into the trap conspiracy theories often represent. In respect of this particular theory it needs to be stated clearly that, from the published minutes of Pius XII's Commission for Liturgical Reform, there is simply no evidence that the then Fr Annibale Bugnini CM was the driving force behind, or made substantial contributions to, the 1951 *ad experimentum* reform of the paschal vigil or indeed to the 1955 definitive reform of Holy Week.[17]

Rather, the minutes reveal evidence to the contrary: the Vice-Relator of the Historical Section of the Congregation of Rites, Fr Joseph Löw CSsR, drafted the proposals for reform presented to the Commission then under the guidance of Fr Antonelli.[18] Furthermore, it is clear that Fr Löw worked with the Professor of Liturgy at the Pontifical Gregorian University, Herman Schmidt SJ, for whose two-volume work *Hebdomada Sancta*, published in 1956 and 1957, Löw provided a glowing preface.[19] The second and largest volume of this publication, comprising 1,058 pages, consists of historical sources and commentary—material which had, presumably, been at least part of that which was put before the members of the Commission during their work on the Holy Week reform.

The young Bugnini—only 36 when the Commission first met in June 1948—was an assiduous secretary, certainly, but he was not in the Commission's driving-seat engineering its reforms with prepared and purportedly perfidious ends in view. Later, Bugnini was certainly not without influence as Secretary of the Preparatory Conciliar Commission (1960–62) and there is evidence in this period of his politicking so as to

---

16. Nicola Giampietro, *The Development of the Liturgical Reform: As Seen by Cardinal Ferdinando Antonelli from 1948–1970* (Fort Collins: Roman Catholic Books, 2009), p. 57. This same phrase was used in Antonelli's September 1956 paper at the Assisi Congress: "The Liturgical Reform of Holy Week: Importance, Realisations, Perspectives," in *The Assisi Papers: Proceedings of the First International Congress of Pastoral Liturgy, Assisi-Rome, September 18–22, 1956* [no editor] (Collegeville: Liturgical & St John's Abbey, 1957), pp. 149–66.

17. See: ibid., pp. 224–33, 245–52, 274–75, 284–89.

18. See: ibid., pp. 245 n. 343; 274 n. 654.

19. Hermanus A. P. Schmidt SJ, *Hebdomada Sancta*, 2 vols. (Rome: Herder, 1956–57).

influence the proposals put to the Council.[20] This may well have led to his marginalisation under Pope John XXIII. In my judgement, however, the historical facts indicate that his great "opportunity" personally to drive liturgical reform in a particular direction arrived with his rehabilitation by Paul VI in January 1964.[21] As responsible historians, then, I submit that we must set aside the a-historical theory that Pius XII's Holy Week reforms must necessarily be prefaced with the seemingly intrinsically pejorative adjective "Bugnini."

a. *Some New Sources*

I have outlined the 1951 and 1955 Holy Week reforms and the relevant clarifications and emendations of these made at the time by the Holy See in detail in *The Organic Development of the Liturgy*, and I respectfully direct those unfamiliar with these reforms to that account and to the sources from which it draws.[22] For familiarity with these reforms in even more detail I would also recommend the "Compendium of the 1955 Holy Week Revisions of Pius XII" by Gregory DiPippo, Editor of the New Liturgical Movement website. The Compendium is freely available online at that site. The widely disseminated 2010 article of Fr Stefano Carusi IBP, "The Reform of Holy Week in the Years 1951–1956," merits attention.[23] Fr Carusi's description of these changes is informative and revealing. His commentary is frequently insightful but could, perhaps, benefit from the making of further distinctions in support of his conclusion that "the entire *raison d'être* of the reform seems to be permeated with the whiff of rationalism and archeologism, with at times dollops of pure imagination."[24] An older piece, a 1960 conference on the Pian reform by Msgr Léon Gromier (1879–1965), a canon of the Vatican Basilica, consulter to the Sacred Congregation of Rites and ceremonial author (though *not*, as widely reported, a former papal Master of Ceremonies), is also available (in English translation) on the Internet. Msgr Gromier's account registers

---

20. See my forthcoming work: *Continuity or Rupture? The Second Vatican Council's Reform of the Liturgy*.

21. See: Bugnini, *The Reform of the Liturgy*, p. 49.

22. See: Reid, *The Organic Development of the Liturgy*, pp. 172–82, 219–34.

23. Originally published in Italian on the blog "Disputationes theologicae" on 28 March 2010. http://disputationes-theologicae.blogspot.fr/2010/03/la-riforma-della-settimana-santa-negli.html, subsequently in English translation on the blog "Rorate Caeli." http://rorate-caeli.blogspot.com/2010/07/reform-of-holy-week-in-years–1951–1956.html.

24. Ibid.

at least an octave higher than those of most other commentators, but it is informative and, although unfortunately not engaging in critical analysis, does highlight some valid concerns.[25]

Since *The Organic Development of the Liturgy* was published other material has become available. It is upon these sources that I would like to draw here.

(1) *Francis Cardinal Spellman*

The first of these is the correspondence of the Archbishop of New York, Francis Cardinal Spellman (1889–1967).[26] Communications in 1955 were not what they are today. The text of the 16 November 1955 Decree *Maxima Redemptionis Nostrae Mysteria* was not instantaneously available to the world's bishops; they relied on secular news reports in the first instance. By 30 November, however, a copy had arrived in Chicago and its Archbishop, Samuel Cardinal Stritch (1887–1958), wrote to Cardinal Spellman to correct the impression created in the press and to advise His Eminence that "one thing…is clear, and that is that the Decree strictly binds all who follow the Roman rite." Cardinal Stritch had consulted Edward Cardinal Mooney (1882–1958), the Archbishop of Detroit, who proposed that they should "have a very useful conversation on what to do about some difficulties which our conditions may present."[27] This aroused Cardinal Spellman's concern. On 6 December he replied, "I would be pleased to associate myself in any action which Cardinal Mooney, Cardinal McIntyre [1886–1979, Archbishop of Los Angeles] and yourself desire," noting that "the comments were that some bishops have requested this change but I do not think that any American bishops would sanction it because it will destroy many of our traditional

---

25. One might highlight the abolition, rather than the restoration, of the ancient Vigil of Pentecost as an astonishing and commonly overlooked feature of this reform; see: *Maxima Redemptionis Nostrae Mysteria*, n. 16. See also Gromier's later articles: "Simples réflexions sur des choses restaurées," *Opus Dei* (1961), pp. 248–54; "La Semaine Sainte restaurée," *Opus Dei* (1962), pp. 76–90. A 1936 letter of Mgr Gromier on the possible restoration of the celebration of the paschal vigil is also of interest; see: Robert Amiet, *La Veillée Paschale dans l'Église latine* (Paris: Cerf, 1999), pp. 95–96. The Introduction to his major work, *Commentaire du Caeremoniale Épiscoporum* (Paris: Vieux Colombier, 1959), makes clear his opinion of "les exposants d'une nouvelle école, les conducteurs d'un mouvement liturgique…" (p. 13).

26. I am profoundly grateful to Frs Jon Tveit and Michael Morris of the Archdiocese of New York for facilitating this research.

27. Typewritten letter, 30 November 1955, Archives of the Archdiocese of New York [AANY] S/C 65 f 9.

well attended Holy Week devotions."[28] Following an airport meeting with Cardinal Stritch en route to Korea,[29] Spellman travelled to Rome to make representation to the Sacred Congregation of Rites.[30] Indeed he raised the matter with Pope Pius XII in a private audience and in a subsequent letter, asserting to the Pope that "It is my certain knowledge that those who applauded the Decree are in the very definite minority, while the bishops and priests of my own region are appalled at the confusion that will be caused by the application of such a revolutionary edict." "Not one of the bishops of this country claims to have been consulted," he writes, adding that, "of this fact I am not certain, but I do know that Cardinal Mooney, the only American Cardinal on the Congregation of Rites, has told me he was not consulted." Spellman adds: "After I left Rome to return to the United States I learned with astonishment that many of the bishops and priests of France feel exactly as do the bishops and priests of the United States."[31]

It would appear that Cardinal Spellman was not objecting to the *details* of the liturgical reform itself; whether folded chasubles are retained or not, or whether it is the paschal candle or the triple candle that goes to the fire at the vigil, seems to be of little concern to him. Rather, what worries him is the fact that the reform interfered with people's devotional practices. Only one Mass was to be permitted on Maundy Thursday, in the evening, and the distribution of Holy Communion at other times in the day was not allowed (the faithful were not permitted to receive at the newly restored Chrism Mass). Cardinal Spellman petitioned Pius XII for an indult to distribute Holy Communion to the faithful at the Chrism Mass, and for an indult "transferring one or two of the evening Masses permitted in parish churches to the morning for permitting the faithful to receive Holy Communion." "Otherwise," he wrote to the Pope, "millions of those accustomed to receive Holy Communion on Holy Thursday will be deprived of the opportunity."[32]

---

28. Typewritten letter, 6 December 1955, ibid.

29. See: typewritten letter, 8 December 1955, ibid.

30. Cardinal Spellman's letters prove the oft-repeated story of the English liturgist J. D. Crichton (1907–2001) that "Cardinal Spellman of New York was on his way to Rome to stop it [the Decree] and it had already been published while he was upon high seas" to be false. See: Reid, *Organic Development of the Liturgy*, p. 231.

31. Typewritten letter, 28 January 1956, AANY, S/C 65 f 9.

32. Typewritten letter, 9 March 1956, ibid. The letter continues: "In the cities women are frightened to go out at night because of many and frequent attacks and robberies."

An indult was duly received, but in August 1956 Cardinal Spellman reflected further in a reply to a request from Archbishop Amleto Cicognani (1883–1973), the veteran Apostolic Delegate to the United States, for comments on the new Order of Holy Week:

> I would say that some of the changes were good and some were confusing. It was especially unfortunate that the bishops of this country were not consulted...
>
> The official indult granting permission for Masses on Holy Thursday morning saved the day from creating a most unfortunate situation because it permitted the children to receive Holy Communion. The fact that Holy Communion could only be distributed at these Masses or immediately after resulted in many people being deprived of the opportunity to receive Holy Communion. And it wrung my heart when priests were obliged to decline to give Holy Communion to the faithful who previously had been permitted to receive Holy Communion both at Mass and outside of Mass.
>
> When only one Mass is permitted on the Saturday vigil it is impossible to accommodate all the faithful... The result was that many churches had to close the doors with hundreds of people remaining outside not hearing Mass and naturally disappointed and some irritated and even angry.[33]

In September 1956 Spellman felt "obliged" to write to the Prefect of the Sacred Congregation for Rites, Gaetano Cardinal Cicognani (1881–1962), in view of the approaching International Congress on Pastoral Liturgy that was to be held in Assisi later that month:[34]

> In my opinion and in the opinion of many of my associates, the extremists in the Liturgical movement [sic] have created great confusion not only among the faithful but also among the clergy. The Holy Father is quoted as wishing greater participation of the laity in the Holy Sacrifice of the Mass and other functions, and therefore, some who belong to the school of Cardinal Lercaro wish a greater use of the vernacular. This is a dangerous tendency, your Eminence, for it is just what the communists are doing in trying to foster national churches...
>
> Some of the revisions and adaptations in the Holy Week liturgy can be carried out in monasteries or other religious houses or in small compact parishes, but they create confusion and sometimes pandemonium in our large parishes with thousands of parishioners...

33. Typewritten letter, 3 August 1956, ibid., S/C 65 f. 11.
34. See: Reid, *The Organic Development of the Liturgy*, pp. 237–53.

If we would have our people receive our Blessed Lord on Holy Thursday, why should unnecessary restrictions be placed upon them? Why not permit every priest to say Mass on the day that commemorates the institution of his priesthood and permit the faithful to receive communion at these Masses?[35]

Cardinal Spellman welcomed the 1 February 1957 Decree of the Congregation of Rites containing *Ordinationes* clarifying certain aspects of the reform, but still pressed Pope Pius XII over the issue of "the accommodation, in a reverent manner, of the vast throngs of people, literally millions of persons, who traditionally receive our Eucharistic Lord on the anniversary day of the institution of the Blessed Sacrament and cannot do so in the evening," petitioning for "permission for the celebration of Mass on Holy Thursday morning and the distribution of Holy Communion during the morning hours of that day."[36] Archbishop Cicognani indicated that he had written to the Sacred Congregation for Rites in the same vein.[37]

In 1959, on behalf of the bishops of the Province of New York, Spellman sought and gained another indult so that the faithful could receive blessed palms at the first Mass of the morning. The practice of blessing them only at the later principal Mass meant that "many are deprived of the opportunity of returning to church to receive their palm," he wrote, adding that "this has caused considerable irritation, particularly among mothers of families who are obliged to go to early Mass in order to prepare their children to attend a later Mass."[38]

Cardinal Spellman's papers include a July 1956 letter from Archbishop Edwin O'Hara, Bishop of Kansas City, enclosing a booklet *Favourable Comments on the Restored Holy Week Ordo from the Reports of the Archbishops and Bishops of the United States*. It reports that "of the 19 Archdioceses and 72 dioceses sending in reports, all but two report general enthusiasm for the New Ordo, and the majority GREAT enthusiasm."[39] Perhaps unsurprisingly the booklet contains no comment in the name of the Archdiocese of New York. Indeed, the editor of *Worship*, Godfrey Diekmann OSB, wrote to Fr Antonelli in 1955: "the unfavourable stand taken by Cardinal Spellman of New York is rather well known."[40]

35. Typewritten letter, 11 September 1956, AANY, S/C 65 f 11.
36. Typewritten letter, 25 February 1957, ibid., f 12.
37. Typewritten letter, 28 February 1957, ibid.
38. Typewritten letter, 21 April 1959, ibid. S/C 65 f 9. See also: typewritten letter, 16 March 1960, ibid. S/C 65 f 14 and the appended decree of the Sacred Congregation for Rites dated 18 January 1960, Prot. D. 1/960.
39. Typewritten letter, 19 July 1956, ibid. S/C 65 f 9.
40. See: Reid, *The Organic Development of the Liturgy*, p. 219.

And yet we have seen Spellman write in 1956 that "some of the changes were good" whilst insisting that "some were confusing." It is clear that Spellman was no liturgist: he does not engage in a discussion of the merits of the use of purple or red vestments on Palm Sunday, the number of collects to be used in the blessing of palms, if or where the *Mandatum* should take place or whether or not the Good Friday liturgy should still include the ancient rites of the Mass of the Presanctified. His concerns are practical and pastoral in the sense of wishing to do all in his power to ensure that his people's devotional and sacramental practices are not disturbed or curtailed.

In this Cardinal Spellman serves to highlight one aspect of the Holy Week reform of 1955 that is often missed—that it frequently necessitated a drastic change in people's practice, particularly devotional ones, and that such sudden change could have an adverse pastoral result. The English novelist Evelyn Waugh detested what he called "the triumph of the 'liturgists' in the new arrangement of the services for the end of Holy Week and for Easter."[41] This does not mean that no reform of Holy Week should have taken place. It is evident that in the 1950s the great majority of the faithful were not habitually acquiring "the true Christian spirit...from its foremost and indispensable font, which is the active participation in the most holy mysteries and in the public and solemn prayer of the Church,"[42] let alone from the great liturgical rites of Holy Week.

Something did need to be done, therefore, though rites reformed by a committee working in secret and rapidly imposed with consummate positivism are unlikely to be a recipe for success on the ground, howsoever pleasing they looked on paper. As an Ecumenical Council would later assert about the desire that the people acquire the true Christian spirit through optimal liturgical participation, "it would be futile to entertain any hopes of realizing this unless the pastors themselves, in the first place, become thoroughly imbued with the spirit and power of the liturgy, and undertake to give instruction about it" (*Sacrosanctum Concilium* 14).[43] It seems, though, that little attention was paid to this reality in the preparation and implementation of the 1950s Holy Week reforms.

41. See: Alcuin Reid (ed.), *A Bitter Trial: Evelyn Waugh and John Carmel Cardinal Heenan on the Liturgical Changes*, 3rd edn (San Francisco: Ignatius, 2011), p. 36.

42. Pius X, motu proprio *Tra le sollecitudini*, 22 November 1903; see also: Second Vatican Council, Constitution on the Sacred Liturgy, *Sacrosanctum Concilium*, 4 December 1963, 14.

43. See also: Reid, "Thoroughly Imbued with the Spirit and Power of the Liturgy."

Thus, Cardinal Spellman rightly protested, "it was especially unfortunate that the bishops…were not consulted," as presumably their pastoral wisdom would have mitigated, contributed to and even possibly improved the reform produced by Pius XII's Commission, which was based largely on historical and academic considerations. So too, a consultation and the taking of a prudent amount of time in preparing for the implementation of any truly necessary and desirable reform permits the essential and lengthy foundational work of liturgical formation at least to commence.

As it was, the bishops read news reports in mid-November 1955, saw the Decree some weeks later, received the actual *Ordo Hebdomodae Sanctae* even later still, and were expected under obedience and without question to have all of these changes in place in time for Holy Week in the last week of March 1956.[44] All of this in just over four months! It is no wonder that pastors such as Cardinal Spellman reacted adversely.

Some reform of the Holy Week rites may well have been justifiable in terms of liturgical and historical principles, and also in respect of facilitating true participation in the liturgical rites themselves placed once again at the heart of the spiritual life of the whole Church, as St Pius X desired,[45] but the sudden imposition of this reform impacted quite severely on the piety of clergy, religious and laity.[46] Cardinal Spellman's stance serves at least as a loud and clear reminder that a "pastoral reality-check" is a prerequisite for authentic and fruitful liturgical reform.

44. In a letter to the Apostolic Delegate, Cardinal Spellman complains that "not sufficient time was allowed for the printing and distribution of the Ordo"; typewritten letter, 3 August 1956, AANY, S/C 65 f 11.

45. Some do not see the importance of this principle of Christian life (that the Sacred Liturgy has and should be given the primary place), or appear to dismiss it because it was badly applied in this reform. For an account of the 1955 reform that would appear to give devotional practices priority over the Sacred Liturgy, see: Joseph Shaw (ed.), *The FIUV Position Papers on the 1962 Missal*, 2nd edn (n.p.: Lulu, 2014), pp. 131–50, esp. 139–40. This account gives little consideration to whether any legitimate progress was made in the reform and draws principally on secondary sources (including this author's own work), operating from the assumption that "there is a widespread desire among those attached to the [*usus antiquior*] that the earlier form of these [Holy Week] rites…be allowed for optional use"; p. 131. That there is in fact such a "widespread desire" amongst the parishes, societies and religious institutes celebrating the *usus antiquior* (beyond the uncritical rhetoric pervading some—largely Anglophone—Internet sites, comment boxes and sacristy corners) is a moot point.

46. Lambert Beauduin and Pierre Jounel described it in *La Maison-Dieu* as "une véritable révolution dans leur piété," 45 (1956), p. 7; reproduced in: "La Semaine Sainte en 1955: Un regard d'anticipation," *Notitiae* 24 (1988), pp. 77–78 (77).

(2) *Carlo Braga CM*

The second new source available to us is the recollections of Fr Carlo Braga CM (1927–2014). Whilst Braga was not a member of the Commission for Liturgical Reform until 1960,[47] according to the autobiographical memoir of Archbishop Bugnini published in 2012 he was assigned by his superiors to help his confrère Fr Bugnini around 1950, whilst but a theological student in his early twenties.[48] Their close collaboration in matters of liturgical reform was to last more than two decades.

In November 2005 Fr Braga gave a conference commemorating the 50th anniversary of the 1955 Holy Week reform.[49] His discourse articulates the guiding principles of the Commission's work. The first is "to make the rites of the central days of the liturgical year more comprehensible and to render participation in them easier, and by this to revivify the recurring weekly celebration [of the liturgy]."[50] The second is to restore valuable elements of the rites lost in tradition and to purify the rites from other elements which do not correspond well to the nature of the liturgy or which do not facilitate the full participation of the people. This, Fr Braga asserts, was "a work involving many risks, but one to confront with courage."[51]

The restoration of the *veritas horarum*—of the true times of the celebration of the Holy Week rites—was a primary principle, and one which was seen as crucial in promoting the participation of the faithful. To this is added a "pastoral" principle, indeed a "pastoral preoccupation with a conscious and active participation by the Christian community," which is seen as justifying the introduction of new elements. Fr Braga tells us that "that is what the faithful were asking for, especially those more sensitive to the new spirituality that was manifesting itself and promoting renewal."[52] Overall, Braga asserts: "the Commission, having welcomed the well-founded aspirations of the people of God, addressed

47. See: Bugnini, *The Reform of the Liturgy*, p. 9.
48. See: Annibale Bugnini CM, *Liturgiae Cultor et Amator, Servì la Chiesa* (Rome: Edizione Liturgiche, 2012), p. 52.
49. Published as: Carlo Braga CM, "*Maxima Redemtionis Nostrae Mysteria, 50 Anni Dopo*," *Ecclesia Orans* 23 (2006), pp. 11–36. I am grateful to Fr Paul Gunter OSB for his assistance in obtaining this article.
50. "Rendere più comprensibile e più facile la partecipazione nei riti del giorno centrale dell'anno liturgico, doveva ravvivare la celebrazione della ricorrenza settimanale"; ibid., p. 16.
51. "un lavoro con molti rischi, ma da affrontare con corragio"; ibid., p. 17.
52. "era cio che chiedevano i fedeli, sopratutto quelli piu sensibili alla nuova spiritualita che andava manifestandosi e favorendo il rinnovamento"; ibid., p. 18.

the most delicate part of its work by showing how one could realise a genuine reform of the liturgy in full and scrupulous fidelity to the best liturgical traditions."[53]

In respect of specific days of Holy Week, Braga deprecates the medieval *missa sicca* for the blessing of palms and its anticipation or duplication of rites that would come later in the actual Mass. The use of red vestments for the whole rite is seen as underlining the unity of the entire celebration. He praises the separation of the blessing and consecration of the Holy Oils from the evening Mass of the Lord's Supper—i.e. the restoration of a distinct "Chrism Mass" on Holy Thursday morning—but recognises the problem articulated by Cardinal Spellman above, that following the 1955 reform not all priests were able to celebrate Mass themselves on the very day on which the Church recalls the institution of the sacred priesthood. In this respect he laments that the mentality of certain members of the Commission was not yet open to the introduction of sacramental concelebration. Ceremonial concelebration, for which there is some basis in tradition, was ruled out.[54] The direction that priests attending should wear the stole over choir dress for the entire Mass and should receive Holy Communion was the resultant compromise.

Braga asserts that the reform of the Good Friday liturgy respected the rites coming from a sound tradition, making only small, if significant, changes.[55] He notes that the solemn prayers of the rite were slightly modified (though he says—clearly *a posteriori*—that the completion of this work, for example in respect of the prayer for the Jews, would have to wait until the reform of Paul VI). The simplification of the adoration of the Cross and the introduction of a collective adoration where members of the faithful were large in number is praised. So too is what he calls the "true novelty of the reform of Good Friday," the introduction of the reception of Holy Communion by all the participants. On this question Braga reveals that the Commission had recourse to Pope Pius XII himself, who saw no difficulty in its introduction.[56]

53. "La commissione, ha accolto le aspirazioni fondate del popolo di Dio e, affrontando la parte più delicata del suo lavoro, ha mostrato come si potesse realizzare una vera revisione della liturgia in fedeletà piena e scrupulosa alle migliori tradizioni liturgiche"; ibid., p. 18.

54. On the history of concelebration see: Alcuin Reid, "Concelebration Today, Yesterday and Tomorrow," in *The Holy Eucharist—The World's Salvation*, by Joseph de Sainte-Marie OCD (Leominster: Gracewing, 2015), pp. xvii–xxxix.

55. "La riforma ha rispettato i riti provenienti da una tradizione santa. I cambiamenti sono stati pochi, anche se significativi"; Braga, "*Maxima Redemtionis Nostrae Mysteria*, 50 Anni Dopo," p. 29.

56. See: ibid., p. 32.

There was, however, a difficulty in the eyes of the Commission with the existing rite containing the Mass of the Presanctified with its offertorial rites, use of incense and the sanctification of unconsecrated wine in a chalice—Braga rather blithely asserts that maintaining all this was simply "not possible."[57] Whereas "the linearity and the severity of the [restored] rites of Good Friday," Braga states, "come from the earliest tradition. The addition of sacramental communion was a sign of full participation in the mystery of the Body and Blood of the Lord immolated for us."[58]

The reformed paschal vigil of 1951, with the refinements made by the 1952 *Ordinationes*, is not discussed in detail, but is described, if not celebrated, as "the head of the battering-ram which penetrated the fortress of our hitherto static liturgy."[59] Such violent language is nothing if not telling in the approach it has to received liturgical tradition and to liturgical development. Indeed, it betrays a defective understanding of liturgical tradition which was shared by others at the time.[60]

Overall, Fr Braga underlines the fundamental aspect of the reform, in principal and in its realisation, as being of a "pastoral and spiritual nature,"[61] noting that it brought about "a simplification of rites that had become prolix in a manner to render participation easier and more understandable."[62] Writing in 2005, he adds that the rites of Holy Week enjoyed a "surge of openness and of true renewal" following the Council.[63]

b. *Some Analysis*
It is clear that for Braga the achievement of liturgy that is truly pastoral and participative requires the simplification of rites, indeed their purging of anything that is not seen as *directly* serving those aims. In *The Organic*

57. "Non si poteva mantenere il rito vigente ne si poteva inserivi materialmente il rito della communione fuori dell a Messa"; ibid.

58. "La linearità e la severità dei riti del venerdì santo vengono mantenute della tradizione pimitiva. Vi si agguinge l'atto sacramentale della comunione, come segno di partecipazione piena al mistero del corpo e del sangue del Signore immolato per noi"; ibid., p. 33.

59. "la testa d'ariete che è penetrate nella fortezza della nostra liturgia ormai statica"; ibid.

60. For an analysis of this see: Reid, *The Organic Development of the Liturgy*, pp. 204–5; also pp. 287–89.

61. "aspetto fondamentale di principio e di realizzazione...la sua natura pastorale e spirituale"; Braga, "*Maxima Redemtionis Nostrae Mysteria*, 50 Anni Dopo," p. 35.

62. "una semplificazione dei riti divenuti prolissi, in modo da renderne più facile el più comprensibile la partecipazione"; ibid., n. 25.

63. "dopo il Concilio ha subito uno slancio di aperture e di vero rinnovamento"; ibid.

Development of the Liturgy I named this stance "pastoral expediency." This is undoubtedly a prominent feature of elements of the 1955 reform of Holy Week and of some if not many of the reforms that would follow. Almost *anything* that was not deemed pastorally expedient was at risk of abolition (hence the loss of many ancient and beautiful customs and ceremonies) and *any* innovation that seemed to serve a directly pastoral or participative end was welcomed, at times regardless of liturgical or theological reservations.[64]

This stance assumes the impossibility of full and fruitful participation in the unreformed rites. In a way it patronises both the clergy and the faithful by absolving them of any need to work toward the one true requirement for full, conscious and actual participation in the Sacred Liturgy, namely liturgical formation—thorough immersion in the spirit and power of the liturgy. In its inherent haste, reform by pastoral expediency does not take the time necessary to lay down deep or solid foundations, and this is its danger. "Modern man" needs these foundations, even more perhaps than his ancestors. There is little point in giving him hastily constructed new rites if he does not yet have the habit of fruitful participation in the existing ones. And if he is in fact habituated thus, the "urgency" of ritual reform itself recedes. This assumption—that new, simplified rites will automatically bring about fruitful participation—is, I submit, the greatest flaw of liturgical reformers and reforms from the 1950s onward.

Indeed, it is clear today that the liturgical formation that many of those attached to the *usus antiquior* have gained amidst, and at times in spite of, the liturgical turmoil of the recent decades is more than sufficient to achieve fruitful participation in the Sacred Liturgy—I am referring here to much more than only the rites of Holy Week. Indeed it is a significant contemporary phenomenon that many young Catholics find the unreformed rites (of the Mass and sacraments) entirely new, rich and challenging in an otherwise rather bland liturgical environment. With the aid of some clergy, and in particular of information technology, they form themselves and slake their thirst from the riches of our tradition.[65]

To return to the Pian Holy Week reform: in the 1950s something did need to be done. The restoration of the *veritas horarum* for the times of the celebration of the liturgical rites is most certainly one area where

---

64. Such as the introduction of the renewal of baptismal vows by the people at the paschal vigil; see: Reid, *The Organic Development of the Liturgy*, p. 176.

65. See: Matthew R. Menendez's contribution to the present volume, "Youth and the Liturgy." The danger of being malformed by erroneous practices and opinions uncritically reproduced on the Internet needs to be guarded against. Authoritative sources should be checked before imitating what one sees online.

reform was necessary, reasonable and likely to truly bring about greater and more fruitful participation in the Sacred Liturgy. We know from Cardinal Spellman that the very sudden imposition of the new times of the Holy Week rites caused significant turmoil and that in hindsight it would have been prudent, pastorally, to have both consulted over this and taken time to prepare laity and clergy for the required changes. Taking that legitimate criticism into account, nevertheless the reform of the times of the celebration of the Holy Week rites was and is an example of legitimate progress, indeed an example of the restoration of sound tradition where it had been lost over the centuries.

The restoration of the Chrism Mass is another example, though the Mass formula in the 1955 *Ordo* is not beyond criticism.[66] So too, permitting the reception of Holy Communion on Good Friday, albeit an innovation, may be considered a justifiable pastoral reform that clearly facilitates greater participation in the rites—nothing less than the sacramental reception of Holy Communion—and in the very mystery at the heart of the Church's Good Friday liturgy. It was, after all, Pius XII himself who judged this to be apposite. To this (non-exhaustive) list I would add the removal of the historically and liturgically dubious duplication of the readings by the priest celebrant, the removal of the prayers for the long-since non-existent Roman Emperor and even the recognition that at the time the ancient custom of the use of folded chasubles and the broad stole was simply not a possibility in most parishes or churches—because they did not have them.[67] In my opinion it is always better to allow such customs which augment and do no violence to the liturgy and can be very beautiful (such as the use of folded chasubles) to die a natural death if they must, or indeed to live on where they can, for at least then one is not guilty of a form of positivistic liturgical slaughter. But of course the existence of "options" in liturgical rites, whilst something with which we are very familiar today, was a foreign category for rubrics then.[68]

---

66. See: Bugnini, *The Reform of the Liturgy*, pp. 116–17.

67. See: Bugnini and Braga, *Ordo Hebdomadae Sanctae instauratus commentarium*, pp. 56–57 n. 28. Their commentary concludes: "Proprium indumentum diaconi est dalmatica et subdiaconi tunicella, non planeta. Tempus poenitentialis satis distinguitur a tempore festivo diversitate coloris."

68. It is somewhat ironic, and not well understood, that a traditional principle of not permitting options in the rubrics, combined with the reality that very few churches had folded chasubles and a broad stole to use, combined to bring about their replacement by the dalmatic and tunicle. That this was anything more than a natural and reasonable historical shift is difficult to demonstrate.

The great question in respect of the 1955 Holy Week reform amongst some Catholics today is whether or not we can or should return to the use of the pre-1955 rites. I submit that the question may itself be somewhat problematic because of an uncritical traditionalism from which it often arises: some legitimate progress was made in this reform and that can and should not be jettisoned.[69] Are we truly to re-impose the celebration of the paschal vigil in the early hours of Holy Saturday morning and remove the other ceremonies from their authentic times? Are we now, sixty years after it has been given annually, to deny people Holy Communion on Good Friday? Is the Chrism Mass summarily to be abolished?[70]

I would suggest, therefore, that the question should rather be: How could the legitimate progress made in the 1955 reform be retained, and how could some of the beautiful and valuable rites that were lost be restored to the celebration of these rites today? An answer is, I would think, not at all impossible, but it would involve much critical and dispassionate study as well as a good deal of liturgical and pastoral maturity and prudence.[71] A simple return to the "pre-1955" package is not an option liturgically, devotionally or culturally at the beginning of the twenty-first century. It is our task to pray and work, according to God's Providence and our particular vocation, for the retention—and, where necessary, the

69. It is, I think, instructive that as renowned a traditionalist as Michael Davies (1936–2004) would write of the Pian Holy Week reforms: "There were sound reasons behind all the reforms and the continuity with the previous ceremonies was evident"; *An Open Lesson to a Bishop: On the Development of the Roman Rite* (Rockford: TAN Books, 1980), p. 28. So too, as Davies points out, it is instructive that Archbishop Marcel Lefebvre (1905–1991) used the 1955 reformed rites of Holy Week in his seminary and priestly society. The "traditionalist" credentials of neither can be doubted; nor can their ability to make critical distinctions in the history of the liturgy. Whilst neither used the phrase, one may assert that they found the Pian reforms to be sufficiently in substantial continuity with received liturgical tradition regardless, perhaps, of some of the problems of that reform. The post-conciliar reform, however, one may assert, they found to be a substantial rupture.

70. Before the Pian reform the oils were blessed and consecrated at the one pontifical Mass of Holy Thursday (in the morning); i.e. there was no separate "Chrism" Mass.

71. Though such a delicate work is made increasingly difficult by the stance of the Pontifical Commission *Ecclesia Dei* that its competence solely to implement the liturgical books in force in 1962 precludes its involvement in any such question. The Congregation for Divine Worship and Discipline of the Sacraments is held to be the competent dicastery. The bureaucratic *impasse* that this reality creates could, realistically, only be overcome by higher authority.

recovery—of *sound* tradition as well as to be open to the true pastoral good that legitimate progress in the development of the Sacred Liturgy can and does bring.

4. *The Reforms of Paul VI*

The *Constitution on the Sacred Liturgy* of the Second Vatican Council, *Sacrosanctum Concilium*, does not specifically mention further reform of the Holy Week rites. On the Council floor the closest the Fathers came in the consideration of chapter 5, on the liturgical year, were some considerations on the extension of the Lenten fast to the evening of Holy Saturday that had been effected by the restoration of the *veritas horarum* of the paschal vigil.[72] Thus article 110 of the Constitution calls for the fast to be prolonged throughout Holy Saturday "where possible." The authoritative commentary on the Constitution, edited by Frs Bugnini and Braga, is similarly silent on any further Holy Week reform.[73] There is no doubt that the various liturgical reforms of the previous decade had impacted significantly on the Council Fathers and one might reasonably infer from their silence *in aula*, and the silence of contemporary commentators, that many if not most of the assembled bishops did not see a need to revise Holy Week once again.

Nevertheless, the Constitution on the Sacred Liturgy called for "a general restoration of the liturgy" (*ipsius Liturgiae generalem instaurationem*, n. 21) and stated that "the liturgical books are to be revised as soon as possible" (n. 25). It is therefore no surprise that the organisation of the *Consilium ad exsequendam Constitutionem de Sacra Liturgia* included a study group (n. 17) "On particular rites in the liturgical year," which would consider the Holy Week rites in the light of the principles of liturgical reform articulated in *Sacrosanctum Concilium*.[74]

---

72. See: Francisco Gil Hellín, *Concilii Vaticani II Synopsis: Constitutio de Sacra Liturgia Sacrosanctum Concilium* (Vatican City: Liberia Editrice Vaticana, 2003), pp. 332–35.

73. See: A. Bugnini CM and C. Braga CM (eds), *The Commentary on the Constitution and on the Instruction on the Sacred Liturgy* (New York: Benziger Brothers, 1965).

74. Relator, Msgr Pietro Borella; secretary, Adrien Nocent OSB; members, Msgr Joseph Pascher, Pierre Jounel, John H. Miller CSC, Ferdinand Kolbe, Rinaldo Falsini OFM and Abbot Jean Gaillard OSB. In 1965 Msgr Mario Righetti became relator and François Vandenbrouke OSB secretary. Anton Hänggi was subsequently appointed a second relator; Msgr Pascher took Hänggi's place after his consecration as Bishop of Basel in 1968; see: Bugnini, *The Reform of the Liturgy*, p. 402.

Archbishop Bugnini recalls that "a further updating of the whole week so that it would be in harmony with the style of the restored liturgy" was needed.[75] This seems a little curious and to be an entirely *post-factum* assertion, as surely "the style of the restored liturgy" was not a known quantity when the study groups were established early in 1964. That curiosity aside, he states that:

> The group had to be concerned to save elements dear to the tradition and the devotion of the faithful without at the same time overburdening the liturgy of these sacred days. [It] began with a careful theological, historical, and pastoral study of the entire matter, with a view to restoring the rites to their authentic original form and making them pastorally more effective.[76]

That another "careful theological, historical, and pastoral study of the entire matter" was necessary just ten years following the last reform of Holy Week seems to be either an astounding indictment of the work of the Pian Commission in the 1950s, or a clear indication that, in spite of all the work done in the previous decade, after the Council another spirit (or set of personal agendas) prevailed and that *everything* needed to be conformed to it.

The first fruit of the Study Group was the March 1965 *Variationes in ordinem Hebdomadae Sanctae Inducendae*,[77] which promulgated new texts and rites for the Chrism Mass and some revised solemn prayers for Good Friday in the light of certain contemporary ecumenical and inter-faith sensibilities. This is a small retouching of the 1955 rites, displaying certain tendencies to be sure, but it is not another root-and-branch reform. In the same month an indult was granted by the Sacred Congregation for Rites permitting non-deacons to sing the Passion where necessary.[78]

The post-Vatican II reform of Holy week was the product of the ongoing work of Study Group 17, and this requires detailed analysis. Their 15 working documents (*schemata*) produced from 1964 and 1968 show that, in a manner similar to the *schema* of Group 10 working on the new *Ordo Missae*, the members were proposing a more radical reform earlier on and somewhat tempered their desires as time went on.[79] The task of

75. Ibid.
76. Ibid.
77. (Vatican City: Typis Polyglottis Vaticanis, 1965).
78. Dated 25 March 1965; see: *L'Osservatore Romano*, 28 March 1965, p. 1.
79. Coetus XVII—De ritibus peculiaribus in anno liturgico: Schema n. 51 (de anno liturgico, 1), 25 iunii 1964; Schema n. 51 (de anno liturgico, 1 bis), sept. 1964;

a detailed examination of their work is not possible here. Nevertheless we should note that it is one of the supreme ironies of twentieth-century liturgical history that the paschal vigil of the 1970 missal of Paul VI contains at least the option of more readings from Sacred Scripture than that promulgated in the reform of Pius XII. The Study Group did, at least in this instance, address one of the unfortunate aspects of the 1955 reform.

Another small but not insignificant element of the post-conciliar reform worth noting is the transformation of the Chrism Mass into a "feast of the priesthood." Archbishop Bugnini reveals that this idea originated with Paul VI himself, "who, as Archbishop of Milan had annually emphasised this special meaning of Holy Thursday..." Bugnini continues:

> The more austere liturgists were vexed by the new turn. They reluctantly resigned themselves to saying farewell to the centuries-old liturgy that had focussed the Chrism Mass on the consecration of the oils as the foundation of all consecrations in the Church and as an immediate preparation for the baptism of catechumens during the Easter Vigil. Gradually, however, the new approach made its way, and finally everyone acknowledged that the pastoral reasons for it were persuasive and justified the sacrifice of a cherished tradition.[80]

Archbishop Bugnini also recounts the motivation for the alteration of the solemn prayers of Good Friday:

> In the ecumenical climate of Vatican II, some expressions in the *Orationes sollemnes* of the Good Friday service had a bad ring to them. There were urgent requests to tone down some of the wording.
>
> It is always unpleasant to have to alter venerable texts that for centuries have effectively nourished Christian devotion and have about them the spiritual fragrance of the heroic age of the Church's beginnings. Above

---

Schema n. 51 (de anno liturgico, 1 ter), 30 nov. 1964; Schema n. 55 (de anno liturgico, 2), 27 feb. 1965; Schema n. 55 (de anno liturgico, 2 bis), apr. 1965; Schema n. 104 (de anno liturgico, 3), 10 sept. 1965; Schema n. 246 (de anno liturgico, 4), 4 oct. 1967; Schema n. 246 (de anno liturgico, 4—addendum I), 13 nov. 1967; Schema n. 246 (de anno liturgico, 4—addendum II), 20 nov. 1967; Schema n. 246 (de anno liturgico, 4—addendum III), 27 nov. 1967; Schema n. 278 (de anno liturgico, 5), 21 martii 1968; Schema n. 278 (de anno liturgico, 5—addendum), 24 apr. 1968; Schema n. 304 (de anno liturgico, 6), 2 sept. 1968; Schema n. 304 (de anno liturgico, 6—addendum), 8 oct. 1968. I am grateful to the ICEL Secretariat, Washington, DC, for making a number of these documents available from their archive.

80. Bugnini, *Reform of the Liturgy*, p. 117.

all, it is difficult to revise literary masterpieces that are unsurpassed for their pithy form. It was nevertheless thought necessary to face up to the task, lest anyone find reason for spiritual discomfort in the prayer of the Church.[81]

In its development down the centuries the Sacred Liturgy, most especially in its pregnant and charged rites of Holy Week, preserved "venerable texts [and rites] that for centuries...effectively nourished Christian devotion" and indeed had about them "the spiritual fragrance of the heroic age of the Church's beginnings," and for good reason. Whilst we may regret the loss of some such rites and texts in the reforms of the 1950s, their purging according to the spirit prevailing following the Council in the 1960s—evidenced by Archbishop Bugnini above—moves liturgical reform from what may be regarded as an overly pastorally expedient and antiquarian revision in the 1950s to what appears to be, at least in part, an intentional theological and ritual deconstruction and an ideological reconstruction in the 1960s.[82]

There is indeed very much to be studied about the post-conciliar reform of the rites of Holy Week, and any such study needs to address precisely this issue, the question of development in continuity or of intentional discontinuity and its extent. For it seems to become clearer and clearer that after the Council:

> Some have set up their self-made liturgy. They have stepped out of the living process of growing and becoming and gone over to making. They no longer wanted to continue the organic *becoming* and *maturing* of something that had been alive down the centuries, and instead they replaced it—according to the model of a technical production—with *making*, the insipid product of the moment.[83]

81. Ibid., p. 119. A list of the revisions made to each prayer follows.

82. Goddard's assertion, that "the 1955 reforms, though they introduced some profound changes in the rites...made few changes to the text and rubrics, so that the character of the Holy Week services was hardly affected at all. By contrast, the 1970 changes, and the manner in which they were carried into effect in individual churches, were of such a radical nature that the services as performed today frequently bear little resemblance to the traditional ones" (*Festa Paschalia*, p. 289), may be somewhat clumsy in its analysis, but it does point to a discontinuity that is real, particularly in the manner in which the rites are celebrated today—an important consideration which takes us beyond the liturgical books as promulgated and which, perhaps, brings us back to the reality of cotton-wool paschal fires or YouTube recordings of "creative" Holy Week rites.

83. Joseph Ratzinger, *Theology of the Liturgy*, Collected Works, vol. 11 (San Francisco: Ignatius, 2014), pp. 537–38.

5. *Conclusion*

Has sound tradition been retained and legitimate progress made? In truth, I think it is difficult to say. In the Pian reforms elements of progress are certainly identifiable, but so too are questionable innovations and unfortunate if not unnecessary losses. I think we can say that in the Pian reform of Holy Week the Roman rite suffered injuries—some minor ones and some that were larger—whilst also being healed of some longstanding lesions. What was introduced into the organism was not sufficiently disproportionate to kill it. In the Pauline reforms we seem to find much more substantial injuries, even theological ones, as well as far greater—if not indeed substantial—innovation. Whether in total these were more than a living body is able to tolerate is the crucial question for future scholarship.

What I would observe is that several decades later neither the reforms enacted on the rites of Holy Week in particular nor the liturgical reform in general have resulted in the liturgical and ecclesial renewal their architects and promoters anticipated. The current Cardinal Archbishop of New York is not troubled by the numbers unable to receive Holy Communion on Holy Thursday, or having to close the doors of churches on Holy Saturday because they are overfull—he is permanently closing churches that have long since been empty. There are many reasons for this, including social and demographic ones. But there are liturgical ones also: it is evident that the rites constructed half a century ago are not, of themselves, a vital part of the solution to the absence of "modern man" from our churches.

In respect of this issue I would like fervently to repeat my appeal for further study of the reforms of Holy Week. We are urgently in need of studies that seek to understand the riches of the rites received in tradition and that seek to conserve all that is good in them; studies that are open to legitimate progress and are critical and balanced, which neither disproportionately idolise smaller elements of the tradition nor dismiss them with undue haste; studies which respect the reality that we cannot take short-cuts in the development and reform of the Sacred Liturgy and which presume and promote the work of formation necessary for true, conscious and fruitful participation in the Holy Week rites, or indeed in any rites whatsoever.[84]

---

84. It is encouraging that at least one study of these reforms has been attempted in recent years; see: Shawn P. Tunink, *Holy Week in the 1950s: The Liturgical Reforms of Pope Pius XII*, unpublished STL thesis (Mundelein: University of St Mary of the Lake, 2013). See also: idem, "Restoring the Easter Vigil: A Look at One of the Holy Week Reforms of Pius XII," *Thesauri Ecclesiae* 8 (2013), pp. 19–29.

Only with this perspective, I submit, can our judgments on the reforms of Holy Week in the past, and our decisions on the celebration of these rites today and in the future, enjoy that integrity and share in that truth of which St Cyprian of Carthage insisted—an integrity and truth which is due to the Sacred Liturgy and to our Lord and God Himself, present and acting in a singular and privileged way in our world in and through the Church's sacred rites.

LITURGICAL FORMATION AND CATHOLIC IDENTITY

Christopher Smith

1. *Introduction*

Pope Pius XII's encyclical *Mediator Dei* is often seen as the Magisterium's stamp of approval on the liturgical movement.[1] This document charted a course for the Church between archaeologism and restorationism, on the one hand, and innovation and experimentation, on the other. The central insights of the liturgical, biblical and patristic movements in the theology of the first half of the twentieth century were enshrined in an official document of the Church. Today, liturgical traditionalists look back at *Mediator Dei* and see in it a positive force integrating the main principles of the classical liturgical movement, as well as a prophetic voice warning against the excesses of calls for reform removed from the tradition. What many people fail to notice, however, is that Pius XII makes a revolutionary claim that, the closer we examine it, might be said to be in some way responsible for the current situation in which we find ourselves: namely, where liturgical "wars" of sixty years have produced deep divisions among Catholics.

In *Mediator Dei* n. 48, Pius XII claims, "If one desires to differentiate and describe the relationship between faith and the Sacred Liturgy in absolute and general terms, it is perfectly correct to say, 'Lex credendi legem statuat supplicandi'—let the rule of belief determine the rule of prayer." Earlier in the same paragraph, the pontiff quotes Prosper of Aquitaine: "legem credendi lex statuat supplicandi."[2] He goes on to state:

> The Sacred Liturgy, consequently, does not decide or determine independently and of itself what is of Catholic faith. More properly, since the liturgy is also a profession of eternal truths, and subject, as such, to the supreme teaching authority of the Church, it can supply proofs and testimony, quite clearly, of no little value, towards the determination of a particular point of Christian doctrine.

1. 20 November 1947; Acta Apostolicae Sedis 39 (1947), pp. 521–95.
2. De gratia Dei "Induculus," quoted at footnote 45 of *Mediator Dei*.

The context of the paragraph makes it clear that Pius is bolstering an argument for the right of the hierarchical Church to reform the liturgy, contrary to those who wish to introduce changes on their own.[3] What Pius does not seem to be doing here is making a theological assertion that the law of belief is antecedent chronologically, logically or theologically, to the law of prayer. But the unfortunate consequence of the way in which this assertion is proposed, when removed from its proper context, is that it effectively reverses the old axiom, *lex orandi, lex credendi.* The use of the quotation from the *Induculus* removes it from its context as well, which was in discussing orthodox faith and prayer on grace against the Pelagian heresy, not as a theological truth of the relationship between the *regula fidei* and the *Ecclesia orans. Mediator Dei* makes an assertion about the priority of faith over prayer based on a reversal of the axiom: in the original quote, it is the law of prayer which establishes the law of belief. In the Pian recension, it is the law of belief, seen as the deposit of faith guarded by the hierarchical Church, which establishes the law of prayer, which, because it is subject to the authority of the hierarchical Church, is obviously secondary.

Aidan Kavanagh (1929–2006), an influential Benedictine liturgical theologian, not ordinarily associated with restorationist liturgical circles, comments upon this quote:

> To reverse the maxim, subordinating the standard of worship to the standard of belief, makes a shambles of the dialectic of revelation. It was a Presence, not faith, which drew Moses to the burning bush, and what happened there was a revelation, not a seminar. It was a Presence, not faith, which drew the disciples to Jesus, and what happened there was not an educational program but His revelation to them of Himself as the long-promised Anointed One... To reverse this is to cancel out the meaning of the maxim

---

3. See: *Mediator Dei* nn. 59–60: "The Sacred Liturgy, consequently, does not decide or determine independently and of itself what is of Catholic faith. More properly, since the liturgy is also a profession of eternal truths, and subject, as such, to the supreme teaching authority of the Church, it can supply proofs and testimony, quite clearly, of no little value, towards the determination of a particular point of Christian doctrine. The use of the Latin language, customary in a considerable portion of the Church, is a manifest and beautiful sign of unity, as well as an effective antidote for any corruption of doctrinal truth. In spite of this, the use of the mother tongue in connection with several of the rites may be of much advantage to the people. But the Apostolic See alone is empowered to grant this permission. It is forbidden, therefore, to take any action whatever of this nature without having requested and obtained such consent, since the Sacred Liturgy, as We have said, is entirely subject to the discretion and approval of the Holy See."

in its original formulation. The law of belief does *not* constitute the law of worship. Thus the creeds and the reasoning which produced them are not the forces which produced baptism. Baptism gave rise to the Trinitarian creeds. So too the Eucharist produced, but was not produced by, a scriptural text, the Eucharistic prayer, or all the various scholarly theories concerning the Eucharistic presence. Influenced by, yes. Constituted or produced by, no.[4]

What does this mean for Catholic identity? With the hindsight of almost seventy years since *Mediator Dei*, it appears that there are now three general trends that can be identified among Catholics. First, there are those who have accepted the Pian reversal of Prosper in such a way as to maintain that, as long as the Catechism enshrines orthodox doctrine on faith and morals, the hierarchical Church can do whatever it wants with the liturgy, because it is secondary, and it really does not matter.[5] Second, there are those who have downplayed Pius's cautions against the reform and argued that the renewal sought by Vatican II still has not happened, and further reform is needed.[6] Third, there are those who argue that the priority of the *Ecclesia Orans* over the *regula fidei* necessitates a restoration of some previous liturgical books or the reform of the current legally promulgated ones in a way as to reverse the reversal.[7]

It is easy to see that each of the three concepts is productive of, and responsive to, very different ecclesiologies. They also produce and are responsive to very different ideas of Catholic identity. The first school of thought is difficult to sustain because it is essentially founded on an equivocation of an ancient text, and as such, flawed *ab initio*. The second is unsustainable as well, because it argues for a further development of the Pian revolution, without regard to an inherently rationalist spirit within it contrary to both *regula fidei* and *Ecclesia orans*. Here, we hope to explore how Catholic identity can be restored through a thorough examination of the liturgical reform and how authentic renewal can re-establish the axiom of Prosper and assist the liturgy in recovering its true nature within a Church which discovers its identity from it.

4. A. Kavanagh, *On Liturgical Theology: The Hale Memorial Lectures of Seabury-Western Theological Seminary 1981* (Collegeville: The Liturgical Press, 1992), p. 92.

5. This seems to be the argument in J. Likoudis and K. Whitehead, *The Pope, the Council and the Mass* (Boston: Christopher Publishing House, 1981).

6. This seems to the argument in P. Marini, *A Challenging Reform: Realizing the Vision of the Liturgical Renewal* (Collegeville: The Liturgical Press, 2007).

7. This seems to be the argument in L. Dobszay, *The Restoration and Organic Development of the Roman Rite* (London: T&T Clark, 2010).

2. *The Authentic Interpretation of Vatican II's Mandate for Liturgical Reform*

a. *Ecumenical Councils and Liturgical Reform:* Potestas Reformandi *Belongs to the* Munera Regendi *and* Sanctificandi

As mentioned above, Pius XII was careful to protect the hierarchy's right to reform the liturgy.[8] In doing so, however, he was not innovating. The Council of Trent in its 25th session mandates a commission of Council Fathers to "consider what ought to be done" and then "commands whatever has been done by them be given over to the most holy Roman pontiff" as regards the catechism, the missal and the breviary.[9] It was not the first time the Pope had taken it on his own authority to do something to the liturgy,[10] but it is the first time an ecumenical council mandated a group of Fathers to make recommendations to the Pope on the revision and publication of liturgical texts for the use of the Church at large.

As Pius XII had succinctly stated in *Mediator Dei,* based on the 1917 Code of Canon Law: "the Sovereign Pontiff alone enjoys the right to recognize and establish any practice touching the worship of God, to introduce and approve new rites, as also to modify those he judges to require modification."[11] This right of the Sovereign Pontiff has been reiterated closer to our own time in the 1983 *Code of Canon Law:*

8. *Mediator Dei* n. 44: "Since, therefore, it is the priest chiefly who performs the Sacred Liturgy in the name of the Church, its organization, regulation and details cannot but be subject to Church authority." N. 58: "The Sovereign Pontiff alone enjoys the right to recognize and establish any practice touching the worship of God, to introduce and approve new rites, as also to modify those he judges to require modification. Bishops, for their part, have the right and duty carefully to watch over the exact observance of the prescriptions of the sacred canons respecting divine worship. Private individuals, therefore, even though they be clerics, may not be left to decide for themselves in these holy and venerable matters, involving as they do the religious life of Christian society along with the exercise of the priesthood of Jesus Christ and worship of God."

9. See: https://www.ewtn.com/library/COUNCILS/TRENT25.HTM#8.

10. For a discussion of Pope St Gregory the Great's (590–604) reforms of the liturgy, see: F. Holmes Dudden, *Gregory the Great: His Place in History and Thought* (London: Longmans & Co., 1905), pp. 264–83. For a discussion of the contributions of Leo the Great and Gelasius to liturgical reform, see: J. Jungmann, *The Early Liturgy to the Time of Gregory the Great* (Notre Dame: University of Notre Dame Press, 1959), p. 236.

11. *Mediator Dei* n. 58, footnote 50, refers to the 1917 *Codex iuris canonici Pii X Pontificis Maximi iussu digestus Benedicti Papae XV auctoritate promulgatus* (Rome: Typis Polyglottis Vaticanis, 1917), para. 1257.

> The direction of the Sacred Liturgy depends solely on the authority of the Church which resides in the Apostolic See and, according to the norm of law, the diocesan bishop... It is for the Apostolic See to order the Sacred Liturgy of the universal Church, publish liturgical books and review their translations in vernacular languages, and exercise vigilance that liturgical regulations are observed faithfully everywhere. (c. 838§1–2)

The *Catechism of the Catholic Church*, however, recognizes limits to that power: "Even the supreme authority in the Church may not change the liturgy arbitrarily, but only in the obedience of faith and with religious respect for the mystery of the liturgy" (n. 1125).

From a theological point of view, this means that the Roman Pontiff has a *potestas*, as part of his immediate and universal jurisdiction, as an exercise of the Petrine primacy, to engage in liturgical reform, but only in accord with the nature of the liturgy itself. The exercise of this power is intimately linked to the *munus sanctificandi*, because, as the 1983 Code of Canon Law states, "the Church fulfills its sanctifying function in a particular way through the Sacred Liturgy" (c. 834§1). It is also intimately linked to the *munus regendi*, because the Pope, as the Code makes clear, "possesses supreme, full, immediate, and universal ordinary power in the Church, which he is always able to exercise freely" (c. 331).

Therefore, it is clear that the Roman Pontiff has the power to change and regulate the liturgy of the Church, and he can be assisted in this by Ecumenical Councils, the work of the Roman curia, and the collaboration of episcopal conferences and individual bishops.

b. *What Sacrosanctum Concilium Mandated*

The exercise of this power was evident in the Constitution on the Sacred Liturgy of the Second Vatican Council. In chapter III of *Sacrosanctum Concilium*, the Council Fathers mandated: "In order that the Christian people may more certainly derive an abundance of graces from the Sacred Liturgy, holy Mother Church desires to undertake with great care a general restoration of the liturgy itself" (n. 21). They were careful to reiterate that this was to happen only under the guidance of Rome: "Regulation of the Sacred Liturgy depends solely on the authority of the Church, that is, on the Apostolic See" (n. 22§1). But what is this mandate for?

> That sound tradition may be retained, and yet the way remain open to legitimate progress careful investigation is always to be made into each part of the liturgy which is to be revised. This investigation should be theological, historical, and pastoral. Also the general laws governing the structure and meaning of the liturgy must be studied in conjunction with the experience

derived from recent liturgical reforms and from the indults conceded to various places. Finally, there must be no innovations unless the good of the Church genuinely and certainly requires them; and care must be taken that any new forms adopted should in some way grow organically from forms already existing. (n. 23)

First of all, the document asks for a restoration of the Sacred Liturgy. This implies that there was something lacking in the Church's experience of worship which had been there at one time, and needed to be returned to, but the document does not explicitly say what needs to be restored. The context seems to suggest that the active participation of the faithful is what should be restored. The mandate of the Council is to retain what promoted that goal, and to change, only after study, only what did not promote that goal and in such a way as it would promote that goal.

The document then goes on to give certain principles that would guide the reform: noble simplicity of rites that could be understood by the faithful, more access to scripture in the rites and preaching, the preservation of Latin and permission for the vernacular in readings, directives and some prayers and chants (nn. 34–36). Subsequent chapters give general guidelines for the reform of the ritual (n. 63b), the restoration of the catechumenate (n. 64), the revision of the sacraments (n. 66–70) and sacramentals (nn. 79–82), the Divine Office (nn. 89–93) and the liturgical year (n. 107).

c. *The Consilium versus the Congregation of Rites*

The Sacred Congregation for Rites had been established by Pope Sixtus V in 1588 in order to assist the Pope in exercising his power over matters liturgical. It was expected that the Congregation would oversee the reform mandated by *Sacrosanctum Concilium*. On 25 January 1964, however, Pope Paul VI issued a motu proprio, *Sacram Liturgiam*, that established "a special commission whose principal task will be to implement in the best possible way the prescriptions of the Constitution on Sacred Liturgy."[12] This committee was known as the *Consilium ad exsequendam Constitutionem liturgicam Sacrosanctum concilium*, or *Consilium*, for short.[13]

---

12. See: A. Bugnini, "Commentary on *Sacram Liturgiam*," *The Furrow* 15 (1964), pp. 356–60.

13. For a list of the members of *Consilium*, see: A. Bugnini, *The Reform of the Liturgy (1948–1975)* (Collegeville: The Liturgical Press, 1990), pp. 942–52. Italian original: *La riforma liturgica (1948–1975)* (Rome: Centro Liturgico Veneziano, 1983).

Ferdinando Cardinal Antonelli (1896–1993), who was a member of the *Consilium*, in his diary records his impression of the spirit within which the group was working:

> [The *Consilium*] is merely an assembly of people, many of them incompetent, and others of them well advanced on the road to novelty. The discussions are extremely hurried. Discussions are based on impressions and the voting is chaotic. What is most displeasing is that the expositive *Promemorias* and the relative questions are drawn up in advanced terms and often in a very suggestive form. The direction is weak.[14]

Also:

> Many of those who have influenced the reform…and others, have no love, and no veneration of that which has been handed down to us. They begin by despising everything that is actually there. This negative mentality is unjust and pernicious, and unfortunately, Paul VI tends a little to this side. They have all the best intentions, but with this mentality they have only been able to demolish and not to restore.[15]

Antonelli records that tension grew between the Sacred Congregation for Rites, which was the organ of the Roman curia tasked with assisting the Pope on matters liturgical, and the *Consilium*. Far from being a merely consultative study circle that would propose to the congregation changes to be made, Antonelli noted that the *Consilium* "arrogated to itself functions which logically inhered in the Congregation of Rites."[16]

As the *Consilium* transformed from a consultative body to one that implemented the reforms it was originally tasked only to study, the complaints of the Congregation which was responsible for the implementation fell on deaf ears. The Congregation's desire to chart a course for liturgical reform in close fidelity to the text of the liturgical constitution was effectively nullified by the unchecked assumption of power by *Consilium* determined to construct a much wider berth than that which the Council Fathers envisioned in voting to approve *Sacrosanctum Concilium*.

---

14. Nicola Giampietro, *The Development of the Liturgical Reform: As Seen by Cardinal Ferdinando Antonelli from 1948 to 1970* (Fort Collins: Roman Catholic Books, 2009), pp. 166–67. Italian original: *Il cardinale Giuseppe Ferdinando Antonelli e gli sviluppi della riforma liturgica dal 1948 al 1970* (Rome: Pontificio Istituto Liturgico, 1996).

15. Ibid., p. 192.

16. Cited in ibid., p. 181 n. 12.

What the Council Fathers thought they were voting for, and what ended up coming forth from the *Consilium*, were very different things. As late as 5 November 1962, shortly before that vote, the Fathers were assured that "the current *Ordo Missae*, which has grown up in the course of the centuries, is to be retained."[17] But, as Alcuin Reid has pointed out:

> The *Consilium* were working on a completely new *Ordo Missae*, calendar, lectionary, etc., from 1964. As Antonelli said, they were not working from a desire to restore but from a wish to demolish and build anew. Hence the radical differences in the lectionary, calendar, order of Mass and other rites—something not intended by the Council but, alas, something enacted by enthusiastic reformers and promulgated by the authority of a pope.[18]

What makes the reform of the liturgy after Vatican II different from the reform of the liturgy after Trent is that the competent organ set up for the direction of that reform was marginalized by a group whose aims were far broader than the much narrower scope envisioned by the conciliar document itself. The subsequent ratification of the liturgical books and documents produced as a result of this novel event in Church history does not take away from the history of their production. The liturgical expression which has molded the vast majority of Catholics since the Council was itself the fruit of a quite intriguing history which few can credibly sustain is consonant with the principles for reform delineated in the liturgy Constitution itself.

3. *An Assessment of the Fidelity of the Implementation of* Sacrosanctum Concilium *to the Council*

a. *Received Widely By the Faithful: Statistical Evidence to the Contrary*
There are those, however, who will argue that, regardless of the way the liturgical reform was brought about, the vast majority of Catholics have enthusiastically embraced the reform. The 1985 Synod of Bishops reported that "the liturgical renewal is the most visible fruit of the whole work of

---

17. A. Reid, "The 'Consilium ad Exsequendam' at 50—An Interview with Dom Alcuin Reid (Part 1)," 7 February 2014 at: http://www.newliturgicalmovement. org/2014/02/the-consilium-ad-exsequendam-at–50_6845.html#.VSWVAlz4v8s.

18. A. Reid, "The 'Consilium ad Exsequendam' at 50—An Interview with Dom Alcuin Reid (Part 2)," 12 February 2014 at: http://www.newliturgicalmovement. org/2014/02/the-consilium-ad-exsequendam-at–50_12.html#.VpVGvbYrK9I.

the Council."[19] The fact that the vast majority of Catholics throughout the world continue to worship according to the reformed books seems to be an indication of its enthusiastic acceptance. At the same time however, there are also signs that measurable indicators of Catholic belief and practice demonstrate a precipitous decline or even collapse of the faith in many Western countries, particularly those where aspects of the reform less continuous with pre-conciliar practice were embraced.

In 2003 Kenneth Jones published a book entitled *Index of Leading Catholic Indicators: The Church Since Vatican II*, about standards of Catholic practice in the United States. Two statistics are particularly salient: one, the number of seminarians dropped from 49,000 to 4700 from 1965 to 2002, a decline of 90%; and two, in 1958 an estimated three out of four Catholics went to Mass every Sunday, as opposed to one in four at the time of writing.[20] The Center for Applied Research in the Apostolate at Georgetown produced a report in 2013 which paints a similar picture of decline.[21] Even more drastic declines are documented in Western Europe.[22]

It is clear that, in many countries with overwhelmingly high rates of Catholic practice before the reform, Catholic identity has suffered serious losses. The question arises: if the objective of the reform was, according to *Sacrosanctum Concilium*, "to impart an ever increasing vigor to the Christian life of the faithful" (n. 1), it must be frankly observed that the goal of the Council has not been achieved.

b. *The Roman Liturgy As We Know It Is Destroyed*
If the reform of the liturgy has not yielded the hoped for fruit of vibrant Catholic faith and practice, can we say that the reform was truly in accord with the vision of the Council Fathers at Vatican II? Is it possible that the decline of Catholic identity had something to do with a change of identity in the liturgy responsible for forming that identity? As we have seen, *Sacrosanctum Concilium* envisions modest changes to the Roman rite as it then existed for the purpose of fostering greater active participation. Apart from the question of what constitutes active participation,[23] it is clear that

19. Final Report of the Extraordinary Assembly of the Synod of Bishops (7 December 1985), II, B, b, 1.

20. K. Jones, *Index of Leading Catholic Indicators: The Church Since Vatican II* (Fort Collins: Roman Catholic Books, 2003).

21. See: https://www1.villanova.edu/content/dam/villanova/VSB/centers/church/21conference/Schools%20and%20Sacraments%20-%20Mark%20Gray.pdf.

22. "The Fate of Catholic Europe: The Void Within," *The Economist*, 5 August 2010. http://www.economist.com/node/16740795.

23. For two opposing viewpoints on this question see: R. Skeris, "*Participatio actuosa* in Theological and Musical Perspective: Theological and Musical

what the faithful were supposed to participate in had drastically changed. As Father Joseph Gelineau (1920–2008), an influential mid-century Jesuit liturgist, stated approvingly:

> If the forms change, the rite changes... In fact, it is a different liturgy of the Mass. We must say it plainly: the Roman rite as we knew exists no more. It has gone... It would not be right to identify this liturgical renewal with the reform of the rites decided on by Vatican II. This reform goes back much further and forward beyond the conciliar prescriptions. The liturgy is a permanent workshop.[24]

Others who were involved in the liturgical reform such as French Oratorian Louis Bouyer (1913–2004) confirmed this assertion of Gelineau, although not as approvingly.[25]

c. *The Hermeneutic of Rupture Guiding the Liturgical Reform Contrary to the Mandate*

So how is it possible that the liturgical reform produced something, which not only far exceeded the bounds of the Council which ordered it, but which its very architects claimed destroyed the historical Roman rite itself? When Pope Benedict XVI gave his Christmas greetings to the Roman Curia on 22 December 2005, he suggested that there were two opposing interpretative methodologies at work suggesting two opposing views of the Council and its work:

> On the one hand, there is an interpretation that I would call "a hermeneutic of discontinuity and rupture"; it has frequently availed itself of the sympathies of the mass media, and also one trend of modern theology. On the other, there is the "hermeneutic of reform," of renewal in the continuity of the one subject-Church which the Lord has given to us. She is a subject which increases in time and develops, yet always remaining the same, the

Considerations," in R. Skeris (ed.), *Divini cultus stadium* (Altotting: Alfred Coppenrath, 1990), pp. 25–34 and *Sacred Music* 117 (1990), pp. 15–23; and M. Faggioli, *True Reform: Liturgy and Ecclesiology in Sacrosanctum Concilium* (Collegeville: The Liturgical Press, 2012), pp. 73–75. See also an analysis in Laurence Paul Hemming, *Worship as a Revelation: The Past, Present and Future of Catholic Liturgy* (New York: Burns & Oates, 2008), pp. 31–33.

24. Joseph Gelineau, *The Liturgy: Today and Tomorrow* (New York: Paulist, 1978), p. 11; French original: *Demain la liturgie: Essai sur l'evolution des assemblees chretiennes* (Paris: Cerf, 1976), pp. 9–10.

25. "There is practically no liturgy worthy of the name today in the Catholic Church." Louis Bouyer, *Decomposition of Catholicism* (Chicago: Franciscan Herald, 1969), p. 105.

one subject of the journeying People of God. The hermeneutic of discontinuity risks ending in a split between the pre-conciliar Church and the post-conciliar Church. It asserts that the texts of the Council as such do not yet express the true spirit of the Council. It claims that they are the result of compromises in which, to reach unanimity, it was found necessary to keep and reconfirm many old things that are now pointless. However, the true spirit of the Council is not to be found in these compromises but instead in the impulses toward the new that are contained in the texts.

The chief problem with this, the Bavarian pontiff continues, is that:

> The nature of a Council as such is therefore basically misunderstood. In this way, it is considered as a sort of constituent that eliminates an old constitution and creates a new one… The Fathers had no such mandate and no one had ever given them one; nor could anyone have given them one because the essential constitution of the Church comes from the Lord and was given to us so that we might attain eternal life and, starting from this perspective, be able to illuminate life in time and time itself.

Seen in this light, Pope Benedict appears to suggest that rupture in the Church's life results from a view of ecumenical councils which is revolutionary in nature and not evolutionary. Applied to the liturgy, this principle suggests that an hermeneutic of rupture alone can fabricate a liturgy entirely on the ashes of a previous one. Applied to ecclesiology, it means that not even the Roman Pontiff can legitimately proscribe the traditional liturgy of the Church without contradicting the faith itself. Applied to Catholic identity, it is unsurprising that the supplanting of the traditional liturgy of the Church in violation of the Church's essential constitution cannot but have disastrous consequences for Catholic identity.

d. *Attempts at Exercising a Hermeneutic of Continuity: The Magisterium of John Paul II and Benedict XVI on the Liturgy*

Even though this discourse on the hermeneutic of continuity versus rupture was pronounced in 2005, it is clear that the Magisterium has exercised its power of vigilance over the liturgy with a hermeneutic of continuity. In his 4 December 1988 apostolic letter *Vicesimus Quintus Annus* commemorating the 25th anniversary of *Sacrosanctum Concilium* St John Paul II noted, "It must be recognized that the application of the liturgical reform has met with difficulties…one has to acknowledge with regret deviations of greater or lesser seriousness in its application" (nn. 11, 13). The Polish pope admitted that the implementation of the liturgical reform had been applied in some places according to a hermeneutic of rupture. His encyclical *Dominicae Coenae* of 24 February 1980 and the Instruction of the Congregation for Divine Worship *Redemptionis Sacramentum* of 25 March 2004 were authentic exercises of the Magisterium to affirm Catholic teaching on the Eucharistic liturgy and promote sound celebrations of the Mass in continuity with what went before. The 2002 third typical edition of the post-conciliar *Missale Romanum* included in its General Instruction certain small revisions with a view to strengthening a hermeneutic of continuity. Pope Benedict XVI's 22 February 2007 Post-synodal Apostolic Exhortation *Sacramentum Caritatis* was another step in this direction.

In all of these official documents, the Roman Pontiff exercised his universal jurisdiction in a hermeneutic of continuity over the liturgy. But in all of them, the official texts of the liturgical reform were taken as givens. Abuses contrary to the texts and to existing liturgical norms were decried, but nowhere do they indicate a questioning of the liturgical reform as such. The proliferation of documents from the Congregation for Divine Worship raises the question: If the reform had been faithful to the intentions of the Council, why the need for so many documents?

4. *An Ongoing Consideration of a Possible Reform of the Reform*

a. *Ratzinger and the Possibility of a Reform of the Reform?*
But could it be possible for anyone, from Pope to baptized Catholic, to look at the liturgical reform itself, not only at abuses of it but in its essence, and suggest that it too was in need of re-examination? Would doing so amount to a betrayal of the Council?

In 1997, then Cardinal Joseph Ratzinger acknowledged the demise of Catholic identity and attributed it to the decomposition of the liturgy: "The crisis in the Church that we are experiencing today is to a large extent due to the disintegration of the liturgy."[26] Ratzinger acknowledged that there had indeed been a rupture in the organic development of the liturgy: "After the Council...in the place of Liturgy as the fruit of development came fabricated Liturgy. We abandoned the organic, living process of growth and development over centuries, and replaced it."[27]

---

26. J. Ratzinger, *Milestones: Memoirs: 1927–1977* (San Francisco: Ignatius, 1999), p. 148. Italian original: *La mia vita: Ricordi (1927–1977)* (Milan: San Paolo, 1997).

27. See K. Gamber, *La Reforme liturgique en question* (Le Barroux: Sainte Madeleine, 1992), p. 8.

He raised the question as to whether a restoration, seen as a "new balance after all the indiscriminate opening to the world" was necessary.[28] Already in 1975, he had stated: "a real reform of the Church presupposes an unequivocal turning away from the erroneous paths whose catastrophic consequences are already incontestable."[29] The call for a "reform of the reform" by Professor Robert Spaemann (b. 1927)[30] at the 2001 Fontgombault Liturgical Conference was elaborated upon by then Cardinal Ratzinger: "It would be an important step...if the missal were freed from these areas of creativity, which do not correspond to the deepest levels of reality, to the spirit, of the liturgy. If, by means of such a 'reform of the reform,' we could get back to a faithful, ecclesial celebration of the liturgy...the *ecclesial dimension* of the Liturgy would once more be clearly apparent."[31] One wonders if Cardinal Ratzinger had in mind that the reform of the reform could restore the *Ecclesia orans* to its primacy over the *regula fidei*.

b. *The Argument of Geoffrey Hull on the Seeds of Destruction within the Church*

Even as there were calls for greater fidelity to the reformed liturgical books with an eye to the previous liturgical tradition and for the reform of that reform, other thinkers were arguing that the way forward had to involve an examination much greater than the documents of Vatican II and the post-conciliar liturgical books themselves.

Geoffrey Hull (b. 1955), an Australian ethnologist, suggested in a book published in 1995 that the crisis of liturgy and Catholic identity had roots much older than the mid-twentieth-century liturgical crisis. In *The Banished Heart*, he claims that there was, in the post-Tridentine period, an increasing secularization of the Catholic mindset: "a liturgical indifferentism which separated the ethos and the doctrine of Catholic worship."[32] The practical

---

28. J. Ratzinger with V. Messori, *The Ratzinger Report* (San Francisco: Ignatius, 1985), pp. 37–38.

29. Ibid., p. 30.

30. R. Spaemann, "The Reform of the Reform and the Old Roman Rite," in Alcuin Reid (ed.), *Looking Again at the Question of the Liturgy with Cardinal Ratzinger: Proceedings of the July 2001 Fontgombault Liturgical Conference* (Farnborough: St Michael's Abbey, 2003), pp. 115–23. French original: *Autour de la question liturgique avec le Cardinal Ratzinger* (Fontgombault: Association Petrus a Stella Abbaye Notre Dame, 2001).

31. J. Ratzinger, "Assessment and Future Prospects," in Reid (ed.), *Looking Again*, pp. 145–53 (151).

32. Geoffrey Hull, *The Banished Heart* (Sydney: Spes Nova League, 1995), p. 148. New edn, T&T Clark, London, 2010.

consequence of this liturgical indifferentism was "provided that the validity and integrity of the rite itself were preserved, it might be performed in whichever way the Church saw fit at that particular time."[33] This would explain how the Roman Missal of St Pius V "might be celebrated in the style of grand opera in the seventeenth and eighteenth centuries, in an entirely artificial mock-Gothic style in the nineteenth, and, on the eve of the Pauline revolution, with electric guitars and pop tunes."[34]

One might argue that the liturgy will always reflect in some way the ethos of the people who celebrate it, and that, as long as it is celebrated by people, their culture will always influence its celebration, for better or worse, in a more or less secular direction depending on how secular those who celebrate it have become. Hull's central intuition, though, is that the emphasis on validity and integrity of the rite, and of what constitutes the Eucharist, became increasingly separated conceptually from the liturgical context in which the rites were celebrated, to such a degree that the rites themselves, and the ethos which accompanies, them, became secondary. It is arguable whether such a distinction *could* be present in a world that had not yet known the fine distinctions of Scholasticism or the need of the Church to elucidate her teaching against Protestant deviations from orthodox doctrine regarding the Eucharist. It is further arguable that such a distinction necessarily had to develop in such a way as to marginalize the liturgical context and ethos of the rites. But if Hull is correct in his assertion that this is indeed what actually happened, two things follow.

First of all, the *Ecclesia orans*, the Church in her life of public prayer, had already become subjugated in practice to the *regula fidei*, orthodox doctrine on faith and morals as expressed in the catechism, long before Pius XII's reversal of Prosper of Aquitaine's axiom in 1947. The school of thought mentioned in the first section above, which sees the liturgy as secondary to the catechism, is therefore not a novel one by a stretch of centuries. This situation would then explain why the Pian revolution failed to elicit contrary commentary at the time it launched.

Secondly, obedience to the liturgical norms of the Church becomes secondary to obedience to the data of revelation on faith and morals. In consequence, they can easily be seen as not important, and indeed, insistence upon them may be dismissed as legalism. Ironically, it also centralizes the formulation and regulation of liturgical norms at increasingly higher levels of hierarchical authority. This produces an incorrect positivism of liturgical law by which, as long as something is properly promulgated by legitimate authority, it is then considered inconsequential,

33. Ibid.
34. Ibid.

whether or not the reality the norm is designed to protect is in accord with faith or morals. Since, in the Pian recension, it is belief which conditions prayer, the legal framework surrounding the common worship of the Church does not actually have to be consonant with the inner essence of the mystery being celebrated. If this is the case, it would explain why there are those for whom the way the liturgy is celebrated, from music and art to texts and ceremonial actions, is never a stable and perduring thing, and hence always capable of being endlessly reinvented according to the creativity of those for whom the law allows scope to be creative.

c. *Is Modern Man Capable of a Liturgical Act?*
Hull crafts a history according to which the true spirit of the liturgy has been lost in the ethos of the Church. That intuition is present even in other thinkers who may not ascribe the same series of historical events as causes of such a loss. As early as 1964, Italo-German theologian Romano Guardini (1885–1968) rhetorically asked in an open letter to Johannes Wagner: "Would it not be better to admit that man in this industrial and scientific age, with its new sociological structure, is no longer capable of a liturgical act?"[35] As Robert Barron (b. 1959) has pointed out,

> the liturgical establishment got it backward: Guardini was not implying that we abandon the liturgy or its reform, but he was implying that we ought perhaps to turn our back on modernity... The project is not shaping the liturgy according to the suppositions of the age, but allowing the liturgy to question and shape the suppositions of any age...for our goal is not to accommodate the liturgy to the world, but to let the liturgy be itself—a transformative icon of the ordo of God.[36]

The liturgical movement saw its fulfillment in the conciliar consti-tution on the Sacred Liturgy, enshrining in the Magisterium its objective of promoting active participation in the liturgy as a means of renewing Christian life. But the liturgical reform, in going beyond the provisions of *Sacrosanctum Concilium*, started, not from letting the liturgy be itself and transform the world in God, but from what was considered by some to be

---

35. "A Letter from Romano Guardini," *Herder Correspondence* 1 (1964), p. 24. German original: "Der Kultakt und die gegenwartige Aufgabe der liturgischen Bildung. Ein Brief," in *Liturgisches Jahrbuch* 14 (1964), pp. 101–6. See: also T. Bogler (ed.), *Ist der mensch von heute noch liturgiefähig Ergebnisse einer Umfrage*, Liturgie und Mönchtum, Laacher Hefte 38 (Maria Laach: Ars Liturgica, 1966).

36. R. Barron, "The Liturgical Act and the Church of the Twenty-First Century," in *Bridging the Great Divide: Musings of a Post-Liberal, Post-Conservative Evangelical Catholic* (Lanham: Rowman & Littlefield, 2004), pp. 53–67 (65).

the most effective way to change the liturgy to suit modern attitudes. The contention of Guardini that modern man was no longer even capable of a liturgical act was used, not for a more incisive critique of modernity, as he intended, but as a tool to further an increasing secularization within the Church that Hull opines had already been germinating for centuries and Antonelli observes was at work in the reform.[37]

So, as Charbel Pazat de Lys asked in 2001 at Fontgombault, "What are the correct methods of applying the criteria of reform?"[38] In other words, what are the principles that can guide a reform to accomplish the goal of the Council? We have already seen that certain aspects of the reform sought to conform the liturgy to the world, and not vice versa. Enshrining an essentially Enlightenment spirit of rationalism as a foundational principle upon which the liturgical reform of the mid-twentieth century proceeded did not yield the expected fruit. So the answer must lie in exposing the rationalist tendencies in the reform and eliminating them from the liturgical ethos of the Church. In doing so, it is important to remember that such rationalism is not merely an invention of the middle of the last century. Its effects were apparent already, in Hull's analysis, in the way that the pre-conciliar rites were celebrated.

Laurence Hemming has defined rationalism as "the understanding that everything, all truth, arises on the basis of what can be foreseen by man."[39] He asserts that in the period 1965–1970, "the call for liturgical reform... was driven by an underlying rationalism."[40] Hemming recognizes that Guardini's subjectivist notion of the human individual in relation to the worshipping community has echoes in *Sacrosanctum Concilium* n. 1's call for the liturgy to be adapted "more suitably to the needs of our own times."[41] But he also points out the consequences of that anthropology: "Guardini speaks of the problem of the particularity of the liturgy in its address to every individual, but in such a way that suggested to later liturgical thinkers not that the individual should adapt himself to the liturgy, but that the liturgy may need to be adapted to modern man."[42] In a new twist on the ancient axiom, the order seems to be that the law of the needs of modern man establishes the law of prayer. That modern man can adequately assess on his own what those needs are and the corresponding

37. See: Giampietro, *The Development of the Liturgical Reform*, p. 177.
38. C. Pazat de Lys, "Towards a New Liturgical Movement," in Reid (ed.), *Looking Again*, pp. 98–114 (103).
39. Hemming, *Worship as a Revelation*, p. 24.
40. Ibid.
41. Ibid., p. 30.
42. Ibid., p. 31.

change in prayer is precisely an example of the rationalism Hemming claims is at work behind the scenes in both Guardini and the first lines of *Sacrosanctum Concilium.* As Hemming points out, "This is the thoroughly modern, subjective, understanding of the human being—that one who, independent and self-established, *then* enters into social (here conceived as liturgical) relations."[43] Hemming goes on to submit that it is the liturgical rite of Baptism that enters us into the relationships of the Church. This view, which asserts the priority of prayer over the law of belief or the law of self-established individuality, is "radically different to the self's self-understanding in contemporary culture."[44]

The Guardini notion of Catholic identity seems to presuppose that there is a pre-existing person who at some point later enters into the social realm of worship. It is essentially individualistic, modern, subjective and rationalist. The Hemming notion of an ecclesial person constituted as such by the liturgical experience of Baptism is communal, time irrelevant, objective and Trinitarian.

Hemming shows that the human person can indeed be capable of a liturgical act, of being incorporated into a Catholic identity, not on the basis of a rationalist conformity of liturgy with perceived needs, but on the basis of the liturgical reality of Baptism as incorporation into Christ. Hemming asks, "Is modern man—the man for the sake of whose require-ments our liturgy came to need adaptation—the subject of the liturgy because the 'subject' is that by whom everything is measured? Or is the real subject of the liturgy…none other than Christ himself?"[45]

The purgation of rationalism necessary to conform the world to the liturgy, and not vice versa, can only emerge after the subject of the liturgy is clearly perceived of as not the human person, but Christ in whose Mystical Body the human person is incorporated by the sacrament of Baptism. This refocus of the Church's efforts from the revision of liturgical rites to suit ever-changing contemporary demands rationally considered, to entering into the mystery of the Christ of faith in the liturgy which makes that happen, re-establishes that it is the law of prayer which indeed grounds belief. The primacy of the communal worship of the Church, the primacy of Christ, reverses the anthropocentric obsession of man with his own perceived needs and gives him the space to transcend them to something infinitely greater.

43. Ibid., p. 30.
44. Ibid., p. 35.
45. Ibid., pp. 49–50.

d. *The Reform of the Reform Cannot Ignore the History of the Production of the Reformed Books*

Any reform of the reform, or any consideration of appropriate principles of liturgical restoration, must start from re-establishing Christ, and not man, as the subject of the liturgy. In doing so, whatever in liturgical theory or practice, in whatever age, distracts from the Christocentric and Trinitarian nature of the liturgy, must be re-examined. This means that the rationalist presuppositions of the very first paragraph of the conciliar liturgy constitution, as well as much of the liturgical reform of the last century, must be challenged. The history of the production of the reformed books from this period bears the stamp of such rationalism. As that obfuscation of the essential nature of the liturgy becomes clearer, the rites formed in that spirit will become less tenable. More and more people, clergy and laity, as they reflect upon the practical consequences that such a rationalist attitude towards the liturgy and its relationship to faith has had for Catholic identity, will demand that the authority of the Church repair the damage done.

A reform is possible, even if it requires reversals of liturgical books and ideas that have become prevalent. As Klaus Gamber (1919–1989) pointed out, "Historical development of our liturgy has not always proceeded evenly and not always had happy results. Wrong decisions were made on a number of occasions... It will be some time until we will be in a position to measure fully the pastoral damage caused to the faithful by the reforms."[46] And as Alcuin Reid has stated, "The task of a thorough assessment of whether this law [of organic development] was respected in the reform enacted following the Second Vatican Council...remains."[47]

e. *The Reform of the Reform Must Start from a Hermeneutic of Continuity*

But where can this reform begin? Theology and canon law both indicate that the Roman Pontiff alone can take discussion on these points and translate them into a reality which can be grasped in the life of the Church. No individual initiative or eccentric experimentation can supplant the hierarchy's duty to assure the conformity of the Church's public worship with the mystery it celebrates. This question cannot be separated from the larger question of the interpretation of the Second Vatican Council, even though, as we have seen, the rationalist spirit, which betrayed the ultimate desire of the Council Fathers, is something not bound by the years 1962–1965.

46. K. Gamber, *Reform of the Roman Liturgy: Its Problems and Background* (Harrison: Foundation for Catholic Reform, 1993), p. 109.

47. A. Reid, *The Organic Development of the Liturgy*, 2nd edn (San Francisco: Ignatius, 2005), pp. 310–11.

Marc Cardinal Ouellet (b. 1944) in his book length interview with Geoffroy de la Tousche on *The Relevance and Future of the Second Vatican Council* asserts, "The Council, in its general plan of reform in continuity, desired to reexamine the liturgy to make it more accessible, more comprehensible."[48] Professor Roberto De Mattei (b. 1948) argues that this was certainly the goal of the Council, but that its implementation was conceived of "within the perspective of a radical secularization of the liturgy."[49] De Mattei's thesis is that secularizing theology has found "confirmation of its own truth in practice" through the liturgical reform.[50] Much earlier Cardinal Antonelli had observed that this secularizing and rupturing vision of liturgical reform "has, in its turn, been absorbed into a wider problem, which is fundamentally doctrinal."[51] This great crisis of doctrine and the Magisterium, brought about in part by the rationalist spirit of a liturgical reform conceived within a hermeneutic of rupture with respect to Vatican II, caused the cardinal to remark, "accepit liturgia, recessit devotio."[52] He saw disastrous results for the devotion of the people, for the formation of their Catholic identity, stemming from a reform proceeding as it was under *Consilium.*

But is it possible to extract the Second Vatican Council and its liturgical reform from the spirit Antonelli feared would shipwreck Catholic identity? Blessed Paul VI (1963–1978), who was the pontiff responsible for guiding the Council after St John XXIII's death in 1963, certainly saw his work in an hermeneutic, not of rupture, but of continuity: "It would not be the truth for anyone to imagine that Vatican II represented any kind of a break, interruption, or 'liberation' from the teaching of the Church: or that the Council promoted or authorized any kind of accommodation or conformism with the mentality of our times in its negative and ephemeral aspects."[53]

---

48. G. de la Tousche (ed.), *The Relevance and Future of the Second Vatican Council* (San Francisco: Ignatius, 2013), p. 145. French original: *Actualite et avenir du concile oecumenique Vatican II* (Dijon: L'Echelle de Jacob, 2012).

49. R. De Mattei, "Reflections on the Liturgical Reform," in Reid (ed.), *Looking Again*, pp. 130–44 (137). See: L. de Maldonado, *Secolarizazzione della liturgia* (Rome: Paoline, 1972), p. 473: "Man is a being of the world, a profane being, that is how God willed him to be, how God saved him. This is the ultimate reason for secularity, its theological value."

50. Ibid., p. 140.

51. Giampietro, *The Development of the Liturgical Reform*, p. 177.

52. Ibid., p. 170.

53. Cf. *Insegnamenti di Paolo VI*, vol. IV (1966), p. 699, quoted in Agostino Marchetto, *The Second Vatican Ecumenical Council: A Counterpoint for the History*

Archbishop Agostino Marchetto (b. 1940) has suggested that much of what has been done in faithfulness to a certain conception of the "spirit of Vatican II" is less a product of the actual intentions of St John XXIII and Blessed Paul VI as much as it is the fabricated historiography of the Council emanating from what he calls the "Bologna school" under the principal tutelage of Italian historian Giuseppe Alberigo (1926–2007).[54] Marchetto explains: "The idea in question is one of the 'novelty' or 'newness' of everything that had to be decided at the Council: this supposedly represented a break with the past and thereby by-passed ideas of continuity and Tradition that in fact need to be taken into account in cases of true *aggiornamento.*"[55] As a result, "by focusing so much of the conciliar hermeneutics on discontinuity, today's general historiographical tendency…thus favors discontinuity…a tendency…which cannot and must not be accepted, at least not as far as the Catholic Church is concerned—and as far as any history which takes into account her specific nature."[56]

It is important, then, to examine the event of the Second Vatican Council, not through the lens of those who wish to interpret it as an entirely new event in the life of the Church, but in continuity with all that went before. The same principle applies to the reform of the liturgy. Hull remarks that *Sacrosanctum Concilium* indeed "did not explicitly order the drastic restructuring of the Roman liturgy that actually ensued."[57]

While it is clear that the intention of the Second Vatican Ecumenical Council was to bring about liturgical reform in continuity, it must be said that it is harder to discern to what extent the same concern motivated Blessed Paul VI in his oversight of the same reform. On the one hand, there are affirmations of continuity within tradition, as we have seen above. On the other, there are suggestions that Blessed Paul VI had contrary intentions as well. In a 1993 interview, the Pope's close friend Jean Guitton (1901–1999) stated that the intention of Blessed Paul VI "was to reform the Catholic liturgy so that it should approximate as closely as possible to the Protestant Lord's Supper…an ecumenical intention to wipe out or at

---

of the Council (Scranton: University of Scranton Press, 2010), p. 646. Italian original *Il Concilio Ecumenico Vaticano II: Contrappunto per la sua storia* (Vatican City: Libreria Editirice Vaticana, 2005).

54. Ibid., p. 666. For a more extensive critique of the Bologna school see pp. 683–93.

55. Ibid., p. 667.

56. Ibid., p. 663.

57. Hull, *The Banished Heart*, p. 5.

least correct or soften everything that is too Catholic in the Mass and bring [it]…as close as possible to the Calvinist liturgy."[58]

If this is indeed true, it speaks of a tension between rupture and continuity bred into the implementation of the reform. Even though *Sacrosanctum Concilium* "was intended to make actual liturgical practice more fruitful in the life of the Church,"[59] "[n]ot enough attention was paid to certain ambiguities in the history of the liturgical movement either by those who brought about the Second Vatican Council's commitment to the 'liturgical renewal,' in the Constitution *Sacrosanctum Concilium,* or by those who subsequently worked to give that commitment concrete form in the revised liturgical books."[60] As a result, "the liturgy is a 'formality' that can change as time proceeds, provided that the 'eternal' truths of the Church are not harmed."[61] The law of belief, under the liturgical reform of the last century, became effectively disassociated from the law of prayer, which was relegated to being secondary and merely any changeable expression among many. The very way the *Consilium* was constructed, where liturgical experts who were not theologians dictated the revision of rites, echoes this disassociation, even though "every word and gesture in the liturgy expresses a theological idea."[62]

This disassociation came about, according to John Parsons, as a result of a rationalist mentality's response to the fact of "the historical relativity of much of human culture," which attempts to "'dig deeper' beneath existing practice and to 'expose' an ideal order which is really 'true' and 'timeless' as the older forms had spontaneously been assumed to be by pre-critical minds."[63] This rationalist and antiquarian mentality, Parsons claims, is precisely what animated the Synod of Pistoia which was condemned by Pope Pius VI in *Auctorem fidei* of 1794, whose proscribed propositions begin to reappear the very year after Pope Pius XII reiterated their condemnation in *Mediator Dei.* This revived Jansenist liturgical mentality would have significant consequences. Parsons explains:

58. Interview by Francois-George Dreyfus on the French radio program *Ici Lumiere 101,* 13 December 1993, cited in ibid., p. 7.

59. L. Dobszay, *The Restoration and Organic Development of the Roman Rite* (London: T&T Clark, 2010), p. 18.

60. A. Nichols, *Looking at the Liturgy* (San Francisco: Ignatius, 1996), p. 11.

61. Dobszay, *The Restoration and Organic Development of the Roman Rite,* p. 24.

62. N. Bux, *Benedict XVI's Reform: The Liturgy Between Innovation and Tradition* (San Francisco: Ignatius, 2012). Italian original: *La riforma di Benedetto XVI* (Milan: Piemme, 2008), p. 65.

63. J. Parsons, "A Reform of the Reform? Part I," *Christian Order,* November 2001, http://www.christianorder.com/features/features_2001/features_bonus_nov01.html.

> A policy of *aggiornamento*...logically implies that the secularised culture of a decayed Western Christendom shall provide the standard by which the Church is to be updated. It was in this context that the reconstruction of the historic liturgy rapidly became a *damnatio memoriae* of the Church's practice... The symbolic repudiation of the tradition of Christendom...has contributed greatly to an undermining of confidence in the Church in general. While it may be possible *logically* to believe in a Church which is an infallible guide in doctrines of faith and morals but which, for most of the time since its foundation, has promoted, in Archbishop Bugnini's striking phrase, "lack of understanding, ignorance and dark night" in the worship of God, it is not possible *psychologically* to carry out a mental juggling act of this sort for very long.[64]

The reformers' desire to uncover and fabricate an ideal liturgy, in sustaining that the way Catholics had worshipped for centuries had been mistaken, caused a crisis of confidence in the Church's teaching on faith and morals, and the liturgy. As if to confirm the *lex orandi, lex credendi* axiom, to pray according to a liturgy which claims that every previous incarnation of that liturgy is a falsification of the truth, in turn produces a belief that the faith and morals, and sacramental life upon which Catholic identity rests, are also capable of corruption.

It is clear that a restoration of the law of prayer and the law of belief cannot come about by continuing to breathe the spirit of rationalism or of rationalist liturgical reform. But, as we have seen, that spirit pervades not only the books of the liturgical reform around Vatican II, but the indifferentist attitude towards how the liturgy is a vehicle for theological truth, all the way back to the liturgical reform around Trent.

This is why a reform of the reform is not just a matter of eclectic restorations of certain disciplines, music, art or ceremonial present in the pre-conciliar liturgical tradition. It also explains why mere aesthetic adjustments to the *Missale Romanum* of Blessed Paul VI, or wholesale return to the post-Vatican II *Ordo Missae* of 1965, or the *Missale Romanum* of 1962 of St John XXIII or 1570 of St Pius V is insufficient.

5. *The Integral Celebration of the* Usus Recentior *with an* Optimal Ars Celebrandi *(Sacramentum Caritatis 38–42)*

All of that being said, and conscious of our conclusion that the provenance of reformed rites of the post-Vatican II period poses certain difficulties, the authority of the Church has confirmed that these liturgical forms are

64. Ibid.

here to stay. How then, must we approach celebrations of the *ordinary form*?

First of all, we have to affirm that the principle of celebrating the liturgy in a Christocentric, and not anthropocentric, manner, is crucial. Restoring practices which underscore that fundamental orientation of the liturgy towards Christ is paramount. Second, in the formation of our people, mandated by the Conciliar constitution, we must use the riches of the Church's liturgical tradition from all times and places to serve as a vehicle for communicating the *regula fidei*, rather than merely relying on didactic explanations of catechism. Third, we must avoid the assumption, often exacerbated by excessive positivist tendencies and rubricism, that the rubrics of the reformed books are themselves sufficient to revivify Christian life and to impart this return to a Christocentric liturgical approach.

In other words, the Church must cultivate an *ars celebrandi* through which the essential nature of the liturgy can shine, even amidst the shadows cast upon it by the rationalism of the past. To this end, Pope Benedict XVI's 2007 postsynodal Apostolic Exhortation *Sacramentum Caritatis* provides a useful guide to *ars celebrandi* properly considered in paragraphs 38–42.

a. Sacramentum Caritatis *38–42*

As if to anticipate an objection, Pope Benedict is quick to point out in this section that "The *ars celebrandi* is the best way to ensure [the] *actuosa participatio*" of the people (n. 38). He goes on to define the *ars celebrandi* as "the fruit of faithful adherence to the liturgical norms in all their richness" (n. 38). Most importantly, it should "foster a sense of the sacred and the use of outward signs which help to cultivate this sense, such as, for example, the harmony of the rite, the liturgical vestments, the furnishings and the sacred space" (n. 40). In other words, "everything—texts, music, execution—ought to correspond to the meaning of the mystery being celebrated, the structure of the rite and the liturgical seasons" (n. 42).

This restoration of a sense of the sacred is important. If the principle referent for some of the reformers was mythical modern man and his perceived needs, Benedict returns to center stage the category of the sacred. It is an important step in the reversal of the assumption of secularization as necessary to the reform. While he does not here give a definition or description of what is sacred, the renewal of the very category in liturgical discourse is already a great step in unraveling the rationalist discourse based on man and not on God. German philosopher Josef Pieper (1904–1997) as early as 1988 had delineated that the "'desacralization' crusades, especially when theological arguments are used, are ultimately rooted...in just such a denial of any sacramental reality. They rest on the conviction that this action, perhaps still called 'sacred', is in truth a purely human performance in which...*nothing at all happens*, least of all a real presence of the divine."[65]

An *ars celebrandi* which respects the sacred renews the liturgy as a vehicle for incorporating the believer into a sacred, sacramental reality beyond himself. It underscores that the liturgy and the sacramental actions of the Church are not essentially human actions which are the result of all too human processes, but divine actions which are given ritual vesture under the guidance of the Church's celebration of her Redemption in Christ. Thus it also elevates the necessary obedience to the liturgical books to an action beyond a mere exercise in legal positivism. This *ars celebrandi* which respects the sacred is a crucial element in recovering the primacy of divine sacramental action in the nature of the liturgy, and is an important corrective to derivations and deviations from that nature.

6. *An Openness to the Value of the Usus Antiquior in the Church Today*

a. *The Radical Statement of Summorum Pontificum*
In *Sacramentum Caritatis* Pope Benedict XVI charts a way forward for how the post-conciliar liturgical experience can escape the rationalist tendencies that threaten to render it, and Catholic identity along with it, unintelligible. That same year, he also did something else which would help to make the way to recovery clearer.

Ever since the appearance of the reformed liturgical books, there had been a question as to whether one could continue to use the previous editions and still remain in communion with the Church. The painful experience of the separation of the followers of Archbishop Marcel Lefebvre (1905–1991) from the visible unity of the Church, and the harsh tactics used by promoters of the reform against ordinary Catholics who were attached to the "Old Rite," made answering that question vital for an understanding of who is and who is not really a Catholic.

Answering the question became more difficult, Laszlo Dobszay maintains, because the Church herself generated a culture of disobedience, in which it was hard to determine realistically what level of assent was

---

65. Josef Pieper, *In Search of the Sacred* (San Francisco: Ignatius, 1991), p. 29. German original: *Was heisst "Sakral"?* (Ostfildern bei Stuttgart: Schwabenverlag AG, 1988).

required to affirm or reject liturgical reform and still remain a Catholic. He states that the "Church itself is responsible for generating disobedience" in three ways: first, "because the Church permitted" the *Consilium* to "stretch far beyond the limits set" and "enacted new regulations explicitly *against* the higher law"; second, the Church "damaged the sense of stability that belongs to the proper exercise of faith, and…belief in the superhuman and revelatory character of the liturgy"; and third, since "while individual innovations persisted without consequence, those who insisted on the preservation of ecclesiastical traditions were reproached."[66]

In 1986, St John Paul II convened a commission of nine cardinals to answer the question definitively.[67] Their overwhelmingly positive response that the Missal of St Pius V had never been abrogated forms an important part of the background to the motu proprio of 2 July 1988, *Ecclesia Dei Adflicta*, which urged bishops to greater generosity in providing for the celebration of what had come to be called the Tridentine Mass. Almost twenty years later, Pope Benedict XVI issued another motu proprio, *Summorum Pontificum* (7 July 2007), along with an explanatory letter to the bishops of the world (of the same date) on the reasons for issuing the motu proprio.

In his letter the Bavarian pontiff says that the fear that greater access to the pre-conciliar liturgical books calls into question the liturgical reform is unfounded. He then does something quite novel in stating that henceforth there will be two forms of the Roman rite: the *ordinary* form, consisting in the books of the liturgical reform; and the *extraordinary form*, consisting in the books in use at the time of the opening of the Second Vatican Council. He also sets forth the theological rationale for answering definitively that use of the pre-conciliar books is not contrary to full ecclesial communion:

> In the history of the liturgy there is growth and progress, but no rupture. What earlier generations held as sacred, remains sacred and great for us too, and it cannot be all of a sudden entirely forbidden or even considered harmful. It behooves all of us to preserve the riches which have developed in the Church's faith and prayer, and to give them their proper place.

---

66. Dobszay, *The Restoration and Organic Development of the Roman Rite*, pp. 28–29.

67. See: Alcuin Reid, "The *Usus Antiquior*—Its History and Importance in the Church After the Second Vatican Council," in A. Reid (ed.), *T&T Clark Companion to Liturgy* (London: Bloomsbury, 2016), pp. 455–82 (464–65).

Earlier, in February 2007 with *Sacramentum Caritatis*, Pope Benedict XVI exercised the Petrine primacy over the liturgy to restore the sacred to the Mass by urging an *ars celebrandi* that would transform anthropocentric celebrations of the liturgy according to its true theocentric character. He purged the *lex orandi* governing the reformed liturgy of its dubious rationalist vesture, without ever touching the texts themselves. In July of the same year he then extracted the historic Roman liturgy of the Church from marginalization and restored to full citizenship the liturgy which had grown up with the Church organically—a liturgy that was not, unlike the production that is the modern Roman liturgy, characterized by a curious cocktail of antiquarian and rationalist concerns.

In doing so, Pope Benedict XVI allowed the Church to see once again what Dietrich von Hildebrand maintained: "[T]he liturgy, more than anything else, is penetrated with the spirit of continuity, and dispenses this spirit to those who live in it."[68] The exercise of the hermeneutic of continuity to shed the reform of what in it might be inimical to the true spirit of the liturgy, and to open up once again the treasures of the historical Roman liturgy to the entire Church, is a great gift. It also allows for a reflowering of Catholic identity. Even though the "liturgy wars" are far from over, and the spirit of the age, which is often not the spirit of the liturgy, is still prevalent in the Church, the Magisterium, which had been perhaps too optimistic about modern man's ability to conform the liturgy to the world and not denature it, evened the playing field for the true face of the liturgy to emerge once again.

In doing so, the Church has not precipitously proscribed a reformed liturgy which continues to be celebrated by many of her children. She has prudently recognized the pitfalls of the reform and put into place measures by which those who are open can renew their identity in Christ through the Sacred Liturgy which celebrates the mystery of our participation in Christ's life. Mutual enrichment of the two forms of the Roman rite and a deeper look into the essence of the liturgy, of our faith, and of our life in God is happening.

7. *Conclusion*

Pius XII's exaltation of creed and catechism above liturgy, his reversal of the ancient order of *lex orandi* then *lex credendi*, was arguably fruit of a progressive divorce between the liturgy as source and summit of Christian life and the doctrines which make that life intelligible. It also

---

68. D. von Hildebrand, *Liturgy and Personality* (Manchester: Sophia, 1990), p. 145. German original: *Liturgie und Personlichkeit* (Ratisbon: Pustet, 1934).

carried within it, as so much of the well-meaning ideas of the liturgical movement, seeds, if not of destruction, of disorder. Aidan Kavanagh presciently saw that modern liturgical reform started with its meaning for man, rather than the sacramental reality, transformation in Christ, that the liturgy signifies. As Geoffrey Hull interprets Kavanagh's thought:

> Doctrinal and ecclesiological developments, which allow divine and absolute realities to be eclipsed by changing human meanings, are not merely the consequences of the Western subordination of primary theology (the liturgical tradition) to secondary theology (the dogmatic tradition)... The fatal error of Western Christians has been to view the Sacred Liturgy not as the spontaneous celebration of their faith, but as one more means of expounding it. In rudely refashioning the Church's *cultus* in the same way as they reformulated their crude explanations of divine truths, the Reformers—Protestant, Jansenist and modern Catholic—usurped the Holy Spirit's creative role in the *opus Dei*, the thing intended to be the very heart and treasury of Christian life. And so the mysterious life-giving cult of God became the "meaningful" yet lifeless cult of man.[69]

The *theologia prima* of the Sacred Liturgy, free from humanizing corruptions, is the way in which we discover our true identity in Christ. It leads us into that *theologia secunda* of faith and morals which shows us how we should act and what we must believe to be coherent with that sacramental reality of our Baptism, of our renewal in the life of God.

---

69. Hull, *The Banished Heart*, p. 212.

THE REFORM OF THE LECTIONARY

Peter Kwasniewski

1. *Introduction*

While almost every other aspect of the liturgical reform following Vatican II has been the target of serious criticism, the revamped multi-year lectionary is the one element consistently put forward as a notable success, an instance of genuine progress.[1] No less a figure than Pope Benedict XVI, though an outspoken critic of many post-conciliar changes, praised the gains of the new lectionary.[2] There is, all the same, good

1. From countless examples that might be chosen, here is how Scott Hahn speaks of it: "I believe, however, that the most significant change [in the liturgy] came about in 1969, with the introduction of the revised lectionary. The media missed this one because there was so little controversy. Almost everyone agreed that the finished product was a remarkable achievement. And there can be no doubt that it was a major development in the life of the Church. The lectionary was designed specifically for the purpose of highlighting the essential relationship between scripture and liturgy," *Letter and Spirit: From Written Text to Living Word in the Liturgy* (New York: Doubleday, 2005), pp. 2–3. Fr Brian W. Harrison concurs: "It seems likely that, whatever future developments occur in the Roman rite, this extended use and emphasis on Sacred Scripture in Catholic worship may prove to be Pope Paul's most lasting contribution, and, arguably, even the most important long-term gift of his pontificate to the life of the Church," "The Biblical Dimension of Paul VI's Liturgical Vision," *Living Tradition* 154 (2011), pp. 1–6 (6).

2. Pope Benedict XVI's criticisms of innovation and "creativity" are found throughout his writings on the liturgy; for his appreciation of the revised lectionary, see the Post-Synodal Apostolic Exhortation *Verbum Domini* (30 September 2010), n. 57. Robert Moynihan relates this story: "When, for example, I expressed my belief (this was in 1993, so, almost 20 years ago) that the annual cycle of readings should not have been replaced by a three-year cycle of readings (I argued that the annual cycle was in a certain way more 'organic,' more in harmony with the natural cycle of the seasons, and so more deeply penetrating, psychologically and spiritually, into the hearts and souls of ordinary faithful, who would hear the same words on the same Sunday each year, but in the changed circumstances brought by the passage of time and life), he then was quite emphatic that the three-year cycle was an improvement, saying it allowed the faithful to hear more passages of the Word of God, and did not

reason to revisit the lectionary 45 years later, in light of experience and maturity of reflection, and to examine critically the principles guiding its revision and the actual realization of those principles.

2. *The Liturgical Movement and the Second Vatican Council*

There were sound reasons for wishing to supplement the old lectionary. As a simple matter of liturgical history, it must be admitted that Western rites of the Mass, including the Roman, had once contained a wider range of scriptural lessons than we find in the Roman rite codified by St Pius V after the Council of Trent and still in use today as the missal of St John XXIII. As one recent author describes it:

> The 1962 lectionary corresponds (with the exception of newly created feast days) with that of the Roman missal of 1570. This, in turn, is dependent upon the *Missale Romano-Seraphicum* (the Franciscan missal) of the 13th century, which did not include the lections for the non-Lenten ferias found in earlier Roman books, as well as in the books of other rites and usages. Gallican missals with lections for non-Lenten ferias continued in use into the second half of the 19th century. Typically, readings would be given for some, but not all, days of the week, such as Monday, Wednesday, and Friday, and would include, for example, parallel accounts of the pericope used in the Sunday Gospel.[3]

limit them to hearing the same passages each year. This argument made clear to me that Pope Benedict personally does in some ways favor at least certain aspects of the conciliar liturgical reform as an improvement over the traditional liturgy." *The Moynihan Letters*, 12 October 2012. http://themoynihanletters.com/liturgy/letter–28-the-old-mass-returns-to-st-peters. As a counterpoint, one might note that in his Letter to Bishops on the occasion of *Summorum Pontificum* (7 July 2007) Pope Benedict XVI mentioned that "new Saints and some of the new Prefaces can and should be inserted in the old missal," and in the motu proprio itself (art. 6) noted that the vernacular might be used for the readings, but breathed not a word about modifying or substituting the lectionary. This could be a sign that he had begun to rethink his position, or it could be merely a sign that he did not wish to cause difficulties by appearing to approve precipitous change.

3. "The Lectionary in the Extraordinary Form," in J. Shaw (ed.), *The FIUV Position Papers on the 1962 Missal*, 2nd edn (n.p.: Lulu, 2014), p. 156; also at http://www.lms.org.uk/resources/fiuv-position-papers/fiuv_pp_15_lectionary. Monday is listed here as a day for which ferial readings were given, but that is an error; the *Comes* of Wurzburg (ca. 650) assigns ferial readings, very irregularly, to Wednesday, Friday and Saturday, while the *Comes* of Murbach (ca. 750) assigns them only to Wednesday and Friday, but very regularly. Monday does not figure into the scheme. See Gregory DiPippo, "Is the Medieval Liturgy a Source for the Modern Lectionary?" http://www.new liturgicalmovement.org/2013/12/is-medieval-liturgy-source-for-modern.html.

The increasing prominence of the sanctoral cycle and the great popularity of votive Masses tended to displace these ferial readings to such an extent that, from the thirteenth century onwards, it seemed nugatory to include in the missal readings that would only rarely be used. This fact, together with a desire to include everything needed for Mass in one conveniently printable and portable volume, explains why it was deemed sufficient for the 1570 missal to contain a reduced selection of readings.[4]

By the middle of the twentieth century, there was widespread agreement among participants in the liturgical movement that the Roman rite would benefit from an increase in the variety and extent of biblical lections—a judgment that emerged, in large part, from the contemporaneous biblical movement, with its renewed emphasis on salvation history. Fr Gaston Morin, a friend of Louis Bouyer, stated in 1944: "Whether we rejoice in it or deplore it, the liturgy is…biblical. To claim to make anyone under-stand it without initiating him into the Bible is a contradiction in terms."[5] Liturgists at Maria Laach were talking in 1951 about having a three- or four-year lectionary cycle.[6] In a 1956 meeting of Pius XII's Commission for the Reform of the Sacred Liturgy, a new *Capitulare lectionum et evangeliorum* for the Roman missal was examined. The conversation touched on a triennial cycle of readings. To Cardinal Cicognoni's formal query, "In general terms, should the scriptural pericopes of the Mass be expanded?" the Pian Commission unanimously replied in the affirmative.[7]

Given this background, it is hardly surprising that the Fathers of the Second Vatican Council discussed the revision of the lectionary but did not give it a great deal of attention. If one is looking through the *Acta Synodalia Sacrosancti Concilii Oecumenici Vaticani Secundi* for sensational speeches

4. "The Lectionary in the Extraordinary Form," p. 156.

5. Cited in J. Pepino, "Cassandra's Curse: Louis Bouyer, the Liturgical Movement, and the Post-Conciliar Reform of the Mass," *Antiphon* 18 (2014), pp. 254–300 (267 n. 54). In Austria, Fr Pius Parsch's publication *"Bibel und Liturgie*, founded in 1926, promoted the relationship between scripture and liturgy and encouraged wider readership of the Bible among Roman Catholics," "Liturgical Movement, The," in P. Bradshaw (ed.), *New SCM Dictionary of Liturgy and Worship* (London: SCM, 2013), p. 285.

6. A. Reid, *The Organic Development of the Liturgy: The Principles of Liturgical Reform and Their Relation to the Twentieth-Century Liturgical Movement Prior to the Second Vatican Council*, 2nd edn (San Francisco: Ignatius, 2005), p. 188.

7. The meeting took place on 6 July 1956; during it Msgr Dante and Fr (future Cardinal) Bea sparred over the idea, a taste of things to come. The minutes are published in N. Giampietro, *The Development of the Liturgical Reform: As Seen by Cardinal Ferdinando Antonelli from 1948 to 1970* (Fort Collins: Roman Catholic Books, 2009), pp. 297–98.

in the aula where Council Fathers sparred over scripture in the Mass, one will be somewhat disappointed.[8] A number of Fathers were concerned about the inconvenience of spreading out scripture over multiple years and therefore requiring multiple volumes for the celebration of Mass. Others suggested the compromise of enriching the annual cycle with weekday readings, particularly from the New Testament. Still others noted that the Sunday readings were lacking in some of the most touching passages of the Gospels.[9] But it was not a matter on which many had much to say. Modifications to the *Ordo Missae* and the retention of Latin were far more controversial and time-consuming subjects of debate.

In the end, the great majority of Fathers voted to approve the following provisions in the Constitution on the Sacred Liturgy, *Sacrosanctum Concilium*:

> 24. Sacred Scripture is of the greatest importance in the celebration of the liturgy. For it is from scripture that lessons are read and explained in the homily, and psalms are sung; the prayers, collects, and liturgical songs are scriptural in their inspiration and their force, and it is from the scriptures that actions and signs derive their meaning. Thus to achieve the restoration, progress, and adaptation of the Sacred Liturgy, it is essential to promote that warm and living love for scripture to which the venerable tradition of both eastern and western rites gives testimony.

8. In Henri De Lubac's journal, we see intervention after intervention tackling paragraphs of the liturgy schema that reaffirmed Latin as the language of the Roman rite and yet conceded the use of the vernacular for the needs of modern times; see: H. De Lubac, *Vatican Council Notebooks*, vol. 1 (San Francisco: Ignatius, 2015), pp. 175–286. There was perhaps no other single topic in the liturgy schema to which the Council Fathers more frequently returned. On the other hand, we will need to be cautious about trusting De Lubac's judgment. For example, a subtle and beautiful intervention on scripture by Bishop Agostinho Lopes de Moura on 5 November 1962, in General Congregation XII (see the following note for an excerpt), is given one line by De Lubac: "At no. 38: everything is fine already." This is not an accurate summary of what the good Bishop said!

9. As noted by Bishop Agostinho Lopes de Moura: "Igitur seligendi videntur textus in quibus via ad Patrem apprime demonstratur, v. g. parabolae de filio prodigo et de divite et Lazaro; colloquium Christi cum Nicodemo, ordinem supernaturalem innuens; cum muliere adultera et Zachaeo, misericordiam extollens; cum Samaritana, oecumenismo favens; necnon colloquium de iudicio finali habiturum, etc.—quae omnia, incredibile dictu, in Missa dominicali usque adhuc omnino desiderantur," *Acta Synodalia Sacrosancti Concilii Oecumenici Vaticani Secundi*, Vol. 1. *Perioda Prima*, Part 2. *Congregationes Generales* X–XVIII (Vatican City: Typis Polyglottis Vaticanis, 1970), pp. 125–26.

35. That rite and word may be clearly seen to be intimately conjoined in the liturgy:

1) In sacred celebrations a more abundant, more varied, and more suitable reading from Sacred Scripture should be restored [*instauretur*].

2) The best place for a sermon, since it is part of the liturgical action, is to be indicated even in the rubrics, as far as the rite will allow, and the ministry of preaching is to be fulfilled most faithfully and well. The sermon, moreover, should draw mainly from the fonts of scripture and the liturgy, as a proclamation of God's wonderful works in the history of salvation or the mystery of Christ, which is ever made present and active within us, especially in liturgical celebrations.

51. The treasures of the Bible are to be opened up more lavishly, so that richer fare may be provided for the faithful at the table of God's word. In this way a more representative portion of the Holy Scriptures will be read to the people in the course of a prescribed number of years.[10]

3. *The Consilium's Revised Lectionary*

The carrying out of these conciliar mandates was left in the hands of the *Consilium ad exsequendam Constitutionem de Sacra Liturgia*.[11] If the committee in charge of the lectionary, Coetus XI, had diligently followed two important principles of *Sacrosanctum Concilium*—namely, section 23, "There must be no innovations unless the good of the Church genuinely and certainly requires them; and care must be taken that any new forms adopted should in some way grow organically from forms already existing," and section 50, "elements which have suffered injury through accidents of history are now to be restored to the vigor which they had in the days of the holy Fathers, as may seem useful or necessary"—the result would have looked significantly different. For in that case, the process of lectionary

---

10. Translation from the Vatican website, modified in light of the Latin original. Something similar is said in *Sacrosanctum Concilium* 92 about the reform of scripture in the Divine Office: "As regards the readings [in the Divine Office], the following shall be observed: a) Readings from Sacred Scripture shall be arranged so that the riches of God's word may be easily accessible in more abundant measure. b) Readings excerpted from the works of the fathers, doctors, and ecclesiastical writers shall be better selected. c) The accounts of martyrdom or the lives of the saints are to accord with the facts of history."

11. A detailed although far from unbiased account may be found in A. Bugnini, *The Reform of the Liturgy 1948–1975* (Collegeville: The Liturgical Press, 1990), Chapter 26, "The Lectionary of the Roman Missal," pp. 406–25.

revision would have involved, first and foremost, restoring to the Roman rite lessons that once *actually* belonged to it, and second, cautiously introducing new lessons in a manner harmonious with the genius of the rite itself.[12]

But it was not to be so. In this area as in so many other areas, the ambitions of the *Consilium* were monumental and innovative. It was not enough to enhance what already existed; the entire lectionary was to be recast from the ground up.[13] The Council Fathers never debated the merits or demerits of such a plan because nothing had ever been said in the aula about scrapping the existing lectionary and starting more or less from scratch. As was true of other liturgical metamorphoses, it would have been unthinkable to the vast majority of the Council Fathers that the liturgy would soon be treated as in a laboratory experiment, whose parts could be removed, replaced, and fabricated *ad libitum*.[14]

Coetus XI's work resulted in the Novus Ordo lectionary with which we are all familiar: a three-year cycle of Sunday readings, a two-year cycle of weekday readings, and a veritable mountain of reading options for feasts, sacramental rites, and other special occasions. A fairly full account of the

12. The English version of *Sacrosanctum Concilium* found on the Vatican website contains a misleading translation of n. 35.1: "In sacred celebrations there is to be more reading from Holy Scripture, and it is to be more varied and suitable." A more precise translation would be: "In sacred celebrations a more abundant, more varied, and more suitable reading from Sacred Scripture should be restored [*instauretur*]." The former version implies that one simply adds on scripture; the latter, that one *restores* scripture to its original (historic) place.

13. There was talk in Coetus XI of retaining the existing lectionary as one of the years in the new lectionary. Ultimately, however, the group told the *Consilium* that it "must not without good reason consider itself bound to the old lectionary," with the main reason for a complete overhaul being that "this is the first time in the history of the Church that the opportunity has arisen of revising it, and this in hitherto unparalleled favorable circumstances and with hitherto unavailable tools," Bugnini, *Reform of the Liturgy*, p. 416. Prior to the promulgation of the *Consilium*'s lectionary for the entire Roman rite in 1969, several episcopal conferences had been given permission to experiment with expanded weekday lectionaries. The German model (adopted also in the British Isles) and the French model (which first introduced the responsorial psalm) proved particularly influential; Bugnini claims that they influenced the final shape of the universal lectionary. See the resources available at Matthew Hazell's "Lectionary Study Aids," http://catholiclectionary.blogspot.com/.

14. It is true that the bishops should have been forewarned of the possibility of some such sea change when the venerable ceremonies of Holy Week, as celebrated by the Latin Church for a millennium at least, were severely altered by Pope Pius XII in the 1950s.

principles behind the reform and many of the practical decisions made was offered in the document called *General Introduction to the Lectionary*, the first edition of which appeared in 1969, and a second, revised and expanded, in 1981.[15] In the pages that follow, I will be engaging ideas explicitly stated in this *General Introduction.*

4. *Critique of the Revised Lectionary*

To be sure, there are gains in the new lectionary, such as the splendid selection of prophetic readings for the ferias of Advent, the selection of readings for Paschaltide, and the felicitous pairing of certain Old Testament and New Testament pericopes.[16] Nevertheless, lone voices over the decades have pointed out various problems with it, ranging from the selection, length, and sheer number of readings, to the academic structuring of the cycles, to worrying omissions, to incidental problems that have arisen in practice.[17]

Here, I will re-examine four guiding principles of the lectionary revision, namely: the lengthening of the readings; their arrangement as a multi-year cycle; the general preference for *lectio semi-continua* or

15. For the first edition, see: *Documents on the Liturgy 1963–1979: Conciliar, Papal, and Curial Texts* (Collegeville: The Liturgical Press, 1982), pp. 573–86. The current second edition of the *General Introduction to the Lectionary* may be found at https://www.ewtn.com/library/CURIA/CDWLECT.HTM or http://www.liturgyoffice. org.uk/Resources/Rites/Lectionary.pdf. The Latin text of the *Praenotanda* for the *Ordo Lectionum Missae* is available at http://www.ccwatershed.org/media/pdfs/14/05/05/11–44–20_0.pdf.

16. No less a scholar than László Dobszay suggested that these Advent and Paschaltide ferial readings be considered for inclusion in a future edition of the *usus antiquior* missal: see *The Restoration and Organic Development of the Roman Rite* (London: T&T Clark, 2010), chapter 17, pp. 142–58.

17. While many books on the liturgy contain passing criticisms of the new lectionary, more substantive critiques may be found in L. Dobszay, *The Bugnini-Liturgy and the Reform of the Reform* (Front Royal: Church Music Association of America, 2003), pp. 121–46; idem, *Restoration and Organic Development*, pp. 142–58; A. Cekada, *Work of Human Hands: A Theological Critique of the Mass of Paul VI* (West Chester: Philothea, 2010), pp. 247–74; P. Kwasniewski, *Resurgent in the Midst of Crisis: Sacred Liturgy, the Traditional Latin Mass, and Renewal in the Church* (Kettering: Angelico, 2014), pp. 124–38 and passim; K. Gamber, *The Reform of the Roman Liturgy: Its Problems and Background* (San Juan Capistrano: Una Voce, 1993), pp. 69–75; J. Robinson, *The Mass and Modernity: Walking to Heaven Backward* (San Francisco: Ignatius, 2005), pp. 328–37.

continuity of readings over the readings of the sanctoral cycle; and the decision to omit "difficult" readings. Then I will consider how the new lectionary was implemented in the flesh, namely the *ars celebrandi* it inaugurated.

a. *The Purpose of Scripture in the Mass*

Before examining any particular principle behind the new lectionary, however, one must engage the more fundamental question of the very purpose or function of the reading of scripture in the Mass. Is it a moment of instruction for the people, or is it an element of the latreutic worship offered by Christ and His Mystical Body to the Most Holy Trinity? It can and should be both, but in a certain order.[18] The Word of God is proclaimed at Mass as part of the spiritual preparation for the Sacrifice of our Redeemer and the communion of God and man in the sacrament of His Passion. Because it is the sacrifice of the Mystical Body, head and members, it is also the sacrifice we, as children of the Church militant, offer to God in union with the Church triumphant and on behalf of the Church suffering. Consequently, the lessons have an ecclesial identity, a sacerdotal orientation, and a eucharistic finality, all of which ought to determine which lessons are the best for their purpose and how they are best to be proclaimed. The readings at Mass are not so much didactic as iconic, pointing the way beyond themselves.[19]

---

18. See P. Kwasniewski, "In Defense of Preserving Readings in Latin," *The Latin Mass* 22 (Summer 2013), pp. 10–13; also at http://www.newliturgicalmovement. org/2013/07/in-defense-of-preserving-readings-in_16.html. The readings in the old rite of Mass, treated more as doxology than instruction, paradoxically *gain* in formative power over the minds and hearts of the faithful. See Dobszay, *Restoration and Organic Development*, p. 144, esp. n. 8; idem, *Bugnini-Liturgy*, pp. 121–24.

19. The *General Introduction to the Lectionary* acknowledges the Eucharistic finality of the reading of scripture in the Mass—reiterated by Pope Benedict XVI in *Verbum Domini* 55, citing n. 10 ("It can never be forgotten that the divine word, read and proclaimed by the Church, has as its one purpose the sacrifice of the new covenant and the banquet of grace, that is, the Eucharist") and again at *Verbum Domini* 86—but it does not seem that the revised lectionary embodies this principle in a realistic and obvious way, for all the reasons that will be given in this essay. Far from never being forgotten, the eucharistic orientation of scriptural proclamation has been reversed, such that the Holy Eucharist itself is all too often viewed as a mere sign, a collective symbol of being gathered together in God's name. It is as if the liturgy of the Eucharist has fallen into the gravitational field of the liturgy of the Word, such that the flesh and blood reality is reduced to the conceptual status of a sign of identity and belonging. The proliferation of "celebrations of the Word of God," i.e., liturgies in the absence of a

The goal of liturgy is not to make us familiar with scripture in the manner of a bible study or catechism class—which, of course, ought to be taking place at some other time—but to give us the right formation of mind and heart with regard to the *realities* of our faith so that we may worship God in spirit and in truth. In the traditional rites of East and West, scripture serves as a *support* to the liturgical action; it illustrates or magnifies something else that the worship is principally about.

b. *Caution Regarding the Length of Readings*

As we saw, the Council Fathers desired that there be more scripture in the Church's liturgies. The first way to pursue this goal is to put *more* scripture into *each individual* liturgy. This was done both by adding a reading to Masses on Sundays and feasts and by lengthening the readings on average in all Masses. In light of scripture's purpose within the Mass, however, I believe we should reconsider the wisdom of increasing the readings *within* a given Mass. It is a truism that more is not necessarily better, but there are specific reasons to be concerned about what one might call the ecology of the Mass, the delicate balance of its interacting parts.

The generally longer readings of the revised lectionary, together with a new emphasis in *Sacrosanctum Concilium* on the homily as an integral part of the liturgy, have contributed to what one might call "verbal imperialism," that is, the tendency of words and wordiness to take over at many Masses, suffocate silence and meditation, and obscure the centrality of the Eucharistic Sacrifice.[20] It happens all too frequently that the homily will last a good fifteen minutes or more whereas the most solemn part of the Mass will last approximately three minutes due to the choice of the second Eucharistic prayer.

We must keep in mind that, in the ordinary form, nearly everything in the Mass is said aloud from start to finish. From the greeting to the collect to the readings to the homily to the Eucharistic prayer and so on until the end, everything is placed on the same level phenomenologically; done badly, it can be like going point by point through the items on a meeting agenda. This means that sheer length translates inevitably into emphasis. In this world of total exposure and extroversion, the Eucharistic prayer

priest that end up looking somewhat *like* Masses to the untrained faithful, only furthers this process of inverse gravitation. If there is to be such a celebration, it should take the form of the Divine Office, the original and authentic "liturgy of the Word."

20. See Kwasniewski, "The Word of God and the Wordiness of Man," in *Resurgent in the Midst of Crisis*, pp. 33–46; idem, "Blessed Silence," *Sacred Music* 141 (Spring 2014), pp. 47–52; Benedict XVI, *Verbum Domini* nn. 21 and 66.

tends to be the loser; it simply does not have enough prominence to hold its own. In the *usus antiquior*, the silent Roman canon provides a center of gravity that no text or talking can outshine. It was and will always be the great counterbalance to lengthy sermons or sub-optimal music—or even sumptuous music.

The total size of the Sunday liturgy of the Word, if one takes into account the two readings, a responsorial psalm, the Gospel, a possibly bloated homily, the Creed, and the prayer of the faithful, when followed by a diminished liturgy of the Eucharist, has left far too many Catholics with a false impression of what the Mass primarily *is*. It seems like the main thing we do together is read scripture and talk about it. A reenactment of the Last Supper is then added on so that everyone gets to receive something before going home. As we know, Catholics like to get something at Mass, whether ashes or palms or bulletins, and, in a way, the lamentable phenomenon of everyone lining up to receive communion fits in with this pattern. The Mass as a true and proper sacrifice has therefore been almost entirely eclipsed by the Mass as "a table of the Word and a table of the Eucharist from which we are fed."[21] Obviously there is some truth in this language, but when it becomes the central way of understanding the Mass, we are looking at a profound distortion.

If the purpose of the readings at Mass is to prepare people for and lead into the great Eucharistic Sacrifice, then the danger of verbal imperialism is obvious: by unduly prolonging the readings, the words have broken off and become their own thing, a center of gravity that *dominates* the liturgy. At this point, the readings are no longer in harmony with their purpose at Mass but are militating against it. Here we see, for the first time, the possibility of scripture *in tension with* the Eucharist rather than serving it as a handmaid. The lengthening of the readings and the overemphasis on the homily, coming together with other liturgical changes (more often than not, abridgements or simplifications) made after Vatican II, has disturbed the balance of the Mass, just as excessive farming can lead to soil erosion and the destruction of an ecosystem.

c. *The Fittingness of an Annual Cycle*
We have considered some of the problems of increasing the readings *within* one Mass. A second way of putting more scripture into the Mass would be to extend the readings over a greater *number* of Masses. While this could be done even within the scope of one year, it seems that the

21. See, for examples of official uses of this language, *Sacrosanctum Concilium* nn. 48 and 51; Constitution on Divine Revelation *Dei Verbum* n. 21; Benedict XVI, *Verbum Domini* n. 68.

liturgical reformers quickly moved to the assumption of a multi-year cycle. With multiple years at its disposal, the new lectionary is able to cover a remarkable portion of scripture, comprising the whole of salvation history and offering a remarkable array of important biblical passages. This, more than anything else, is seen as the great achievement of the reform.

However, I would like to urge caution even here. A one-year cycle of readings can be considered not only with regard to the *quantity* of scripture it presents but also with regard to the *way* in which it presents the scripture it contains. One year is a natural unit of time, with a satisfying completeness, like that of a circle.[22] Historically, Western and Eastern rites have always had a one-year cycle of readings,[23] as does synagogue worship.[24] Indeed, every culture has linked the rhythms of human life to the combined rhythms of the sun and the moon, joining the human to the cosmological.

22. *Sacrosanctum Concilium* itself furnishes a convincing account of why the liturgical year is just that—a *year*: "Holy Mother Church is conscious that she must celebrate the saving work of her divine Spouse by devoutly recalling it on certain days throughout the course of the year. Every week, on the day which she has called the Lord's day, she keeps the memory of the Lord's resurrection, which she also celebrates once in the year, together with His blessed passion, in the most solemn festival of Easter. Within the cycle of a year, moreover, she unfolds the whole mystery of Christ, from the incarnation and birth until the ascension, the day of Pentecost, and the expectation of blessed hope and of the coming of the Lord... In celebrating this annual cycle of Christ's mysteries, holy Church honors with especial love the Blessed Mary, Mother of God, who is joined by an inseparable bond to the saving work of her Son... The Church has also included in the annual cycle days devoted to the memory of the martyrs and the other saints" (nn. 102–4).

23. The position paper quoted earlier also makes this point: "The [traditional] lectionary's limited size allows the faithful to attain a thorough familiarity with the cycle, particularly in the context of the use of hand-missals and commentaries on the liturgy, which expound the passages and their connection with the season, and the proper prayers and chants of the day. The association of feasts and particular Sundays with particular Gospel or Epistle passages echoes the practice of the Eastern churches, where Sundays are often named after the Gospel of the day" ("The Lectionary in the Extraordinary Form," p. 155 n. 5).

24. The Torah was held to have been divided by Ezra the scribe into an annual reading schedule of 54 "parashot" or sections. These are distributed across the available Sabbaths. Some Jewish congregations follow a three-year cycle of Torah readings, but the one-year cycle is the more ancient and common. See, nevertheless, Paul Bradshaw's cautions about arguing from ancient Jewish liturgical practice in *The Search for the Origins of Christian Worship: Sources and Methods for the Study of Early Liturgy*, 2nd edn (Oxford: Oxford University Press, 2002).

With the one-year cycle comes repetition and its fruit of familiarity, which leads to internalization—the planting of the seed deep in the soil of the soul. One who immerses himself in the traditional liturgy becomes aware that its annual readings, over time, are becoming bone of one's bone, flesh of one's flesh. One begins to think of certain days, months, seasons of the year, or categories of saints in tandem with their particular readings, which open up their meaning more and more to the devout soul. If the Word of God has an infinite depth to it, the traditional liturgy bids us stand beside the same well year by year, dropping down our bucket into it, and in that way *awakening* us to an inexhaustible depth that may not be so clear to someone who is dipping his bucket into different places of a flooding stream over the course of two or three years.

The fundamental elements of faith and habits of prayer need to be inculcated week after week, day after day; and thus it is pedagogically most appropriate to have readings repeated annually: the age-old Epistle and Gospel assigned for the various Sundays after Pentecost, the readings for the Easter Octave, the readings for certain categories of saints—Martyrs, Apostles, Confessors, Doctors, Popes, Virgins. In this way, the Christian people are strongly *formed* by a set of "core texts" throughout the cycle of the year, rather than being carried off each day into new regions of text—especially some of the drier historical narratives or longer passages of the Prophets, from which it may be hard to benefit except by extra-liturgical study.

It seems inarguable that the faithful need more scripture in their lives. But it does not follow that we must cover as much scriptural ground as possible at Mass. Consider the matter from a psychological point of view. The reading at Mass is a "feature of an event": the mind does not easily connect yesterday's reading to today's, or today's with tomorrow's. A bunch of things are happening in the course of the liturgy and in the rest of my day, and unless the priest very deliberately connects the readings, each day is an entity unto itself. The daily Mass is the discrete unit, and so the readings should be proportioned to *it*, not to a larger time sequence (apart from the general character of the liturgical year and its seasons). The result is that with an expanded lectionary people will hear and *forget* more scripture than they did before; whereas on the old one-year cycle, people hear things repeatedly and have the opportunity to become familiar with them. We stand to get more, spiritually, out of *one* inspired passage that becomes familiar than from a long-term cycle attempting to "get through" a lot of scripture.

The situation is quite different with *lectio divina*, where each day one is focused exclusively on the Bible, and so it is easier to connect days to each other. Because they essentially practice *lectio divina* or at least some form of concentrated bible study as they prepare their homilies, priests are the ones who stand to benefit the most from the two-year/three-year cycles, which could explain the enthusiasm of many of the clergy for the lectionary. But what about the laity? Note that the Catholic biblical renewal in recent years is largely from Protestant converts who have introduced salvation history and *lectio divina* into parish programs. This suggests that the work we need to be doing is more at home *outside* the Mass than *inside* it.

Thus, although it is common to praise the new lectionary for containing much more scripture than its predecessor, experience with both could lead one to the opposite conclusion—namely, that the multi-year lectionary is unwieldy and hard to absorb, whereas the old cycle of readings is beautifully proportioned to the rhythm of the natural cycle of time and the fullness of the ecclesiastical year of grace that builds upon nature. And we can say, in general, that an annual cycle of well-chosen readings is more suited to the iconic and latreutic purpose of scripture in the Mass as articulated earlier.

d. *The Primacy of the Sanctoral Cycle*

Having looked at the extension of the readings both within a given Mass and over many Masses, I turn now to a third guiding principle of the revised lectionary, namely, the preference for continuous reading or *lectio semi-continua*, in other words, that we read sequentially from a certain book or letter or Gospel over a period of time, and that maintaining this continuity for the most part trumps the sanctoral cycle. This is a distinct and important principle.

Everything said above about the impracticality of continuity in readings could be repeated here, but I want to draw attention to the special relationship the saints have to scripture and to the Mass. Since the goal of Christian faith is not a *material* knowledge of scripture but personal sanctification and conversion, which is the *formal* content and aim of scripture itself, the saints are rightly put forward in the liturgy as our example of how to live, how to believe, how to love—and scripture is rightly pressed into service for this purpose, by the traditional correlation of specific readings with specific saints or classes of saints. On account of both their more limited number and their memorable (and mandated) alignment with particular saints, these lessons and gospels facilitate *familiarity* with the Word of God as it illustrates or teaches us about the triumph of God's holy ones.

The saints are, one could say, scripture in flesh and blood, and that is why the written word is so appropriately called upon to minister to them and reflect their existential primacy.[25] Scripture, by itself, is a dead letter. It is the saints who are the ultimate proof and most glorious manifestation of the truth of the Christian faith. The saints demonstrate that scripture is not a lifeless book but a living paradigm.[26] We must understand the role of scripture at Mass in reference to its embodiment in the lives of the saints and its continual directing of our gaze to the supreme reality of Jesus Christ, Eternal and Incarnate Wisdom.

Allow me to offer just one example. On 4 May, the feast of St Monica in the *usus antiquior*, the Epistle of the Mass is St Paul speaking of the honor due to true widows (a reading Monica shares with other holy widows), but the specially chosen Gospel recounts when Jesus raised the weeping widow's son from the dead and restored him to his mother.[27] What more

25. It bears mentioning that scholarship on the history of the Christian liturgy has established with certainty that, apart from Easter, the very earliest liturgical commemorations were *not* those of the great feasts of Our Lord and His Mother, but rather those of the martyrs, like St Stephen and St Lawrence. For example, as Dom Gregory Dix notes, "the feast of S. Stephen, December 26th, seems to have originated at Jerusalem in the fourth century (before December 25th had been accepted there as the date of our Lord's birth)," *The Shape of the Liturgy*, new edn (London: Continuum, 2005), p. 378; for a fascinating account of the development of the liturgical calendar and the cycles within it, see Dix's entire chapter, "The Sanctification of Time," pp. 303–96. The special feastdays that ornamented the primitive Eucharistic liturgies with proper readings, prayers, and antiphons were nearly always those of the saints; the sanctoral cycle enjoyed a *de facto* pride of place for many centuries. On the basis of respect for tradition, therefore, this cycle deserves at the very least to be allotted a place of honor within the framework of the later emphasis on Sundays and holy days honoring the mysteries of Christ. This the *Novus Ordo* calendar and rubrics have, regrettably, failed to do.

26. Seen in this light, it is more than slightly concerning that the cult of the saints was downplayed by the *Consilium* and liturgists of the period: the systematic elimination of asking for the intercession of the saints in the collects, *super oblata*, and postcommunions of the reformed missal; the square brackets in the Roman canon; the elevation of the weekday cycle of readings over the commons, and so on. What we are witnessing here is one among countless examples of the protestantization of the Mass—something Bugnini openly talks about when he says, on almost every other page of his *Reform of the Liturgy*, that this or that course of action was evaluated for its ecumenical advantages and disadvantages, and that the *Consilium* consistently tried to pattern the reform of the Catholic liturgy off of, or gear it towards, the concurrent reforms and noises of reform in other Christian communities.

27. 1 Tim 5:3–10; Luke 7:11–16. Although virtually the same Gospel pericope (Luke 7:11–17; see: *Ordo Lectionum Missae* 1969, p. 234) is stated to be an option

perfect Gospel could there be for the mother of St Augustine! What could better impress both the Gospel *and* Monica's life on our minds than this striking juxtaposition! Each year, throughout her sojourn on earth, no matter how many thousands of years will pass by, Holy Mother Church will thus commemorate the mother who never lost faith in God and eventually regained her son, dead in sin and error, risen in the life of grace.

e. *The Coherence of the Mass Propers and the Ordinary*

The three guiding principles of the new lectionary that I have examined so far have to do with the quantity of scripture in the Mass. Before moving on to a fourth guiding principle that does not concern quantity, I want to pause and raise a question about the category of quantity itself as regards scripture in the Mass.

We can take the question of the sanctoral cycle as an example of what I mean. The use of an all-embracing proper or common of the Mass within the sanctoral cycle has the effect of knitting an entire liturgy together as a seamless garment: the prayers honor and invoke the saint; the readings and antiphons extol the virtues of the saint, who is put forward as our example and teacher; the Eucharistic Sacrifice links the Church Triumphant, represented by the lists of saints in the Roman canon, to all of us pilgrims in the Church Militant. The whole liturgy acquires a unity of sanctification, showing us both the primordial Way of sanctity—Jesus in the Holy Eucharist—and the models of sanctity achieved.

The feast of St Thérèse of Lisieux[28] (see: Appendix A) can serve as a particular example of the immense literary and theological richness of the traditional *Missale Romanum*, which centers the variable parts of the Mass around the saint whose memory we celebrate on earth. As can be easily seen, the elements of the Mass connect with one another like links in a chain, providing the worshiper with a focused spiritual formation and a powerful incentive to prayer.[29]

---

in the new lectionary for the Feast of St Monica on 27 August, the fact that there are still other options in the common of holy women and, more tellingly, that the *General Introduction to the Lectionary* strongly discourages substituting a sanctoral reading for the ferial reading, will in most cases conspire to eliminate the special Gospel for St Monica.

28. See Kwasniewski, "Loss of Riches," for more discussion of the propers for this particular feast and how they compare with the propers given in the modern Roman missal and *Graduale Romanum.*

29. It could be due to my own limitations, but the same number of years of immersion in the new lectionary and the new Mass has simply not produced in me the same depth of remembrance, association, resonance, and penetration into the texts of the liturgy.

If we take a step further back and look at the antiphons, prayers, and readings against the backdrop of the presence of scripture throughout the *Ordo Missae*, we can see just how impressive is the result (see: Appendix B). One might call this phenomenon "biblical permeation" or "scriptural suffusion," a suffusion supported by the unchanging *Ordo Missae*. Because the Order of Mass is not subject to a plethora of options, it is much easier to connect the variable parts to the invariable. For example, the characteristic use of Old Testament texts in the antiphons strongly harmonizes with the Roman canon's express mention of Abel, Abraham, and Melchizedek and with its hieratic language of sacrifice, so reminiscent of the Mosaic Law. The solidity and stability of the canon is like a massive foundation of rock on which the carefully hewn stones of the propers are built up into a spacious edifice for prayer.[30]

As Appendix B shows, scripture permeates the *usus antiquior* at every level. Even though many of the prayers are said silently, Catholics who are well acquainted with the old rite follow along in their missals and make these rich prayers their own. This has certainly been my experience: I have come to cherish not only the changing propers but also the fixed verses from Psalms 42, 25, 15, and the Prologue of John's Gospel.

In the new liturgy, by contrast, the prayers, readings, and Eucharist are awkwardly situated vis-à-vis one another: they no longer fit together into a single flow of action. The biblical lessons are extrinsic and accidental to the celebration of most saints' days, in tension with scripture's inner purpose. The general problem here is the overall *integrity* of the liturgical service. Going beyond the formal "readings" at Mass, we should also look to how scripture is present throughout the *rest* of the liturgy. How "saturated with scripture" is the liturgy *as a whole*? Do the proper antiphons, prayers, and readings cohere with one another and with the *Ordo Missae*?[31]

30. For extensive reflections on the theological, liturgical, and mystico-ascetical value of the propers of the Mass, see: W. Mahrt, "The Propers of the Mass as Integral to the Liturgy" and S. Weber, "Singing the Propers of the Mass: A School of Christian Prayer," in J. Rutherford (ed.), *Benedict XVI and Beauty in Sacred Music* (Dublin: Four Courts; New York: Scepter, 2012), pp. 149–62 and pp. 163–74; L. Dobszay, "The *Proprium Missae* of the Roman Rite," in U. M. Lang (ed.), *The Genius of the Roman Rite: Historical, Theological, and Pastoral Perspectives on Catholic Liturgy* (Chicago: Liturgy Training Publications, 2010), pp. 83–118.

31. The elements in the *Novus Ordo* are more disparate for a reason—namely, a different *coetus* was responsible for each area of the reform, and it appears at times they did not communicate very well; see Lauren Pristas's remarks on the treatment of Septuagesimatide by Coetus I and XVIIIbis in *The Collects of the Roman Missal* (London: Bloomsbury, 2013), pp. 97–104, 110–11. Of course, the work of reform

Accordingly, while there is obviously a vastly greater *extension* of scripture in the new rite, one may still raise a question about its *intensity*. Is the new Roman missal as deeply imbued with the language, imagery, and spirit of scripture as the old *Missale Romanum*?

f. *The Omission or Dilution of "Difficult" Passages*

To this point I have called into question those guiding principles behind the reform of the lectionary that concerned the quantity of scripture in the Mass. I want to look briefly at one of the *non*-quantitative aspects of the reform, namely, the decision to omit or marginalize "difficult" passages.

It might be assumed that once the reformers allowed themselves three years of Sundays and two years of weekdays, they would certainly not fail to include in their new lectionary *all* the readings that are found in the traditional Roman liturgy, and that in their march through various books of the Bible they would not omit any key passages. Instead, they made a programmatic decision to avoid what they considered "difficult" biblical texts.[32] What kind of texts did they have in mind? I will offer a couple of examples.

In the vast new lectionary, the following three verses from 1 Cor 11 *never appear*, not even once: "Therefore whosoever shall eat this bread, or drink of the chalice of the Lord unworthily, shall be guilty of the Body and of the Blood of the Lord. But let a man prove himself; and so let him eat of that bread, and drink of the chalice. For he that eateth and drinketh unworthily, eateth and drinketh judgment to himself, not discerning the Body of the Lord" (vv. 27–29). St Paul's warning against receiving the Body and Blood of the Lord unworthily, that is, unto one's damnation, has not been read at any ordinary form Mass for almost half a century. And yet, in the *usus antiquior*, these verses are heard at least *three times every year*, once on Holy Thursday (where the Epistle is 1 Cor 11:20–32),[33] and twice on

---

needed organizing, but the *Consilium* was organized for sheer speed, to achieve reform as quickly as humanly possible, because, as Bugnini recognized so well, there was only a short window of time in which to achieve their promethean goals.

32. *General Introduction to the Lectionary*, n. 76; see: Cekada, *Work of Human Hands*, pp. 265–72.

33. On Holy Thursday in the *Novus Ordo*, the second reading is 1 Cor 11:23–26, simply narrating the institution of the Eucharist. The longer reading found in the *usus antiquior* provides the full context for what St Paul is saying and makes clearer the connection between the institution of the Holy Eucharist and the present gathering of Christians for the celebration of the Mass. Given that the *General Introduction to the Lectionary* claims that the new selection of readings embodies the idea that readings should form one action with and lead to the Eucharist, this particular omission of

Corpus Christi (where the Epistle is 1 Cor 11:23–29 and the Communion antiphon is 1 Cor 11:26–27).[34] Catholics who attend the *usus antiquior* will never fail to have these challenging words placed before their consciences. Let us be frank: the concept of an unworthy communion has simply disappeared from the general Catholic consciousness, and the new lectionary must share some of the blame.

It is well known that the cursing or imprecatory psalms were removed from the liturgy of the Hours, but it is less well known that selective psalm suppression affected the Mass as well.[35] There are a surprising number of psalm verses *prominent* in the old missal that are either *absent* in the new lectionary or much more rarely found. For example, the moving lines of Ps 42 with which nearly every celebration of the *usus antiquior* begins were, in the new lectionary, exiled to Friday of the 25th week of Ordinary Time in Year 1 and a couple of verses in the Easter Vigil. That's it. Psalm 34 [35], so beloved to our ancestors for its Passiontide language and ascetical images, was whittled down from eight appearances in the *usus antiquior* to a single appearance in the *usus recentior*—*if*, that is, the Introit is said or sung, which is optional (see: Appendix C).[36]

---

1 Cor 11:27–29 from the lectionary seems inconsistent with the reformers' own account of the purpose of scripture in the Mass. On the other hand, perhaps it was thought that any talk of damnation in connection with the love feast of the Eucharist was "difficult for the faithful to understand."

34. If the faithful happen to attend a votive Mass of the Blessed Sacrament—a popular choice among votive Masses—they will encounter them yet again.

35. Because the various aspects of liturgical reform were farmed out to a large number of groups working under the *Consilium*, the disappearance of many psalm verses from the liturgy cannot be laid to the charge of just one group and does not appear to have been centrally planned. For example, Coetus XI was responsible for the Gospel acclamation verses and the replacement of Graduals/Tracts with responsorial psalms, while Coetus XXV was responsible for the revision of the chant books, which would have included the entrance, offertory, and communion antiphons (as well as the great interlectional chants, which were allowed to remain as options). Nevertheless, the passing-over or removal of "difficult" psalms clearly reflects a widespread mentality of scholars of the time, and in that sense the resulting lacunae are anything but accidental.

36. It is true that one can recover some of these verses by singing the propers from the *Graduale Romanum*; but, alas, communities that chant the full Gregorian propers in the context of the ordinary form are rarer than hen's teeth. *De facto*, this psalm has dropped out of the Church's public worship. It may someday be different. If Fr Samuel Weber's *The Proper of the Mass for Sundays and Solemnities* (San Francisco: Ignatius, 2015) catches on, we will see a number of neglected biblical verses reappearing in the context of the ordinary form.

What is happening in such examples (and they are numerous) is quite simple. Embarrassed by a divinely revealed doctrine or spiritual attitude, certain members of the Church do what they can to ensure that it is either never, or only very rarely, mentioned. The men of Coetus XI knew what the traditional lections were, and it appears that they deliberately suppressed some of them.[37] The novelty of the multi-year cycles and the monumental fact of "more scripture" distracted our attention from the subtler question of what was lost in the transition. A similar process of doctrinal attenuation can be seen in the *Consilium*'s editing of the collects, whose post-conciliar versions frequently omit or downplay mention of "unpleasant things."[38]

g. *The* Ars Celebrandi

Everything I have said to this point has to do with the lectionary itself: what led to its creation, what principles guided its formation, and how particular readings were selected or excluded. But how scripture is *treated*, how it is reverenced by the ministers, how it is integrated into the entire liturgy, is arguably no less important than the selection and quantity of readings. A metaphor would be the contrast between the modern printed book and the medieval illuminated manuscript. A Bible that has been written out by hand in a beautiful script ennobled with an elaborate initial and surrounded by lavish ornamentation is a certain way of *viewing and treating* the Word of God, no less than a cheap modern paperback that crams the words onto thin sheets with a drab, uniform layout and no special images. In this final portion of my critique, I would like to turn our attention to the domain of the *ars celebrandi*.

One sign of whether we are grasping the Eucharistic nobility and finality of the readings is whether the lections are proclaimed with due solemnity. They should be surrounded by a rich ceremonial, including the *chanting* of the sacred text, candles, and incense. At a sung Mass in the *usus antiquior* the priest's (and cleric's) chanting of the readings elevates them in a

---

37. Could some of the omissions have been accidental or subconscious—motivated, for example, by the idea of a "liturgy for modern man," which was an unquestioned *desideratum* of the reformers? From the way Bugnini describes it in his memoirs, Coetus XI had a huge amount of well-organized information in front of them as they worked on the new lectionary, including detailed lists of the lections included at that time in the *Missale Romanum* and in other traditional rites (see: *Reform of the Liturgy*, pp. 412–14). The conclusion that these omissions were deliberate seems unavoidable.

38. See: Pristas, *Collects of the Roman Missal*; Cekada, *Work of Human Hands*, pp. 219–45.

manner fitting to the depth and beauty of God's own words and fitting, also, to the public act of transmitting divine revelation. The chant is like musical incense. At a solemn Mass, the hierarchical chanting, first by the subdeacon, then by the deacon, wonderfully expresses the metaphysical relationship of the elements: the lower minister sings the Epistle, the mid-level minister sings the Gospel, and the highest minister, the one who directly represents Christ the High Priest, whispers the words of conse-cration that infinitely exceed any song on earth. In such ways, the classical Roman rite brings out forcefully the fact that when we are handling scripture, we are not handling mere human verbiage, but precious secrets proceeding from the mouth of God. Paradoxically, the *usus antiquior* treats the Word of God with tremendous veneration and yet decisively subordi-nates that written Word to the *Mysterium Fidei*, the Word made flesh.

At a sung Mass, the chanting of the Epistle and Gospel and the slow-moving elaborate beauty of the interlectional chants—the Gradual and the Alleluia or Tract—prompt us to receive the Word *as God's Word* and to meditate on it.[39] While theoretically available to the *usus recentior*, chanted readings and the chants between the readings are encountered extremely rarely.[40] Rather, the delivery of the Sunday readings—up to four of them in a row, read aloud in the manner of a lecture, and all too often with monotonous elocution—treats these words as merely human, not divine, and discourages meditation. (Low Mass in the *usus antiquior* is a separate question, but I would argue that the overall atmosphere of silence and reverence characteristic of the low Mass endows the readings and antiphons with a similarly meditative poignancy, and their being read at the altar by the priest serves a function similar to their solemn chanting at a sung Mass.)

39. See, in addition to the articles mentioned in footnote 30, the profound exposi-tion of the role of chanted lections and the proper antiphons, especially the Gradual and Alleluia/Tract: W. Mahrt, *The Musical Shape of the Liturgy* (Richmond: Church Music Association of America, 2012).

40. See P. Kwasniewski, "Why Are the Readings Not Sung at Mass?" (http://www.ccwatershed.org/blog/2014/nov/20/why-are-readings-not-sung-mass/). If we take up the earlier metaphor of a liturgical "ecosystem," the modern responsorial psalm can be seen as an invasive species that has choked out the more sophisticated and delicate species of Gregorian chant. And while there are acceptable plainchant settings of the responsorial psalms, they cannot compare artistically with the inter-lectional chants of the *Graduale*, nor can they emulate the quality of the chants as a musical *lectio divina.*

We saw earlier that the Council had stated, in words that warmed the hearts of Fr Bouyer, Fr Morin, and others of their generation: "To achieve the restoration, progress, and adaptation of the Sacred Liturgy, it is essential to promote that warm and living love for scripture to which the venerable tradition of both eastern and western rites gives testimony" (*Sacrosanctum Concilium* 24). How, in a manner proper to liturgy, do we best promote a *warm and living love for scripture*? We treat scripture in a special ceremonial way: we enclose it in a silver or gold case; we chant the readings; we incense and kiss the Gospel and flank it with candles. With its simultaneous introduction of a multitude of readings and of lay lectors, the ordinary form has ironically rendered a sung and solemn liturgy of the Word extremely rare, and, as we know too well, the spoken version tends to be unremarkable and eminently ignorable, when it is not positively annoying due to well-meant attempts to declaim the readings with dramatic flair.

Finally, we can ask ourselves: Does there *need* to be a homily at a weekday Mass? Cannot the Word of God, or better yet, the liturgy as a whole, sometimes be allowed to "speak for itself"? We need to find ways to make our liturgies less centered on human wisdom and the personalities of the actors and more centered on Jesus Christ, His Word, His Sacrifice.

5. *Conclusions*

The criteria we have considered—the function of scripture in the Eucharistic Sacrifice, the internal cohesion of the Mass as an "ecosystem," the psychology of memory, the natural unit of the year, the due place of the sanctoral cycle, the spiritual role of difficult passages, the aesthetic and ceremonial treatment suited to the divine Word, and, not least of all, the authority inherent in traditional practice—permit us to draw a number of general conclusions.

First, like much else in the liturgical reform conducted under Pope Paul VI, the new lectionary exhibits signs of unseemly haste, overweening ambition, and disregard of principles approved by the Council Fathers.[41]

41. As to haste, one may get a glimpse into the rushed chaos of the lectionary process by reading an eyewitness account of just a little piece of it: P. Inwood, "The Scandalous (but True) Story Behind ICEL's 1969 Lectionary for Mass" (http://www.praytellblog.com/index.php/2015/04/13/the-scandalous-but-true-story-behind-icels–1969-lectionary-for-mass/). In his notes on the first and seventh meetings of the *Consilium*, Cardinal Antonelli expressed considerable dismay at how rushed things were: "I am not enthusiastic about this work. I am unhappy at how much the Commission has changed. It is merely an assembly of people, many of them

The Council's call for "more scripture" was open to different and even conflicting realizations. The revised lectionary, while it does represent one possible implementation of numbers 35 and 51 of *Sacrosanctum Concilium*, ends up contradicting outright numbers 23 and 50 of the same Constitution, which enunciate the controlling principle of continuity with tradition as well as the request that elements already present in our tradition be *restored*. It is worth noting that the bulk of the readings in the pre-conciliar *Missale Romanum* represent an inheritance from the early centuries of Catholic worship, a stable body of lessons on which generations of pastors, preachers, theologians, and laity had been nurtured, a tradition deserving of immense respect for its venerable antiquity.[42] It is, to speak plainly, outrageous that this unbroken tradition, which had withstood all the ravages of time, fell victim to the scalpels of liturgical specialists. The result has been an obvious rupture and discontinuity at the very heart of the Roman rite, in spite of legal fictions and constructs necessary to help us through this period of crisis.[43]

Second, quite apart from whether or not it can be seen as faithful to the Council's desiderata, the *Novus Ordo* lectionary is gravely flawed because of its overall conception, its unwieldy bulk, its politically correct omissions, and its watering down of key spiritual goods emphasized in the old readings.[44] No human mind can relate to so great a quantity of biblical text spread out over multiple years: it is out of proportion to the natural cycle

---

incompetent, and others well advanced on the road to novelty. The discussions are extremely hurried. Discussions are based on impressions and the voting is chaotic"; Giampietro, *Development of Liturgical Reform*, p. 166. "I have the impression, however, that the body which decided in the matter, in this case 35 members of the *Consilium*, were not competent enough to deal with the question. There is also a negative factor: the haste to drive on simply because *tempus urget*"; p. 172.

42. For some indications of this antiquity and stability, see: J. Baudot, *The Lectionary: Its Sources and History* (London: Catholic Truth Society, 1910); Dix, *Shape of the Liturgy*, pp. 360–69, 470–72.

43. I am assuming, for the sake of argument, that the provisions of *Sacrosanctum Concilium* are mutually compatible with each other and with the universal principles of liturgy enunciated in the first chapter—an assumption that can be difficult to maintain at times.

44. As a result of the loss of a one-year cycle with its frequent repetition of certain scripture passages (including passages unique to the old rite), a Catholic attending Mass in the *usus recentior* is going to receive a different spiritual formation characterized by different emphases. This will be true whether we are talking about Catholics who attend on Sundays only, or about those who also attend on weekdays. The comparison of the resulting differences in spirituality is a cutting-edge area of research that deserves further study.

of the year and its seasons; it is out of proportion to the supernatural cycle of the liturgical year. The revised lectionary does not lend itself readily to the sacrificial finality of the Mass but, inasmuch as it appears to serve a didactic function, sets up a different goal, quasi-independent of the offering of the Sacrifice.[45] The use of the names "liturgy of the Word" and "liturgy of the Eucharist" underlines the problem: it is as if there are two liturgies glued together.[46] They are seldom joined by the obvious connection of being related to one and the same *feast*, since the new lectionary prefers to ignore the saints in its march through the books of scripture.[47] Nor has it often been the custom to join the two liturgies by means of ceremonial practices that show the chanting of scripture to be one phase of the journey towards Jerusalem and the hill of Calvary (see: Luke 9:51).

Third, in light of this critique, we are in a better position to acknowledge that the *usus antiquior* possesses what is, in many ways, a superior lectionary, and Catholics who rejoice to worship in this form of the Roman

45. As William Mahrt writes: "The anthropocentric approach may well have stemmed from a misconception about the liturgy—that its principal purpose is didactic. If the liturgy is primarily to instruct the people, then the interaction between priest and people is quite appropriate. But if the principal purpose is the worship of almighty God, the joining in Christ's sacrifice to the Father, then the theocentric approach makes more sense. This does not mean that there are not didactic elements in the liturgy, particularly in the lessons and the sermon. But even then, the function of the reading—that is, the singing—of the lessons is much more than simple instruction. It is a celebration of the history of our salvation, the telling of the foundation narrative of our religion, articulated particularly by the gospel readings through the course of the liturgical year. I would even venture to say that the best instruction for the people is to lead them into an intense participation in the sacrifice of Christ"; "Solemnity," *Sacred Music* 142 (Spring 2015), pp. 3–7 (5–6).

46. I have gone into this more in my article "Why 'Mass of the Catechumens' Makes Better Sense Than 'Liturgy of the Word,'" http://www.newliturgicalmovement. org/2014/12/why-mass-of-catechumens-makes-better.html.

47. Indeed, the *General Introduction to the Lectionary* expressly recommends that the cycle of readings *not* be interrupted by special readings on saints' memorials, unless there is some compelling pastoral reason to do so: "The first concern of a priest celebrating with a congregation is the spiritual benefit of the faithful and he will be careful not to impose his personal preference on them. Above all he will make sure not to omit too often or needlessly the readings assigned for each day in the weekday lectionary: the Church's desire is to provide the faithful with a richer share at the table of God's word" (n. 83, citing *Sacrosanctum Concilium* 51). N. 82 also notes that the weekday readings are to be used on their assigned days "in most cases...unless a solemnity, feast, or memorial with proper readings [i.e. where the saint is mentioned in the reading] occurs."

rite should be unafraid to maintain and argue this advantage. We have a magnificent treasure to conserve and to share generously with our fellow Catholics.[48]

Fourth, the current *usus antiquior* readings are less varied and numerous than they have been at earlier points in the Roman rite's history, and there is no inherent reason why the annual cycle could not be judiciously enriched with daily readings for certain seasons and by the selection of appropriate new readings for certain saints' feasts, all the while scrupulously respecting and maintaining the cycle of readings already in place. In this way, the primacy of the liturgical year and the coherence of the sanctoral cycle could both be maintained, and neither sound tradition nor valuable spiritual goods would have to be compromised.[49]

48. "St Gregory the Great...made every effort to ensure that the new peoples of Europe received both the Catholic faith and the treasures of worship and culture that had been accumulated by the Romans in preceding centuries. He commanded that the form of the Sacred Liturgy as celebrated in Rome (concerning both the Sacrifice of Mass and the Divine Office) be conserved... In this way the Sacred Liturgy, celebrated according to the Roman use, enriched not only the faith and piety but also the culture of many peoples... The Roman missal promulgated by St Pius V and reissued by Bl. John XXIII...must be given due honour for its venerable and ancient usage" (Motu Proprio *Summorum Pontificum*, introduction and art. 1). "What earlier generations held as sacred, remains sacred and great for us too... It behooves all of us to preserve the riches which have developed in the Church's faith and prayer, and to give them their proper place" (Letter to Bishops, 7 July 2007). The Instruction *Universae Ecclesiae* (30 April 2011) states in n. 8 that the first aim of *Summorum Pontificum* is "to bestow on all of the faithful the Roman liturgy in the *usus antiquior,* as a precious treasure to be preserved" ("Liturgiam Romanam in Antiquiori Usu, prout pretiosum thesaurum servandum, omnibus largire fidelibus").

49. It is even conceivable that one might retain the one-year cycle for Sundays, Holy Days, and privileged octaves or seasons, while adopting a two-year cycle of daily readings for the remainder of the time, yet without a forced plan of continuous readings and without eclipsing readings assigned for saints' days, which would always take precedence, in keeping with the system attested by the most ancient Roman lectionaries. Such an arrangement could be a better way of fulfilling the desiderata of the Council Fathers in *Sacrosanctum Concilium* 35 and 51 while avoiding the problems critiqued here. Of course, every feast or feria would need to have *assigned* readings rather than a set of options. "Optionitis" is the bane of liturgy correctly understood as an objective, formal, and public cult offered to God by the entire Church. On this point of fundamental importance, see: R. Guardini, *The Spirit of the Liturgy* (New York: Crossroad, 1998), Chapter 1, pp. 17–35; J. Ratzinger, *The Spirit of the Liturgy* (San Francisco: Ignatius, 2000), pp. 166–69, also in idem, *Theology of the Liturgy*, Collected Works, vol. 11 (San Francisco: Ignatius, 2014), pp. 102–5.

Fifth, *now* does not seem to be the best time to undertake this task. Those who love the classical Roman liturgy deeply appreciate the stability and serenity of the old missal and often (quite reasonably, in my opinion) feel shell-shocked by changes, small or great. And those who are in charge of liturgical matters in the Church still seem doggedly committed to the defense (one might say, at all costs) of the novelties of the 1960s and 1970s. It is not an environment favorable to the preservation of tradition *or* to its legitimate and prudent development.[50] I sympathize with those who say we need a breathing space, a season of refreshment, in which we rediscover and rejoice in the traditional liturgy of the Church, with the notion of change far from our minds. The Lord in His kindness may someday provide a peaceful opportunity for gently supplementing the lections of the *usus antiquior*. We should neither try to rush the advent of that day, nor close off our minds to that possibility.

6. *Practical Steps*

Since we are also interested here in practical steps, there are several things we can be doing right now to address at least some of the problems that have been raised.

First and foremost, we must celebrate the *usus antiquior* ever more widely, and learn again from our own tradition the properly *liturgical* function, configuration, and ceremonial of the readings. In this realm, it is crucial to promote the sung Mass and, where possible, the solemn Mass, so that all things, including the proclamation of God's Word, may be done beautifully and nobly.

Again, pastors in charge of *usus antiquior* communities ought to promote *lectio divina* and bible studies and not be afraid to base their preaching on Sacred Scripture, while not neglecting texts from the missal, the catechism, and other classic homiletic sources. The tight integration of

---

50. There is a spiritual danger, too: reformatory arrogance, one of the curses of modern progressivism. Our age does not seem to be especially talented at subtle or judicious improvements; we are an age of demolitions with wrecking balls. Nor should we be surprised that something put together in a matter of a few years would not be as solid and coherent as something that developed organically for many centuries. As Dietrich von Hildebrand says: "We live in a world without poetry, and this means that one should approach the treasures handed on from more fortunate times with twice as much reverence, and not with the illusion that we can do it better ourselves"; *The Devastated Vineyard* (Chicago: Franciscan Herald, 1973; repr. Roman Catholic Books, 1985), p. 70.

the propers of the Mass often make it easy to fulfill the Council's request that "the sermon...should draw its content mainly from scriptural *and liturgical* sources."[51]

Within the sphere of the ordinary form, there are many things that can be done.[52] First, since one of the most notable characteristics of the historic Roman rite is its permeation with the Word of God, we should be singing the proper antiphons at Mass—at least the Entrance, Offertory, and Communion chants.[53] In this way we can overcome one of the greatest ironies of the post-conciliar period, namely, that while the Council, like scripture, bestows praise on sacred song, the liturgy of the Word today is rarely chanted, and, even worse, our authentically *scriptural* songs, the propers, have been replaced with hymns of notoriously variable quality and fidelity to the Bible.

Second, we should take a hermeneutic of continuity approach to the modern lectionary. On memorials and feasts, we might choose from the optional readings those that correspond to the former missal, or in any case, those that fit well with the saint in question. During the suppressed Octave of Pentecost, we should celebrate Votive Masses of the Holy Spirit, selecting appropriate readings, once again emulating the old rite as closely as possible. The proclamation of the readings should be heightened with ceremonial features such as chanted lessons (whenever lectors, deacons, and priests can be sufficiently trained), incense, and candles.

Third, we should *not* use the so-called "short forms" of readings, which are often ruses for omitting the uncomfortable bits—as when the American and British lectionaries provide for the silencing of the verse "Wives, be subordinate to your husbands, as is proper in the Lord."[54] If a

---

51. *Sacrosanctum Concilium* 35§2, emphasis added. How rare it is to hear sermons that comment at any length on prayers of the Mass, whether proper to the day or from the Ordinary! Is it not strange that, apart from baptisms, first communions, and other special events, priests so rarely draw their themes from the immense treasury of the liturgy itself?

52. A number of these recommendations are also mentioned by Pope Benedict XVI in *Verbum Domini* (see, e.g., nn. 58, 67, 70).

53. While there might have been some excuse in times past for neglecting the sung propers inasmuch as good musical resources and the requisite pastoral support were not on hand, recent years have seen an explosion of plainchant settings in both Latin and English, at varying skill levels. Fr Samuel Weber's *The Proper of the Mass* provides four settings, from a more challenging melismatic adaptation of the Gregorian exemplar to simple psalm tones, for the Introit, Offertory, and Communion antiphon of all Sundays and major feasts of the modern Roman rite.

54. The *General Introduction to the Lectionary* n. 75 states that "In the case of certain rather long texts, longer and shorter versions are provided to suit different

priest sees that "difficult" verses of scripture have been altogether omitted under the pressure of liberalism and secularism, he would do well to bring up those very verses in his homily.

Fourth, lectors should be more carefully selected and trained for their purpose, and suitably vested, as befits the dignity of their office. A deliberate effort to increase the number of male lectors would also be a worthy endeavor.[55]

Fifth, to counterbalance the problem of "verbal imperialism," the liturgy of the Eucharist should be given due weight and dignity by the sacred music employed, by the adoption (whenever possible) of an eastward orientation at the altar, and by the use of the Roman canon,[56] so that this part of the liturgy truly appears to be the Mass's point of arrival—in the words of the poet Richard Crashaw, "the full, final Sacrifice / On which all figures fix't their eyes. / The ransomed Isaac, and his ram; / The Manna, and the Paschal Lamb."

situations. The editing of the shorter version has been carried out with great caution." This provision seems to have in mind readings such as the Gospels for Lent 3A, 4A, and 5A, and Palm Sunday ABC (the Gospels for Lent 3A and 4A are specifically mentioned by Bugnini in his summation of the new lectionary as examples of longer passages that may be shortened; see: Bugnini, *Reform of the Liturgy*, p. 418). However, a reading as brief as Matt 13:44–52 (Sunday 17A) also has a short form (vv. 44–46). Is this text, and others like it, really so long that it warrants a short form? Of course not—but a glance at the omitted text explains why the short form option is there. The *General Introduction to the Lectionary* n. 75 does not mention that short texts will be made even shorter due to their controversial material. This is another example of the subtle ways in which the Word of God has been muzzled in the new lectionary. It is true that proclaiming the longer form can augment the problem of "verbal imperialism" described above, but, in the balance, the preaching of true doctrine takes precedence until such time as the lectionary can be appropriately slimmed down.

55. It is high time bishops paid attention to Pope Paul VI's Apostolic Letter *Ministeria Quaedam* (15 August 1972) by instituting lectors and acolytes on a stable, permanent basis, which, by creating a pool of properly deputed and well-trained liturgical ministers, would go some way towards aiding a dignified celebration of the liturgy of the Word and of the Eucharist. The fact that only men can receive these ministries (see: *Ministeria Quaedam* 7) would not only restore to a place of honor a custom of almost 2,000 years' standing in the Catholic Church, but also help reverse the ubiquitous take-over of liturgical ministries by women and the progressive decline of male participation in Catholic worship that has coincided with it. See: M. Foley, "Male Subjection and the Case for an All-Male Liturgical Ministry," *Antiphon* 15 (2011), pp. 262–98.

56. See: *General Instruction of the Roman Missal* n. 365, one of the most sinned-against paragraphs of that frequently violated document.

Lastly, the Catholic parish, like the life of every Catholic, should manifest a variety of prayer forms and a breadth of education. The vast increase in the quantity of scripture at Mass reflects a mentality that sees Mass as the only time when Catholics are ever going to be in church or anywhere near a Bible, so one has to pack everything one can into that time.[57] This mentality obviously neglects the role of the Divine Office or liturgy of the Hours, which is and has always been a dedicated liturgy of the Word of God and deserves its important place—for example, in publicly celebrated vespers. Moreover, nothing can substitute for extraliturgical formation in catechism classes, prayer groups, and bible studies, through pamphlets, books, and DVDs distributed to the faithful, and even through well-written bulletins. As Pope Benedict XVI reminded us, *lectio divina* should be taught and encouraged.[58] The formation of the faithful in the Word of God is not a burden that the Mass was ever meant to carry or is even well-suited to carry.

Allow me to close with the moving words of Cardinal Ratzinger in his preface to Dom Alcuin Reid's *The Organic Development of the Liturgy*—words that apply extremely well to the revision of the lectionary:

> [G]rowth is not possible unless the liturgy's identity is preserved, and… proper development is possible only if careful attention is paid to the inner structural logic of this "organism." Just as a gardener cares for a living plant as it develops, with due attention to the power of growth and life within the plant, and the rules it obeys, so the Church ought to give reverent care to the liturgy through the ages, distinguishing actions that are helpful and healing from those that are violent and destructive. If that is how things are, then we must try to ascertain the inner structure of a rite, and the rules by which its life is governed, in order thus to find the right way to preserve its vital force in changing times, to strengthen and renew it.[59]

57. See: P. Kwasniewski, "Lingering in the Courts of the Great King: The Sanctification of Time Through Prayer," *The Latin Mass* 22 (Winter/Spring 2013), pp. 14–19.

58. See, inter alia, *Verbum Domini* nn. 86–87; Angelus, 6 November 2005; Message to Youth of the World, 22 February 2006; Question and Answer with Young People, 6 April 2006; Homily at the Chrism Mass, Holy Thursday, 13 April 2006; Homily at Vespers in Altötting, 11 September 2006; Question and Answer with Seminarians, 17 February 2007; General Audience, 28 October 2009.

59. Ratzinger, "Preface"; Reid, *Organic Development*, p. 9; also *Theology of the Liturgy*, pp. 589–90. The author wishes to thank Jeremy Holmes, Matthew Hazell, Gregory DiPippo, Fr Samuel Weber OSB, and Fr Innocent Smith OP for their detailed critiques of an earlier version of this paper.

Appendix A:
Proper of the Mass for the Feast of St Thérèse of Lisieux
*(*Missale Romanum *1962, 3 October)*

Veni de Líbano, sponsa mea, veni de Líbano, veni: vulnerásti cor meum, soror mea sponsa, vulnerásti cor meum. Laudáte, púeri, Dóminum: laudáte nomen Dómini. Gloria Patri, et Filio, et Spiritui Sancto... Veni de Líbano...	Come from Libanus, my spouse, come from Libanus, come: thou hast wounded my heart, my sister, my spouse, thou hast wounded my heart. Praise the Lord, ye children: praise ye the name of the Lord. Glory be to the Father... Come...	*Introit* Song 4:8–9; Ps 112:1
Oremus. Dómine, qui dixísti: Nisi efficiámini sicut párvuli, non intrábitis in regnum cælórum: da nobis, quæsumus; ita sanctæ Terésiæ Vírginis in humilitáte et simplicitáte cordis vestígia sectári, ut præmia consequámur ætérna. Qui vivis et regnas...	Let us pray. O Lord, Who hast said: Unless ye become as little children, ye shall not enter into the kingdom of Heaven, grant unto us, we beseech Thee, so to follow the footsteps of saint Teresa, virgin, in lowliness and simplicity of heart that we may gain everlasting rewards. Who livest...	*Collect*
Léctio Isaíæ Prophétæ. Hæc dicit Dóminus: Ecce ego declinábo super eam quasi flúvium pacis, et quasi torréntem inundántem glóriam géntium, quam sugétis: ad úbera portabímini, et super génua blandiéntur vobis. Quómodo si cui mater blandiátur, ita ego consolábor vos, et in Jerusalem consolabímini. Vidébitis, et gaudébit cor vestrum, et ossa vestra quasi herba germinábunt, et cognoscétur manus Dómini servi ejus.	Lesson from Isaias the Prophet. For thus saith the Lord: Behold I will bring upon her as it were a river of peace, and as an overflowing torrent the glory of the gentiles, which you shall suck; you shall be carried at the breasts, and upon the knees they shall caress you. As one whom the mother caresseth, so will I comfort you, and you shall be comforted in Jerusalem. You shall see and your heart shall rejoice, and your bones shall flourish like an herb, and the hand of the Lord shall be known to His servants.	*Epistle* Isa 66:12–14

Confíteor tibi, Pater, Dómine cæli et terra: quia abscondísti hæc a sapiéntibus, et prudéntibus, et revelasti ea párvulis. Dómine, spes mea a juventúte mea.	I confess to Thee, O Father, Lord of heaven and earth, because Thou hast hid these things from the wise and prudent and hast revealed them to little ones. My hope, O Lord, from my youth.	*Gradual* Matt 11:25; Ps 70:5
Allelúia, allelúia. Quasi rosa plantáta super rivos aquárum fructificáte: quasi Líbanus odórem suavitátis habéte: floréte flores, quasi lílium, et date odórem, et frondéte in gratiam, et collaudáte cánticum, et benedícite Dóminum in opéribus suis. Allelúia.	Alleluia, alleluia. Bud forth as the rose planted by the brooks of waters. Give ye a sweet odor as Libanus. Send forth flowers, as the lily, and yield a smell, and bring forth leaves in grace, and praise with canticles, and bless the Lord in His works. Alleluia.	*Alleluia* Sir 39:17–19
In illo témpore: Accessérunt discípuli ad Jesum, dicéntes: "Quis, putas, major est in regno cælórum?" Et ádvocans Jesus párvulum, státuit eum in médio eórum, et dixit: "Amen dico vobis, nisi convérsi fuéritis, et efficiámini sicut párvuli, non intrábitis in regnum cælórum. Quicúmque ergo humiliáverit se sicut párvulus iste, hic est major in regno cælórum."	At that time, the disciples came to Jesus saying: "Who, thinkest Thou, is the greater in the kingdom of Heaven?" And Jesus calling unto Him a little child, set him in the midst of them and said: "Amen I say to you, unless you be converted and become as little children, you shall not enter into the kingdom of Heaven. Whosoever therefore shall humble himself as this little child, he is the greater in the kingdom of Heaven."	*Gospel* Matt 18:1–5
Magníficat ánima mea Dóminum: et exsultávit spíritus meus in Deo salutári meo: quia respéxit humilitátem ancíllæ suæ: fecit mihi magna qui potens est.	My soul doth magnify the Lord. And my spirit hath rejoiced in God my Savior. Because He hath regarded the humility of His handmaid: He that is mighty hath done great things to me.	*Offertory* Luke 1:46–49

Sacrifícium nostrum tibi, Dómine, quæsumus, sanctæ Therésiæ Vírginis tuæ precátio sancta concíliet: ut in cujus honóre solémniter exhibétur, ejus méritis efficiátur accéptum. Per Dominum...	We beseech Thee, O Lord, that the holy intercession of saint Teresa, Thy virgin, may make our sacrifice agreeable to Thee, so that it may be made acceptable by the merits of her in whose honor it is solemnly offered. Through our Lord...	*Secret*
Circumdúxit eam, et dócuit: et custodívit quasi pupíllam óculi sui. Sicut áquila expándit alas suas, et assúmpsit eam, atque portávit in húmeris suis. Dóminus solus dux ejus fuit.	He led her about and taught her: and He kept her as the apple of His eye. As the eagle, He spread His wings and hath taken her, and carried her on His shoulders. The Lord alone was her leader.	*Communion* Deut 32:10–12
Illo nos, Dómine, amóris igne cæléste mystérium inflámmet quo sancta Therésia Vírgo tua se tibi pro homínibus caritátis víctimam devóvit. Per Dóminum...	May the heavenly mystery, O Lord, enkindle in us that fire of love, whereby the saint Teresa, Thy virgin, offered herself to Thee as a victim of charity for men. Through our Lord...	*Postcommunion*

Appendix B:
Biblical Permeation in the Mass—Missale Romanum *1962,*
Laetare *Sunday, Solemn Mass*

Roman canon	*Order of Mass /*	*Proper of Mass*
Asperges	Ps 50:9, 1 (Asperges me) Ps 84:8 (Ostende nobis) Ps 101:2 (Domine, exaudi)	
Prayers at the Foot of the Altar	Ps 42 (Judica me) Ps 123:8 (Adiutorium nostrum) Ps 84:7 (Deus tu conversus) Ps 84:8 (Ostende nobis) Ps 101:2 (Domine, exaudi) Ezek 42:13; Heb 9:3 [sancta sanctorum]	

Entrance antiphon	Isa 66:10–11 (Laetare, Jerusalem) Ps 121:1 (Laetatus sum)
Kyrie	Ps 122:3; Isa 33:2; Matt 20:30-31; Luke 17:13; Jdt 7:20; Est 13:15; Tob 8:10
Epistle	Gal 4:22–31 (Scriptum est)
Gradual	Ps 121:1, 7 (Laetatus sum)
Tract	Ps 124:1–2 (Qui confidunt)
Prayer before the Gospel	Isa 6:6–7 [tetigit os meum]
Gospel	John 6:1–15 (Abiit Jesus trans mare)
Offertory antiphon	Ps 134:3, 6 (Laudate Dominum)
Offertory of the Mass	Ps 115:4 [calicem salutaris] Exod 29:41; Lev 2:9; 8:28; 17:16; Num 15:7; Eph 5:2; Phil 4:18, etc. [odorem suavitatis] Dan 3:39–40 (In spiritu humilitatis) Luke 1:11 (a dextris altaris incensi) Rev 8:3–4 [angelus venit] Ps 32:22 (misericordia tua super nos) Ps 140:2–4 (Dirigatur, Domine, oratio mea) Ps 25:6–12 (Lavabo inter innocentes)
Sanctus	Isa 6:3 (Sanctus) Mark 11:10 (Hosanna in excelsis) Ps 117:26; John 12:13 (Benedictus qui venit)

Roman Canon	*Of the elaborate tapestry of biblical allusions,*
	  here are a few threads:
	Tob 8:9; Pss 49:14; 49:23; 106:22 (sacrificium
	  laudis)
	Pss 49:14; 55:12; 60:9; 65:13; 115:5 [redde
	  vota/reddam vota]
	Luke 6:20; John 11:41 (elevatis oculis)
	Matt 26:26; 1 Cor 11:25, etc. {institution/
	  consecration}
	Gen 4:4; 22:7–13; 14:18 {Abel, Abraham,
	  Melchisedech}
	Eph 1:3 [omni benedictione spiritali in
	  caelestibus in Christo]
	Pss 50:3; 68:17 (multitudinem miserationum
	  tuarum)

The Lord's Prayer	Matt 6:9–13
Agnus Dei	John 1:29 (Agnus Dei, qui tollit)

Prayers before communion	John 14:27 (Pacem relinquo vobis) Matt 16:16 [Filius Dei vivi] Gal 1:4 [secundum voluntatem...Patris] 1 Cor 11:29 [indigne...iudicium]
Prayers at communion	Ps 77:4; John 6:31, etc. [panem de caelo] Ps 115:4 (nomen Domini invocabo) Matt 8:8 (Domine non sum dignus) Ps 115:3–4 (Quid retribuam... Calicem salutaris accipiam) Ps 17:4 (Laudans invocabo)
People's communion	John 1:29 (Ecce, Agnus Dei) Matt 8:8 (Domine non sum dignus)
Communion antiphon	Ps 121:3–4 (Jerusalem, quae aedificatur ut civitas)
Placeat tibi	Dan 3:40 (Placeat tibi)
Blessing	Gen 28:3 [Deus omnipotens benedicat tibi]
Last Gospel	John 1:1–14 (In principio erat Verbum)

On days that call for a Gloria, one might note the following criptural allusions:

Gloria	Luke 2:14 (cp. 19:38); 1 Chr 29:13; Tob 8:17; John 4:22; Rev 11:17; Rom 8:34; Eph 1:20; Heb 1:3; Ps 82:19; Phil 2:11

Appendix C:
Psalm 34 [35] in the Mass of the Roman Rite

In the *usus antiquior* (*Missale Romanum* 1962)

Friday in Passion Week	Gradual (Ps 34:20, 22)	Mine enemies spoke peaceably to me: and in anger they were troublesome to me. Thou hast seen, O Lord, be not Thou silent: depart not from me.
Saturday in Passion Week	Gradual (Ps 34:20, 22)	Mine enemies spoke peaceably to me: and in anger they were troublesome to me. Thou hast seen, O Lord, be not Thou silent: depart not from me.

Monday in Holy Week	Introit (Ps 34:1–3)	Judge Thou, O Lord, them that wrong me, overthrow them that fight against me; take hold of arms and shield, and rise up to help me, O Lord, the strength of my salvation. Bring out the sword, and shut up the way against them that persecute me; say to my soul: I am thy salvation.
	Gradual (Ps 34:3, 23)	Arise, O Lord, and be attentive to my judgment, my God and my Lord, [be attentive] to my cause. Bring out the sword, and shut up the way against them that persecute me.
	Communion (Ps 34:26)	Let them blush and be ashamed together, who rejoice at my evils: let them be clothed with shame and fear, who speak malignant things against me.
Tuesday in Holy Week	Gradual (Ps 34:13, 1–2)	But as for me, when they were troublesome to me, I was clothed with sackcloth, and I humbled my soul with fasting, and my prayer shall be turned into my bosom. Judge Thou, O Lord, them that wrong me, overthrow them that fight against me; take hold of arms and shield, and rise up to help me.
September 15 (Seven Sorrows of BVM)	Gradual (Ps 34:20, 22)	Mine enemies spoke peaceably to me: and in anger they were troublesome to me. Thou hast seen, O Lord, be not Thou silent: depart not from me.
September 18 (Joseph of Cupertino)	Offertory (Ps 34:13)	But as for me, when they were troublesome to me, I was clothed with sackcloth, and I humbled my soul with fasting, and my prayer shall be turned into my bosom.

In the *usus recentior* (*Missale Romanum* 1970/2008)

Monday in Holy Week	Introit (Ps 34:1–2)	Contend, O Lord, with my contenders; fight those who fight me. Take up your buckler and shield; arise in my defense, Lord, my mighty help.

The Reform of the Calendar and the Reduction of Liturgical Recapitulation

Michael P. Foley

1. *Introduction*

Context is everything. You may have heard that several years ago the Cardinal of Washington DC was approached by an aide to then-House Speaker Nancy Pelosi and offered $1,000,000 if he would declare in his next homily that Nancy Pelosi was a saint. The Cardinal adamantly refused but after the aide repeatedly pointed out how many poor people could be fed with the help of a million dollars, His Eminence reluctantly agreed.

The next day Nancy Pelosi and her aide were sitting in the front pew of the basilica for Mass. At the start of his sermon, the Cardinal pointed out that the Speaker of the House was present. "While Congresswoman Pelosi's presence is probably an honor to some," the Cardinal said, "it is not to me. Some of her views are egregiously contrary to the tenets of the Church, and her policies continue to scandalize the faithful. Nancy Pelosi is a petty and self-absorbed hypocrite, a serial liar, a cheat, and an advocate of legalized mass murder. She is a disgrace to her office and the worst example of a Catholic politician I have ever seen." The Cardinal drew a breath and concluded: "But compared to Barack Obama, Nancy Pelosi is a saint."

Context can also help to explain an odd pattern in the 1962 liturgical calendar. A biblical reading, theme, event, or saint appears on a particular day. Then, later in the year, the same reading, theme, event, or saint reemerges, only not quite in the same manner. This "repetition" can occur because both the Temporal and Sanctoral cycles happen to include an identical element, but it can also occur within the same cycle, be it the Temporal or Sanctoral.

To offer a few preliminary examples: Palm Sunday, especially its blessing of palms and procession, celebrates Christ's Kingship, but there is also a feast of Christ the King. Holy Thursday celebrates the gift of the Eucharist, but there is also a feast of *Corpus Christi*. Good Friday commemorates the blood that our Lord shed for us on the Cross as well as His pierced heart, but there is also a feast of the Precious Blood, a feast of the Holy Cross,[1] and a feast of the Sacred Heart. 27 September is the feast of Saints Cosmas and Damien, but we also pray to these saints on the Thursday of the Third Week of Lent.[2] The Ember Wednesday of Advent focuses on the Annunciation, but there is also a feast for it on 25 March.

One would think that since the 1962 Roman missal has an annual cycle of readings (as opposed to the three-year cycle of the new lectionary), there would be a minimum of repetition in order to expose the faithful to as much of the Holy Bible as possible. But instead, we find a startlingly different strategy. What is it?

The answer to that question is the subject under examination here, namely, the identification and explanation of a pattern that can be accurately labeled "liturgical recapitulation." My argument will be organized into four parts. First, I will summarize two key concepts: "recapitulation" and "mystery." Second, following Pope Benedict XVI, I will apply this understanding to the Roman calendar and offer several concrete examples of liturgical recapitulation. Third, I will trace the reduction of recapitulation in the 1962 and 1970 calendars. And fourth, I will offer possible reasons for the relatively recent decline in liturgical recapitulation.

2. *Recapitulation and Mystery*

The first step is to be clear about our terminology. In Latin *recapitulatio* can have the same meaning as "recapitulation" in English, that is, a return to the heading (caput) as a way of summarizing or restating an argument or narrative. In late ancient and even ecclesiastical Latin, *recapitulatio* can be synonymous with both *repetitio* and *collectio*.[3] But there is also a specialized meaning of the word. In neo-Platonic thought, *recapitulatio* describes the

---

1. And in the calendar before 1962, there were two feasts for the Cross: one on 3 May (dropped in 1960) and one on 14 September.

2. We do so because the stational church for that day is that of Sts Cosmas and Damian.

3. "Recapitulatio," in Charlton Lewis and Charles Short (eds), *A Latin Dictionary* (Oxford: Clarendon. 1879), p. 1529C.

ascent of the philosopher to ever higher principles, "to categories of Being ever prior, both temporally and existentially, ever higher in dignity and more comprehensive in scope, until it completes its 'return to the One.' Each higher mode of contemplation subsumes those beneath it, and so it 'recapitulates' them from its encompassing perspective."[4]

Recapitulation is also part of the specialized language of Sacred Scripture and the Church Fathers. In his epistle to the Ephesians, St Paul writes that God the Father has revealed the mystery of His will so that "in the dispensation of the fullness of times" He might "recapitulate all things in Christ"—*anakephalaiōsasthai ta panta en tō Kristō* (1:9–10). That term, *anakephalaiōsis*, which like the Latin *recapitulatio* literally means a "reheading," is later picked up by Greek Fathers such as St Irenaeus, who use it for Christ's redeeming all human experience.[5] Some modern commentators have gone so far as to suggest that the notion of *anakephalaiōsis* or *recapitulatio* designates the very "essence of the Christian theory of history."[6] Although that may be an exaggeration, the concept as modified by the Church Fathers does indeed point to a distinctively Christian understanding of how God is present in human history; for unlike the neo-Platonic notion, Christian recapitulation is not simply an atemporal return to the higher or a going back to a beginning outside of space and time, but a going *forward in time* towards the end as a way of integrating oneself with the beginning.

The use of the term *recapitulatio* in Latin Christianity is somewhat more complicated. The *Vetus Latina* or Old Latin translations of the New Testament did not use *recapitulare* for Eph 1:10 but *instaurare*, to renew or restore. This decision puzzled St Jerome:

> In the Latin manuscripts, *instaurare* is written instead of *recapitulare*, and I wonder why the translators did not use this Greek word, even though by the same license they adopt *dialectica* and *philosophia* as they stand in the Greek. In fact, even orators, in their concluding arguments or before their concluding arguments at the end of the case, on account of either the

---

4. Robert M. Durling, "Platonism and Poetic Form: Augustine's Confessions," public lecture, Princeton, March 1982; cited in Robert McMahon, *Augustine's Prayerful Ascent: An Essay on the Literary Form of the* Confessions (Athens, GA: University of Georgia Press, 1989), p. 142.

5. See: *Apostolic Preaching* 6.

6. John Freccero, "The Significance of Terza Rima," in Rachel Jacoff (ed.), *Dante: The Poetics of Conversion* (Cambridge: Harvard University Press, 1986), p. 266. Origen, as we will soon see, also uses the term.

judges' memory or of those who are hearing the transactions, usually make a replaying, that is, an *anakephalaiōsin*, so that what they had earlier been disputing more broadly, they could later encapsulate in a brief discourse, and so that each person could begin to remember what he had heard.[7]

Despite his personal disagreement with the choice, however, Jerome kept *instaurare* in his own translation, and hence the Vulgate renders Eph 1:10 *instaurare omnia in Christo*, or as the Douay Rheims translation puts it, "to reestablish all things in Christ."

Both the word and the concept of *recapitulatio*, however, continued to survive in the Latin West in other ways. Tertullian self-consciously uses *recapitulare* instead of *instaurare* when discussing Eph 1:10,[8] and Rufinus uses it when translating Origen's homilies on Leviticus.[9] But *recapitulatio*'s survival in ecclesiastical Latin is owed chiefly to St Augustine, who learned of it from the Donatist Tyconius. For Tyconius, as for Origen, recapitulation signifies not only God's gathering up of all things in Christ but a literary device employed in Sacred Scripture where "certain things are said in such a way that it looks as if they are proceeding in chronological order or in the order of events, whereas the narrative is [really] secretly recalling prior things which had been overlooked."[10]

Augustine gives as an example the fact that the book of Genesis first mentions the LORD God planting a garden of paradise and then adds that He formed out of the ground "all manner of trees, fair to behold, and pleasant to eat of" (2:8–9). The second statement, that God formed trees, "recapitulates" the first statement that God planted a garden by making explicit something that was at best implied, namely, the precise manner in which God planted the garden. Centuries later St Thomas Aquinas would

---

7. "Pro recapitulare in latinis codicibus scriptum est, instaurare et miror cur ipso uerbo graeco non usi sint translatores, cum istiusmodi licentia, dialectica et philosophia sicut in graeco habentur, assumptae sint. nam et oratores in epilogis, uel ante epilogos, in fine causarum propter memoriam iudicum et eorum qui audiere negotia, recordationem, id est, ἀνακεφαλαίωσιν solent facere, ut quae prius latius disputarant, breui postea sermone comprehendant, et unusquisque recordari eorum incipiat quae audiuit;" Jerome, *Commentariorum in epistolam ad Ephesios* 1.1.vers. 10. All translations, unless otherwise noted, are mine.

8. Tertullian, *adversus Marcionem* 5.17.

9. Origen, *In Leviticum homiliae* 6.2.

10. *De doctrina Christiana* 3.36.52. See also: *civ. Dei* 15.21, 16.5, 16.10, 20.21. According to Robert McMahon, the principle of recapitulation also explains the organization of the *Confessions*; see: McMahon, *Augustine's Prayerful Ascent*, pp. 142–55.

still be using *recapitulatio* in the same manner, as a means of designating a particular technique in biblical poetics.[11]

It may seem that the Latin sense of recapitulation moved away from its scriptural and Greek Patristic moorings by focusing on exegesis rather than history, but I would argue that it was not so much a relinquishing of the older usage as it was an application of it to a particular field. The common thread uniting the two is the idea of a paradoxical movement whereby in moving forward we move both backwards and upwards. As we move forward in time (or in our reading) towards our goal, we move backwards towards the first principles; but in moving towards first principles, we are also moving up towards a reality that is "higher" by virtue of the fact that it is either more encompassing or ontologically superior. In other words, *recapitulatio* is more than just a "recap," a summary or an abridged repetition; it is a recurring encounter with a sacred mystery.

And when I assert that recapitulation is a recurring encounter with a sacred mystery, I must specify what I mean by "mystery," since a mystery can designate: (1) something proportionate to our understanding, (2) something below our understanding, or (3) something above our understanding.[12] A detective novel, for example, is usually about a mystery that is proportionate to our understanding: that is, it is about a crime that is currently unsolved but, thanks to the genius of the protagonist, is eventually solved. And once it is solved, there is no mystery left, for the crime (or rather, the identity of the criminal) was a puzzle with a clear and determinate answer, an answer that even a sluggish mind like Inspector Lestrade's is capable of grasping once the facts have been unearthed and explained by a brilliant Sherlock Holmes. Tellingly, the phrase for solving a mystery in Latin, *solvere mysterium*, also literally means dissolving a mystery. Once we know "who done it," no residue of mystery is left, as the mind is now satisfied by the full disclosure of the reality it was seeking.

But there are some mysteries that cannot be solved or dissolved. A mystery that is below our understanding, for instance, is a mystery that by its very nature lacks intelligibility. The Scriptures speak of the "mystery of iniquity" (2 Thess 2:7) in this sense, for the key to understanding evil is understanding that it cannot be fully understood. Since evil is not a good but the privation of a good,[13] and since our minds cannot understand or grasp privation any more than our eyes can see darkness,[14] our minds

---

11. See: *Summa Theologiae* I.70.1, I.102.1.ad 5.

12. See: Michael P. Foley, "The Mystery of the Mystery Genre," *Anamnesis* 2 (2012), pp. 53–74.

13. See: Augustine, *Confessiones* 7.12.18–16.22.

14. See: Augustine, *De ordine* 2.3.10.

can only dimly fathom evil, more by what it is not rather than by what it is. Put differently, understanding the essence of evil is far different from "solving for X" as we do with a murder mystery or a formula in algebra. Evil is by its very nature absurd, and hence its mysterious element can never be resolved.

The third kind of mystery lies on the opposite end of the spectrum of being, for unlike the mystery of iniquity that flies below the radar of human reason, the third kind flies above it, outstripping the human mind's ability to comprehend it. It is not that the mystery in question is only temporarily unknown (like an unsolved crime) or that it lacks intelligibility (like evil or darkness) but that it superabounds in intelligibility, and that consequently, it can have a paradoxically blinding effect on our intellects. The example that Aristotle and St Thomas Aquinas give of this phenomenon is of an owl blinded by the noonday sun.[15] Such is the nature of God, and such is the content of the Beatific Vision.

When, therefore, we speak of recapitulation as an encounter with "mystery," it is important to keep in mind that what is being designated is mystery in this third sense, as the encounter with divine and superabundant intelligibility. Consequently, every time we encounter the mystery, we can learn something more from it or be further enriched by it; and no matter how many times we encounter it or how deeply we delve into it, we will never be able to exhaust its riches or plumb its depths. An element of meaningful mystery will always remain, even in the Beatific Vision itself.[16]

Further, mystery's inexhaustibility applies not only to the essence of the Triune God but to the person of Jesus Christ in particular *and to everything He did*, even to the smallest of his human acts. For by virtue of the great mystery of the hypostatic union, every act performed by our Lord was performed by a Divine Person, and hence every act of Jesus Christ is both infinitely efficacious and mysterious.[17] It is fitting, then, that we refer to the episodes of Christ's life upon which we meditate while praying the rosary as "mysteries."[18] Furthermore, the intelligible and infinite mystery

15. See: Aristotle, *Metaphysics* II, 1 993b 7–10; St Thomas Aquinas, *Summa Theologiae* I.1.5.ad 1.

16. See: St Thomas Aquinas' distinction between "seeing" and "comprehending" God's essence in *Summa Theologiae* I.12.7; I.12.8; Suppl. 92.3.ad 2; Suppl. 92.3.ad 6.

17. For Christ's human acts as infinitely efficacious or satisfactory, see: Bl. Columba Marmion, *Christ the Life of the Soul* (St Louis: Herder, 1925/Angelico, 2012), pp. 59–64.

18. It is possible that the use of the word "mystery" to designate the subject of devotion while praying the Holy Rosary is, like the medieval "mystery plays," derived not from *mysterium* but *ministerium*, an act in a play; see: Georges Bertrin, "Miracle

of Christ is poured forth into His saints and into His Church moving through history: as the Second Vatican Council teaches, "By celebrating the passage of these saints from earth to heaven the Church proclaims *the paschal mystery achieved in the saints* who have suffered and been glorified with Christ" (*Sacrosanctum Concilium* 104, emphasis added). The life of a saint or a significant event in Church history, therefore, is more than just "food for thought"; it too is a privileged encounter with mystery. All sacred mystery, both in general and in its particular historical incarnations, is like a brilliant diamond with innumerable facets that can be appreciated increasingly but never fathomed completely.

3. *Liturgical Application*

Although neglected for centuries,[19] the language of recapitulation was adopted by Pope Benedict XVI during his pontificate. Following the example of the Greek Fathers, Benedict used the term to designate Christ's activity, who "recapitulates all the world" to Himself.[20] But instead of

Plays and Mysteries," in Charles G. Herbermann (ed.), *Catholic Encyclopedia*, vol. 10 (New York: Robert Appleton, 1911), pp. 348–50 (348). That said, understanding the mysteries of the rosary vis-à-vis our third definition of mystery is entirely appropriate, for these events in the life of Christ or His Mother are sacred mysteries, revealed by God and inexhaustible by human reason. See the First Vatican Council. "If any one say that in Divine Revelation there are contained no mysteries properly so called (*vera et proprie dicta mysteria*), but that through reason rightly developed (*per rationem rite excultam*) all the dogmas of faith can be understood and demonstrated from natural principles: let him be anathema" (Sess. III, Canons, 4. *De fide et ratione* 1).

19. The centuries between St Thomas Aquinas and Pope Benedict XVI show little distinctive theological use of the term *recapitulatio*. One exception is St Lawrence of Brundisi (1559–1619), whom we shall quote below, and another is Hans Urs von Balthasar, about whom Veronica Donnelly writes: "This theme of recapitulation [which he took from St Irenaeus] is a pervading one in Balthasarian christology [*sic*], imbued as it is with the Pauline and Johannine Christocentrism. In fact he views recapitulation in Christ as the purpose of revelation because 'the revelation in Christ was to bring together in one divine and human Head everything heavenly and earthly'"; citing Balthasar, John Riches (ed.), *The Glory of the Lord*, vol. 1 (San Francisco: Ignatius, 2009). Donnelly also cites Balthasar's *Glory of the Lord*, vol. 2 (San Francisco: Ignatius, 2009), pp. 51ff. and W. G.- Doepel (trans.), *Man in History* (London: Sheed & Ward, 1968), pp. 107–8. See: Veronica Donnelly, *Saving Beauty: Form as the Key to Balthasar's Christology* (Bern: Peter Lang AG, 2007), p. 102 and p. 102 n. 25.

20. "Because Christ was not born as an individual among others. He was born to create a body for himself: he was born—as John says in chapter 12 of his Gospel—to draw all things to him and in him. He was born—as the letters to the Colossians and to the Ephesians say—to recapitulate all the world, he was born as the first-born of

applying this primary sense to biblical poetics like St Augustine, the Holy Father also applied it to another area: the liturgical calendar. Hence the Pope described the Solemnity of the Most Holy Trinity as a feast that "recapitulates, in a sense, God's revelation in the paschal mysteries: Christ's death and resurrection, his ascension to the right hand of the Father and the outpouring of the Holy Spirit."[21]

Given what we have seen about the nature of recapitulation and about the nature of sacred mystery, such an application is, in my opinion, eminently defensible. It puts us in a position to see certain alleged redundancies in the liturgical calendar as instances of a dynamic of recapitulation, where the Church militant, recognizing that every sacred *factum* is also a *mysterium* (to paraphrase an important line from St Augustine and Pope St Gregory the Great),[22] returns to the same person, event, or thing she had celebrated earlier in the year but from a different perspective. Since there are often too many facets or layers to be taken in at once by our feeble and temporally conditioned intellects, the Church wisely allows the faithful to experience the mystery in a way they might not have been able to before. When, for example, the Church meditates on the Annunciation during Ember Wednesday of Advent, her thoughts are dominated by the impending celebration of the Nativity. But when she meditates on the Annunciation during Lady Day (25 March), she is freer to consider other dimensions of this great event: the mystery of the Incarnation, the role of the Holy Spirit, and not least, the *fiat* of the Blessed Virgin Mary.

many brothers, he was born to reunite the cosmos in himself, such that he is the head of a great body. Where Christ is born, there begins the movement of recapitulation, the moment of the calling, of the construction of his body, of the holy Church. The Mother of '*Theós*,' the Mother of God, is Mother of the Church, because she is Mother of the one who came to reunite all in his risen body." Pope Benedict XVI, "Reflection of the Most Holy Father in the Course of the First General Congregation of the Special Assembly for the Middle East of the Synod of Bishops," 11 October 2010: "ricapitolare tutto il mondo, è nato come primogenito di molti fratelli, è nato per riunire il cosmo in sé, cosicché Lui è il Capo di un grande Corpo. Dove nasce Cristo, inizia il movimento della ricapitolazione." The version published on the Vatican website infelicitously though unofficially translates *ricapitolare* as "summarize."

21. 30 May 2010, Angelus address, Joseph G. Trabbic (trans.), *Zenit News*, http://www.zenit.org/en/articles/on-the-trinity. Alas, the Vatican again translates *ricapitola* as "sums up" rather than "recapitulates" (http://w2.vatican.va/content/benedict-xvi/en/angelus/2010/documents/hf_ben-xvi_ang_20100530.html).

22. See Augustine, *Tractatus in Johannem* 50.6; Gregory, *Moralia* 20. For a scholarly assessment of this principle, see: Christian Mohrmann, "Confessions as a Literary Work of Art," in *Etudes sur le Latin des Chrétiens*, 2nd edn, Tome I (Rome: Edizioni di Storia e Letteratura, 1961), pp. 371–81 (378).

Let me offer three other examples in greater detail taken from our current season of summer: *Corpus Christi*, the Precious Blood, and the Transfiguration.

a. *Corpus Christi*

Holy Thursday is the original feast of *Corpus Christi*, the celebration of the institution of the Eucharist. Yet as a part of the sacred Triduum, Maundy Thursday is mixed with other considerations: the institution of the priesthood, the call to service dramatized by the washing of the feet, Judas's betrayal of our Lord, the agony in the garden, the impending Passion of Our Lord, etc.

Fittingly, the first person to see the need for an additional feast to honor the Blessed Sacrament was our Lord Himself. In the thirteenth century, a humble sixteen-year-old girl began having dreams of a bright moon marred by a small black spot. After years of seeing this perplexing vision, Jesus Christ appeared to her and revealed its meaning. The moon, He told her, represented the Church calendar, and the black spot the absence of a feast in honor of His Blessed Sacrament. That nun was St Juliana, Prioress of Mont Cornillon (d. 1258), and the feast she was commissioned by our Lord to promote was that of *Corpus Christi*.

Even before its universal promotion in 1314, *Corpus Christi* was one of the grandest feasts of the Roman rite. By request of Pope Urban IV, the hymns, Mass propers, and Divine Office were composed or selected by St Thomas Aquinas, whose teaching on the Real Presence was so profound that the figure of Jesus Christ once descended from a crucifix and declared to him, "Thou hast written well of me, Thomas." The mastery with which Aquinas weaves together the scriptural, poetic, and theological texts of this feast amply corroborates this judgment.

One of the most conspicuous features of *Corpus Christi* is the procession after Mass, for which Holy Church grants a plenary indulgence (under the usual conditions) to all those who take part in it. This public profession of the Catholic teaching on the Real Presence, which was solemnly encouraged by the Council of Trent, was traditionally accompanied by ornate pageantry and much celebration. The streets would be elaborately decorated with garlands and images, and the procession would wind through the whole town.

The Eucharist is, of course, both the Body and Blood of our Lord, and so the collect for the feast as well as several other prayers and antiphons make mention of both. Nevertheless, two things can be said about the traditional feast of *Corpus Christi*: first, even though the Eucharist as a whole is adored, the focus leans more towards Our Lord's Eucharistic Body rather than His Precious Blood. We think of food for our souls, the

Panis angelicus, the great spiritual nourishment prefigured by the manna from heaven and by the multiplication of the loaves. We also think incarnationally: Emmanuel, "God is with us," was once among us veiled in a body and is now among us veiled in the appearance of bread. Finally, we think eschatologically, of how the Host, which makes present the Risen Christ, is a foreshadowing of the glorified bodies the elect will enjoy at the end of time. Hence, the Magnificat antiphon for Vespers on *Corpus Christi* speaks of the Body of Christ as the "pledge of our future glory."

Second, even when we adore the Precious Chalice as well as that of the Host on *Corpus Christi*, the focus again tends to lean towards that which both have in common, namely, the miracle of Transubstantiation, the Real Presence, and the great appropriateness of both bread and wine as the matter of the sacrament, of how crushed grains and crushed grapes die to sustain us and rise again transfigured as a new creation.

b. *The Precious Blood*

On the other hand, when Catholics hear the phrase "Precious Blood" by itself, they do not tend to think primarily in terms of symbolism, transubstantiation, or the nourishment that is analogous to earthly food or drink. For although we consume the Blood of our Lord at Holy Communion (even if we are receiving under the species of bread alone), the mention of His Blood by itself invites us to meditate on four other topics.

The first is ablution and aspersion, washing and sprinkling. The flesh of the sacrificial lamb may have been eaten during the feast of Passover, but its blood was sprinkled on the doorposts, thereby averting the Angel of death. Similarly, St Peter speaks of being sanctified by "the sprinkling of the Blood of Jesus Christ" (1 Pet 1:2), while the book of Revelation describes the Blood of the Lamb of God as washing clean the white robes of the saints (7:14; see: 1:5).

Second, the red Blood that washes white also redeems, buying us back from the slave block of the devil. In the Epistle to the Hebrews we read that "neither by the blood of goats or of calves, but by His own blood [Christ] entered once into the Holies, having obtained eternal redemption" (Heb 9:12).[23] One of the earliest epithets for the Savior's Blood in Church parlance is *pretium redemptionis nostrae*, the "price of our redemption."

Third, we remember the Atonement, with its teaching on sin and propitiation. The Blood forcibly reminds us of our shared responsibility in spilling It and of God's mercy in accepting It as our reconciliation with Him. In the book of Genesis, the blood of Abel "speaks" from the ground (4:10). What does it say? That Cain is guilty. Similarly, the Epistle to

---

23. See: Acts 20:28; Rev 5:9.

the Hebrews states that the Blood of Christ "speaks better" than Abel's (12:24). What does it say? That we are guilty, but that we are also reconciled. Christ was wounded for our iniquities (Isa 53:5), but it is by these stripes that we are healed (1 Pet 2:24).[24] Hence, God proposes His Son as "a propitiation, through faith in His blood...for the remission of former sins" (Rom 3:25).

These awesome themes and more are explored on the feast of the Most Precious Blood (July 1). The feast began in Spain in the sixteenth century and was promoted by St Gaspar del Bufalo (d. 1837), founder of the Missionaries of the Most Precious Blood. When Pope Pius IX was exiled from Rome, one of his companions, Don Giovanni Merlini, third superior general of the Missionaries, suggested that he vow to extend the feast to the entire Church if he regained possession of the Papal States. But the Pope decided instead to extend the feast immediately to all Christendom on 30 June 1849. That same day, the French drove out the Italian nationalists who had captured Rome. Since 30 June was a Saturday before the first Sunday of July, Pius IX decreed on 10 August of that year that every first Sunday of July would be dedicated to the Most Precious Blood (the date was later changed to 1 July).[25]

In 1934, to commemorate the nineteenth centenary of our Lord's death, Pope Pius XI raised the feast to the rank of a double of the first class (according to the pre-1960 system). The feast was also extolled shortly before Vatican II by Pope John XXIII in *Inde a Primis*, an apostolic letter on promoting devotion to the most Precious Blood of our Lord Jesus Christ.[26] While those laboring under archeologism (the presumption that older means better) might contemn this "recent" feast, John XXIII saw in it traces of God's ongoing love for His Church: "The Church's wonderful advances in liturgical piety match the progress of faith itself in penetrating divine truth," he writes. "Within this development it is most heart-warming to observe how often in recent centuries this Holy See has openly approved and furthered" this devotion.

---

24. See: Pope Benedict XVI, *Jesus of Nazareth: Holy Week: From the Entrance into Jerusalem to the Resurrection* (San Francisco: Ignatius, 2011), p. 187.

25. See: Ulrich F. Mueller, "Feast of the Most Precious Blood," in Charles G. Herbermann (ed.), *Catholic Encyclopedia*, vol. 12 (New York: The Encyclopedia Press, 1913), pp. 373–74.

26. 30 June 1960. The Latin text may be found at https://w2.vatican.va/content/john-xxiii/la/apost_letters/1960/documents/hf_j-xxiii_apl_19600630_indeaprimis.html. An English translation under the title, "On Promoting Devotion to the Most Precious Blood of our Lord Jesus Christ," may be found at http://www.papalencyclicals.net/John23/j23pb.htm.

Of course, our Lord's Blood was considered earlier on Good Friday, but our hearts on that day were filled with such sorrow that it was difficult for us to appreciate Its magnificence. It is therefore appropriate that we recapitulate the theme and under a more triumphant and jubilant banner. After noting that the Church has already celebrated Good Friday and *Corpus Christi*, Dom Guéranger asks, "How is it…that holy Church is now inviting all Christians to hail, in a particular manner, the stream of life ever gushing from the sacred fount?" His answer: "What else can this mean, but that the preceding solemnities have by no means exhausted the mystery?"[27]

c. *The Transfiguration*
Another feast fittingly celebrated after the Triduum and *Corpus Christi* is that of the Transfiguration of our Lord on 6 August. As Pope Benedict XVI notes in his Apostolic Exhortation *Sacramentum Caritatis* (22 February 2007), the transubstantiation of bread and wine into Christ's Body and Blood is not only a profound miracle in its own right, but it also "introduces within creation the principle of a radical change, a sort of 'nuclear fission'" that sets off a chain reaction that will ultimately culminate in the "transfiguration of the entire world, to the point where God will be all in all" (n. 11). And one of the first hints of this cosmic transfiguration at the end of time is the personal transfiguration of our Lord, when His face shone as the sun and His garments became white as snow (see: Matt 17:2).

The Gospel reading for the Second Sunday of Lent is also of the Transfiguration. According to tradition, our Lord deigned to be transfigured before three Apostles—Peter, James, and John—in order to fortify them for the brutal and demoralizing spectacle of His forthcoming crucifixion[28] (note that it is these same three Apostles that He wanted with Him in the Garden of Gethsemane). The Transfiguration was meant to give the Apostles a foretaste of the Resurrection in order to help them overcome the trauma of the Crucifixion. By the same logic, the Church wisely anticipates the glory of Easter during the penitential season of Lent by calling to mind the Transfiguration, as if to give the faithful a glimpse of the light at the end of the tunnel.

27. Prosper Guéranger, *The Liturgical Year*, vol. 12 (Great Falls: Bonaventure, 2000), p. 386.
28. See St Thomas Aquinas, *Summa Theologiae* III.45.1.

But Lent is not the time to savor the glory of Easter, and there is so much more to glean from the Transfiguration than a mere means of steeling one's courage. How appropriate, then, that the Church recapitulates the event during the more jubilant Time after Pentecost. It is there that she can ruminate on at least three other aspects of this mystery:

First, as with *Corpus Christi*, she can consider our future glory. One of the Breviary hymns for the feast speaks of the event as a "sign of perennial glory."[29] As Peter the Venerable teaches, the Resurrection is already prefigured in the Transfiguration; and the Resurrection, needless to say, is a "sneak peek" at the amazing, luminous, space-and-time-defying bodies that the elect will acquire on the Last Day.[30]

Second, she can reflect on the relationship between the two Testaments. When Jesus is transfigured, Moses and Elijah, representatives of the two main branches of the Old Testament (the Law and Prophets), accompany Him. The triptych of Moses, Elijah, and Jesus therefore represents the sum of biblical history. But eventually, Moses and Elijah disappear and only Jesus remains. The High Priest of the new Covenant is in continuity with the Old but also greater than it.

Third, she can speculate on the "social" dimension of the transfiguration. What does it mean to say with Pope Benedict that the world will be "transfigured"? What does it mean to have human living transfigured by the Catholic call to action,[31] under the social kingship of our transfigured Lord? How should our lives, our social interactions, and our politics be transfigured in light of the "nuclear fission" of Christ's Eucharistic Body? Interestingly, the date of the feast was chosen for a socio-political reason, to commemorate the Christian victory over the Turks at the Battle of Belgrade in July 1456, news of which reached the Pope's ears on 6 August of that year.[32]

---

29. The hymn is *Quicumque Christum quaeritis*, and the verse is *Signum perennis gloriae.*

30. Those bodies will possess the four gifts of impassibility, agility, subtlety, and clarity.

31. See: Bernard J. F. Lonergan SJ, *Insight: An Inquiry into Human Understanding* (San Francisco: Harper & Row, 1978), pp. 742–43.

32. As Pope Calixtus III later wrote: "If this fortress [at Belgrade] had been lost, the very existence of the entire Christian republic would have been in danger" (Letter to a Burgundian Bishop, http://www.ucalgary.ca/applied_history/tutor/endmiddle/bluedot/belgrade.html).

4. *Reduction of Liturgical Recapitulation*

One of the effects of almost every major reform to the general calendar since 1950 has been a reduction in recapitulation.[33] In 1955, all of the octaves of the saints (as well as the octaves of Epiphany, Ascension, *Corpus Christi*, the Sacred Heart of Jesus, the Immaculate Conception, and All Saints) were eliminated. Now it is debatable whether an octave fulfills the strict criteria of recapitulation as we have defined it, but it can at least be argued that the octave day of a feast in particular often functions as a kind of recapitulation. When the Church celebrates the feast of Stephen on 26 December, for instance, she calls to mind the great deacon's martyrdom, but because the hearts of the faithful are still filled with the joy of Christmas, it is difficult to contemplate the martyrdom on its own terms. Usually our thoughts tend to be drawn to Stephen's status as one of the *comites Christi*, that privileged group of martyrs who mystically stand guard at the crib of our Lord by virtue of their feast days' proximity to Christmas. But when the octave day of Stephen was celebrated on 2 January as well, it gave us an opportunity to make up for any deficiencies in venerating the saint that may have occurred on 26 December.

In 1960, a number of recapitulated saints' days were eliminated or combined, despite the antiquity of a number of them. The Finding of the Holy Cross on 3 May, St John Before the Latin Gate on 6 May, the Apparition of St Michael on 8 May, St Peter in Chains on 1 August, and the Finding of St Stephen on 3 August were eliminated, while St Peter's Chair in Rome on 18 January and St Peter's Chair in Antioch on 22 February became St Peter's Chair on 22 February. That at least some of the faithful had understood these extra feasts as part of a process of liturgical recapitulation (despite the fact that they did not use the term) can be seen in the way in which they described or explained these liturgical events.

Writing in the nineteenth century about the feast of St John Before the Latin Gate, Dom Guéranger states: "The beloved Disciple John, whom we saw standing near the crib of the Babe of Bethlehem, comes before us to-day [6 May]; and this time he pays his delighted homage to the glorious Conqueror of death and hell." Note the image: we first encountered St John as witness to the Birth of our Lord; we now encounter him as witness to the Resurrection. It is the same person but recapitulated by being seen in a different light, specifically, a different facet of the mystery of the life of Christ.

---

33. I wish to express my gratitude to Mr Stephen Higgins for his significant contributions to this part of the chapter.

Similarly, writing in the 1950s, Maria Von Trapp states the following about the feast of the Finding of the Holy Cross on 3 May and the feast of the Triumph of the Holy Cross on 14 September:

> On the third of May the Church has us celebrate the feast of the Finding of the Cross. It is connected with the old tradition that the Empress Helena discovered the True Cross of Christ in the fourth century and built a church on that place. We may rest assured that this legend alone would not be reason enough for Holy Mother Church to install not only one but two feasts. For in September we celebrate the Exaltation of the Holy Cross. What the Church wants to bring home to us is this that we must take the word of Our Lord seriously: "Whosoever wants to become my disciple, let him take up his cross and follow Me."...When we celebrate these feasts of the Cross in May and September in our family, this leads to talk about the different crosses in our life, small ones, big ones.[34]

The Second Vatican Council (1962–1965) did not address the issue of recapitulation directly. Its constitution *Sacrosanctum Concilium* merely states that "The rites should be distinguished by a noble simplicity; they should be short, clear, and unencumbered by useless repetitions" (n. 34).[35] The phrase "useless repetitions" (*repetitiones inutiles*) could be taken as a call to reduce the number of feasts in the Church calendar, but I would argue that since liturgical recapitulation is neither useless nor a repetition, *Sacrosanctum Concilium* 34 does not apply to feasts that are constituents in a pattern of recapitulation. Further, it is unclear whether this paragraph is intended to be applied to the calendar, since it does not appear in the Constitution's fifth chapter on the liturgical year (nn. 102–11). The only explicit principle of reform grounded in article 34, that the saints' days not "take precedence over the feasts which commemorate the very mysteries of salvation" (n. 111), no doubt contributed directly to the eventual loss of seventy saints from the universal calendar and indirectly to a decline in liturgical recapitulation, but the laudable goal of keeping the Sanctoral cycle from overshadowing the Temporal Cycle is not *per se* opposed to liturgical recapitulation.

---

34. Maria Augusta Trapp, *Around the Year with the Trapp Family* (New York: Pantheon, 1955), pp. 241–42.

35. "Ritus nobili simplicitate fulgeant, sint brevitate perspicui et repetitiones inutiles evitent, sint fidelium captui accommodati, neque generatim multis indigeant explanationibus."

Whatever the cause, the 1969 calendar evinces a further loss of recapitulation. The feast of the Precious Blood that was so dear to Pope John XXIII was abolished, or rather combined, with the feast of *Corpus Christi* to create the Solemnity of the Most Holy Body and Blood of Jesus Christ. Similarly, the feasts of St Gabriel and St Raphael were eliminated in order to form a combined feast together with that of St Michael. While there is certainly nothing wrong with praising all of the archangels together, and while it is true that with these three archangels there was a certain transference of veneration not unlike that of Sts Peter and Paul (whereby celebrating the memory of one calls forth a celebration of the other)— nevertheless, each of these three archangels has a different name with a different meaning and a different mission in the economy of salvation, and the separate legacy of each one is therefore not inappropriately singled out by a separate feast day. The feast of St Gabriel, for example, fell on 24 March, a fitting preparation for the feast of the Annunciation on 25 March.

Other examples of reduced recapitulation in the 1969 calendar include the suppression of the Second feast of St Agnes on 28 January (which fell eight days after the first feast of St Agnes on 21 January), the suppression of the feast of the Stigmata of Saint Francis on 17 September, and the suppression of the first of the two feasts of the Seven Sorrows of the Blessed Virgin Mary. In 1962, the Seven Sorrows fell on the Friday before Good Friday and again on 15 September, the day after the feast of the Holy Cross. As *The Saint Andrew Daily Missal* points out:

> The first feast of her Sorrows in Passiontide recalls our Lady's share in Christ's sacrifice on Calvary; this second one [in the Season after Pentecost] recalls also the other events when she suffered with Jesus. Moreover, she also shares in the sufferings of the Church, His Spouse, who is crucified in her turn and in this time of suffering renews her devotion to His Mother's sorrows.[36]

Another valid way to view the relation between these two feasts is that the first, only one week away from the Passion of Our Lord on Good Friday, invites us to meditate on the compassion of Holy Mary, on her "suffering with" her Son during His Passion, while the second, only one day after the Triumph of the Cross, allows us to return to the theme of compassion in a more triumphant, victorious key.

---

36. Dom Gaspar Lefebvre OSB (ed.), *Saint Andrew Daily Missal* (St Paul: E. M. Lohmann Co., 1953), p. 1557.

The transference of some feasts in 1969 also had an effect on recapitulation. On the one hand, moving the feast of St Monica from 4 May to 27 August, the day before her son's feast day on 28 August, is understandable, as the hagiographies of Sts Monica and Augustine are notably intertwined. On the other, St Augustine's death on 28 August, AD 430, occurred decades after his mother's and in the midst of a vastly different world than the one described in the *Confessions*; for when Augustine was dying, the Roman Empire was crumbling and the barbarians were literally at the gates of his city of Hippo Regius. Monica's original feast day on 4 May, which had been kept since the thirteenth century, more naturally calls to mind her crucial role in Augustine's baptism, which took place in the springtime; indeed, there were some local medieval calendars that once celebrated 5 May as the feast of the Conversion of Augustine. Celebrating Monica's heavenly birthday and Augustine's ecclesiastical birthday as a "double header" on 4 and 5 May is therefore appropriate. But turning the heavenly birthdays of Monica and of the aged bishop of Hippo into a double header in late August is, in my opinion, less appropriate, and it has the additional disadvantage of depriving the faithful of the opportunity to recapitulate liturgically after the passing of several months the lives of these two extraordinary saints.

In addition to the elimination, conflation, and transference of feast days, there are at least three additional developments contributing to the reduction of recapitulation in the 1969 calendar:

First, the *de facto* elimination of the Ember Days.[37] We have already noted how the feast on 25 March and the Ember Wednesday of Advent are recapitulations of the mystery of the Annunciation.

Second, the elimination of the station days from the 1970 Roman missal. In the 1962 *Missale Romanum*, there are eighty-nine Masses on eighty-six days of the year with a designated stational church. Although the 1968 *Enchiridion of Indulgences* assumes that the Roman missal would

---

37. Although *Sacrosanctum Concilium* 50—that liturgical elements "which have suffered injury through accidents of history are now to be restored to the vigor which they had in the days of the holy Fathers"—could have been used to reinvigorate the quarterly observance of Embertide, the Sacred Congregation of Divine Worship's 1969 *General Norms for the Liturgical Year and the Calendar* removed Ember Days from the universal calendar and left it to bishops' conferences to "arrange the time and plan for their celebration" (n. 46). Some national episcopal conferences, like Germany's, followed this instruction, but most did not, a neglect that has left over 90% of the Roman Catholic population worldwide without an annual observance of Ember Days. See Michael P. Foley, "The Glow of the Ember Days," *The Latin Mass* 17 (Fall 2008), pp. 36–39.

still include the station churches, the 1970 edition makes no reference to them and has a cycle of readings that abstracts from them entirely (in the 1962 missal, by contrast, the prayers and readings of a given day are often heavily influenced by a particular stational church). The station days are currently observed in Rome during the season of Lent—most notably by the North American College—but this still leaves 99.6% of the world's Catholics who do not live in Rome without a liturgical observance of the station days. And even the 0.4% that has the opportunity to observe the station days only has it during the forty days of Lent—less than half the number in the 1962 missal.[38]

Finally, the three-year lectionary cycle of the 1970 Roman missal eliminates, two-thirds of the time, several of the readings that created recapitulated a biblical event, such as the Transfiguration.[39]

On the other hand, it can be argued that the institution of Divine Mercy Sunday by Pope St John Paul II in 2000 is an instance of liturgical recapitulation, with Easter focusing on the event or reality of our Lord's bodily resurrection and Divine Mercy Sunday focusing on both the cause and effect of that great miracle.

5. *Reasons for Decline*

There are, in my opinion, a number of possible reasons for the modern under-appreciation of recapitulation. The first is an assault on the notion of *mysterium* in modern philosophical thought, either by flattening and evacuating it (in the manner of Descartes) or by making it utterly inscrutable and unknowable (in the manner of Kant). Either extreme has fatal repercussions for recapitulation, for the former makes it unnecessary and the latter makes it impossible.

Second, the emphasis in *Sacrosanctum Concilium* on ease of comprehension, as when the document calls for rites that "should be within the people's powers of comprehension, and normally should not require much explanation" (n. 34; see n. 62), *may* to some degree have unwittingly contributed to a flattening of a sense of mystery and hence mitigated

---

38. See Michael P. Foley, "Making the Stations," *The Latin Mass* 18 (Winter 2009), pp. 38–41.

39. It may, however, be the case that the increase of biblical readings in the new missal has created new instances of recapitulation. Perhaps further study can be done in this area. If indeed there is more recapitulation thanks to the new lectionary, it is imperative that the faithful be shown these instances and taught their value *as instances* of liturgical recapitulation.

any perceived need for recapitulation—this despite the Council's solid affirmations on the Sacred Liturgy's relation to the mystery of our Faith in other passages (see: nn. 5, 6, et passim).

Third, Catherine Pickstock contends that the authors of *Sacrosanctum Concilium* and the architects of what is now called the ordinary form of the Roman rite were operating under a soft Cartesianism that construes all advancement in knowledge as a linear and univocal progression rather than a tentative and "stuttering" participation in the mystery of the numinous.[40] *If* Pickstock is right, it is not difficult to see why the *Concilium* under Pope Paul VI would have been indifferent to the benefits of recapitulation or why Annibale Bugnini, even years before the opening of the Second Vatican Council, would have encouraged or countenanced a reduction of liturgical recapitulation in the Roman calendar.

Fourth and lastly, the Great Texts professor in me cannot help but speculate that another cause is a possible failure to read the liturgical year as a grand and unified "book," where recurring elements, far from being redundant, are seen as vital clues into the author's meaning or at the very least as a means of underscoring crucial themes. In a great book, when an author "repeats himself," it is for a reason, but the assumption of many twentieth-century liturgical reformers (to say nothing of contemporary literary critics) seems to have been that any recurrence, especially where an ancient text is concerned, must be the product of accident or carelessness. While I cannot deny this possibility, I nevertheless maintain that it is safer and more productive to begin with a hermeneutic of modesty and a respect for the integrity of the object being studied before passing judgment on the value of its elements.

a. *Timeless Value?*

It is my conviction that despite contemporary neglect, liturgical recapitulation is a valuable tool both anthropologically and theologically. Anthropologically, it is ideally suited to the way in which we human beings grow in wisdom and love. Man is monogastric in terms of his body, but he is a ruminant in terms of his intellect, a creature who, to borrow a colorful image from St Augustine, calls things up from the stomach of his mind in order to chew on them more.[41] Liturgical recapitulation stems to some extent from a recognition that because we see now through a glass darkly and know only

---

40. Catherine Pickstock, *After Writing: On the Liturgical Consummation of Philosophy* (Oxford: Blackwell, 1998), pp. 170–76.

41. Augustine, *Confessions* 10.14.21.

in part, we need to circle around and survey the same phenomenon several times. Returning to the same reality but in a new light or from a different perspective deepens our experience and knowledge of that reality.

Theologically, liturgical recapitulation is not simply a concession to the littleness of our minds but a witness to the greatness of the sacred and the supernatural. Realities such as those narrated in Scripture or defined by Catholic dogma or actuated in the life of a saint are too august to be captured in a single sitting or by a single snapshot but require being revisited again and again. Consequently, just as there is a second account of the Mosaic Law in the Old Testament known as Deuteronomy, and just as there are four different Gospels rather than one "definitive" biography of our Lord, it is fitting that there be a calendar of worship in which mysteries are recapitulated.

On a different theological note, observing and understanding recapitulation in the liturgical calendar can serve to illuminate other forms of recapitulation that the Church cherishes. As we have already noted, liturgical recapitulation is evocative of the biblical technique defined by Tyconius and Augustine; even more, recapitulation broadly understood can be seen as the principle undergirding all typological exegesis.[42] St Lawrence of Brundisi once described man as the "recapitulation of all creation" and the dogma on the Last Judgment as the "recapitulation of all of the mysteries of our Faith."[43] And most importantly, Paul's depiction of Christ as the recapitulation of all things finds apt elaboration in the soteriology of St Irenaeus, which understands redemption as the recapitulating activity of the Son of God.

6. *Conclusion*

Our reference to St Paul returns us to Eph 1:9–10 and to the Apostle's claim that God the Father wishes to make known to us the mystery of His will by recapitulating all things in Christ, in the fullness of times—or put simply, that God reveals a mystery in order to recapitulate temporally

---

42. See Hans Boersma, "Spiritual Imagination: Recapitulation as an Interpretive Principle," in Hans Boersma (ed.), *Imagination and Interpretation: Christian Perspectives* (Vancouver: Regent College, 2005), pp. 13–33.

43. St Lawrence writes that just as the creation of man on the sixth day illustrates that he is both a recapitulation and a microcosm of all creation, so too is "the last and universal mystery of the Judgment like the peroration and recapitulation of all the mysteries of our faith" (mysterium finalis et universalis iudicii, est veluti peroratio et recapitulatio omnium mysteriorum fidei nostrae). See: *Quadragesimale quartum*, vol. 10, pars I, par. 14 (in feria secunda infra hebdomadam primam quadragesimae).

all things in Christ. As a result of this divine initiative, the Church both receives these mysteries and, among other things, recapitulates them in time through her annual calendar. And so, just as God recapitulates all things in Christ, let us lovingly respond by recapitulating Christ in all things, starting with our observance of His sacred time.

Living the Liturgy: A Monastic Contribution to Liturgical Renewal

Philip Anderson OSB

1. *Introduction: Living the Liturgy*

When Dom Prosper Guéranger, founder of the Benedictine Congregation to which my abbey belongs, took up residence in the abandoned buildings of the little French priory of Solesmes at the dawn of the nineteenth century, he surely had no intention of founding a liturgical movement, and even less of becoming the "father" or "grandfather" of what blossomed in the twentieth century under that name.[1] However, being already a promising liturgist and church historian, he certainly *did* realize how much the monastic order in general, and, in particular, the family of Saint Benedict, had done and could do to promote the liturgical life of the Church. Dom Lambert Beauduin, whom many, including his *confrère* at the Abbey of Mont César (Louvain), Dom Botte, regard as being a principal actor of the modern liturgical movement (beginning with the famous Malines Congress of 1909), heaps high praises on his predecessor in the liturgical science:

> The abbot of Solesmes was a man of a great and single idea. He had from the start the genial intuition of his mission, and he devoted himself entirely to it: that of restoring to our disinherited age all the scattered treasures of the thousand-year tradition of Christianity, and above all the forgotten riches of antiquity that the Church preserves in her liturgy. Such was the luminous star that guided him in all his ways. And he envisaged this ideal in all its aspects...the study and the love of liturgical institutions; the pastoral value of the liturgical year and its ever varied teachings; the doctrinal foundations of this theological locus of first order; the treasures of asceticism and of mysticism which the liturgical seasons and the lives of the saints bring us

---

1. See: Cuthbert Johnson, *Prosper Gueranger (1805–1875): A Liturgical Theologian* (Rome: Studia Anselmiana, 1984), pp. 13–14.

every day. In sum Dom Guéranger placed himself from the beginning at the center of the temple, and he contemplated its every part and all its elements: he is the unequaled liturgist.[2]

Here I will not attempt to retrace the history of liturgical institutions or add its voice, except in passing, to specific debates that have animated theologians and liturgists in the post-conciliar era. Leaving to pastors and specialists these discussions, I hope rather to provide a glimpse of how monks live their liturgical life, day by day, and thereby show what a monastery has to offer to liturgical renewal.

As has been said, not without a dose of English humor, that "liturgy is too important to be left to liturgists."[3] My first point is something along those lines: whatever they are, monks are not primarily liturgists. They are, indeed, actors, agents of the liturgy, but not liturgical specialists. I mean not to offend. Perhaps what I *do* mean will become more apparent as we go along. None of what I have to say, by the way, about a monastic contribution to liturgical renewal will be of my own invention. It derives, rather, from the founts of wisdom originating in the monastic adventure started at Solesmes about one hundred and eighty years ago and from the living tradition of our monastic family as it moves forward today.

One might say that the monastery is less a liturgical "think-tank" than a liturgical laboratory. But neither term really expresses the thing. Using a more monastic metaphor, taken from the *Rule* of Saint Benedict, it would be truer to say that the monastery is a workplace, a workshop, where the Holy Spirit is the fire in the sacred forge whence come spiritual works: *ora et labora* (pray and work).

Now among these holy works forged by the monk the foremost is the *Opus Dei* (the Work of God), the holy liturgy. This is not for us merely a subject for study, but rather a good work to perform and to live every day. The liturgy is what we do, the life of which we live. Granted this is the case of all Christians in a sense, it is no less certain that few can dedicate their lives to liturgical prayer with the same completeness that is possible for members of the monastic order, since even the most fervent of the faithful living outside the cloister walls, including priests and religious, though their existence be centered around the celebration of Holy Mass, have other preoccupations in life, notably the multi-faceted efforts of the apostolate. The monk, like the bishop in his cathedral, but in a different way, is truly *homo liturgicus*.

2. Lambert Beauduin, "Dom Marmion et la liturgie," *La Vie Spirituelle* 78 (1948) pp. 33–45 (44–45).

3. Aidan Nichols, *Looking at the Liturgy* (San Francisco: Ignatius, 1997), p. 9.

2. Custos, quid de nocte?

So who exactly is the monk? Who is this monastic artisan in the liturgical workshop? Well, he is, for one thing, a sentinel, a watchman. "Watchman, what of the night? Watchman, what of the night?" asks the prophet Isaiah with insistence (21:11). Long before dawn this monastic watchman makes his way to a kind of wooden bench, a seat or stall in the church, where he stands and sits alternatively, perhaps making use of the famous—or infamous—"mercy seat." It is his workbench and his cross, his special place in the Church. He comes to praise God in the night, as he keeps watch. Tertullian refers to the early Christian gathering as "*Antelucani coetus*" (the predawn assembly).[4] The expression describes rather well the monastic choir. The monk fulfils, according to St Hildegard, an "angelic function, the divine service, the same service the angels perform in heaven."[5] Abba Bessarion, a Desert Father, goes as far as to assert that monks "should always be looking at the same object at which the cherubim and the seraphim are looking."[6]

But why does the monk do this? In order to answer this fundamental question, a few doctrinal considerations are in order. After all, is not the liturgy itself, with its *lex orandi*, a privileged source of theology? Is it not true that "the sanctuary precedes the *aula* of theological discourse" and that "the altar confers authority upon the academic chair," as Dom Daniel Kirby of Silverstream Priory points out?[7]

St Thomas Aquinas suggests there is a kind of cycle in creation. This is not the cyclical sense of history as in Oriental religions, but rather a single cycle or return of all things to their source. When God creates, it is as if things come out, proceed from Him (in Latin, *exitus*). Creatures drawn *ex nihilo* do not come out of God in any material way; there is no emanation from the divine substance.[8] Of course! But the reality is hard to express without these concrete images. God certainly is the absolute origin of creation, and in this sense it proceeds from Him. Furthermore,

---

4. See: Prosper Guéranger, *Institutions Liturgiques*, vol. 1 (Paris: Société Générale de Librairie Catholique, 1878), p. 48.

5. Saint Hildegard, *Scivias* II, 5 (Jacques Paul Migne [ed.], *Patrologia Latina* [Paris, 1841–1855], vol. 197), pp. 485–86.

6. Abba Bessarion, *Apophthegm* (Migne, *Patrologia Latina*, vol. 73), p. 934.

7. Daniel Kirby, *Liturgy, Doctrine, and Discipline: The Right Order*, Vultus Christi Blog, 7 November 2014.

8. See: First Vatican Council, Dogmatic Constitution *Dei Filius* (24 April 1870), canons 2–4; Heinrich Denzinger, Peter Hünermann, Robert Fastiggi and Anne Nash (eds), *Enchiridion symbolorum definitionem et declarationem de rebus fidei et morum*, 43rd edn, Latin–English (San Francisco: Ignatius, 2012), nn. 3022–24.

it is fitting, says the Angelic Doctor, that this marvelous work of God's hand returns to Him in some way, completing the cycle (in Latin, *reditus*). The philosopher Plotinus had said something similar.[9] But how can this happen? How can creation, especially material creation—that of tree-toads or of elephants, for example—return to its Creator? Well, precisely, through man, that microcosm, that summary of things, that walking world. The monk is a watchman. He is also a little bit of everything and presides over the visible world. Here we might recall Pascal's remark:

> Man is but a reed, the weakest thing in nature, but he is a thinking reed. The entire universe need not arm itself to crush him. A vapor, a drop of water suffices to kill him. But, if the universe were to crush him, man would still be nobler than that which killed him, because he knows that he dies and the advantage which the universe has over him. The universe knows nothing of this.[10]

In effect, man (i.e. man and woman) includes in himself something of inert matter: in this he represents the lower world of rocks, minerals, crystals and less complex matter. He has features that are proper to plants: his bodily tissue grows like that of any vegetative life. Man is obviously a kind of animal, having limbs and sensory knowledge. He is even part angel, so to speak, owing to his spiritual faculties of intellect and will. Thus it is that man, and man alone, is the creature that can collect in his heart all the voices of creation and bring them back to God through praise.[11] "The heavens declare the glory of God,"[12] exclaims the psalmist. Yes, but they do not appreciate their own praise. Man does. He sees the stars; he wonders; he gives praise—especially if he happens to be a monk or a nun.

As the night gives way to dawn and the first rays of sunlight filter through the widows to the east, when the monk, still in his choir stall, moves from matins or vigils to the office of lauds, he is invited by means of the liturgy to pass in review the great order of the cosmos we have been evoking, proceeding from top to bottom. We see this especially in the Canticle of the Three Young Men in the book of Daniel: "*Benedicite, omnia opera Domini...* Bless the Lord, all works of the Lord... Bless the Lord, you heavens...You angels of the Lord, sing praise to him and highly

---

9. See: Andrew Louth, *The Origins of the Christian Mystical Tradition* (Oxford: Clarendon, 1981), p. 38.

10. Blaise Pascal, *Pascal's Pensées* (New York: E. P. Dutton & Co., 1958), p. 97 n. 347.

11. See: Paul Delatte, *The Rule of St Benedict: A Commentary* (New York: Benziger Brothers, 1921), pp. 131–43.

12. Ps 19 (The Jerusalem Bible).

exalt him forever… All waters above the heaven…sun and moon…stars of heaven…rain and dew," etc. (3:35–42). And the series continues all the way down to the whales and all that moves in the waters, to all the wild beasts and cattle. The same cosmic "parade" occurs in the *laudate* psalms (148, 149, and 150) that we chant every day in our monastic office: "Praise the Lord from the heavens, praise him in the heights! Praise him, all his angels, praise him, all his host!… Praise him, sun and moon, praise him, all you shining stars!" (Ps 148:1–3). And so forth in descending order, following the hierarchal order of the cosmos, from the highest creatures to the lowest.

Unfortunately this exquisite harmony of praise, as it existed from the beginning in the first man and woman in Eden, was fragile, breakable, and through sin was in fact broken. Once expelled from the primal garden Adam could no longer function adequately as intermediary of the universe, as the priest of creation. A Redeemer was wanted and awaited for many centuries. Then, with the accomplishment of the great effort of God to save mankind, a whole new spiritual world of grace came into existence. Thenceforth, the Sacrifice of Mass replaced the praise once given to God by Adam and later by the inefficacious sacrifices of the Mosaic Law. Now, at last, a source of infinite grace allowed man, through the Sacrifice of the Messiah and through offices of the ordained priesthood, to offer to God a worthy praise, one infinitely more precious: the Most Holy Body of Christ and His Precious Blood. All of this is simply the substance of our Catholic faith. Christ, the Messiah, coming in the fullness of time, is the ultimate *leitourgos* (actor of the liturgy).

Monks and nuns, while most of mankind sleeps, accomplish this more complete, this "professional" work of praise, as they keep watch in the night, chanting the psalms under the grace of the New Law, which, according to St Thomas Aquinas, is the grace of the Holy Spirit.[13] So there the monk stands, whether he is a priest or a lay brother, at his post as watchman, offering the Divine Office at night and, at the break of day, the Holy Sacrifice of the Eucharist. He thus accomplishes as never could be done before Christ, the work of bringing back to the Father, to the Creator, the praise of all creation, grouped mystically around the Christian altar.

St Therese of Lisieux, that very contemplative Doctor of the Church and of the "Little Way," found her vocation in the love that is in the heart of the Church and that moves all the other members.[14] The Benedictine monk likewise, but in a specifically liturgical mode, lives at this same contemplative center, from which radiate, like concentric ripples issuing

13. *Summa Theologiæ* I–II, q. 106, a. 1.
14. St Thérèse of Lisieux, *Story of a Soul* (Washington: ICS, 1996), p. 194.

from the impact of a stone falling into a pond, waves of grace that silently move out toward the furthest peripheries of the Church and of the world. *Bonum diffusivum sui* (the Good tends to give of itself) says the scholastic adage. This contemplative charity is nourished by liturgical prayer. Thus the liturgical prayer of monks appears as a powerful form of evangelization, that of the spiritual watchman of the New Israel. "St Benedict," explains Pope Francis, "took up the way of life that he summed up in two words: *ora et labora* (pray and work). It is from contemplation, from a strong relationship with the Lord, that there is borne in us the capacity to live and bear God's love, his mercy, his tenderness to others" (Angelus Address, 21 July 2013).

Unlike other men, the monk is *vowed* to the liturgy. St Benedict bids him to prefer nothing to this liturgical praise, to this "Work of God" (*Opus Dei*), which is his very life, as we have seen. Like all Christians, he is to be "poor in spirit" (Matt 5:3) and thus inherits the Kingdom. Like every member of the faithful, he is to be perfect like His Heavenly Father is perfect.[15] Unlike most Christians, though, he is formally and publically committed to a form of life that involves personal sacrifices aimed at living a frugal and prayerful existence that will enhance the acquisition of perfection. In the end, this watchman is also a kind of pilgrim, moving, climbing the ladder of humility or the mountain of perfection—St Benedict uses both metaphors—in obedience, poverty and chastity, in spirit of faith, charity and immense hope—not just for himself but for the entire Church. And all of this is accomplished to the constant rhythm of the liturgy.[16]

3. *The Hermeneutics of Hope*

At this *Sacra Liturgia* conference we have reflected on the rich and complex reality of liturgical formation and of liturgical renewal as part of the New Evangelization. It was, then, Cardinal Joseph Ratzinger, who, before being elected to the Chair of Saint Peter, called for a "new

---

15. See: Second Vatican Council, Dogmatic Constitution *Lumen Gentium* (21 November 1964), chapter 5.

16. See: Second Vatican Council, Decree *Perfectae Caritatis* (28 October 1965), n. 7: "Communities which are entirely dedicated to contemplation, so that their members in solitude and silence, with constant prayer and penance willingly undertaken, occupy themselves with God alone, retain at all times, no matter how pressing the needs of the active apostolate may be, an honorable place in the Mystical Body of Christ, whose 'members do not all have the same function' (Rom 12:4). For these offer to God a sacrifice of praise which is outstanding."

liturgical movement of the twenty-first century to maximize the strengths and minimize the weaknesses of the 'old' in the century now closing."[17]

To say there has been some controversy on this topic would be quite an understatement. It is clear, in any case, that the teaching of Pope Emeritus Benedict on the subject of the hermeneutics of renewal and organic development has been immensely helpful to those who reflect on the life of the Church in our time. Liturgical tradition, like that of doctrine, must be a living reality, but one which remains quite coherent, in harmony with itself, without loss of identity along the way. There must be no revolution or rupture here, but rather a living continuity that allows for new life without breaking the historical connection with the past. The liturgy is thus like the biblical eagle that renews itself: "Your youth is renewed like the eagle's" (Ps 103:5). It is Dom Alcuin Reid, a principal inspirer and organizer of the *Sacra Liturgia* conferences, who gave to one of his books the suggestive title, *The Organic Development of the Liturgy.*[18] That is precisely the idea.

But what might a monk have to do with this matter of hermeneutics? Well, we, more than most categories of Christians, have had, and continue to have, a privileged role in the area of Tradition. Everyone knows that much of European culture was preserved in monasteries after the breakdown of the structures (and infra-structures) of the Roman Empire. Because monasteries tended to be stable places, where generation after generation of men and women persevered in a life consecrated to God, it is only natural that these institutions played an important role in maintaining a sense of history and, precisely, of continuity.

Leaping ahead to modern times, to the twentieth century, when profound changes were being introduced into the liturgical practice of the Catholic Church, especially during the Second Vatican Council, I recall what seemed to me a telling moment with respect to the hermeneutics of organic development. In his Latin letter, *Sacrificium Laudis* (Sacrifice of Praise),[19] Blessed Paul VI asked that those institutes having the obligation to recite the Divine Office in choir (especially contemplative monastic communities) maintain the use of Latin and of chant, a liturgical tradition he refers to as *gloriosa illa hereditas* (that glorious heritage). He even went

---

17. See: Peter Stravinskas, back-cover praise for: Nichols, *Looking at the Liturgy.*

18. Alcuin Reid, *The Organic Development of the Liturgy*, 2nd edn (San Francisco: Ignatius, 2005).

19. Letter *Ad Moderatores Generales Religionum Clericalium* (15 August 1966). ET: ICEL, *Documents on the Liturgy: 1963–1979* (Collegeville: The Liturgical Press, 1982), n. 421, pp. 1080–81.

so far as to plead with supreme moderators of these religious institutes, saying, "*Sinite Nos, etiam invitis vobis, rem vestram tueri* (Allow Us, even against your inclination, to protect your own interest)." In 2014, at a meeting of Benedictine abbots of North America, His Excellency, Archbishop Rino Fisichella, President of the Pontifical Council for the Promotion of the New Evangelization, in an unofficial but adamant aside, told the Benedictine superiors that they should be preserving Latin and Gregorian chant in their liturgies ("If you do not do this," he asked, "who will?"). All of this underlines the fact that monks have a privileged role to play in maintaining the continuity of the living liturgical tradition.

4. *Adoration in Spirit and in Truth*

Now, the monk, that watchman of the true Israel of God, that spiritual pilgrim, is also a digger—not a digger of graves, but a digger of wells. There is a truly biblical symbolism at play here, both in the water itself and in the depth of the well. Surely, throughout human history, there never was, nor could there be a deeper and more substantial conversation than the one that took place between Jesus and the Samaritan woman next to Jacob's well. No mere poet or philosopher ever dreamed of words so pregnant with meaning. In fact, the whole liturgical question is given an answer here, one that touches our particular questions too, one that springs forth from the depths of Divine Wisdom:

> Woman, believe me, the hour is coming when neither on this mountain nor in Jerusalem will you worship the Father. You worship what you do not know; we worship what we know, for salvation is from the Jews. But the hour is coming, and now is, when the true worshippers will worship the Father in spirit and truth, for such the Father seeks to worship him. God is spirit, and those who worship him must worship in spirit and truth. (John 4:21–24)

The monk labors with his hands, and he prays. But prayer is the first thing. *Ora et labora.* And this prayer, at its deepest level, is worship, adoration in spirit and in truth. This is not only a matter of spirit *or* of truth, but of spirit *and* of truth.

While we have witnessed many efforts aimed at liturgical renewal since the Second Vatican Council, two rather distinct tendencies—or should we say exaggerations?—seem to stand out among the less successful endeavors. The first is a manner of making the liturgy *spiritual*, at least in some striking way, but without sufficient regard to truth. This might take the form of a "charismatic" sort of celebration that generates remarkable enthusiasm, strong emotions, but which does not sufficiently respect liturgical law (truth) set down by the Church. We might also be considering a liturgy based on a more particular intellectual movement, following an ideology such as Marxism or feminism; Americans tend to lump them all together under the term "liberalism." Here too those participating in this sort of liturgy are intensely engaged: their minds and hearts are participating, but the liturgical truth gets lost in the picture, as an ideology takes center stage. Soon enough the inevitable comes about: empty souls and empty pews. The cistern is cracked, and the living waters run away. There is worship in spirit of some sort, you see, but not in truth. This tendency in our part of the world is more typical of the post-conciliar period, than in, let us say, the 1950s.

His Eminence Cardinal Burke has shown that the truth involved in liturgical law is no mere convention but is founded on a form of divine justice (jus divinum).[20] This points us to St Thomas Aquinas's analysis of the moral virtue of religion.[21] Man owes to God, in truth and as a matter of justice, some exterior form of worship, and this worship is something far more important, something infinitely nobler than any mere ideology.

The other exaggeration I shall mention, one affecting a much smaller number of Catholics in our day but who are often among the ones we call "practicing Catholics," those having a keen sense of liturgical law and truth, is characterized by a loss of spiritual content. Here we have adoration in truth this time, yes, but without—or without enough—spirit. This is the more recent version of that to which reference was made in certain controversies of the past by names such as *rubricism* (excessive concern with rubrics) or of *formalism*, where the rubrics are the crucial reference or where exterior form is what commands all the attention. The perfect execution of the prescribed rite is assured, but neither the faithful worshipper in the pews, nor even, perhaps, the priest has a real understanding of the meaning of it all. Here, too, the cistern is cracked, and the waters of divine life are lacking. There is an analogy here with what St Paul calls the "letter" of the law as opposed to the spirit. In this case, "the tree hides the forest" from view, following the popular adage. This tendency would correspond more to imperfections affecting the Church before the Second Vatican Council.

---

20. See: Raymond Cardinal Burke, "Liturgical Law in the Mission of the Church," in Alcuin Reid (ed.), *Sacred Liturgy: The Source and Summit of the Life and Mission of the Church* (San Francisco: Ignatius, 2014), pp. 389–415 (398–99).

21. See: *Summa Theologiæ* II–II, q. 81, a. 4 and a. 7.

Now, we must not promote caricatures. Dom Prosper Guéranger, in his *Institutions Liturgiques*, strongly blames those who would make light of the Church's elaborate rubrics.[22] True enough. Still, anyone who has dealt very much with more traditionally minded Catholics knows the type who is obsessed with the letter of the liturgical law to the point of missing the spirit of the liturgy and finally, perhaps, the whole point. This attitude, sometimes affecting true intransigence, not infrequently alienates both members of the faithful and certain clergy members who show interest in the *forma antiquior* but who are put off by what looks to them like a new form of pharisaical hypocrisy. A gulf can appear between the Church as a whole and communities making use of the *forma antiquior* if this tendency is not checked. As Cardinal Ratzinger pointed out during the Liturgical Conference held at Fontgombault Abbey in France in 2001: "[I]t would be fatal for the old liturgy to be, as it were, placed in a deep-freeze, left like a national park, a park protected for the sake of a certain kind of people, for whom one leaves available these relics of the past."[23]

In this perspective, it seems to me to be no accident that the future Pope Benedict XVI chose the title *The Spirit of the Liturgy* for his book about this great subject. As he points out, the title was inspired by a book by Romano Guardini,[24] who treated the subject in the early twentieth century. *Adoration, worship in Spirit and in Truth...* What good could a liturgy be, were it to remain a thing without *spirit*, and therefore without life? On the other hand, how can it be inspired by the Holy Ghost, the Holy Spirit, if it is not a *true* liturgy? This seems to be a capital point in assuring an authentic liturgical renewal: holding "both ends of the chain," as they say in French, "Il faut tenir les deux bouts de la chaîne." Only in preserving these two elements can the liturgy be renewed so as to be that "spring of water welling up to eternal life" (John 4:14).

There is an important question that might be considered here, one related to what I have been saying about the spirit of the liturgy. As anyone can see who looks at the history of the liturgical movement of the twentieth century, the *leitmotiv* of this story, the underlying question to which all roads seem to lead, is that of the "active participation" or more precisely the *participatio actuosa* of the faithful attending liturgical celebrations. We monks must agree with the better inspired commentators

22. Guéranger, *Institutions Liturgiques*, vol. 1, p. 379.

23. "Assessment and Future Prospects," in Alcuin Reid (ed.), *Looking Again at the Question of the Liturgy with Cardinal Ratzinger* (Farnborough: St Michael's Abbey, 2003), pp. 145–53 (152).

24. See: Joseph Cardinal Ratzinger, *The Spirit of the Liturgy* (San Francisco: Ignatius, 2000), pp. 7–8.

on this subject, who point out that participation in something as sublime as is the liturgy must be understood as belonging to what is most excellent in man, his spiritual nature, without excluding the body and the material aspect. I am thinking of what Cardinal Ratzinger said in chapter 2 of part four of *The Spirit of the Liturgy*. Father Aidan Nichols OP echoes the question that certain Enlightenment liturgists asked:

> Is the liturgy primarily latreutic, concerned with the adoration of God, or is it first and foremost didactic or edificatory, the conscious vehicle of instruction of individuals and the upbuilding of a community?[25]

It seems to me that for the monastic order, in its vast majority, such a question, excessively focused on practical pastoral concerns—however praiseworthy—has little sense. We must always return to the Gospel, with its call to adoration, to "worship in spirit and in truth." It is precisely from this deep worship that the renewed apostolic activity of the New Evangelization which Pope Francis is urging the entire Church to embrace will flow. Goethe truly set the modern world on a fatal course when he had that troubling character, Faust, write, not "In the beginning was the Word," but "In the beginning was the Deed."[26] True liturgical life can set things straight.

5. *Sailing Between Scylla and Charybdis: A Question of Balance*

Following another biblical metaphor, in addition to being true actors of the liturgy, spiritual watchmen, and diggers of wells, we monks must be, like St Peter, sailors: *duc in altum* (put out into the deep waters) (Luke 5:4). On the great sea, while sailing our liturgical ships, we must avoid, in Homeric terms, both the Scylla of a formalism that tends to fossilize and rob the liturgy of its character as a living tradition (truth without spirit), and the Charybdis of falsely charismatic or ideological celebrations that abandon the objective and necessary reference to the Tradition of the Church with its established forms and laws (spirit without truth). It is precisely in that arduous middle path, avoiding both errors, that the true liturgical renewal must find its course.

---

25. Nichols, *Looking at the Liturgy*, p. 32.

26. Johann von Goethe, A. S. Kline (trans.), *Faust* (online: Poetry in Translation, http://www.poetryintranslation.com/PITBR/German/FaustIScenesItoIII.htm, 2003), part I, scene III, l.1237.

But what does this all mean, practically speaking? Where is this balance to be encountered? How does one chart the course our ship must take in concrete terms? Finally, what help is monastic life here? Without pretending to have all-embracing answers to these difficult questions, I think monastic life can offer, in fact, something unique. In our day, there may be less need for monks to preserve and codify manuscripts as they have done in the past, but monks can offer something essential to the liturgical life of the Church and to liturgical renewal—I might even say something existential.

As we have seen, monks, especially Benedictine monks, live by the liturgy. St Benedict calls the liturgy *Opus Dei* (the Work of God), and directs his disciples to prefer no earthly activity to this liturgical task. Here lies the key to an important contribution to liturgical renewal that monasteries *can* make: that of liturgical hospitality. As, day and night, the monks perform the solemn celebration of the *Opus Dei*, others may also participate in this great treasure of the Church. To the extent that the liturgy of a given monastery reflects an authentic sense of liturgical renewal it becomes a mirror where visitors contemplate this liturgical light and beauty.

Not just anyone can make prolonged visits to a Benedictine monastery, but many can—and probably should—especially those responsible for liturgical formation. Furthermore, priests with important pastoral duties really need to get away from the hectic pace and tension of their daily pastoral duties, and a pilgrimage to a monastery represents an excellent way for them to "recharge" their spiritual batteries, to use a quite unbiblical but expressive image. They will thus bring back to their duties a renewed appreciation of the liturgy.

In principle, the form or template of liturgical celebration is to be found in the cathedral church of each diocese. However, since in modern times, especially in America, there are no longer canons to celebrate daily the Hours of the Liturgy in the cathedral, the mother church of a diocese, as was once the case, it is only in certain monasteries that a complete picture of the liturgy can be encountered on a regular basis. In many churches solemn Masses are celebrated, of course, as are vespers and other liturgical ceremonies often enough. But only in a monastery does one encounter the sort of *laus perennis* or prayer without ceasing that is the complete liturgical life of the Church. Even many Benedictine monasteries, especially those that have taken on considerable duties in the administration of large schools, are unable usually to assure the Holy Liturgy in its fullness. Active religious orders, facing the hard reality of a modern apostolate, must lighten even more their liturgical load. Carmelite and Poor Clare nuns have a beautiful and complete liturgy, but their religious tradition is less focused on liturgy than that of the Benedictines.

As Dr Judith Bowen points out in her introduction to the English translation of Dom Guéranger's autobiography, monasteries have in modern times a vocation as exemplars:

> [W]hat emerges from all Guéranger's writing and actions is the importance of prayer and its public forms if people are to be fully engaged with faith. It is this insight which underpins Guéranger's work, and the autobiography reveals his early appreciation that a monastic community can act as an exemplar for Christian belief. The notion of exemplarity is important for an understanding of Guéranger's writing and explains his belief that, in the aftermath of the [French] Revolution, monastic life could offer to his contemporaries a mirror that would reflect all of the traditions of the Church—a commitment to obedience and to collective prayer, daily reminders of saintly lives, a reaffirmation of mystical experience and the discipline required to observe the liturgical calendar.[27]

This is, no doubt, just as true today as in the early nineteenth century, albeit in a different way.

I would like to quote here a text of Blessed John Henry Newman, who is actually describing in this historical sketch Benedictine monasticism, but does so—interestingly enough—in terms that could well describe a living and authentically renewed liturgy, the object of our quest. It is, I think, as if he were describing what a guest might contemplate during the liturgy at a Benedictine abbey:

> [It is] not...proceeding from one mind at a particular date, and appearing all at once...but it is...diverse, complex, and irregular, and variously ramified, rich rather than symmetrical, with many origins and centres and new beginnings and the action of local influences, like some great natural growth; with tokens, on the face of it, of its being a divine work, not the mere creation of human genius. Instead of progressing on plan and system and from the will of a superior, it has shot forth and run out as if spontaneously, and has shaped itself according to events, from an irrepressible fullness of life within, and from the energetic self-action of its parts, like those symbolical creatures in the prophet's vision, which "went every one of them straight

27. Judith Bowen, "Introduction," in Br. David Hayes OSB and Sr. Hyacinthe Defos du Rau OP (trans.), *In a Great and Noble Tradition, the Autobiography of Dom Prosper Guéranger, Founder of the Solesmes, Congregation of Benedictine Monks and Nuns* (Herefordshire: Gracewing, 2009), pp. xix–xx.

forward, whither the impulse of the spirit was to go." It has been poured out over the earth, rather than been sent, with a silent mysterious operation, while men slept...and thus it has come down to us, not risen up among us, and is found rather than established.[28]

A more particular aspect of this exemplarity proper to monastic communities is the matter of sacred music. In most places, sad to say, the Church's exhortation given in the Constitution on the Sacred Liturgy, *Sacrosanctum Concilium*, has gone unheeded: "The Church recognizes Gregorian chant as being specially suited to the Roman liturgy. Therefore, other things being equal, it should be given pride of place in liturgical services" (n. 116). In our monasteries this treasure of sacred chant can still be experienced in a significant way.

Finally, where should the liturgical pilgrim go? Where can he or she encounter this exemplar? There would be so much to say here, so many possible places to mention, that I had better stick with the houses belonging to our Solesmes Congregation. In addition to the priory of nuns in Westfield, Vermont, and my own Abbey of Our Lady of Clear Creek in Oklahoma, there are two houses in Canada, not far from Montreal. There are numerous monasteries in France (old stones always have their tale to tell...) where the entire liturgy is celebrated each day according to the monastic rite, often in the setting of that truly monastic architecture, the Romanesque. In some places the liturgy is celebrated according to the newer liturgical books (in Latin), especially at Solesmes Abbey. In other places, such as Fontgombault Abbey (not to mention Le Barroux and the Monastère Saint-Benoît in the Diocese of Fréjus–Toulon, where Dom Alcuin is based), the *usus antiquior* is followed. Hospitality has always been one of the hallmarks of the Benedictine Rule, and liturgical hospitality, as we envisage it here, may prove to be a sign of the times. Enough of the tour guide.

6. *A Tale of Two Missals*

In the context of *Sacra Liturgia*, I could hardly fail to mention the peculiar liturgical situation we experience in our day: that of having two forms or usages of the Roman liturgy, especially with regard to the celebration of Holy Mass. This mention seems all the more appropriate since my

---

28. John H. Newman, "The Mission of St Benedict," in *Historical Sketches*, vol. 2 (London: Longmans, Green & Co., 1899), pp. 365–430 (388).

monastic community, in collaboration with the *Ecclesia Dei* Commission (under the Congregation for the Doctrine of the Faith) makes use of the 1962 missal, as provided for by the Apostolic Letter, *Summorum Pontificum* (7 July 2007) of Pope Emeritus Benedict XVI.

Some will find rather odd that monks, whose liturgy incorporates few elements of the liturgical renewal instituted at the Second Vatican Council, may contribute to the current movement of liturgical renewal. All I can say is that, although we certainly hold a conservative position in these matters, we have never intended to throw our lot in with those who would preserve a "fossilized" liturgy, one entirely separated from the living process of a Tradition that proceeds by way of organic development. Whatever any of us thinks of the situation in which there are two forms of the Roman liturgy, it must be admitted that there has to be found, somehow, at the heart of it all, a real unity, a note that is always found in the things of God and of the Church.

I do not have an answer to the question that arises as to what future the Roman rite should have (continue with both forms? eliminate one or the other? blend the two together in a *tertium quid*?). I believe that the authentic development of the liturgy is already showing us, little by little, the solution and that "only time will tell." In his Preface to *The Spirit of the Liturgy*, Cardinal Ratzinger spoke figuratively of an overlay of whitewash that had hidden all too much the fresco of the Church's liturgy.[29] The first abbot I knew in France, Dom Jean Roy, used the image of a layer of dust that needed to be removed. Neither of these men of God desired a rupture with the past, but the renewal of something ever ancient and ever young. It remains to be seen how the next phase of this renewal will "play out."

I should add here that in my experience, the *usus antiquior* exercises a powerful attraction over the young, whether seminarians, young priests, or discerners of a vocation to the religious life, even as they are keen to remain faithful to the authorized discipline of the Church. This reality, one that cannot be denied, at least in the part of the world in which we live, must certainly give us a clue about finding the balance I mentioned above, that arduous middle path between extremes, which allows the Church to put out into the deep of the postmodern world and to flourish. This is for me a sign of great hope.

During the Fontgombault Liturgical Conference mentioned earlier, the then Cardinal Ratzinger expressed his fear that use of two forms of the Roman rite might lead to a state of affairs where each Catholic would choose his or her church à la carte, something that would "damage the

---

29. See: Ratzinger, *The Spirit of the Liturgy*, pp. 7–8.

structure of the Church." He pointed out in this regard the positive role monasteries might play. This complements, perhaps, what was said earlier about exemplarity:

> One ought therefore—it seems to me—to look for a non-subjective criterion, with which to open up the opportunity of using the old missal. That seems to me very simple, in the case of abbeys: this is a good thing…it corresponds to the tradition by which there used to be orders with their own rite, for example the Dominicans. Thus, abbeys which ensure the continuing presence of this rite, and likewise religious communities such as the Dominicans of Saint Vincent Ferrer, or other religious communities…seem to me to offer an objective criterion.[30]

7. Urbs Jerusalem

The liturgy, writes Romano Guardini, has something in it reminiscent of the stars, of their eternally fixed and even course, of their inflexible order, of their profound silence, and of the infinite space in which they are poised.[31] He goes on to show that, far from causing the Church to be disinterested in the lot of the faithful, this profoundly contemplative beauty of liturgical prayer is the best stimulus for courageous action on the part of those who live in the world. A monk of the twenty-first century would not put it differently. An authentic monastic contribution to the liturgy and to its renewal will always be along those lines. There is a need in our liturgical celebrations, one too often forgotten in our day, of beauty ("Beauty will save the world"—Dostoevsky), of wonder, and of transcendence.

There is, perhaps, no liturgical poem that so captures the transcendent and contemplative nature of the liturgy as does the hymn for the Dedication of a Church, especially in its original form, previous to the reform of Urban VIII. In it we hear a very pure echo of the liturgy of heaven, the final destiny of every faithful soul that God calls to His beatific vision. This incomparable meditation on the final end of man, whose author is unknown (is that not significant?) will provide a fitting conclusion, I think, to these considerations about a monastic contribution to liturgical renewal.

---

30. "Assessment and Future Prospects," in Reid (ed.), *Looking Again*, p. 150.

31. Roman Guardini, *The Spirit of the Liturgy* (New York: Sheed & Ward, 1935), p. 210.

Mother Abbess Cecile Bruyère, the first superior of the Benedictine community of women founded by Dom Guéranger in his later years, had a special devotion to the liturgy of the Dedication and to that hymn. She had a particular fondness for the idea that "there is but one Liturgy," that is to say in Heaven and on earth. She speaks of this in her book, *The Spiritual Life and Prayer According to Holy Scripture and Monastic Tradition*. In a mediation centered on the liturgy of heaven as described in the book of Revelation she writes:

> During the days of [the Church's] pilgrimage our Pontiff would not abandon His bride; and by a wonderful way, and with a wisdom all divine, He found the means of identifying the Sacrifice of earth with that of heaven, since there is but one priesthood, that of Jesus Christ, but one Sacrifice on earth and in heaven, but one Victim, namely, the Lamb conquering sins... Thus the Church's hierarchy on earth through the wonders produced by the Sacraments, presents to the ravished gaze of the heavenly citizens a faithful reproduction of that which takes place "within the veil, *ad interiora velaminis.*"[32]

The most important contribution monks can ever make to the work of renewal is their very liturgical life, which is a living and ever renewed witness to God and to the reality of the Faith in the Church. In some monasteries a more traditional accent predominates; in others the aspect of renewal is more evident. But in every community there must be a living tradition that faithfully bears witness to the message of the Gospel.

Modifying somewhat the title Blessed John Henry Newman gave to one of his essays, monastic life could be called a "Grammar of Divine Ascent." We monks say to souls in search of beauty in spirit and truth: Come and take part in this monastic liturgy: it will speak for itself. Maybe you will experience nothing at all. Then again, perhaps God will make His voice heard in the inner sanctuary of your soul. Perhaps, if you listen carefully during the Office of Vigils, you will catch a murmur of the prayer of the first Christians, who would meet before dawn in the catacombs; or again, during the Easter Vigil especially, you might relive something of the liturgical grandeur of the Roman basilicas in the time of Pope St Leo or of St Gregory the Great.

---

32. Cécile Bruyère, *The Spiritual Life and Prayer According to Holy Scripture and Monastic Tradition* (Eugene: Wipf & Stock, 2002, previously London: Art & Book, 1900), p. 413.

If, however, the specter of Romanticism repels you from such poten-
tially nostalgic musings, if you have no interest in gazing backwards, you
might listen, while at the abbey, for an echo from an even better place, one
located outside time and space, from the land of perfect and total renewal,
the place of truly divine liturgy:

> Urbs Jerusalem beata,
> Dicta pacis visio,
> Quae construitur in caelis,
> Vivis ex lapidibus,
> Et Angelis coronata,
> Ut sponsata comite. Amen.

> Jerusalem, the blessed city,
> Vision of peace its name;
> Constructed in the heavenly place
> Of ever living stones,
> And crowned with Angels round about,
> Like unto a bride by her maidens ringed. Amen.[33]

33. Hymn for the Dedication of a Church (translation by the author).

HOMILY AT THE SOLEMN VOTIVE MASS OF THE HOLY ANGELS

Jordan J. Kelly OP

Using the words of the liturgy, it is "truly right and just" that in a Dominican church the votive Mass of the Holy Angels is offered and the theology of the Angels given us by the Angelic Doctor, St Thomas Aquinas, be, in some humble way, offered for our meditation and encouragement.

St Thomas's treatise on the angels is one of the longest treatises in the *Summa Theologiae*, comprising 14 questions of the *prima pars*. Clearly, the Angelic Doctor acknowledges this subject matter is most important; even its placement tells us to listen and take heed of what we are to learn. After considering God in Himself (*De Deo Uno* and *De Deo Trino*) and creation in general, Thomas explicates to us his sublime revelation concerning the angels—in fact, he will speak of the angels before he speaks about man and our destiny.

Our knowledge of the angels shows us Thomas' profound life of faith, as what he knows is by revelation and what we know by faith. The reciprocity of revelation for Thomas and faith for ourselves demonstrates the capital importance of this treatise: the treatise *per se* is like a *Summa* in diminution, treating all the major themes with respect to angels that Aquinas will consider in greater depth with respect to men. By understanding grace and nature in spiritual creatures (angels), we can understand grace and nature in corporeal creatures (men).

This treatise of the *Prima Pars* offers us these most salient points:

1. Man is not the only creature made in the Imago Dei.
2. Man is not the only creature destined for Beatitude.
3. Man is not a purely spiritual being.
4. And, although the angels are of a higher dignity than men in the order of creation, the cosmic changing event of the great gift of the Incarnation, we now have the privilege of seeing our humanity elevated and divinized.

Such knowledge should only lead us with awe and wonder to consider anew the words of the Psalmist: "Lord, what is man that you should keep him in mind...with glory and honor you crowned him...making him little less than a god..." (Ps 8:4–5). The lessons of this treatise remind us of the need for proper humility, and just how gratuitous is the gift of our creation, our nature, and our destiny.

A disposition of humility and the reception of a gratuitous gift... Ten days ago the celebrant of this Mass knelt down in front of his Archbishop and was given the most gratuitous and undeserved gift that can be given to any man—Sean Michael Connelly knelt down, but Fr Sean Michael Connelly, a priest for ever according to the Order of Melchizedek, another Christ, arose—changed and radically configured to Christ the High Priest for all eternity.

Long after question 64 and the theology of the angels, in question 113 of the *prima pars*, St Thomas treats the topic of guardian angels. All angels, and even this lowest rank of angels, act as executors of Divine Providence among men. What is this Divine Providence? God's good and holy will, ordering all things sweetly and drawing them unto Himself. All creatures were made as an expression of His goodness, and it is because *He is good*, not because we are good, that He invites us to communion with Himself.

How does He accomplish this communion? Both angels and men are created to give Him praise—to offer to Him a continual sacrifice of praise. Guardian angels give praise and glory to God by carrying out the plan of Divine Providence and acting as instruments of God, His agents in helping men, guarding and protecting them from dangers, giving them spiritual comforts and consolations, drawing them back to Himself.

My brother priests, is this not what we are called to do: "to share all sufferings; to penetrate all secrets; to heal all wounds; to return from God to men; to bring pardon and hope; to teach and to pardon, console and bless always" (H. Lacordaire OP)? We who have known more than nine days know that this is so very true. And knowing it, how often do we stand in humble awe knowing that we are the unworthy recipients of such a gratuitous gift and even more, God's mercy?

Father Sean, it is this mixed life of offering a continual sacrifice of praise, and of being an instrument to guard, guide, teach, forgive, console and heal God's Holy People that the Lord bestowed upon you just nine days ago. Your fidelity to this gift will be forged in the furnace of regularity—to serve when you would rather retreat; to stand at the altar when you would rather sleep; to raise your hand one more time in absolution; it is in these acts of allowing yourself to be a victim that you will realize how great is the gift you have been given; and may it call you each day to deeper and deeper humility. And, at the end of each day, you will find that as exhausting as this humility may be, you will be somehow refreshed and grateful to God. No priest is worthy of the gift; no priest is an angel; but the grace of the Sacrament of Holy Orders and the graces of your Guardian Angel will conform you more and more each day unto Himself; and order all things sweetly and draw you unto Himself.

It is easy to be humble and filled with gratitude when one celebrates in such splendor; every rubric perfect; angelic music; splendid vesture; a Church full of people filled with zeal and faith. But your humility will be ever greater, your gratitude more complete, your conformity to our Eternal High Priest more perfect, when the vesture is moderately beautiful, the cantor is struggling to find pitch, and the people are numbed from the realities of work and family—in fact that celebration may have infinitely more to do with your eternal salvation than this.

Father Sean, may the intercession of the angels form you more and more each day as another Christ; and, may you find your joy and meaning in being a sacrifice of praise for God and for His People. If you allow this to happen you will have the most glorious life, because you are Priest of Jesus Christ!

INDEX

CPSIA information can be obtained
at www.ICGtesting.com
Printed in the USA
LVHW080815270520
656645LV00003B/19